The Love She Most Desires

LOVE &
RESPECT

The Respect He Desperately Needs

DR. EMERSON
EGGERICHS

THOMAS NELSON
Since 1798

NASHVILLE   DALLAS   MEXICO CITY   RIO DE JANEIRO

Focus on the Family
Colorado Springs, Colorado

Published in Nashville, Tennessee, by Thomas Nelson. Thomas Nelson is a registered trademark of Thomas Nelson, Inc.

Published in association with Yates & Yates, LLP, Attorneys and Literary Agents, Orange, California.

Thomas Nelson, Inc., titles may be purchased in bulk for educational, business, fund-raising, or sales promotional use. For information, please e-mail SpecialMarkets@ThomasNelson.com.

Unless otherwise indicated, Scripture quotations are taken from the New American Standard Bible (NASB), © 1960, 1977, 1995 by the Lockman Foundation. Used by permission.

Other Scripture quotations are taken from the following sources:

The King James Version of the Bible (KJV). The New King James Version (NKJV®), © 1982 by Thomas Nelson, Inc. The Holy Bible, English Standard Version™ (ESV) © 2001 by Crossway Bibles, a division of Good News Publishers. All rights reserved. New International Reader's Version (NIRV) © 1996, 1998 by International Bible Society. All rights reserved worldwide. The Holy Bible, New International Version (NIV). © 1973, 1978, 1984, International Bible Society. Used by permission of Zondervan Bible Publishers. The contemporary english version (CEV). © 1991 by the American Bible Society. Used by permission. *The Message* (MSG) by Eugene H. Peterson. © 1993, 1994, 1995, 1996, 2000. Used by permission of NavPress Publishing Group. All rights reserved.

Cover Design: Charles Brock, UDG/Design Works, Inc.
Cover Photo: Steve Gardner/pixelworksstudio.net and photos.com
Workbook Interior Design: Rainbow Graphics; Kingsport, TN.

ISBN 978-0-8499-4858-9 (book and workbook)

Library of Congress Cataloging-in-Publication Data

Eggerichs, Emerson.
  Love and respect : the love she most desires, the respect he desperately needs / by Emerson Eggerichs.
    p. cm.
  ISBN 978-1-59145-187-7 (hardcover)
  ISBN 978-1-59145-417-5 (hardcover with DVD)
  ISBN 978-1-59145-246-1 (IE)
  1. Spouses—Religious life. 2. Love—Religious aspects—Christianity. 3. Respect—Religious aspects—Christianity. I. Title.
  BV4596.M3E34 2001
  248.8'44—dc22

                                                2004013768

Printed in the United States of America
10 11 12 13 14 RRD 5 4 3 2 1

To Sarah, the love of my life
who has made the writing of this book so much easier.

———

Lord, Your Word calls a husband to
"Enjoy life with the woman whom you love" (Ecclesiastes 9:9).

I have since 1973.
I do right now.
I forever will.

LOVE & RESPECT
CONTENTS

PART THREE: THE REWARDED CYCLE

Love & Respect Workbook
Contents

Workbook Part Two: The Energizing Cycle

ACKNOWLEDGMENTS

For their untold hours of editing and typing, my heartfelt thanks to my good friends, Fritz and Jackie Ridenour. Both are gifts of God to me. They grabbed the vision and would not let go, despite incredible deadline pressures. Without them, this book could not have been completed. They have brought me joy. (Since helping me, Jackie has entered heaven for her eternal reward.)

To the board of Love and Respect Ministries, I express my appreciation. You have made decisions that continue to advance this worthy cause. There is wisdom in many counselors. Your advice is invaluable.

I thank my children, Jonathan, David, and Joy, for standing with Mom and me. You have blessed us as we have watched you promote the Love and Respect message. Thanks for making this vision your vision.

To my sister, I clap my hands in applause. Ann, you have helped me whenever and wherever. I am blessed! Thanks for finding me so many jokes!

My mom and dad are now in heaven. While on earth, both were a testimony to what God can do through two people who open their hearts to Him. Thank you, Mom and Dad, for looking beyond yourselves to God. Later in life, you chose to be faithful to the end.

I am beholden to you who have told me your personal stories of Love and Respect in marriage. Your testimonies will not only help others but have made this book very inviting. Thank you!

Sarah and I will never know on this side of eternity the impact that is being made because of you—our friends—who prayed for us. You know who you are. We humbly thank you. Remember us still.

In the movie *Chariots of Fire*—about the life of Eric Liddell, the Olympic runner who refused to race on Sundays—the Bible is quoted:

"For those who honor Me I will honor" (1 Samuel 2:30). Reader, I wish to acknowledge and honor God. This message of Love and Respect comes from His heart in Ephesians 5:33. This book would not exist if God had not graciously illumined me to His revelation.

Though the application of these two truths is my frail attempt to serve you, the essential truths themselves will never change—not any more than God changes. Lord, I thank You most of all and forevermore.

LOVE ALONE IS NOT ENOUGH

You may remember how the Beatles sang, "All you need is love." I absolutely disagree with that conclusion. Five out of ten marriages today are ending in divorce because love alone is *not* enough. Yes, love is vital, especially for the wife, but what we have missed is the husband's need for respect. This book is about how the wife can fulfill her need to be loved by giving her husband what he needs—respect. Here is the story of one couple who discovered the Love and Respect message just in time:

> My husband and I attended your Love and Respect marriage conference. A few days before we had gotten into another "Crazy Cycle" and decided we had had enough and were going to end our marriage. We were both hurt, sad, angry, and despondent. By the way, we are both believers and I work on the staff of a large church.
>
> We had been seeing a Christian marriage counselor and I can honestly say that your conference not only saved our marriage but actually helped us more and gave us more information and strategies than counseling ever did. We had decided to go as

a last-ditch effort, but my husband really didn't believe it would help and almost didn't go. The truths God has revealed to you are both simple and profound. . . . They started a healing process and revolutionized our marriage. If only we had been given this information thirty years ago, what heartache and pain it would have saved us.

Let me just say, after the close on Saturday, we spent the best afternoon and evening with each other we have had in years. It was like we were in our twenties again and so in love. Emerson, I can honestly tell you, I never ever realized how important, how life-giving, respect was to my husband.

What did this woman and her husband hear at that conference? What revolutionized their marriage? What caused two people ready to divorce on Friday to be walking together the next day like two young lovers? The book you have in your hands is the Love and Respect message this couple heard. Their account is one of thousands of letters, notes, and verbal affirmations I have received that testify what can happen when a husband and wife take a different approach to their marriage relationship.

Do you want some peace? Do you want to feel close to your spouse? Do you want to feel understood? Do you want to experience marriage the way God intended? Then try some Love and Respect!

This book is for anyone: people in marital crisis . . . spouses headed for divorce . . . husbands and wives in a second marriage . . . people wanting to stay happily married . . . spouses married to unbelievers . . . divorcées trying to heal . . . lonely wives . . . browbeaten husbands . . . spouses in affairs . . . victims of affairs . . . engaged couples . . . pastors or counselors looking for material that can save marriages.

I know that I am promising a lot, and I wouldn't dream of doing this unless I fully believed that what I have to tell you works. Following are more examples of how marriages turn around when wives and husbands discover the message of Love and Respect and start living it out daily:

> It has been one year since we attended the Love and Respect conference. It is the single most powerful message on marriage that my husband and I have ever heard. We constantly find ourselves going back to the principles we learned that special weekend. We sit on the couch together and walk through C-O-U-P-L-E and C-H-A-I-R-S and see where we have gotten off track. . . . We have such incredible joy in trying to do things God's way and then seeing Him bless us.

> Just a few days ago I decided to tell my husband that I respect him. It felt so awkward to say the words, but I went for it and the reaction was unbelievable! He asked me why I respected him. I listed off a few things, and I watched his demeanor change right before my very eyes.

> I am sad that I have been married twenty-two years and just now understand the Respect message. I wrote my husband two letters about why I respected him. I am amazed at how it has softened him in his response to me. I have prayed for years that my husband would love me and speak my love language. But when I began to speak his language, then he responded with what I have wanted.

The above letters are typical of those I receive weekly, if not daily, from people who have gained wisdom by understanding the one key verse of Scripture that is the foundation for this book. No husband feels fond feelings of affection and love in his heart when he believes his wife has contempt for who he is as a human being. Ironically, the deepest need of the wife—to feel loved—is undermined by her disrespect.

Please understand, however, that what I have to tell you is not a "magic bullet." Sometimes the glow a couple feels at one of our conferences fades in a few days or weeks, and they succumb to the same old problems—the Crazy Cycle. I like to advise all couples who learn about the power of Love and Respect to give it a six-week test. In that time, they can see how far they have come and how far they still have to go.

The journey to a godly, satisfying marriage is never over, but during three decades of counseling husbands and wives, I have discovered something that can change, strengthen, or improve any marriage relationship. I call it the Love and Respect Connection, and my wife, Sarah, and I are taking this message across America. We are seeing God work in remarkable ways when men and women submit themselves wholeheartedly to this biblical design for marriage. We see it working in our own marriage, where we are still discovering new blessings as we use the Love and Respect Connection to touch each other.

If you and your spouse will practice the Love and Respect Connection, the potential for improving your marriage is limitless. As one wife wrote:

> I wanted to let you know, I GOT IT! God granted me the power of this revelation of respecting my husband. . . . This revelation . . . has changed everything in my marriage—my approach, my response, my relationship to God and my husband. It was the missing piece.

For so many couples, respect is, indeed, the missing piece of the puzzle. Read on, and I'll show you what I mean.

PART ONE

THE CRAZY CYCLE

WITHOUT LOVE

SHE REACTS

THE
CRAZY
CYCLE

HE REACTS

WITHOUT RESPECT

I wrote this book out of desperation that was turned into inspiration. As a pastor, I counseled married couples and could not solve their problems. The major problem I heard from wives was, "He doesn't love me." Wives are made to love, want to love, and expect love. Many husbands fail to deliver. But as I kept studying Scripture and counseling couples, I finally saw the other half of the equation. Husbands weren't saying it much, but they were thinking, *She doesn't respect me.* Husbands are made to be respected, want respect, and expect respect. Many wives fail to deliver. The result is that five out of ten marriages land in divorce court (and that includes evangelical Christians).

As I wrestled with the problem, I finally saw a connection: without love from him, she reacts without respect; without respect from her, he reacts without love. Around and around it goes. I call it the Crazy Cycle— marital craziness that has thousands of couples in its grip. In these first seven chapters I will explain how we all get on the Crazy Cycle—and how we all can get off.

CHAPTER ONE

THE SIMPLE SECRET TO A BETTER MARRIAGE

How can I get my husband to love me as much as I love him?" This was the basic question I heard from wife after wife who came to me for counseling during the almost twenty years I pastored a growing congregation. My heart broke for wives as they wept and told me their stories. Women are so tender. On many occasions I sat there with tears rolling down my cheeks. At the same time I became irked with husbands. Why couldn't they see what they were doing to their wives? Was there some way I could help wives motivate these husbands to love them more?

I felt all this deeply because I had been a child in an unhappy home. My parents divorced when I was one. Later they remarried each other, but when I was five, they separated again. They came back together when I was in third grade, and my childhood years were filled with memories of yelling and unsettling tension. I saw and heard things that are permanently etched in my soul, and I would cry myself to sleep at times. I remember feeling a deep sadness. I wet the bed until age eleven and was sent off to military school at age thirteen, where I stayed until I graduated.

As I look back on how my parents lived a life of almost constant conflict, I can see the root issue of their unhappiness. It wasn't hard to see that my mom was crying out for love and my dad desperately wanted respect.

Mom taught acrobatics, tap dance, and swimming, which gave her a good income and enabled her to live independently of Dad's resources. Dad was left feeling that Mom could get along fine without him, and she would often send him that message. She made financial decisions without consulting him, which made him feel insignificant, as if he didn't matter. Because he was offended, he would react to her in unloving ways. He was sure Mom did not respect him. Dad would get angry over certain things, none of which I am able to recall. Mom's spirit would be crushed, and she would just exit the room. This dynamic between the two of them was my way of life in childhood and into my teenage years.

As a teenager I heard the gospel—that God loved me, He had a plan for my life, and I needed to ask forgiveness for my sins to receive Christ into my heart and experience eternal life. I did just that, and my whole world changed when I became a follower of Jesus.

After graduation from military school, I applied to Wheaton College because I believed God was calling me into the ministry. When I was a freshman at Wheaton, my mother, father, sister, and brother-in-law received Christ as Savior. A change began in our family, but the scars didn't go away. Mom and Dad are now in heaven, and I thank God for their eternal salvation. There is no bitterness in my heart, but only much hurt and sadness. I sensed during my childhood, and I can clearly see now, that both of my parents were reacting to each other defensively. Their problem was they could offend each other most easily, but they had no tools to make a few minor adjustments that could turn off their "flamethrowers."

While at Wheaton, I met a sanguine gal who brought light into every room she entered. Sarah was the most positive, loving, and others-focused person I had ever met. She had been Miss Congeniality of Boone County, Indiana. She was whole and holy. She loved the Lord and desired to serve Him only. She should have had a ton of baggage from the divorce that had torn her family, but she did not let it defile her spirit. Instead, she had chosen to move on. Not only was she attractive, but I knew I could wake up every day next to a friend.

THE JEAN JACKET "DISAGREEMENT"

I proposed to Sarah when we were both still in college, and she said yes. While still engaged we got a hint of how husbands and wives can get into arguments over practically nothing. That first Christmas Sarah made me a jean jacket. I opened the box, held up the jacket, and thanked her.

"You don't like it," she said.

I looked at her with great perplexity and answered, "I do too like it."

Adamant, she said, "No, you don't. You aren't excited."

Taken aback, I sternly repeated, "I do too like it."

She shot back. "No, you don't. If you liked it, you would be excited and thanking me a lot. In my family we say, 'Oh my, just what I wanted!' There is enthusiasm. Christmas is a huge time, and we show it."

That was our introduction to how Sarah and Emerson respond to gifts. Sarah will thank people a dozen times when something touches her deeply. Because I did not profusely thank her, she assumed I was being polite but could hardly wait to drop off the jacket at a Salvation Army collection center. She was sure I did not value what she had done and did not appreciate her. As for me, I felt judged for failing to be and act in a certain way. I felt as if I were unacceptable. The whole jacket scenario took me by complete surprise.

Sarah and I discovered that "those who marry will face many troubles in this life . . ."
(1 Corinthians 7:28 NIV)

During the jean jacket episode, though neither of us clearly discerned it at the time, Sarah was feeling unloved and I was feeling disrespected. I knew Sarah loved me, but she, on the other hand, had begun wondering if I felt about her as she felt about me. At the same time, when she reacted to my "unenthusiastic" response to receiving the jacket, I felt as if she didn't really like who I was. While we didn't express this, nonetheless, these feelings of being unloved and disrespected had already begun to crop up inside.

We were married in 1973 while I was completing my master's degree in communication from Wheaton Graduate School. From there we went to Iowa to do ministry, and I completed a master's of divinity from Dubuque Seminary. In Iowa, another pastor and I started a Christian counseling center. During this time, I began a serious study of male and female differences. I could feel empathy for my counseling clients because Sarah and I, too, experienced the tension of being male and female.

YOU CAN BE RIGHT BUT WRONG AT THE TOP OF YOUR VOICE

For example, Sarah and I are very different regarding social interaction. Sarah is nurturing, very interpersonal, and loves to talk to people about many things. After Sarah is with people, she is energized. I tend to be analytical and process things more or less unemotionally. I get energized by studying alone for several hours. When I am with people socially, I interact cordially but am much less relational than Sarah.

One night as we were driving home from a small group Bible study, Sarah expressed some strong feelings that had been building up in her over several weeks.

"You were boring in our Bible study tonight," she said, almost angrily. "You intimidate people with your silence. And when you do talk, you sometimes say something insensitive. What you said to the new couple came across poorly."

I was taken aback but tried to defend myself. "What are you talking about? I was trying to listen to people and understand what they were saying."

Sarah's answer went up several more decibels. "You need to make people feel more relaxed and comfortable." (The decibels rose some more.) "You need to draw them out." (Now Sarah was almost shouting.) "Don't be so into yourself!"

I didn't respond for a few seconds because I was feeling put down, not only by what she said but by her demeanor and her tone. I replied, "Sarah, you can be right but wrong at the top of your voice."

Sarah recalls that our conversation that night in the car was life-changing for her. She may have been accurate in her assessment of how I was acting around people, but her delivery was overkill. We both dealt with things in our lives due to that conversation. (We still sometimes remind one another, "You know, you can be right but wrong at the top of your voice.") Overall, I think Sarah has improved more from that conversation than I have. Just this past week she coached me on being more sensitive to someone. (And this is after more than thirty years in the ministry!)

That early episode in our marriage planted more seeds of what I would later be able to describe and articulate. I knew Sarah loved me and her outburst was caused by her desire to help me. She wanted me to appreciate her concern and understand that she was only doing it out of love, but the bottom line was I felt disrespected, attacked, and defensive. Over the years, we continued to grapple with this same problem. She would voice her concern about something I was not focusing on as I should. ("Did you return so-and-so's phone call? Did you jot a note to so-and-so?") I would do my best to improve, but occasionally I would slip back, making her feel that I did not value her input.

AND THEN I FORGOT HER BIRTHDAY

A few more years went by, and Sarah's birthday was coming up. She was thinking about how I would respond—would I even remember? She always remembered birthdays, but birthdays weren't big on my radar screen. She knew she would *never* forget my birthday, because she loved me dearly. She wondered, however, if I would celebrate her birthday. She was thinking, *Does he hold me in his heart the way I hold him in mine?*

So what she did was not done in a mean spirit. She was simply trying to discover things about me and men in general. She knew that forgetfulness was a common problem, and she was just being curious. As an experiment, she hid all the birthday cards that had arrived before her birthday. No hints of her birthday existed anywhere, and I was going along in my usual fog, studying and thinking. On her birthday I had lunch with a friend. That evening as Sarah and I had dinner, she softly asked, "So, did you and Ray celebrate my birthday today?"

I can't describe exactly what goes on inside the human body at a moment like that. But it felt as if my blood went out of my heart, down to my feet, and then shot full force into my face. How would I ever explain this one?

I hemmed and I hawed, but I couldn't explain forgetting Sarah's birthday. My forgetfulness had been unloving, and I could see that she was hurt. But at the same time, I had these strange feelings. Yes, I had been wrong to forget, but I hadn't ignored her birthday intentionally. I felt judged, put down—and rightly so. At the time, I couldn't describe my feelings with a word like *disrespected.* During those years, when the feminists were going full blast, men didn't talk about being disrespected by women. That would have been arrogant, and in church circles it would have been considered a terrible lack of humility.

Loving Times and Spats of Ugliness

The years rolled by—a blur of preaching, pastoring, and counseling more married couples. Sarah and I continued to grow in our marriage as we learned more and more about one another, and we had a lot of great times. But along with the loving times were spots (should I say spats?) of ugliness. Nothing was long term; we would almost always pray together afterward, asking forgiveness from one another as well as from the Lord. But what did it all mean? Where was our marriage going? After all, I was a pastor who was paid to be "good." How could I justify all my little slip-ups that were "good for nothing"?

As someone has said, the problem with life is that it's so daily. And Sarah and I irritated each other almost daily with bad habits we couldn't shake. One of mine was leaving wet towels on the bed. At least once a month Sarah would be angry about my wet towel. And every three months or so, I would start drifting back into being preoccupied with other things, neglecting certain duties, and forgetting certain requests.

Every couple learns about daily conflicts, which Solomon calls "the little foxes that ruin the vineyards" (Song of Solomon 2:15 NIV).

When she would critique me, tension would arise and I would come across as blaming her or making excuses.

Sarah periodically coughs and clears her throat, and early on in our marriage when we would be praying, I would get irritated by her coughing. How childish could I be? We were praying to the Lord of heaven, and I was bothered by something she couldn't help. Other times, she wanted me to praise the Lord when I was frustrated. Frankly, I didn't always want to praise the Lord, so did that make me less spiritual? When she was frustrated, I didn't tell her to praise the Lord! Didn't that make me less judgmental and more spiritual?

Tension has a way of tearing down your self-image. On the heels of confrontation, I felt I could never be good enough. And on the heels of family conflict, Sarah felt she was a failure as a mother and wife. As with all couples, the specifics that prompted these tensions weighed heavily on us as a couple. Indeed, life can be "so daily."

It is not Sarah's first choice to travel, study, and teach because that is not her gifting, though she is willing to go for the sake of our ministry. I can't stand fixing things that break in the home since that's not

As God revealed the Love and Respect message, I experienced Psalm 119:130: "The unfolding of Your words gives light; it gives understanding" (NIV).

my talent. So I usually complain when trying to fix something which doesn't get fixed anyway (and that's why I didn't want to do it in the first place!).

I share all these little "secrets" about my wife and me to let you know that we do not deliver our message on marriage from any pedestal of perfection. We have struggled on many fronts and will continue to do so, but now we struggle knowing we can win! Over the years, ever so slowly, we have discovered the "secret" that has made all the difference for us (and for many other couples).

THE "SECRET" HIDDEN IN EPHESIANS 5:33

For more than twenty years I had the privilege of studying the Bible thirty hours a week for my pulpit ministry. I also earned a PhD in family studies, plus a master's in communication. I had a lot of formal training, but when this illumination from Scripture exploded in my heart and mind one day in 1998, it simply blew me away. I literally exclaimed, "Glory to God!" The insight that I finally recognized in Scripture, and which I later confirmed from reading scientific research, explained why Sarah and I would get into our arguments. I finally saw very clearly why Sarah could be crushed by my words and actions, just as my mom had been crushed by my dad. And Sarah could say things that would send me through the roof, just as my mom had said things that would send my dad through the roof.

What was the secret? Actually, it was not a secret at all. This passage of Scripture has been there for some two thousand years for all of us to see. In Ephesians 5:33, Paul writes, "Each one of you also must love his wife as he loves himself, and the wife must respect her husband" (NIV).

Of course, I had read that verse many times. I had even preached on that verse when conducting marriage ceremonies. But somehow I had never seen the connection between love and respect. Paul is clearly saying that wives need love and husbands need respect. As I started sharing my secret in messages and later in seminars and conferences, I would often run into people who would say something like, "This Love and Respect Connection sounds good, Emerson, but isn't it a little theoretical? We have real problems—money problems, sex problems, how to raise the kids . . ."

As I will show throughout this book, the Love and Respect Connection is the key to any problem in a marriage. This is not just a nice little theory to which I added a few Bible verses.[1] How the need for love and the need for respect play off of one another in a marriage has *everything* to do with the kind of marriage you will have.

HOW GOD REVEALED THE LOVE AND RESPECT CONNECTION

In the beginning, when I was struggling to find help for other marriages as well as for my own, I was not searching for any "Love and Respect Connection." But that connection surfaced as I pondered what Ephesians 5:33 is saying. My thought process went something like this: "A husband is to obey the command to love even if his wife does not obey this command to respect, and a wife is to obey the command to respect even if the husband does not obey the command to love."

So far, so good. Then I reasoned further: "A husband is even called to love a disrespectful wife, and a wife is called to respect an unloving husband. There is no justification for a husband to say, 'I will love my wife *after* she respects me' nor for a wife to say, 'I will respect my husband *after* he loves me.'"

At this point I still hadn't seen the Love and Respect Connection. My theory surfaced as God guided me in recognizing the strong link between love and respect in a marriage. I saw why it is so hard to love and respect. When a husband feels disrespected, it is especially hard to love his wife. When a wife feels unloved, it is especially hard to respect her husband.

At that point came the illumination that made sense to me, and it has made sense to a lot of people ever since. When a husband feels disrespected, he has a natural tendency to react in ways that feel unloving to his wife. (Perhaps the command to love was given to him precisely for this reason!) When a wife feels unloved, she has a natural tendency to react in ways that feel disrespectful to her husband. (Perhaps the command to respect was given to her precisely for this reason!)

The Crazy Cycle is, indeed, "the evil of folly and the foolishness of madness" (Ecclesiastes 7:25).

The Love and Respect Connection is clearly within Scripture, but so is the constant threat that the connection can be strained or even broken. And then came what I call the "aha" moment: this thing triggers itself. Without love, she reacts without respect. Without respect, he reacts without love—ad nauseam. Thus was born the Crazy Cycle! (See page 5 for a visual of it.)

Everywhere I share my theory, husbands and wives immediately understand. They see that if they don't learn how to control the Crazy Cycle, it will just go round and round and where it stops nobody knows.

To put this book in brief outline form, I want to help couples:

- Control the Craziness (The Crazy Cycle)
- Energize Each Other with Love and Respect (The Energizing Cycle)
- Enjoy the Rewards of a Godly Marriage (The Rewarded Cycle)

Why Love and Respect Are Primary Needs

Getting on the Crazy Cycle is all too easy. Recognizing that you're on the Crazy Cycle and learning how to keep it from spinning out of control *is* possible if husband and wife can learn how to meet each other's basic needs for love and respect. I have often been asked, "How can you be so sure the wife primarily needs to feel love and the husband primarily needs to feel respect?" My answer comes in two parts.

First of all, my experience as a counselor and as a husband confirms this truth. The wife is the one who asks, "Does my husband love me as much as I love him?" She *knows* she loves him, but she wonders at times if he loves her nearly as much. So when he comes across as unloving, she typically reacts in a negative way. In her opinion, he needs to change into a more sensitive and caring man. Unfortunately, a wife's usual approach is to complain and criticize in order to motivate her husband to become more loving. This usually proves about as successful as trying to sell brass knuckles to Mother Teresa.

On the other hand, a husband does not commonly ask, "Does my wife love me as much as I love her?" Why not? Because he is assured of her love. I often ask husbands, "Does your wife love you?" They reply, "Yes, of course." But then I ask, "Does she like you?" And the answer usually comes back, "Nope."

In many cases, the wife's dislike is interpreted by the husband as disrespect and even contempt. In his opinion, she has changed from being the admiring, ever-approving woman she was when they courted.

Now she doesn't approve, and she's letting him know it. So the husband decides he will motivate his wife to become more respectful by acting in unloving ways. This usually proves about as successful as trying to sell a pickup to an Amish farmer.

Even more convincing is what Ephesians 5:33 teaches about the woman's primary need for love and the man's primary need for respect: The husband *must* love his wife as he loves himself, and the wife *must* respect her husband. Could it be any clearer than that? Paul isn't making suggestions; he is issuing commands from God Himself. In addition, the Greek word Paul uses for love in this verse is *agape*, meaning unconditional love. And the wording of the rest of the passage strongly suggests that the husband should receive unconditional respect. Christian spouses should not read this verse to say, "Husbands, love your wives unconditionally, and wives, respect your husbands only if they have earned and deserve it." As the old saying goes, what is sauce for the goose is sauce for the gander. In this verse, respect for the husband is just as important as love for the wife.

Another writer of Scripture chimes in with Paul on this matter of respect for husbands. The apostle Peter wrote to wives that if any husbands were disobedient to God's Word, "they may be won without a word by the behavior of their wives, as they observe your chaste and *respectful* behavior" (1 Peter 3:1–2; italics mine). Peter is definitely talking about unconditional respect. The husbands he mentions are either carnal Christians or unbelievers who are disobedient to the Word—that is, to Jesus Christ. God is not pleased with a man like this, and such a man does not "deserve" his wife's respect. But Peter is not calling on wives to feel respect; he is commanding them to show respectful behavior. This is not about the husband deserving respect; it is about the wife being willing to treat her husband respectfully *without conditions.*

To say the least, doing something when you don't really feel you want to do it is counterintuitive. Therefore, this passage must be acted on in faith. God has ordained that wives respect their husbands as a method to win husbands to Himself. As a husband opens his spirit to God, he reopens his spirit to his wife. No husband feels affection toward a wife who appears to have contempt for who he is as a human being. The key to creating fond feelings of love in a husband toward his wife is through showing him unconditional respect.

Respect—Unique Feature of This Book

Many books on marriage stress the need for husbands to love wives, but the unique feature about this book is the concept of wives showing unconditional respect toward husbands. My theory is simple, but it is so powerful that I decided to leave the pastorate in 1999 and begin sharing these truths about love and respect full time. Ever since, Sarah and I have shared our message with thousands of married couples and, again and again, we receive confirmation that we are definitely on the right track. Every wife we've met wants her husband to appreciate how much she loves him, and she yearns to feel more love from him. What we try to share is that the best way to love a husband is to show him respect in ways that are meaningful to him. Such respect lets him feel his wife's love for him and ignites in him feelings of love for his wife.

This book will show you the power of unconditional love and unconditional respect. As you and your spouse use these powerful tools, you can save a struggling marriage from the divorce court or a "ho-hum" marriage from boredom and concealed bitterness. If you have a good marriage, you can make it even better. Sarah and I had a good marriage before we discovered the simple secret taught in this book. But now our marriage is *much* better.

How much better is it? Have we reached some kind of marital nirvana and all is perfect? Hardly. We still come across to one another at times as unloving or disrespectful. We still get on the Crazy Cycle like everybody else. But we have made a decision that has changed the course of our marriage for the good. If only my mom and dad could have discovered this. Sarah and I now know how to reduce the number of times we spin on the Crazy Cycle, and we often stop it before it gets started.

What is this life-changing decision we both have made? I have decided to believe that Sarah does not intend to be disrespectful. Oh, she can get nasty, but that isn't how she feels in her heart. I know she respects who I am deep inside. Sarah has decided to believe that I do not intend to be unloving, though I still hurt her at times with my comments and attitudes. She knows that in my heart I love her deeply and would even die for her. So how does all this actually play out? I'd like to illustrate with eggs and towels.

Sarah Can't Stop Peppering the Eggs

Sarah likes pepper on her eggs. I do not. In her view, scrambled or sunny-side-up eggs need to be peppered until black. In the course of our marriage, Sarah has fixed me eggs hundreds of times, and she has put pepper on these eggs just about every time she cooks them, even though she knows I don't like peppered eggs. But I have concluded that Sarah is not doing this to spite me or because I am unimportant to her. I know her heart. She has even muttered in frustration (after peppering the eggs again), "Well, they aren't any *good* if they don't have pepper."

As baffled as I am by this constant peppering, I have not concluded that Sarah is plotting to change me or irritate me. I know Sarah is thinking of other things. She is on autopilot when she peppers my eggs. I have told her hundreds of times, "Please don't put pepper on my eggs." If she really respected me, wouldn't she listen to me? Wouldn't it be natural for me to explode in anger, especially if I can predict this—

again? Wouldn't it be right for me to become doubtful of her good intentions? Wouldn't it be right for me to start keeping track of many annoying things she does like peppering my eggs? All this would prove I really don't matter to her, wouldn't it?

But I am able to interpret Sarah much less negatively than that because I have decided that she does not intend to be disrespectful, not in her deepest soul. I made that decision, and other husbands are making it too. One man wrote:

> It was freeing to reflect on the fact that my wife was well-intentioned and good-hearted toward me, as she acknowledged. Sadly, I could misunderstand her heart. There were lots of things I didn't know about her heart. For example, it turns out she had been going through postpartum depression. Understanding some things like that softened my heart a lot. I started to think more about how she might not be sensing my love for her, even though I was well-intentioned and good-hearted toward her.

This husband "gets it." He has made the right decision about his wife, and so can you regarding your spouse.

EMERSON CAN'T PUT THINGS WHERE THEY BELONG

I leave wet towels where they don't belong. I leave a loaf of bread on the counter. I leave the cupboard doors open. I leave books stacked on the living room floor. I have an excuse, of course: I am mentally preoccupied. As Sarah says, "He is always thinking." Sometimes I stun myself by what I do or don't do. Looking back at the cupboard doors, I realize most of them are still open. I say to myself, *Why didn't I close those doors? Where was my mind?* Or I leave towels lying on the bedroom floor instead of hanging them up in the bathroom. (By the way, this is where we've learned to keep things light, which releases tension. When Sarah dangles the towel in front of my face, I smile and say, "What a coincidence! I was just going to hang that towel up!")

Now don't get me wrong. I am not a pig. But I am married to Sarah, who is the epitome of neatness and cleanliness, and I flunk by her standards. She is not a perfectionist, but she is logical. Why leave a towel on the bed when a rack is in the bathroom waiting for the towel? Why leave a cupboard door open when the hinge functions both ways? Why leave the books on the floor when it would only take a few seconds to put them on the bookshelf?

But Sarah has not concluded that this means I am out to ignore her or irritate her. She knows I am thinking of other things, that I am on autopilot as I come and go. Yet she has told me thousands of times, "Please pick things up and put them away." Wouldn't it be easy for her to say, "If you really loved me, you would listen to me"? Wouldn't it be natural for her to explode in anger? Wouldn't it be right for her to become doubtful of my good intentions? Wouldn't it be right for her to start keeping track of the many things I do like this? After all, surely all this would prove she really doesn't matter to me.

But Sarah is able to see me in a more positive light because she has decided to believe that I do not purpose to be unresponsive and unloving, not in my deepest soul. She has made that decision, and so have other wives. One woman married more than thirty years says:

> As I look back, I realize how disrespectful I've come across. He is a naturally kind and compassionate man, very outgoing, and has the gift of serving (he's always willing to do things for me on a moment's notice) . . . truly a well-meaning, good-hearted man who has had sin in his life, like all of us. . . . I realize that maybe my expectations were too unreasonably high.

Another wife adds:

Since early in our marriage when he came across as really controlling and not listening to concerns that I would have, I didn't
see that he had feelings inside. I started the "in your face" bitter
wife responses. Now I see more of his heart and am starting to
understand what my words have done to him.

These gals "get it" also. They've made a decision to change their
approach, and so can you regarding your spouse.

Yes, Sarah and I both have our faults. The Crazy Cycle always
wants to spin, but we can control it by remembering the Love and
Respect Connection. We know this works, and there is much I want to
share about how and why it works. The first step is understanding just
how husbands and wives communicate.

CHAPTER TWO

TO COMMUNICATE, DECIPHER THE CODE

If husbands and wives are to understand the Love and Respect Connection, they must realize that they communicate in code. And the problem is, they don't know how to decipher the messages they send to one another.

A couple was about to celebrate their tenth wedding anniversary, and the wife began to wonder if her husband would remember. There had been plenty of times during the past decade when he had forgotten their anniversary altogether. No matter what she did—little hints, bigger hints—he would miss it. But on their tenth wedding anniversary, with no hints at all, he remembers! He makes a beeline for Hallmark and is soon gazing upon all those racks full of greeting cards. One colorful card quickly catches his eye. He skims the words—they are perfect! He thinks, *This card is* her—*no doubt about it.* He grabs it off the shelf, pays the clerk, and hurries home rejoicing. Finally, he has remembered their anniversary, and a special one it will be too.

She is there when he arrives at home, so he sneaks the card into another room, signs it, and quickly writes her name on the envelope. He even adds a couple of tiny hearts over her name as an extra touch. Then he comes out and hands his wife her tenth anniversary card. She beams from ear to ear. She is so happy—finally he has remembered! She tears open the card and begins to read . . . and then her face falls. The eyes that had been bright with loving energy turn cold. Her beaming countenance becomes sour and dark.

"What's wrong?" her husband asks. (He's a very sensitive guy, and he can pick up on these things.)

"Nothing."

"There is, too. What's wrong?"

"No, there's *nothing* wrong."

"But there is—I can see it. What is it?"

"Well, it's not bad . . . for a *birthday* card."

As you might guess, the conversation is headed downhill from here. "You're kidding!" says the husband, grabbing the card from her hand. "No way . . . unbelievable!"

"No, *you're* unbelievable!"

The husband blinks in the face of his wife's very real anger. He knows he is full of goodwill. He has remembered their tenth anniversary. He has bought her a present as well as a card. "Well, honey, I made an honest mistake. Give me a break."

"Give you a break? An honest mistake—oh, it was an honest mistake, all right, because you just don't care. Do you know what? If you took your car in to be detailed and they put a stripe on the side that was even a fraction of an inch off, you would notice that, right? Why? Because you *care* about it. But you don't care about our anniversary. You don't care about *me!*"

The husband can't believe it. He is moving from feeling guilty to getting angry. What he thought would be a loving celebration of their tenth anniversary has become a conflict that is escalating fast.

"Hey, I made an honest mistake, all right? Give me a break. Good grief!"

"You buy me a birthday card on our tenth anniversary, and you expect me not to be upset? I'd rather you hadn't bought me any card at all!"

The husband has been on the defensive, but now his pulse rate is up. He has tried to do the loving thing, and all his wife can do is say nasty things.

"You know what? The way you're talking I'm *glad* I got you a birthday card for your anniversary!" And with that brilliant parting shot, he storms out of the room, slamming the door behind him. Approximately two minutes have passed since he handed her the card. This couple, a husband and wife who truly love each other, have come home expecting to spend a wonderful, romantic evening together. Instead, they end up stomping to opposite ends of the house, staring out the windows into the darkness, wondering how it had ever come to this, and thinking, *This is crazy!*

When counseling couples, I often ask, "What causes fights and quarrels among you?" (James 4:1 NIV).

This story is based on an actual incident, and I have collected many others like it from couples Sarah and I have counseled. Angry exchanges are caused when the husband appears careless, depriving his wife of love, and when the wife reacts with criticism and complaints that are vehement, depriving the husband of respect. And why should she be respectful? The stupid oaf doesn't deserve her respect!

"All You Want Me for Is Sex!"

Here's one more example. The husband is gone for a week on a business trip. As his plane lands, he starts envisioning a romantic sexual evening with his wife, so he hurries home as quickly as he can. As he walks in the door, his wife's first words are, "What are you doing home so early? Well, since you're here, I need you to pick up the kids from school. And don't forget, we have parent-teacher meetings this evening.

Oh, yes . . . I want to talk to you about Billy. The teacher called today and said he's been showing off and distracting his friends in class. And on the way to the school, can you pick up my clothes at the cleaners? Oh, I almost forgot. Dinner will be late because my sister is dropping over for coffee."

So much for the romantic evening planned by our knight of the business road who has wound up playing second fiddle to the kids, the cleaning, and his wife's sister. On his way out the back door he calls sarcastically over his shoulder, "Great to see you after a week!"

His wife is bothered by his sarcastic tone, but just as he walks out the phone rings and she doesn't have time to follow him outside to ask him what he meant. Later, during the parent-teacher meetings, she senses he is still angry, but on the way home she says nothing. She is exhausted from all the week's activities, and she is upset because he has never asked her once about all she has had to deal with. She wonders what right he has to be upset with her when *he* is the one being unreasonable.

As they retire into bed that night, the husband decides that he will "make up" with his wife in the most obvious and natural way. As he reaches to rub her back, which is usually a good way to get started, she groans, "Don't. I'm too tired."

Angrily, he rolls away from her without saying a word. Wounded by his anger, she says, "You're so insensitive!"

In disbelief, he replies, "I can't believe you said that. I've been gone for a week. I come home and instead of any kind of greeting, you just go on about the kids and your sister. When I try to get close, you tell me you're too tired. And then *you* call *me* insensitive! Am I just a meal ticket to you?"

By now the wife is very hurt, and she retorts, "You never asked once how I was doing. The only time you get interested in me it's for sex!"

"I was gone a week! When we were first married and I had to travel, you couldn't wait to see me get home. You'd greet me at the door with a smile and a kiss. Now you simply look up and say, 'Why are you home so early?' Thanks. That makes my day."

CRAZINESS—JUST KEEP FLIPPING THE LIGHT SWITCH

Stories like these are not unusual. Every married couple has versions of their own. Around and around it spins. I call it the Crazy Cycle. So many people are on the Crazy Cycle that five out of ten couples in the church are divorcing, and the craziness seems to be getting worse. It's like someone coming into a room, flipping the light switch, and discovering the lights won't come on. If someone tries the switch two or three times with no results, you can understand. He will eventually figure it out—a tripped circuit breaker, a burned-out bulb. But if he stands there and flips the switch constantly for half an hour, you begin to wonder, "Is this guy a little crazy?"

Runaway divorce statistics reveal that "insanity is in their hearts" (Ecclesiastes 9:3).

The point is simple: *Craziness happens when we keep doing the same things over and over with the same ill effect.* Marriage seems to be fertile ground for this kind of craziness. Ironically, there are more books being published on marriage today than ever before. There are books on marital communication, money management, sex, etc. There are even books on how to become a better husband (or wife) in thirty days! But with all our knowledge, the craziness continues. And it doesn't seem to matter if the couples are Christians or unbelievers. Why? I have concluded that those of us in the church, who believe we have the Truth, are not using the whole truth. A crucial part of God's Word has been completely ignored or perhaps simply gone unnoticed when it has been there all the time right under our noses!

Many Christian spouses know Ephesians 5:33 and can at least

paraphrase it. The apostle Paul tells husbands to love their wives as much as they love themselves, and wives are to respect their husbands. But is anyone really listening? Perhaps the first step to better communication between husband and wife is to hear what God's Word clearly says.

Why Do Couples Communicate in Code?

Communication in marriage has been described, discussed, and dissected in hundreds, if not thousands, of books and articles. Why is communication between husbands and wives such a problem? It goes back to the fact that we send each other messages in "code," based on gender, even though we don't intend to. What I say is not what you hear, and what you think you heard is not what I meant at all.

Let's see how this plays out at home as a couple is getting dressed to start the day.

She says, "I have nothing to wear." (She means, she has nothing *new.*)

He says, "I have nothing to wear." (He means, he has nothing *clean.*)

There is no serious danger of conflict here, but the "nothing to wear" line illustrates that we all see things out of our own needs and perceptions. Just the other day, I was working on my computer and Sarah had the radio on in the next room. It was some kind of talk show and just loud enough to derail my train of thought. I yelled to her, "Are you listening to that?" There was no reply. I yelled again, "Are you *listening* to that?" Still no answer. Finally, I yelled louder, "Are you listening to the radio?!" She yelled back, "I have been trying to listen, but you keep interrupting!"

This created a two-minute exchange that almost turned into a serious argument. It seems Sarah was irritated with me because she hadn't even noticed the radio—she was busy with something else. But she thought I had called to her because there was something on this talk show that I really wanted her to hear. Of course, my real intention was that she turn off the radio if she wasn't really listening to it. So I was irritated with her because she hadn't understood me.

Finally, it came to me that I hadn't been very clear about what I had meant, and yelling at her three times wasn't too loving either. So I apologized. I cite this little misunderstanding to point out that things like this can escalate, particularly if husband and wife are a bit upset with one another about something that happened the day before (or possibly just a few minutes ago). In other cases, couples may be experiencing long-term tension, which can escalate when fed by a simple miscommunication.

At a certain point, the issue isn't about turning off the radio, or whatever the miscommunication may be. The wife can get irked with the husband because he isn't being sensitive, something that most wives always anticipate or expect. In less than a minute, the wife can start feeling unloved and accuse her husband of being unloving. Meanwhile, the husband can get displeased with the wife when she starts talking to him as if he's insensitive. He starts reciting the mantra of many husbands: "I can never be good enough." The husband is feeling disrespected or at least unfairly criticized—again. A tiny spark in a dry forest can quickly catch fire, and if a couple doesn't know how to put it out, it can grow into a serious conflagration.

"When the Issue Isn't the Issue"

In almost every case, the issue that seems to be the cause of the craziness is not the real issue at all. Do you ever get into a conflict with your spouse but you aren't sure why? You see your spouse deflate or bristle or go cold, and then you think, *What is wrong here? What's happening?* Typically, you write it off by saying, "If only she weren't so touchy" or, "If only he weren't so childish." Of course, if *you* are the one who is offended, that's different. Your spouse is guilty of stepping on your toes—again.

Just because you may feel unloved or disrespected does not mean your spouse is sending that message. When the wife felt unloved because she got a birthday card for her tenth anniversary, it did not mean that the husband was sending her a message saying, "I really don't care about you or love you." At the same time, when his wife reacted in an angry and disrespectful way, that did not mean her message was, "I don't respect you any farther than I can throw you."

When the traveling businessman came home expecting to be sexually intimate and his wife was unresponsive, the message she was sending was not, "I don't respect you or your needs." And the husband may have become moody or upset, but he was not signaling that he did not love her. Often, we focus on our own needs and simply overlook the needs of the other person. The wife needs love; she is not trying to be disrespectful. The husband needs respect; he is not trying to be unloving. Once you grasp this basic principle—that the "issue" is not the real issue at all—you are on your way to cracking the communication code.

WE'RE AS DIFFERENT AS PINK AND BLUE

When the issue isn't the real issue, it is crucial to understand that one thing is going on in the spirit of the wife and an entirely different thing is going on in the spirit of the husband. The opening chapters of Genesis tell us God created them male and female. That's hardly news. But what it underlines is that men and women are *very* different. For example, Peter notes that difference when he instructs husbands to treat wives in a very specific way "*since* she is a woman" (1 Peter 3:7; italics mine).

Matthew 19:4 tells us "the Creator 'made them male and female'" (NIRV); in other words, very different.

The way I like to picture the difference between men and women is that the woman looks at the world through pink sunglasses that color all she sees. The man, however, looks at the world through blue sunglasses that color all he sees. Men and women can look at precisely the same situation and see life much differently. Inevitably, their pink and blue lenses cause their interpretation of things to be at odds to some degree.

Not only do men and women see differently, but they also hear differently. To carry the pink and blue analogy a little further, God created men with blue hearing aids and women with pink hearing aids. They may hear the same words but get much different messages (as in, "I have nothing to wear!"). Because men and women have sunglasses and hearing aids in different colors, they send each other messages in different codes.

When the spirit of your wife deflates before your eyes, and you suddenly sense an issue, she's sending a code. Of course, if there were a thousand women watching and listening, wearing their pink sunglasses and pink hearing aids, they would quickly say, "Well, I know why that sweet little thing is shutting down on him. She's so sweet and tender. I can't believe it; look at how he's talking to her." To women, the code is obvious as they decipher the message through pink sunglasses and pink hearing aids. No wonder they often think, *Men are so brain dead. They have two brains—one's lost and the other is out looking for it!*

But turn it around. When the wife sees the spirit of her husband deflate, or he gets angry and won't talk, his behavior seems childish to her. But if a thousand men with blue sunglasses and blue hearing aids were watching and listening, they would say, "I know why that guy shut down on her. Good grief! Look at the way she's talking to him. Unbelievable! Get that witch a broom!"

Are you beginning to see why male/female communication can be such a problem? Let's go back to the story of the anniversary card that turned into "Happy Birthday." When the wife sees that her husband has purchased a birthday card, her spirit deflates in an instant. He has forgotten their anniversary many times, but this is the last straw! Obviously, her husband doesn't even love her enough to take the time to *read* a card he bought for her!

So she sends him an angry message, and, of course, it was in code. Does he decode her words and expressions correctly? Of course not. He is wearing blue sunglasses. All he sees is anger, irritation, and disrespect. He feels guilty, then irritated. After all, he made an honest mistake . . . give him a break!

But the wife peers through her pink sunglasses, and she will have none of this "honest mistake" bit. She takes the conflict to a new low by assassinating his character. He thinks more of his car than he thinks of her!

That does it. He is glad he bought her a birthday card—it serves her right. He doesn't have to deal with this. And he walks out. So they both spend their tenth anniversary wondering how a little thing like a card could cause so much craziness. But, of course, the card wasn't really the issue. The real issue was that the wife felt unloved and responded the only way she knew how—by getting in her husband's face and telling him off. (Not all wives do that, but most lean in that direction at such moments!) With her pink sunglasses and pink hearing aids firmly in place, she wanted him to be genuinely sorry —not defensive, but asking forgiveness. Then they could have gone out for a nice dinner. But his blue sunglasses and blue hearing aids wouldn't let that happen. His real issue—which he probably couldn't even verbalize—is that he felt disrespected. He would show her, and so two essentially good-willed people wound up spinning on the Crazy Cycle with no clue about how to slow it down or stop it.

> The good-willed husband is "concerned about . . . how he may please his wife" and the good-willed wife is "concerned about . . . how she may please her husband" (1 Corinthians 7:33–34).

What do I mean by "good-willed people"? Simply that both of these people love each other a great deal. They do not mean real harm; they do not intend real evil toward one another. They are hurt and angry, but they still care deeply for one another. That is why they spent their anniversary evening in separate rooms, miserable, wondering how this whole stupid thing could have happened. (And the reason neither will figure it out is that each blames the other for the whole sorry affair.)

SCIENTIFIC RESEARCH CONFIRMS THE CENTRALITY OF LOVE AND RESPECT

As long as spouses do not learn to decode the pink and blue messages they are sending one another, the Crazy Cycle will spin and spin some more. What is that one thing that is going on inside of her, where the code is obviously pink? What is the one thing that is going on inside of him, where the code is obviously blue? The woman absolutely needs love, and the man absolutely needs respect. It's as simple—and as difficult—as that.

Interestingly enough, scientific research confirms that love and respect are the foundation of a successful marriage. Dr. John Gottman, professor in the Department of Psychology at the University of Washington, led a research team that spent twenty years studying two thousand couples who had been married twenty to forty years to the same partner. These people came from diverse backgrounds and had widely differing occupations and lifestyles. But one thing was similar—the tone of their conversations. As these couples talked together, almost always there was what Gottman calls "a strong undercurrent of two basic ingredients: Love and Respect. These are the direct opposite of—and antidote for—contempt, perhaps the most corrosive force in marriage."[1]

Gottman's findings confirm what has already been in Scripture for some two thousand years. Chapter 5 of Ephesians is considered by many to be the most significant treatise on marriage in the New Testament.

Paul concludes these statements on marriage by getting gender specific in verse 33. He reveals commands from the very heart of God as he tells the husband he *must* love (*agape*) his wife unconditionally and the wife *must* respect her husband, whether or not her husband comes across as loving.[2]

Note, however, that this verse gives no command to a wife to *agape*-love her husband. As I studied this verse over the years, I began to ask, "Why is there no command for a wife to *agape* her husband?" And then it struck me. The Lord has created a woman to love. Her whole approach to nurture, her sensitivity, love, and compassion are all part of her very nature. In short, God designed the woman to love. He's not going to command her to *agape* her husband when He created her to do that in the first place. God is not into redundancy.

Let's go a little further with this and skip over to Titus 2:4. Here, older women are told to encourage younger women to love their husbands and children, but in this case, Paul is not talking about *agape* love. In Titus 2:4, he uses the Greek word *phileo*, which refers to the human, brotherly kind of love. The point is, a young wife is created to *agape* her husband and children. Ultimately, she will never stop unconditionally loving them. But in the daily wear and tear of life, she is in danger of becoming discouraged—so discouraged that she may lack *phileo*. A kind of impatient unfriendliness can come over her. She may scold and sigh way too much. After all, there is always something or someone who needs correcting. She cares deeply. Her motives are filled with *agape,* but her methods lack *phileo.*

Not every woman has this problem, but I have counseled many who admit they do have their periods of negativity concerning husbands or the children. Sometimes this is known as PMS (Pre-Murder Syndrome). Everyone ducks for cover when Mom is in that kind of mood. No one doubts her basic mother love, but sometimes they're not so sure she really *likes* them.

Part of the problem, however, is that women are not at all sure *they* are being loved, especially by their husbands. The question continues to come up: "Does he love me as much as I love him?" It sure doesn't seem like it. When he acts (or reacts) in ways that seem unloving to her, she reacts in ways that feel disrespectful to him. Who started it? Yes!

"You're Stepping on My Air Hose!"

The more I meditated on these two passages of Scripture, the more I realized that if a husband is commanded to *agape*-love his wife, then she truly *needs* love. In fact, she needs love just as she needs air to breathe. Picture, if you would, the wife having an air hose that goes to a love tank. When her husband bounds in and starts prancing around like a ten-point buck looking for someplace to graze, he steps on her air hose. This does not make her a happy camper. In fact, if she can find a baseball bat or some other weapon, she might just whack the big buck and tell him, "Get off my air hose; I can't breathe." Simply put, when her deepest need is being stepped on, you can expect her to react negatively.

In counseling, I tell the husband that when he sees the spirit of his wife deflate, he is stepping on her air hose. She is not getting the "air" she needs to breathe. She is crying out, "I feel unloved by you right now. I can't believe how unloving this feels. I can't believe you're doing this to me."

Not only is the husband commanded to love his wife, but the wife is commanded to respect her husband. You see, the husband needs respect just as he needs air to breathe. He also has an air hose that runs over to a big tank labeled "respect," and as long as the "air" is coming through, he is just fine.

To keep the deer analogy going, suppose the wife, a lovely doe, starts tromping on his air hose with her sharp little hoofs. As we have seen in a story like the tenth anniversary birthday card, the wife may have had good reason to prance all over her husband's air hose, but what's going to happen? As his air hose starts to leak because of all the little cuts her hoofs have made in it, the husband is also going to react because his deepest need (respect) is not being met. And the battle is on.

As I worked out what Ephesians 5:33 is saying, I started doodling with a diagram like the face of a clock. At 12:00 I wrote, "Without love." At 3:00 I wrote, "She reacts." (If she needs love like she needs air to breathe, and she's being suffocated, she *will* react.) Then at 6:00 I wrote, "Without respect," and at 9:00, "He reacts." (If he needs unconditional respect like he needs air to breathe, and he's hearing criticism or being attacked in some way, he *will* react.)

And there you have it—the Crazy Cycle (see page 5). Husbands and wives keep spinning on the Crazy Cycle because they don't understand that what seems to be the issue isn't the issue at all. The real issues are always love and respect. Everything else is just filling in the details.

MEN HEAR CRITICISM AS CONTEMPT; WOMEN FEEL SILENCE AS HOSTILITY

Let me emphasize to wives that when men hear negative criticism, it doesn't take them long to start interpreting that as contempt for who they are as men. Remember, the man is wearing blue hearing aids. When his wife sends out those pink but very pointed messages and his air hose starts to leak, he soon says to himself, *I don't deserve this kind of talk. Everybody respects me except you. You're just picking a fight. I wish you would just be quiet.*

When a husband can take it no longer, he gets up and walks out without a word, and that is the *coup de grâce.* He might as well have screamed at the top of his lungs, "I don't love you!" The wife is dazed. First, she has been treated unlovingly. Second, she has tried to move toward her husband by doing the loving thing. And now he has shown her he is the most hostile, unloving human being on the planet by just walking away and leaving her there! That does it! She is not far from thinking she has all kinds of grounds for divorce. (But if she does stop to think, she will realize that she started the whole thing with her criticism.)

Often both spouses have goodwill but are not deciphering each other's code. She criticizes out of love, but he "hears" only disrespect. He distances himself to prevent things from escalating, which is the honorable thing to do, but she "sees" only his failure to be loving!

Right about now the women reading this are saying, "Well, if husbands just weren't so immature . . . if my husband could just be man enough to talk things out, then we could get somewhere." You can think that kind of thing, and I understand why you would. Unfortunately, it's not going to change men at all. This attitude of men goes a lot deeper than the fact that they might be immature or proud. Men have an honor code. When a wife comes at a husband who has basic goodwill, he doesn't want to fight verbally or physically. As his wife rails at him or criticizes, he sits there quietly, which makes her angrier than ever. Because her frontal attack isn't working, she soon sees him as cold and uncaring. Meanwhile, he's thinking, *I can't believe this. My wife is treating me with disrespect—in fact, it's really contempt. All she can say is that I am unloving.*

The Crazy Cycle continues to spin. As she gets louder, he gets quieter. Soon she may be screaming at him with venomous words that he's never heard in all his life. As a rule, women have learned to fight with words. They are masters of the art, and husbands can feel helpless before the onslaught.

I want to underline that this happens all the time with couples who actually have good intentions—and maybe more so because they feel freer to let down their guard and express what upsets them. Most husbands and wives who are on the Crazy Cycle have basic goodwill toward one another, but they just don't know how to express it. And so the Crazy Cycle eventually spins many of them right into separation and divorce. I've had couples fighting with one another in my office, and I have said, "Time out . . . time out! Sir, let me ask you something, does your wife have basic goodwill toward you and others? Would you entrust the children to her?"

"Oh, absolutely."

"Ma'am, does he have basic goodwill toward you and others, and would you entrust the children to him?"

"Of course."

"Then what is going on with you two? How can two good-willed people treat one another this way?"

The husband and the wife will look at me as if to ask, "Why don't you tell us? All we know is, we fight and fight and fight, and usually we really don't know why."

As I have tried to explain to many couples over the years, a major part of the answer is learning how to decode each other's messages. Whenever a wife is complaining, criticizing, or crying, she is sending her encoded message: "I want your love!" And whenever a husband is speaking harshly or sometimes not speaking at all, he is sending his encoded message: "I want your respect."

We've begun to see how this decoding can start to happen, but there are still problems that stand in the way. Men, for the most part, are masters at stonewalling their wives, who confront them because they feel unloved. And many women are so fed up with husbands who don't seem to want to love them that the last thing they want to grant is respect. These women say the husband has to earn her respect before she will grant it; but, of course, if she continues to disrespectfully hammer at him, especially when he is trying to do the honorable thing, nothing much will happen. We'll look at how all this plays out and how husbands and wives can deal with these problems in the next chapter.

CHAPTER THREE

WHY SHE WON'T RESPECT; WHY HE WON'T LOVE

L earning to decipher your spouse's code isn't always done in a day, a month, or even a year. Listen to this husband who came to me for counsel because he sincerely was trying to love his wife. He writes:

Thanks for all your suggestions and support. [But] I remain perplexed at the chasm that exists between my perception and reality. When I began this endeavor, I had hope but low expectations, and I was happy to see how quick and positive the effects of "loving" behavior are. It was not difficult to bite my tongue and not "fight back" when I prepared myself for it. I think that while I felt apologetic, I can easily be humble and pretty much take anything that comes my way.

The difficulty begins when I begin to see things return to normal. When I let my guard down, I begin to talk or share and it turns out that underneath things are very volatile and sensitive. When things started to go bad last week, it happened extremely fast and I was surprised to hear how all the same issues remain at the same raw and grim level. I hate hearing that I am her enemy. It is painful to hear her ask, "Why do you want

to crush my spirit?" It is extremely difficult to not explode in
despair when I hear her say that she doesn't believe that I love
her, or that I will never change, or that she made a mistake and
I am not the man she thought I was.

It sure makes it seem that the road is long and possibly
fruitless. Amidst getting angry, and blaming her, and the gambit
of contorted emotional upheavals, I hear you saying that it is
rarely the content but rather the manner of delivery that causes
problems and I cringe at my inability to communicate effectively. Things have gotten so grossly out of shape and I feel
shamed that I've been blind and let them get so bad. I also feel a
little overwhelmed that all this effort and tolerance will only get
us to some point of mediocrity, and that at the slightest pertur-
bation everything will come tumbling down again.

*Realizing marriage
demanded permanence
and work, the disciples
complained, "If the rela-
tionship . . . is like this,
it is better not to marry"
(Matthew 19:10).*

Few men can articulate the male struggle
as well as this man does. His wife is crying out
for love, but she isn't helping at all because of
her contempt. Why do some women feel so
free to make comments like, "You're not the
man I thought you were" to their husbands
and expect them to remain unaffected? How
do wives expect husbands to respond with
love to this kind of barrage? At the same time,
how do men get themselves in such a pickle by being so blind in the
first place?

UNCONDITIONAL RESPECT—AN OXYMORON?

When I talk to wives, they have no trouble grasping the concept of
unconditional love. After all, they are wired that way. But when I men-

tion showing unconditional respect for husbands, it's a much harder sell. Few seem to have considered 1 Peter 3:1–2. The apostle Peter reveals that husbands who "are disobedient to the word" (meaning they are undeserving of respect) "may be won . . . by . . . respectful behavior." A simple application is that a wife is to display a respectful facial expression and tone when he fails to be the man she wants. She can give her husband unconditional respect in tone and expression while confronting his unloving behavior and without endorsing his unloving reactions. He may deserve contempt, but that doesn't win him any more than harshness and anger wins the heart of a woman.

The Bible teaches unconditional respect: "Show proper respect to everyone. . . . Not only to those who are good and considerate . . . but . . . harsh"
(1 Peter 2:17–18 NIV).

Interestingly, at first men don't grasp the idea of unconditional respect either. Wives and husbands believe respect ought to be earned. The wife feels her husband doesn't deserve respect. The husband wants to earn respect, but he doesn't feel he deserves the kind of disrespect he's getting from his wife.

To suggest that respect for men should be unconditional gets some wives downright upset. Repeatedly, I hear comments like these from wives: "How can I show respect for him when he comes across as so unloving?" . . . "He doesn't deserve respect; he has hurt me" . . . "I love him, but I get so frustrated and angry I don't want to respect him" . . . "Love is what matters. If he loved me as I need to be loved, maybe I would have stronger feelings of respect" . . . "Yes, I have things to deal with, but the major problem is with him and he needs to change. The truth is he needs to love and respect me far better than he does."

Time and again I've had women tell me they've never heard the two words *unconditional respect* put together in the context of a relationship. For them, it is literally an oxymoron (a term created by putting together two words that appear to be incongruous or contradictory).

A licensed counselor who used my materials and became a thorough believer in the power of the Love and Respect message wrote to say:

> Just yesterday, I talked to two new female clients who were wanting to save their marriages that were barely alive. I asked them if they loved their husbands. Without hesitation they said, "Yes." I then asked if they respected their husbands. I got nothing but hesitation! They sputtered like an old car needing a tune-up. One of them admitted that she was quite the reader, but she had never heard anything like this before. She asked me how she was supposed to respect her husband unconditionally. I told her in the same way that he was supposed to love her unconditionally. It's only with God's help. She smiled.

Note that these two wives had no problem with the concept of unconditional love. Women never think of *that* as an oxymoron. To them, the words *unconditional love* aren't contradictory at all, and when they don't receive love from their husbands, they let them know it. Women are much more expressive-responsive than men, who tend to compartmentalize their emotions. To put it simply, women are much more apt to show how they feel while men shut down. Men don't know how to deal with the fact that they aren't respected, and they can't put a voice to their feelings. The husbands think, *Well, if that's the way she feels, there's nothing I can do. If I have to earn her respect and I'm that bad as a person, then I guess I'll just forget it.*

When the wife flatly says her husband will have to earn her respect before she gives him any, she leaves the husband in a lose-lose situation. Now he's responsible for both love and respect in the relationship. He must unconditionally love his wife *and* he also must earn her respect. Is it any wonder he shuts down in the face of all that?

IT ALL GOES BACK TO PINK AND BLUE

Respect for husbands is an unfamiliar idea for many wives, but there certainly are reasons for their attitude. Part of it goes back to those pink and blue sunglasses and hearing aids. As one wife put it, "We think so differently. I don't even relate to what he considers respect (or the lack of it)."

Another obvious reason for the respect gap in women is the crude and unloving behavior of their husbands. I am well aware that many a wife has good reasons to get in her husband's face—I have heard it all for more than a quarter of a century. But that's not the total picture. There is also the cultural mind-set. For the past forty years, the American church has preached unconditional love. I preached it for many years in my own church, as I remained clueless about the importance of unconditional respect. During those years I was continually frustrated as a male counselor, and so were the women who came seeking my advice. Why couldn't husbands love their wives as their wives needed to be loved? It wasn't that they lacked the knowledge—they showed plenty of that back in courtship days. But now that they were married the husbands seemed to lack motivation to love their wives. They seemed less energized about their marriages. Something was missing.

Then I realized that, in stressing unconditional love, I was teaching the truth but only half the truth. Paul's advice in Ephesians 5:25

By ignoring unconditional respect for husbands, I had not been "accurately handling the word of truth" (2 Timothy 2:15).

and 28 is sound: "Husbands, love your wives, just as Christ loved the church and gave himself up for her. . . . Husbands ought to love their wives as their own bodies. He who loves his wife loves himself" (NIV). But all of the emphasis on unconditional love hadn't motivated or equipped many men to be loving, at least not as loving as their wives would like. What was missing was that very short phrase, "the wife must respect her husband" (Ephesians 5:33 NIV).[1]

As I changed my message to include the whole truth—love *and* respect—I got interesting reactions. In one case I spoke twice to a group of two hundred women on the topic of respecting their husbands. I made myself available for a third talk, but the leadership of the group declined. Instead, they asked a female friend of mine to address the topic: "How to Love Your Husband." My friend had heard me speak, and she dropped me a note: "That was your point! How to love your husband." She could not believe how this group of women had missed it. The way to fully love a husband is to respect him in ways that are meaningful to him.

I survived being "fired" by that group of women and went on to spread the message of unconditional respect everywhere I could. And many wives are getting that message, including one who reported:

> I have led several studies on being a godly wife and have read and hopefully applied lots of biblical marriage resources. But I knew something was still missing even in my own relationship. . . . I could not figure out why my husband was staying somewhat aggravated with me and I was definitely not receiving the love and affection that I so desired. Now I realize that I have been showing him disrespect without ever dreaming that was what was being communicated. . . . I tried . . . respect . . . I was amazed at the result. My husband is definitely not a sweet talker. He is an outdoorsman who hunts all over the world. That's our business. Anyway, I thought this feels kind of silly but I said to him, "Honey, I couldn't sleep very well last night so I spent a lot of time thinking of all the things I respect about you" (which was true). He did not respond but I felt a softening in the air. Two days later, after spending all day in the duck blind with several

men, he said to me, "I missed you today. I wish you could have gone with me. I thought all day about what a sweet girl you are." I nearly laughed out loud—he called me a sweet girl—I'm a grandmother—but, oh, it is so fun to feel loved. I am now aware of so many ways that I was communicating disrespect without meaning to.

Respect does something to the soul of a man. God made him that way.

What about Aretha and R-E-S-P-E-C-T?

I sometimes get the question, "You say women need love and men need respect. Isn't the opposite just as true? Don't gals need respect and guys need love?" My answer is, of course, women need respect and guys need love, but I'm talking about the primary drive in each sex. Sometimes this gets mixed up. Back in the late 1960s, when the feminist movement[2] was hitting its stride, Aretha Franklin released a hit record entitled "R-E-S-P-E-C-T," which clearly sent the message that all women were asking for was a little respect when they got home. Respect is what women needed, and they "had to have it."

"R-E-S-P-E-C-T" became something of a theme song for many women, but what most of them did not realize is that the song was really written by a man—Otis Redding—two years before Aretha ever sang it. Otis released the song as a single on August 15, 1965, as his message to his wife. Does the irony of this strike you as it does me? Aretha had the right to sing "R-E-S-P-E-C-T" from a female point of view, of course. A woman does need respect, and if a man loves her properly, she will get that respect. But the primary meaning in Otis Redding's song is a cry from a *man's* deepest soul that says respect is what he needs and he's "got to have it."

Aretha Franklin's hit song notwithstanding, I still believe that women want love far more than respect and men want respect far more than love. I'll illustrate that from two rather divergent areas: the greeting card industry and the military. They are very different parts of our society, but both serve as examples of men's and women's deepest values.

Greeting Cards Are All about Love

Greeting cards are a clue into the minds and needs of women. Market studies show that, overwhelmingly, the majority of cards in the United States are purchased by women and given to women. Greeting cards are a multimillion-dollar business. Now, the card companies are not interested in ideology. They don't want to change anyone's mind. They are out to make money, so they produce what sells. Knowing that, I challenge you to find a card from a husband to a wife that says, "Baby, I really respect you." You won't see it. That card isn't out there, because that is not what a wife wants to hear. Women are locked into love. Love is their mother tongue. I'm not criticizing that; I'm just pointing out the way God designed women. In fact, if love weren't the woman's deepest value, this world would be in very sad shape. Women are this way, and we men rejoice.

Unfortunately, by that same token, you won't find any greeting cards that wives send to their husbands, saying, "Baby, I really respect you." Why not? Because they don't sell either. When women buy greeting cards for their husbands, they want to express love for them; they don't even think about respect. Sadly, the deepest yearning of husbands goes unmet because wives (and the card publishers) are locked into relaying sentiments of love.

Those of you who have a son, consider how sad he may be never to hear from his wife, "I really respect you." A need created in his soul by God will be overlooked because certain voices claim he doesn't deserve it unless he meets and maintains your daughter-in-law's romantic expectations. If his marriage is typical, after the first year, he will know his wife loves him but will feel she neither likes him nor admires him for who he is as a human being. If the pattern is like most, she will spend her energy seeking to help change him by her loving criticism and complaints, which eventually feel like contempt to him.

Respect Is a Man's Deepest Value

Women need to learn how to understand and use the word *respect* because, in truth, respect is a man's deepest value. Ever since I started developing the Love and Respect approach to marriage, I knew the Scriptures plainly taught about the male need for respect, and my own observations confirmed this. But I was always curious. Would these ideas stand up to statistical analysis? Would this need for respect by men show up in research done by a top-notch survey group? Yes, it would. In one national study, four hundred men were given a choice between going through two different negative experiences. If they were forced to choose one of the following, which would they prefer to endure?

a) to be left alone and unloved in the world

b) to feel inadequate and disrespected by everyone

Seventy-four percent of these men said that if they were forced to choose, they would prefer being alone and unloved in the world.[3]

For these men, the greater negative experience for their souls to endure would be to feel inadequate and disrespected by everyone. I have had numerous men confirm this research by telling me, "I would rather live with a wife who respected me but did not love me than live with a wife who loved me but did not respect me."

These men are not saying that they are indifferent to love. They know they need love, but they need to feel respected even more than to feel loved. Perhaps a good analogy is water and food. We need both to survive, but we can live longer without food than without water. For men, love is like food and respect is like water. Enough said! *Respect is the key to motivating a husband.*

A good illustration of how respect can motivate a man is found in our armed forces—the military. Because I attended a military academy from eighth grade to twelfth grade, I have had an interest in basic principles of military leadership. For instance, my observation is that great leaders motivated their troops through unconditional honor. Envision a U.S. Marine general speaking to his men after observing them in training maneuvers that did not go too well. "Men, I believe in you more than you believe in yourselves. Get your heads up. Look at me. I admire you more than you admire yourselves. Your performance stunk today, but I see more potential in this fighting unit than any in the world. Where you will be in six months will result in the world hearing of this fighting unit, and I am taking you there."

When a general respects his men and believes in them more than they believe in themselves, these soldiers want to improve, they want to get better, they want to fulfill that potential this general sees in them. Such men want to serve. Why do you think they call it the military "service"?[4]

Not only do men want to serve, but they are also willing to die in combat. There is something in many men, placed there by God, to fight and die for honor, to fight and die for women, children, and their buddies. When I attended Wheaton College, the chaplain there was Jim Hutchens, who had also been a chaplain in the Vietnam War. Jim told me that the Vietcong would wound an American soldier, knowing his buddies would seek to rescue him. Vietcong snipers would then seek to kill those who came out to try to drag the wounded man back to safety. He would often hear the heart cry of a GI: "I have to go.

A husband is geared to hear the command, "Take courage . . . be men and fight" (1 Samuel 4:9).

I have to help Joe. I can't leave him there. I've got to go. He's my friend." Honor and love compelled the American GI in Vietnam as it has down through every war in history. One husband wrote to me:

> I have been in the Air Guard for fourteen years with an additional six years of active duty. During your conference you made many references about men willing to die for their spouses or their nation. This certainly made an impression upon both of us. (My wife has always seen military service as equating to war and death. I see it as honor and duty.) I am committed not only to my country, but to the men I serve with. Only men who serve in such a capacity (military, firefighters, police officers) can understand the bonds that are formed and the loyalty you feel to one another.

I am sure this man is not trying to discount the women who serve honorably in various capacities in the military, as well as in firefighting and police work. But I believe he is trying to state a deep truth that is true of most men. I have counseled enough husbands to know the same kind of honor and loyalty that drives the military man is also in action in his home. Unfortunately, there are voices in our culture that have been saying, "Don't show respect to men; they don't deserve it. They'll treat you in a subservient way, or they'll abuse you and even kill you." This is true of a certain number of men, but I believe it is a lie concerning the vast majority. A man who has basic goodwill will serve his wife and even die for her. There is no expectation of the wife to die for her husband.

Of course, there are wives who might push the point a bit. You may have heard the story about the woman who told her husband, "Oh, Harry, you keep saying you'd die for me, but you never do!" That's just a story, of course, designed to get a smile or a laugh, but it isn't funny when men who are willing to die for their wives are treated with contempt and no respect. One woman wrote to me to confess:

> Although a Bible student for most of my life, and a very spiritual person, I had given up, but then I read your statement that says: "Though there is more to love than dying for someone, it is a sad day when a man knows that he'd die for his wife because he loves her, yet he hears her continually complain, ['You don't love me.']" The truth hit me powerfully in my spirit like no other thing has hit me concerning our marriage. I felt the kind of shame one feels when she knows she has done terribly wrong, and she knows not to even ask for forgiveness, and she knows that this one will take a long time to heal, but she knows this is one thing she won't do again.

This lady "gets it."

HUSBANDS ARE TO VALUE WIVES AS EQUALS

Paul's writings clearly command men to *agape*-love their wives (see Ephesians 5:22–33), but is there any place in Scripture where men are instructed to respect their wives as well? After teaching wives to behave respectfully before their husbands (see 1 Peter 3:1–2), Peter goes on to tell husbands to live in an understanding way with their wives "and show her honor as a fellow heir of the grace of life" (1 Peter 3:7). When Peter uses the phrase "show her honor as a fellow heir," he is telling husbands to value and prize their wives as equals within the grace of God. Paul concurs when he writes that in Christ, "there is neither Jew nor Greek, there is neither slave nor free man, there is neither male nor female; for you are all one in Christ Jesus" (Galatians 3:28).

This concept of honoring your wife is also found in Ephesians 5, where Paul says husbands ought to love their wives as they do themselves. As Paul says, "No one ever hated his own flesh, but . . . cherishes it." The passage clearly says that as a husband cherishes his own flesh he is to cherish his wife in the same way (see vv. 28–29). A wife longs to be that special person Paul describes. She wants to be cherished as a princess, not revered as a queen. She longs to be first in importance to him.

It is as though she is the princess and he is the prince. In Ephesians 5:33, a husband has a need to be respected as the head, the one called upon to die. "Christ . . . is the head . . . [and] loved the church and gave Himself up for her" (Ephesians 5:23, 25). The prince goes into battle for the princess, not vice versa. Consequently, the princess does not seek to be respected as the "head." Instead, she yearns to be honored, valued, and prized as a precious equal, "a fellow heir of the grace of life," as Peter unfolds in 1 Peter 3:7.

To carry further the word picture of the prince and princess, I believe the biblical order of things is that, as prince, the husband is to be considered "first among equals." By that I mean he is her equal, but he is called upon to be the first to provide, to protect—and even to die if necessary. This is graphically illustrated on any sinking ship as lifeboats are put over the side. The cry is always, "Women and children first!"

It's not an accident that in every culture, as a rule, men are bigger and stronger than women. Is this not God's visual aid concerning His purpose for men? When Nehemiah led his men in rebuilding the wall and fighting off the enemy, he urged them to "fight for your brothers, your sons, your daughters, your wives" (Nehemiah 4:14). Something in a man longs for his wife to look up to him as he fulfills this role. And when she does, it motivates him, not because he is arrogant, but because of how God has constructed him. Few husbands walk around claiming, "I'm first among equals." The husband with goodwill (and good sense) knows this isn't his right, but it is his responsibility. She, on the other hand, possesses something within that thirsts to be valued as "first in importance." Nothing energizes her more! She is not self-centered. God placed this in her by nature.

When he honors her as first in importance and she respects him as first among equals, their marriage works. When he expects her to look up to him yet puts her down, he deflates her. When he feels she is trying to be a bossy queen, he cannot detect her real heart. When she expects him to protect her but then accuses him of being paternalistic (too fatherly) or condescending, she deflates him. When she feels he is trying to be "more than equal" or greater, she cannot detect his real heart.

HUSBANDS: DO NOT SAY, "I TOLD YOU SO!"

A word of caution must be given to husbands at this point. For many wives, hearing that the Bible teaches women to give unconditional respect to their husbands is a huge piece of information. It is often something wives may never have heard before in any form. A wise husband will not use this information as a weapon. Instead, he will be humble. He will let his wife process what she has learned and then let her act upon it. When she does, miracles can happen.

In a marriage especially, "thoughtless words cut like a sword" (Proverbs 12:18 NIRV).

In many cases, couples report that the Crazy Cycle grinds to a screeching halt. And more often than not, this change is triggered by the wife as she tries to give her husband unconditional respect. As a wife gets used to the idea of respecting her husband, she likes doing it and, of course, her husband is pleased also (after he gets over the shock). But most important, the husband is triggered to give his wife unconditional love. The lose-lose situation turns into a win-win, as the following letters from two much happier husbands indicate: One man who had attended numerous marriage seminars during twelve years of marriage wrote:

> While most marriage seminars concentrate on the husband's need
> to love his wife unconditionally and sacrificially, few delve in
> any detail into the wife's encouragement to respect her husband.
> Dr. Eggerichs understands this intrinsic need men have and how
> important the fulfillment of this need is to marriage communi-
> cation. My wife and I heard things that explained why we "argue"
> and why we feel the way we feel. . . . I have never left a marriage
> seminar more excited and encouraged about my marriage.

Another husband who had attended one of our conferences said:

> Having participated in several marriage seminars over the past
> seventeen years, I was not anticipating any earth-shattering or
> thought-provoking ideas. If anything, I expected the typical
> reproof commonly granted to men at these conferences. Instead,
> I walked away enlightened with a deeper sense of God's design
> for men and women within the context of marriage. Rather
> than seeing our differences as deficiencies or reasons to divide,
> I began to appreciate and celebrate the uniqueness with which
> God has "wired" us. Although I was convicted of my short-
> comings, I was also moved and inspired. I walked away encour-
> aged and refreshed as I received a deeper understanding of who
> I am, and how that translates into my role as husband.

These men are among a growing number of husbands who are receiving respect and responding to their wives with positive understanding dialogue. And their wives are seeing that their husbands don't have to "earn respect" any more than they don't have to "earn love."

But I have encountered many women for whom the words *unconditional respect* are a red flag. They have been bombarded for so long by the wrong interpretation of biblical submission that they are suspicious and even hostile toward the whole idea. "It will never work" . . . "It's a man's world" . . . "Unconditionally respecting men will just give them more power to grind us down."

I understand these concerns, but I respond that husbands who have goodwill toward their wives are not looking for ways to have power and superiority over them. On the contrary, many husbands don't feel that powerful at all. Deep down they have a basic fear that can keep the Crazy Cycle spinning. As the next chapter will show, wives have far more power to change their marriage than many ever imagined.

CHAPTER 4

WHAT MEN FEAR MOST CAN KEEP THE CRAZY CYCLE SPINNING

In chapter 2, I mentioned that many husbands interpret criticism as contempt, and contempt is something men do not handle well. Wives must grasp that their husbands aren't half as big and strong and impervious to being hurt as they might seem. A woman may envision herself as a sweet little dewdrop and her man as a big, strong bear who should be able to absorb any kind of punishment. One huge fellow was stunned by his beloved's attack and said to her, "You hate me."

Frustrated, she replied, "When I scream 'I hate you,' you should know I don't mean it. You are 6'9" and weigh 260 pounds, for goodness' sake. I do that because you can take it." The truth is, however, a lot of men can't take it. No matter how big they may be physically, emotionally they are vulnerable to what sounds like contempt.

The male fear of contempt is dramatized in the first chapter of Esther. What was the fear? That wives would start to despise their husbands and defy them. The result: there would be no end to the contempt and anger poured out by wives on their husbands throughout the king's realm (see Esther 1:18). This is not to justify the male fear of contempt in the book of Esther or anywhere else. But as women fear being unloved, men fear being disrespected (held in contempt). The yearning and need of husbands is that their wives give them honor and respect.

CONFLICT MAKES MOST MEN FEEL DISRESPECTED

When Decision Analysts, Inc., did a national survey on male-female relationships, I had the opportunity to contribute a question that was asked of a large representative sampling of men. The question read:

> Even the best relationships sometimes have conflicts on day-to-day issues. In the middle of a conflict with my wife/significant other, I am more likely to be feeling:
>
> (a) that my wife/significant other doesn't respect me right now.
> (b) that my wife/significant other doesn't love me right now.

Not surprisingly, 81.5 percent chose "(a) that my wife . . . doesn't respect me right now."[1]

The survey substantiated what I already had discovered in my years of working with married couples. Men need to feel respected during conflict more than they need to feel loved. This does not mean men do not need love. As I already mentioned, men know deep down that their wives love them, but they are not at all that sure that their wives respect them. Perhaps that's why they favored answer (a) over answer (b) by such a great majority. Whatever the reason, during marital conflict, it is clear that men place a higher value on feeling respected than on feeling loved. Many women cannot imagine this because they are still tuned into the love wavelength.

Practically every woman I have met or counseled would be willing to say, "I just want somebody to love me, to make me special, to make me the most important one in his life." No one seizes on these words and accuses women of being prima donnas or egomaniacs. Yet when a man says he needs to be respected, he is often labeled, especially in our culture, as arrogant.

But it's amazing what happens when a woman gives a man respect and admiration. Just go back to your days of courting. During courtship the woman may have thought that her man was motivated to ask her to marry him because of her love. After all, love is what motivated her. In fact, her love was huge; there is no question about that. But more than she ever realized, it was her unique and intimate admiration that won her man's heart. The old saying puts it: "Every man does what he does for the admiration of one woman." Back in courtship days, she became that woman and he bowed the knee and proposed. He felt deep feelings of love for her, but they came out of his being convinced that she respected him and admired him. She was striking a chord deep within him that literally drove his life then as it drives his life today.

Wives virtually ask to be unloved when they "look down on their husbands" (Esther 1:17 NIRV).

I believe that men hold respect and honor as almost equal values. My experience as a man, and with other men, tells me that in our arena we have an honor code, and if we don't live by that honor code, we're in big trouble. We have learned from boyhood that there are certain things you just don't do, certain things you just don't say. A woman will talk to a husband in the home in the way that a man would never talk to him. He can't believe she can be so belligerent, so disrespectful.

The husband will often look away, wanting to drop the argument and move on. He doesn't want to talk about it. Why? Because he feels engulfed and overpowered by his wife's dark countenance, negative emotions, and combative words. All this annoys and incites him. So he withdraws. To him, that is the honorable thing to do.

Are You a Criticizer or a Stonewaller?

According to John Gottman's extensive research, 85 percent of husbands eventually stonewall their wives during conflict. For a man, tension builds faster because his blood pressure and heart rate rise much higher and stay elevated much longer than his wife's.

During tense exchanges, a wife's negative criticism can overwhelm the husband and he has little appetite to deal with it. The wife sees such exchanges as potentially increasing love between them, and her heart-beats per minute (BPM) do not escalate. The husband, on the other hand, sees the exchange as an argument in which he is apt to lose respect, and this revs up his BPMs.

David's wife asked for the Crazy Cycle when "she despised him in her heart" (2 Samuel 6:16).

In an attempt to calm himself down, the husband will stonewall—become quiet, say nothing, or go off by himself. If asked why he has stonewalled, the husband will say something like, "I'm trying not to react." The wife may see her husband's stonewalling as unloving, but he does not. He is simply trying to do the honorable and respectable thing, but his wife thinks he's rejecting her. How could he possibly want to withdraw and stonewall her when all she has done is given him a minor criticism or two?

Gottman states, "Such interactions can produce a vicious cycle, especially in marriage with high levels of conflict. The more wives complain and criticize, the more husbands withdraw and stonewall; the more husbands withdraw and stonewall, the more wives complain and criticize."[2] Gottman adds that if a wife becomes belligerent and contemptuous, the marriage is in serious danger. If this cycle isn't broken, it will probably end in divorce.[3]

HOW WOMEN DEAL WITH CONFLICT BETWEEN THEMSELVES

My experience in counseling hundreds of marriages over the years confirms that husbands are, indeed, masterful stonewallers as a rule. Their wives, of course, are usually the ones who are the criticizers, the confronters, the ones who want to get things out on the table and get them settled. There are wives who stonewall at times, but in my experience, they are in the minority. My view is that when a wife does stonewall, she does so because she has lost confidence that her husband will hear her heart. She longs to connect but has given up hope. While his heart rate may be going through the roof, hers is slow and steady because her heart is broken. (See appendix D, p. 317.)

In the majority of cases, a wife who is in love with her husband will move toward him when she feels unloved. For example, it's the first year of marriage and he has been late to dinner two nights in a row without calling. She says to herself, *This is wrong. How can he be so insensitive? Am I last on his priority list? This is so unloving.* Instinctively, she proceeds to say what she believes is the loving thing when he comes through the door: "We need to talk. We need to talk right now. Please sit down and talk to me!"

In approaching her husband in this fashion, the wife is using the same approach she would use with a best girlfriend. When women have conflicts with each other, they both usually verbalize their feelings. They share what is on their hearts because instinctively they know it will eventually lead to reconciliation. At some point, one of them will say, "Well, I was wrong." Then the other will say, "No, I was wrong too. Will you forgive me?" And the other one says, "Yes, of course I'll forgive you. I'm really sorry." Then they hug, shed a few tears, and pretty soon they're laughing.

That's what I call bringing things full circle. Unfortunately, women think this approach will work with their husbands just as well as it does with their best girlfriends. When a problem arises and something feels unloving, the wife instinctively moves toward her husband to share her feelings. Her eventual goal is that both of them will apologize and then embrace. This is the way she keeps her marriage up-to-date—a high value for her. Her heart longs to resolve things and to reconcile. Her husband matters to her more than any other adult on earth. In truth, her confrontation is a compliment. She thinks, *Oh, that he could see my heart! Why does he close himself off from me?*

What a wife usually fails to see is that a big difference exists between her best girlfriend and her husband. A wife will be more judgmental toward her husband than toward her best girlfriend. She feels free to do this because, as his loving helpmate, part of her mission, in her mind, is to "help" change him into a loving man. She knows that if she can just get her criticisms out on the table, he can change. And if he'll change to be a bit more loving, she knows she will still outlove him.

A Wife's Self-Image May Depend on Her Husband's Approval

The typical wife also fails to realize that her self-image often rests on what she believes her husband thinks of her. This is not the case with a girlfriend. Her girlfriend's opinion of her is important, but not as vital as her husband's opinion.

Also, the marriage relationship, unlike her relationship to a girlfriend, is a topic of ongoing discussion between her and other women. Women want to report to each other how wonderful their marriages are. So a wife's negativity can intensify when her husband stonewalls her efforts to get him to change. He isn't making her feel good, and she can't report to her friends the joys of her marriage. If her negativity intensifies, she is in danger of becoming even more belligerent and contemptuous, and then her husband will close her off completely.

Proverbs 21:19 says, "It is better to live in a desert land than with a contentious and vexing woman." The sad irony is that a wife can become "contentious and vexing" because her husband misinterprets her. He doesn't decipher the code in which she cries, "I need your love." Instead, he hears, "I don't respect you." This sweet, tender, godly woman is misunderstood. When she gets too negative, she does herself—and her marriage—no favors.

Thankfully, some women are becoming aware that negative confrontation doesn't work. As one wife said:

> My strength and verbal skills aren't helping my marriage. I have come across to my husband as too strong and too controlling and too demanding and too critical. I have been his mommy and his teacher and his holy spirit. It's my own personal nature to lead and direct and control and fix and do right and make others do the same. He is scared of my tongue.

A Wife's Scolding Can Start the Crazy Cycle

When a man begins to feel that his wife no longer looks up to him but is looking down at him, the Crazy Cycle kicks in. The Crazy Cycle often starts when women start scolding in their homes. The word *scold* is often associated with mothers bawling out their children; the dictionary definition, however, says that scolding means to reprimand or criticize harshly and usually angrily and even openly. When a wife

A wife "who brings shame" on her husband "is like sickness in his bones" (Proverbs 12:4 NIRV).

comes at a husband with repeated reprimands and "scolding," this is a surefire way not only to annoy him but to treat him with disrespect. Wives, however, tend not to see this. As mothers, correction is part of their maternal nature. Unfortunately, they tend to mother their husbands also, as this mother admits:

> As I sat at the conference and listened to you speak about love for a wife, I had no problem hearing and agreeing with everything you were saying. Then on Saturday when you started talking about respect and the lack thereof, I have to be honest, I was taken aback. I was so focused on why he couldn't understand me that I was totally missing that he was feeling put down. I think this is especially true for me. As a mother of young children, I am forever trying to make them understand right from wrong. I never realized that I had been projecting that onto my husband as well. In all honesty, I don't think my husband really knew how to explain how my behavior was making him feel.

When a wife scolds her husband, she's only trying to help correct things, to keep things on an even keel. And there is no doubt at times men need this kind of help. But when a man begins to feel that what his wife is saying reduces him to a child being scolded, there can be trouble. He doesn't necessarily see his wife's heart; he only hears her words, which are saying that she's looking down on him. To paraphrase Proverbs, he would rather live in the wilderness than with this irritating woman. While many wives do not intend to be disrespectful, they appear that way to their husbands, and their husbands take refuge in stonewalling them. (For tips on how not to criticize or stonewall your spouse, see appendix A, p. 305.)

I've asked any number of businessmen, "Do you want your associates to love you or respect you?" They all laugh and say, "I could care less if they love me, but respect me? Absolutely!" Right or wrong, men interpret their world through the respect grid, and a wife's softened tone and facial expressions can do more for her marriage than she can imagine.

Sarah was talking to a wife about controlling her verbal venom toward her husband. The wife was showing disdain for him, which she knew was not wise. But her husband did things that made her so angry. In her view, the problem was strictly with him. He didn't clean up the kitchen right, he didn't put the dishes in the dishwasher correctly, and he didn't pick up after himself the way she expected, so she had turned sour and negative. The wife heard what Sarah was trying to say, but she felt overcome by her anger and hurt.

So Sarah asked this wife a question she asks many women who arrive at our conferences full of contempt for their husbands: "What if your son grew up and married someone like you?" The woman's mouth fell open. She was stunned. For the first time, she saw it! She would *never* want any woman to treat her son the way she was treating her husband. She realized that when her son became a husband, if his wife treated him with such anger and contempt, his spirit would be crushed and he would shut down in defeat. When she heard it put this way, a completely new view surfaced. She saw herself more clearly than ever before, and she vowed to change.

As a retort to his wife's contempt, David communicates that he "will be held in honor" (2 Samuel 6:22 NIV).

This lady is a vivid example of many wives who come to our conferences. They have mixed emotions. They love their husbands, yes, but respect them? No. That is why we constantly encourage wives to ask themselves one question: "Is what I'm about to say or do going to come across as respectful or disrespectful?" This prevents a wife from misrepresenting her heart by coming across too negatively.

This whole idea of the male need for respect is new information to many women. In seminar sessions women sit in disbelief when I tell them that Scripture commands wives to give their husbands unconditional respect. I understand their confusion. They are so wired to love, and the culture has so radically enforced this whole idea of love-love-love, that they don't really know the men they are married to. In fact, they often respond, "This is totally foreign to me."

To speak his language, remember: "the wife must respect her husband" (Ephesians 5:33 NIV).

And that's exactly the problem. When a wife does not speak "respect language," after a while her husband isn't interested in communicating. Who wants to keep talking to someone who doesn't speak your language? So the husband goes quiet and walks away. Even though wives are told that husbands feel, "My wife doesn't respect me," their response is, "What's that got to do with anything?" The answer, quite obviously, is: *everything.*

It is high time for women to start discovering how their husbands really feel. One wife was shocked when she asked her husband, "Do you want me to tell you that I love you or that I respect you?"

Without hesitation he replied, "Respect." She couldn't believe her ears. She had never realized that though he needed her love, what he lacked was assurance of her respect. Learning this is hard on many a wife, and I am sorry that they have to feel everything from amazement to shame. No one is trying to shame wives. On the contrary, our Love and Respect message is designed to help wives see that their big, powerful husbands are really in need of something that wives can give—respect. When a husband receives unconditional respect from his wife, those fond feelings of affection will return, and he will start giving her the kind of love she has always hoped to receive.

"So That's It . . . I Need Respect!"

But not all men are conscious of their need for respect. Even significant leaders adept at assessing many different people in many different situations are not always in touch with why they react the way they do in their marriages. I had lunch with a man who ran for the United States Senate and, as I explained the Love and Respect Connection, he said, "Now that you've put it that way, that is exactly how I feel. That's it. I want respect."

A CEO of a large company attended our conference and, as he reflected on what he had heard, he realized he was reacting to his wife because he felt disrespected. He started voicing this to her, and though it created some tension for a while, it eventually resulted in a deeper understanding between them. In his words, "It helps me and her. When I humbly voice my feelings, we both know what's going on, instead of me just being moody and withdrawing. Now as she seeks to understand me, her appeal to me to understand her need for love really makes sense. It feels fair."

I have an acquaintance who has a PhD in educational psychology. As he went over the Crazy Cycle material with me, he said, "That is exactly what I feel when things get heated between my wife and me. For years it was something I was feeling down deep but wasn't in tune with. I was reacting all right, but neither of us knew why."

The common thread in what these three men said is that they couldn't articulate their need for respect, but once it was pointed out, they understood. Early on they quite possibly may have thought to themselves at times, *I don't deserve this disrespect.* But they soon suppressed those feelings. This is quite typical of today's male because the culture has told him it isn't right to express feelings of being disrespected, and if he dared to do so, his wife would not accept it because to her he would sound "arrogant."

Another thing that may stop a man from voicing his need for respect is hearing from his wife, "You don't deserve my respect." With his vocabulary rejected as archaic and his attitude criticized as arrogant, it doesn't take long for a male to file away his essential need for respect in a compartment labeled, "Do Not Bring Up." And there it will stay—but if another woman admires him, then look out. As one wife shared after her husband strayed into an affair:

> I realized that my husband had cheated with this woman, not because of her looks or her personality, or because she was anything so great, but rather because she was his captiv[e] audience. She thought he hung the moon. Every remark he made to her was witty; everything he did was perfect. In her eyes, he was the most handsome, intelligent, funny man in the world. He needed an ego boost, and she was ready and willing to be that for him.

ARE LOVE AND RESPECT THE SAME THING?

There are many wives who tell me, "Respect and love are the same thing." I respond, "No, they aren't, and you know they aren't. For instance, you respect your boss. You don't love your boss." I have been in counseling sessions with couples, and with her mate sitting there listening, the wife will readily say, "I love my husband but don't feel any respect for him." But when I turn this around and ask the wives how they would feel if they would hear their husbands say, "I respect you but don't love you," they are horrified. They exclaim, "I would be devastated."

I asked one wife, "How long would it take you to get over that?" She quickly answered, "Forever."

The typical wife would be up in arms if she heard, "I respect you but don't love you." That is taboo! She would view her husband as a very unloving human being. Yet this same wife feels she can readily say to him, "I love you but don't respect you." What she doesn't understand is that her husband is equally devastated by her comment and it also takes him "forever" to "get over it." The bottom line is that husbands and wives have needs that are truly equal. She needs unconditional love, and he needs unconditional respect.

ALL THIS SHOULD BE OBVIOUS, RIGHT?

Almost every time Sarah and I teach our seminar about the Love and Respect Connection, people tell us, "Why, of course; this is so obvious." And then either the husband or the wife adds, "But why doesn't my spouse get it?" Whether it's a husband or a wife who "doesn't get it," the answer is the same: *we often don't see the obvious.*

A door-to-door salesman rang the bell and waited. A boy who looked about ten years old answered. He was smoking the biggest cigar the salesman had ever seen. After a few seconds of stunned silence on the salesman's part, he finally asked, "Is your mother home?" The ten-year-old puffed a couple of times, blew smoke in the salesman's face, and said, "What do *you* think?"

And that's the point. If the salesman had been thinking at all, he would have known that Mother wasn't at home. But for some reason we don't always think, particularly when something is shocking or distracting. When a wife feels unloved, it can be such a shock to her heart that she is oblivious to her disrespectful reactions toward her husband, though any man watching could see it plainly. When a husband feels disrespected, it can provoke him so quickly he doesn't see his unloving reaction, which would be obvious to any woman. Words of wisdom for all husbands and wives are these:

WE EASILY SEE WHAT IS DONE TO US
BEFORE WE SEE WHAT WE ARE DOING TO OUR MATE.

When sorting out how to slow down the Crazy Cycle, it helps to remember that men are commanded to love because they don't love naturally, and on the other side, women are commanded to respect because they don't respect naturally. If the Love and Respect Connection is to make sense and work in a marriage, the wife, in particular, must conquer any feelings about her husband needing to earn her respect. I have counseled many wives who love to love, but they do not love to respect. When these women feel unloved, often they will try to improve the situation with even more love. That's natural. But when these women feel unloved, it is hard for them to show respect. That's unnatural. They act disrespectfully, but they don't really want to. They are merely reacting to their built-in feelings. Not realizing how contemptuous she sounds, a wife might say, "He's blowing this 'respect thing' out of proportion. He's too sensitive. My scolding and sour look stay. That's who I am at times. He needs to get over it! This is *his* problem."

But, of course, it isn't his problem; it's *their* problem. How would this wife feel if her husband would say, "You're blowing this love thing out of proportion. You're just too sensitive. You're always telling me I'm too harsh. You need to get over it"?

Husbands, of course, also have their work cut out for them. Because they are feeling disrespected, they can lose sight of the heart of their wives. It is easy to lose fond feelings of affection in the face of what appears to be contempt. But is her goal to emasculate you? Not if she is good-willed. Even if she is unfairly nasty, this is no excuse for a man of honor to refuse to obey God's command to love his wife. I believe the men who are reading this book are men of honor, and my appeal to them is this: *Love your wife. Always try to see what is in her deepest heart.*

If a husband has any honor and goodwill at all, he must step up to the plate and start figuring out this business of "being loving." And he must conquer any fears he may have of her contempt. Her criticisms may not be contempt at all; they are simply her way of crying, "Please love me." When a husband can decode that cry and respond to his wife with understanding and love, he will experience the joy of a fair and balanced approach to marriage, and those fond feelings of affection will return. I have talked to many men who say they want to try but are clueless as to how to go about it. Fortunately, there are plenty of clues, which I am always happy to share with any husband who is willing to listen, learn, and then change his approach to his wife. (See especially chapters 5 to 7, as well as chapters 8 to 14.)

MARRIED COUPLES ARE AT A CROSSROADS

Today married couples are at a crossroads. Will she appreciate her husband's need for respect, or will she denounce his feelings? Will she discover that the best way to love a husband is by respecting him in ways that are meaningful to him? Or will she focus totally on what she feels is the key to a happy marriage—her womanly feelings—and dismiss his needs as antiquated or male arrogance?

At the same time, will the husband appreciate his wife's need for love or just continue to ignore her feelings? Will he discover the best way to love a wife is to look beyond her criticisms and complaints to see why she isn't feeling loved? Or will he just cower before her apparent contempt and retreat to the shelter of his "stone wall"?

In a marriage, the wise person give[s] thought to their ways" (Proverbs 14:8 NIV).

Increasing numbers of couples who are at the crossroads are taking the right fork—the one labeled "Love and Respect." One wife, a strong-minded career woman, wrote to tell us of how she and her husband were using the Love and Respect Connection concepts and that their Crazy Cycle is slowing down and has all but stopped. She wrote:

My husband was able to see that when he would withdraw (often because I was disrespectful), I would feel abandoned or unloved. So I would go after him with a vengeance that would make a warrior cower . . . which would disrespect him and hurt him deeply, causing him to withdraw even more severely—the whole "Crazy Cycle." But he, for the first time, was willing to see that he had acted "unlovingly." He was able to own some part of it. I think he was able to see that I was more delicate (even though I try really hard to sell my strength to everyone, including him) and that I do need him and want his support and strength. I asked him to forgive me for being so disrespectful. We have been talking and things have been gradually changing. Mutual understanding is setting in.

At some points in this chapter I may sound as if I'm trying to hammer the wives on their lack of unconditional respect for their husbands. But I'm not trying to hammer wives—*I'm trying to help them*, because I know how pivotal the wife's respect can be in slowing down the Crazy Cycle. Yes, many men are unloving clods to one degree or another, but they can change. In fact, many of them want to change, and the best way to get them to change is treating them with unconditional respect.

In our conferences and counseling situations, we deal constantly with husbands and wives who quickly grasp the concept of the Crazy Cycle. They would like to get off—as soon as possible—but there are still a few reservations. They have been spinning for so long they wonder, *Can this stuff really work?* In chapter 5, we will start looking at answers to some typical questions and give practical advice for stopping the Crazy Cycle.

CHAPTER FIVE

SHE FEARS BEING A DOORMAT; HE'S TIRED OF "JUST NOT GETTING IT"

I have counseled many wives who want to try the unconditional respect approach, but they are still not totally convinced that it will work. That old, "The rat needs to earn my respect" attitude dies hard. And I have counseled many husbands who truly want to be loving men. They are willing to try but are wary of looking like unloving fools—again.

Questions from wives and husbands who want to try to stop the Crazy Cycle, or at least slow it down, usually focus in three general areas:

1. She wonders, *Won't I wind up just being a doormat?*
   He wonders, *Why can't she see I'm tired of hearing, "You just don't get it!"?*

2. She thinks, *But if I don't really feel respectful, I'll be a hypocrite.*
   He thinks, *I get no respect—what's the use?*

3. She thinks, *Can I really ever forgive him?*
   He thinks, *I blew it again . . . nobody can love that woman!*

I want to deal with all these reservations to show husbands and wives that, while these concerns are typical and natural, there are answers that can give them courage and motivation to start using the Love and Respect Connection to stop the Crazy Cycle. As we will see, in each of these areas the wife's concern is a mirror image of her husband's concern in many ways.

WHO SHOULD MAKE THE FIRST MOVE?

But before we start, there is one critical question for husband and wife to consider. As we think about stopping the Crazy Cycle, who makes the first move? As a wife, whatever you do, don't say, "Emerson is right. I need your love, so start loving me and I'll show you respect." That simply won't work because that attitude is in itself disrespectful, and it triggers an unloving reaction. You are making your husband responsible for both the love and respect in the marriage. He will simply shut down.

On the other side, as a husband, never say, "Emerson is right. If you respect me, all will be well and I will be more loving." That won't work either because that attitude is in itself unloving, and it triggers a disrespectful reaction. You are making your wife responsible for both the love and the respect in the marriage. She will simply shut down.

So who should make the first move? In our marriage conferences, I explain that I prayed about this, and here is the answer God gave me: *the one who sees himself or herself as the most mature.* You see, you can't wait for your spouse to go first, even though it's preferable. All of us want our spouse to be the first to start doing the respecting or the loving. But can you afford to wait passively for this to happen, like some kind of neutral bystander? Can a husband wait for his wife to respect him before he becomes more loving? Can a wife wait for a husband to really love her so she will then show him respect?

The fear, of course, is that you will show love or respect to your spouse, as the case may be, and get a bad response. So you tend to pull back, waiting for the other person to move first. But what are your options? Holding back your love or respect will just keep the Crazy Cycle spinning away, but being mature and making the first move could slow it down.

Think about it this way. It is absolutely ineffective for a husband to shout, "I'm not loving that woman until she starts respecting me!" It is pointless for a wife to scream, "I'm not respecting him until he starts loving me!" Taking the role of the mature mate and moving first may be risky, but it is very powerful. Rarely can you lose. Think about it. You know if your spouse acted first, you would respond positively. Knowing that, do you really believe that your spouse doesn't have enough goodwill to react lovingly or respectfully if *you* make the first move? When you touch your spouse's deepest need, something good almost always happens. The key to energizing your spouse is meeting your spouse's heartfelt desire. (For how to say it, see appendix A, p. 305.)

In your marriage, be the first to "seek peace and pursue it" (1 Peter 3:11).

In this chapter, and in chapters 6 and 7, we will be looking at three general areas of concern held by husbands and wives who would like to stop the Crazy Cycle but still have a few reservations. The first concern is one we hear a lot in our conferences: the wife fears that unconditionally respecting her husband will guarantee that she will wind up being a doormat.

NOT A DOORMAT BUT A WOMAN WITH POWER

As I encourage some wives to use unconditional respect, I can tell they suspect that I am a chauvinist in sheep's clothing trying to set them up for a life of subservience. I remind such a wife to be patient. I'm trying to help her get her husband to love her *more,* not run rough-shod over her.

When I talk about respecting your husband, I do not mean being a doormat. I do not mean burying your brains, never showing your leadership ability, or never disagreeing in the slightest way. I do not mean that he is superior and you are inferior in some way. Nor do I want you to ignore your hurts and vulnerabilities.

Despite my assurances, some wives fear that taking a respectful atti-tude during a conflict with their husbands will render them powerless. These women do not believe a husband will change into a loving man unless he is awakened to his flaws. And the only way he will awaken to his inadequacies and faults is to hear his wife's grumblings, corrections, and contempt. One wife confessed, "I would listen in on phone con-versations (or conversations in a group of people) to 'correct' any mis-statements he might make."

Another wife admitted "mothering" her husband. "As mothers, it is built into us to be instructors—that's a major part of motherhood. But it is extremely difficult to differentiate our roles between mother and wife. For instance, when baby comes along, Dad seems at a loss as to what to do and we 'instruct' Dad. Over time, we start instructing in many areas."

> Wives, "do what is right and do not give way to fear"
>
> (1 Peter 3:6 NIV).

The typical wife knows instinctively that correcting and mothering her husband are not good ways to approach him, but what else can she do? If she keeps win-ning battles this way, it could help her win the war of changing him into the kind of man she feels he ought to be. She keeps on using neg-ativity because she feels empowered by it. She thinks it gets through to him. She knows being nice doesn't get through to him because he just seems to ignore that. Her disrespect gets his attention and she seems to win the skirmishes, which are usually about the same problems: being late, working too much, poor parenting, insensitivity, etc. But none of these problems is the root of the issue. Lack of love and respect is at the heart of it all. (To evaluate your approach to your spouse, see appendix B, p. 309.)

As John Gottman observes, "The major goal is to break the cycle of negativity."[1] One wife confessed, "Most people would label me 'one of the happiest, most positive people I know,' but then something happens behind closed doors. I can yell and scream and rant on about little issues forever."

Unfortunately, the wife who feels empowered by negativity isn't even aware she needs to break that cycle. But she may sense that her criticisms don't motivate him to be more loving, so she tries to apologize after an argument or a conflict. He may accept her apology because he knows she is a good-willed woman who feels badly. But as the Crazy Cycle spins again the next month (or week) and then continues in a distinct pattern, he begins to believe that she has contempt for him as a human being—that she secretly despises him.

Because he is confused, he doesn't ask the question, "Don't you respect me?" for fear she'll say, "No, I don't." That frightens him so he avoids it. As a result, she gets locked into disrespect as a way of communicating her irritation and goading him to change. But over the course of the marriage, something slowly dies between them. She wins the battles, but deep down she knows she is losing the war.

WHAT IF YOU'RE AFRAID TO TAKE THE RISK?

But suppose she attends a Love and Respect Conference and learns what can happen if she begins showing her husband unconditional respect. She sees a glimmer of hope, but possibly she is afraid to "take the risk." I talk to many wives who find themselves in this state of mind after hearing our message for the first time. A wife wrote, "I am willing to try this approach as a key to improve my marriage relationship. It's a risk because I do not know what my husband's response will be. I am holding God's hand and trusting him."

In ages past, wives were "holy women . . . who hoped in God" (1 Peter 3:5), and today God calls wives to do the same.

To this dear woman, and to all others like her, I say taking the risk is the way to achieving your goal! If a wife can trust her husband's basic goodwill and his good intentions (even though he may be acting unloving at times), she can turn her marriage around, as the following reports testify. One woman wrote to admit she was sad because she had been married twenty-two years and was just starting to understand the Love and Respect message. She said:

> I wrote my husband two letters about why I respected him. I am amazed at how it has softened him in his response to me. I have prayed for years that my husband would love me, and speak my love language. But when I begin to speak his language, then he responds with what I have wanted.

Another wife who had attended our Love and Respect Conference with her husband wrote:

> I am nearly in shock at the changes in my husband in the last several days. To give you some background . . . we had a major fight last January and Round Two came in May. That was when he told me he didn't know how he felt about me, and didn't know what our future was together. Talk about a Crazy Cycle! We had jumped on and were running to our death.
>
> The thing that struck me was your comment that a man can feel the loss of respect so deeply but not be able to give voice or vocabulary as to what is wrong. As a man who is not given to voic-

ing his emotions much on a good day, I believe this is how my husband was affected. He was able to tell me I had pushed him too hard, but I didn't understand what button I had pushed. As a result, a lot of my efforts to reach out over the last six months backfired.

So, on New Year's Eve I left a card in his lunch box. Nothing mushy, just a "You give me many reasons to smile" message, to which I added "and many things about you I respect," then I said thanks for Christmas and Happy New Year. The next day he got up from the table and brought a chair for me! This last Sunday he suggested going to a movie in the evening, sat and talked before the movie started, proposed going to a musical in town next week. In general, he has been much more open and communicative. . . .

While it would be simplistic and untrue to say all our problems are magically solved, there is a bridge between us that did not exist a week ago. I have yet to hear the "L" word from his lips, but his actions are such that I know it still exists in his heart, and I intend, with God's help, to fan that flame as much as possible.

Following are comments from three different women who have also discovered the power of respecting their husbands:

I didn't know something from God could be so easy. I have believed in God my whole life [but] I was not taught this before. But it does make so much sense. If you respect your husband, he will love you. It may not always be in the ways I love him but he does in his own special way. I thank God every day for letting me learn this.

I was so "in the dark" about a man's number one need being respect . . . even over love. Now, instead of just telling him that I love him, I have begun telling him what I appreciate and admire about him. He eats it up!

———

A close friend called to tell me God wanted me to listen to what you were saying about respect. My husband and I have gone to numerous marriage conferences and read many books together but nothing remotely like this has ever been mentioned. I think this is the key to understanding my husband and to a joyful marriage. It is amazing what God does when you obey Him.

All these wives have "gotten it." They have decoded the messages their husbands were sending. They have learned how vulnerable a man can be to a wife's anger and contempt. Best of all, they have adjusted their pink sunglasses and pink hearing aids and are aware that when a wife respects her husband she does *not* become a doormat. In fact, he starts rolling out the red carpet for her!

But what about husbands who need to adjust their blue sunglasses and blue hearing aids and do their part to make the Love and Respect Connection? I have talked to many men who would be willing to try, but they feel clueless about how to begin. We'll look at their problems below.

HUSBANDS, REMEMBER ONLY ONE IDEA—LOVE

In the last few years, I have counseled with not a few men who say they are tired of hearing the relentless mantra, "You men just don't get it. You're stupid." They admit they don't grasp certain things, but being labeled "neanderthal" and "caveman" is demeaning and discouraging. If the cave existed, these men would favor going there to hide! They would agree with the biblical proverbs that say it is better for a disrespected man to live in a corner of the roof or in a desert land than with a contentious and vexing woman (see Proverbs 21:9, 19). As one husband plaintively but aptly put it: "I have spent the last twenty years literally consumed with trying to figure out what is going on in our marriage."

I sympathize with these husbands because there were plenty of times in the last thirty years when I felt the same way! But I want to remind all husbands that their wives are basically good-willed women. They are only acting critical, contentious, and disrespectful because they are crying out for love. The honorable husband who is man enough to try to turn things around must learn how to respond when he's feeling disrespected and offended. He must learn what to do in the face of his wife's negative reactions and accusations that he is unloving.

No matter how hard it gets, "husbands, love your wives" (Colossians 3:19).

The good news is that the husband need only focus on two questions. First, he must ask, "Is my wife coming across to me disrespectfully because she is feeling unloved?" Good things are in store when he learns to decode his wife's deepest cry: "Please love me!" To do this decoding, a husband must ask himself what his wife has against him—*why* she feels rejected and even abandoned. The husband may or may not completely decode the wife's message, but the point is he will be trying to understand her, not attack her back. Second, a husband must ask, "Will what I say or do next come across as loving or unloving to my wife?"

In Genesis 29 and 30 we read of the marriage of Jacob and Rachel. First, they were madly in love. He was willing to work seven years for her, and it only seemed as if it were a "few days." Then, after being tricked by his uncle Laban into marrying Rachel's sister, Leah, Jacob was required to work seven *more* years before Rachel could become his wife. But when Leah had children and Rachel didn't, Rachel became jealous and confronted Jacob, pleading, "Give me children, or else I die" (Genesis 30:1). Instead of comforting Rachel, Jacob got angry and said, "Am I in the place of God, who has withheld from you the fruit of the womb?" (v. 2) Instead of getting angry, Jacob could have tried to decode Rachel's demand. Was she really expecting him to be in the place of God? Or was she ventilating her inner pain over her barrenness and the social struggle she was having with her sister to be closest to Jacob's heart?

As a husband, I am always seeking to decode what my wife is feeling. Suppose Sarah confronts me in a way that leaves me feeling offended, disrespected, or described as unloving. I can react defensively and say, "Women! Who can ever understand them?" Or, because I know the Crazy Cycle is always ready to spin, I can realize Sarah is actually crying out to me. She needs me. She isn't trying to emasculate me.

In the heart of every wife is this cry: "surely now my husband will love me" (Genesis 29:32).

True, when I feel offended, it just goes against my natural grain for me to say, "Oh, I get it. Sarah wants me to love her." But I know that is precisely what is going on because I am sure I'm married to a good-willed woman. She isn't deliberately trying to be disrespectful and contemptuous; she is simply letting me know that I have stepped on her air hose—again—and she needs my love more than ever.

THIS HUSBAND DECODED IN JAIL

One husband learned how to decode his wife the hard way. Here is how he described his "epiphany" experience:

> On a Saturday evening, I threw a dish in anger that hit my wife in the face and left a small cut. She called the police and I was handcuffed and taken off to jail. A magistrate thought it best for me to

sit out the weekend there and held me over on a LOT of bond. I wouldn't pay it . . . [and] after about four hours on a steel cot the novelty wore off and I really started to think hard about why I was there. With nothing to read, no place to go, and not able to sleep any more, I basically paced and prayed for two days. One single Scripture stayed in my mind the whole time: "Husbands, love your wives as Christ loved the church . . ."

For two days, God replayed the memories I had of our arguments and in each one I was acutely aware of how I had failed to love my wife. It was like pausing a video and having Someone point to it and say, "See, right here you could have reached out to her and reassured her, but you were too busy trying to prove your point."

At one point I was seeing her face, all distorted with rage as she screamed at me, but totally without any sound . . . the mute button had been pushed on this memory, and then little by little the sound came up so I could hear it. Only the words were not what my wife had been screaming at me. Instead, they were replaced with other words that I needed to hear: "I want you to LOVE me, why won't you LOVE me? I'm afraid and insecure and I need you to hold me and LOVE me. . . ."

And that's when I began to weep. All this time I had been so totally wrapped up in my own needs—to demand respect, to be right at any cost, to win a petty argument—this hurt our priceless relationship. I had been so caught up in the words that I had totally missed her heart, her need.

This was my epiphany, and this is why Scripture commands me to love my wife as Christ loved the church. In my conversations with men since then, I have seen the color drain from their faces as I tell them about my experience, and I see the dawning of their own awareness as they realize how they have blown it, too. We NEED this command, but not many of us know just how badly.

Anyway, God sat me down for two days in jail, took away all the distractions, and forced me to look at myself in a way I had never done before. By the end of it, I had been totally emotionally ruined and rebuilt, and I could hardly wait to get home and share with my wife what God had shown me! My last evening in my cell I was freer than I had ever been. I knew the Lord had spoken to me and I knew I was going to do something about it, first in my own marriage, and then in others if the Lord allowed.

Although the husband and his wife reconciled, the court ordered him to attend domestic violence counseling, which he was happy to do. He waited over a year after his experience to validate the changes in his life and then, with the blessing of his pastor, he began to invite other men to discuss the topic of marriage with him. Now he and his wife meet with couples who come to them with domestic issues like the ones they had. He adds, "I'll forever be grieved at what I did to my wife, and forever grateful for what He has done for our marriage since."

There are many reasons I like this man's story, but perhaps best of all is that the wife was the first one to contact us when she ordered our resources to learn more about unconditionally respecting her husband. In her e-mail request, she said absolutely nothing about the abusive incident. She only wrote that she was:

> . . . mightily convicted about my need for learning this vital aspect of my wifely role. My husband has a men's Bible study where, naturally, the focus is on loving and leading your wife God's way. There is a dearth of material on the other important aspect of a godly marriage, namely, wives and respect. Lots on submission, but not much on respect. My husband and I have been married, very badly (and without God) . . . and we are

committed to making our relationship one that honors and glorifies His presence and grace in our lives.

There was not one hint of how she took a dish in the face and how he had to go to jail. I was curious about the kind of Bible study her husband was conducting, so I e-mailed him and asked him to explain what he was doing and why. That's when he told me the whole story about hitting his wife, going to jail, and figuring things out as he paced up and down in his cell. What a woman! What a man! He had changed so much that she yearned to do her part and now they work together to help other marriages.

Can a husband understand? In serious conflict, if a husband reassures his wife that he truly loves her in spite of the argument they are having, and he avoids like the plague sending the message, "I don't love you," all will be fine. One man wrote to tell us how he finally learned to decode:

> Later that night, in my mind, I went over what she said and what you taught. I prayed for wisdom. By this time a good deal of the hurt had worn off (I have been through this many times before), but this time there was something different. There was a peace and reassurance I had not felt before, as if the Holy Spirit was saying, "Stay calm, don't push it, just relax." And I did. I did not sleep very well at all that night and spent a lot of time thinking. It was then I was able to decode what she was really saying. She was trying to express the pain she felt in our marriage. . . .
>
> It took all night for me to understand what was behind her words; her words were not respectful or loving, but what she was trying to say was deeper and I began to "decode" that. I started off by telling her what I thought was behind what she said, and that it

was her way of expressing the pain she felt. It started an hour-long discussion that ended up with my wife sitting in my lap with her arms around me weeping and weeping. It was an emotional release of sorrow. It was a very sad time of grief, but it was HEALING. It was the first time that she had ever done that. This was the first time she felt that I had understood her.

What did this husband do to get to this "breakthrough" point in his marriage? He stayed calm. He prayed for wisdom. He relaxed—and he adjusted his sunglasses. Instead of just seeing blue, he tried to see some pink, and his wife's pain became clear. As we saw in chapter 2, a key to decoding one another's messages is to be aware of her pink sunglasses and hearing aids and his blue ones. But both spouses can adjust their lenses if they want to try. As another husband wrote to tell me:

> I believe that the Holy Spirit is revealing (polite way of saying "hit between the eyes with a 2x4") my inability to "decode." I see only through my own lens and fail to see through hers. I fail to get behind "her eyes."

The Crazy Cycle can be slowed—and stopped—if only we would have eyes to see and ears to hear.

CHAPTER SIX

SHE WORRIES ABOUT BEING A HYPOCRITE; HE COMPLAINS, "I GET NO RESPECT!"

She had been married for thirty-eight years, and it hadn't been easy. Her husband had served in reconnaissance with the U.S. Marines in Vietnam and had returned with post-traumatic stress disorder. For years following the war he dealt with his memories by being an over-achiever, and he became very successful. Although a Christian, he eventually got into an affair and became an alcoholic, ruining his health.

"He is unable to work," her letter continued. "He is away from the Lord. For years I have been 'stuck' on the command for wives to respect their husbands. If the Lord said it, I believe it's true, but I did not want to be a hypocrite. . . ."

Many wives find themselves in similar situations, and they often tell me that, while they want to be respectful and obedient to the Lord, they don't want to be hypocritical, going through motions that don't mean anything. Gently but firmly I respond that I'm not asking wives to be hypocrites by respecting their husbands even if they don't "feel respectful." This really isn't about feelings. It's about how wives can help control the Crazy Cycle by doing what the Scriptures teach. Peter calls wives to respectful and chaste behavior in order to win husbands who are being disobedient to God's Word (see 1 Peter 3:1–2). Obviously, wives can go on "winning the battles" by attacking, criticizing, or lecturing husbands who are drinking, straying, or whatever their problems may be, but they will eventually lose the war.

When a man is harsh, uncaring, or unaware, the wife can say he is unloving and needs to change; that he needs to correct himself— and I agree completely. Obviously, the man needs to understand her womanliness and need for love. If her spirit deflates and she becomes grieved, he is called to be a man of honor and serve her needs. But here is the rub: such a man may be called, but he won't necessarily answer. At this point a wife faces two basic choices. She can try to make personal adjustments and treat her husband respectfully according to what Scripture says, or she can continue with a sour look and a negative, disrespectful attitude. She can continue to contend, "If he feels disrespected, that's his problem. How can I feel respect for him when he is so unaware of me and my feelings? That would be hypocritical."

I understand why a wife could feel hypocritical about respecting a man who has been treating her badly. But to continue with disrespect only means shooting herself in both feet. Few wives have real malice in their hearts, but their negative emotions can get the better of them. The deepest yearning of their hearts—for love—is clouded by negativity. Not only do husbands feel they can never fulfill a wife's expectation of love, but now they feel disrespected for who they are.

The typical man cannot put a voice to this, but he feels responsible to meet his wife's need for love and somehow try to meet his own need for respect. This kind of man shuts down in the face of it all. It is simply too overwhelming. Does the disrespected husband let his wife know how he feels? No. As a rule, a man doesn't complain and he doesn't cry. He simply grits his teeth and compartmentalizes his feelings. He may be dying inside, but he won't tell his wife for fear she'll say, "You don't deserve my respect." So he grows silent. He withdraws, possibly walks away in anger. She has won another battle but feels even more unloved.

We are called to follow Jesus, who "kept entrusting Himself to Him who judges righteously" (1 Peter 2:23).

She feels caught. She doesn't feel any love coming from him, so showing respect for him seems phony. Besides, if she shows respect, she feels he will "get his way." I asked one woman, "Are you afraid that your respectful manner will lessen your chances of motivating your husband to change?" Here is her response:

> After pondering that, I have concluded that this is where the rubber hits the road. If I trust my feelings (or previous experiences where contempt has seemed effective), I will be afraid to do it differently. If I step out in faith, claiming God's Word as the basis for my action, then I am trusting God to bring to pass what He said He would do. I can't go wrong with that! I've determined that is the path I am going to take no matter how unfamiliar it seems.

Amen! This wife "gets it"! Obeying God's Word does not make a wife a powerless hypocrite. Actually, it makes her a woman who loves and reverences God.

This can happen even in the most difficult situations. The lady whose letter opened this chapter put aside her fears of being a hypocrite and tried to be respectful to her husband. Her letter continues:

I am asking the Lord to show me ways to show [my husband] genuine respect. I have definitely seen a difference in his attitude toward me. I believe that more good things will come as I continue to show him unconditional respect, and after all, the Lord is responsible for the outcome. I have only to be obedient to Him, and He will handle what concerns me.

Exactly. We are not called to change everything or everyone. We are only called to be obedient, and God will handle it from there. I would never claim that this is simple and effortless. It takes tremendous faith, courage, and fortitude. But it can pay off in incredible ways, as one wife who read our Love and Respect materials learned. She writes:

It's amazing what can happen when a man feels respected. I knew that I needed to show unconditional respect for my husband whether I felt like it or not. I started going through the actions, even though the feelings weren't there. After a while, the feelings started to follow, especially now! My husband has been serving just as you said. This last weekend we had our neighbors over for dinner [and] my husband offered to cook the dinner. He also washed my car this weekend (he has never done that before) and out of his Christmas bonus, he gave me $500 to spend, no questions asked. He's also cleaned the kitchen and has done the dishes twice now. I've been sending him e-mails at work about once a week just to let him know I'm so thankful that, because of him and his hard work, I can be a stay-at-home mom to our two children. I've made sure the house is clean and dinner is done when he gets home from work. I've also made sure that I'm not wearing sweats and looking "ratty" when he comes home. I'm more pleasant and excited.

Trusting and obeying God's Word because we love and reverence God never, ever makes us a hypocrite! When the alarm goes off in the morning, we get up, even when we don't feel like getting up. Because we do what we don't feel like doing, does that make us hypocrites? No, it is a sign we are responsible people. Showing respectful behavior when we don't "feel respectful" is evidence of maturity, not hypocrisy.

Trust God to handle it. "The eyes of the Lord are on" those who do right, "and his ears are attentive to their prayer" (1 Peter 3:12 NIV).

REFUSE TO PLAY RODNEY DANGERFIELD— DON'T STONEWALL!

To the husband who may sense that his wife thinks being respectful to him is hypocritical, my advice is this: do not give up! And do not go into your well-worn Rodney Dangerfield mantra: "I just don't get no respect!" Instead, be a man of honor and move toward your wife even if you are receiving what feels like verbal deathblows. Call on that same sense of male honor that makes men willing to take a hit for their buddies in combat. Be willing to take a hit from your wife. You won't die (although at times death may seem preferable).

You can be the mature one who makes the first move toward your wife, even though she has seriously wronged you. As you engage her, you can take the verbal deathblows to stop the craziness. Yes, it will be hard and even humiliating, but you can win the heart of your wife! Scripture says, "A fool's anger is known at once, but a prudent man conceals dishonor" (Proverbs 12:16). Suppose your wife is being horribly disrespectful. There is no question that you have the "right" to be offended. But as a man of wisdom *you choose to conceal the dishonor.* You hear God calling you to take a different approach, and you *can* do it. If you keep saying that you can't, then you will persuade yourself this is impossible. You must distinguish between "I can't" and "I won't."

I USED TO SAY, "I'LL SHOW HER!"

In my own marriage, there was a season when it was important to me to get in tune to why I reacted to Sarah. As this notion of uncondi-tional respect surfaced in my soul, I still felt embarrassed to say directly

When offended, husbands should "act like men, be strong" (1 Corinthians 16:13).

to her, "I feel disrespected." That appeared to me to be self-centered and, admittedly, I was uncertain of Sarah's reply. Would she snap, "Well, you don't deserve respect"? I don't recall her ever saying that, but I distinctly recall thinking it would be dangerous to express feel-ings of being disrespected. It was much easier for me to send my mes-sage indirectly in code—by getting angry or going silent. In my anger, I was thinking, *She can't treat me this way. I'll show her!*

So I withdrew. Strangely, that never seemed to work. I didn't real-ize it at the time, but because I wanted respect I was trying to motivate her to be respectful by being unloving. (Sort of like trying to urge her to be more watchful by poking her in the eye with a sharp stick.)

There came a time, however, when I knew I had to be clearer. I had to grow up and be more mature. But how could I respond to Sarah so she could get my real message? As a man of honor, I needed to intro-duce some kind of change. The phrase I came up with was: "Honey, that felt disrespectful. Did I just now come across as unloving?" (For more ideas on what to say or not say, see appendix A, p. 305.)

I did not say, "Sarah, you are a disrespectful black widow spider using your venom to devour me!" Personal attacks never, ever work with anybody. The phrase, "That felt disrespectful," removed the per-sonal attack. I was not saying she was a disrespectful person. I was only describing what I felt. My new approach allowed me to express my feelings without claiming Sarah was wrong and I was right. I could say to Sarah, "I'm not saying I am right for feeling this way, nor am I saying you caused me to feel this way. I am only saying that I feel this way." I was not necessarily confessing these feelings were sinful, nor was I saying Sarah was an angel.

The line, "Honey, that felt disrespectful," has many possible applications. Sometimes I needed to grow up and not personalize things Sarah did or said as "disrespect." On other occasions, Sarah needed to be a little more positive about the man she married.

"The heart of the wise instructs his mouth, and adds persuasiveness to his lips" (Proverbs 16:23).

But the icing on the cake is when I would add, "Did I just come across as unloving?" This gave Sarah the benefit of the doubt, and often she returned the favor. Too many times in the past I had put her on the defensive. Countless times, Sarah had said in defeat, "It's always me. I'm always to blame. You are always right. You never do wrong."

My new approach gave Sarah a break. I didn't say I was always right and could never do wrong. I owned up to my part of the blame, and for her this was a breath of fresh air! Sarah quickly decided she loved hearing me say, "Honey, that felt disrespectful. Did I just now come across as unloving?"

Granted, these two sentences can feel a bit awkward the first time or two you use them. They are forcing you to be transparent and even to lead with your chin in some respects. But if a couple wishes to address the deepest issues when conflicts arise, this gets to it very quickly. If a couple wants to get off the Crazy Cycle, this speeds up the process. It certainly has for us.

True, there is a risk that Sarah might say, "Well, yes, I felt unloved because you are unloving and you don't deserve respect." For most couples that never happens. The power of these simple Love and Respect sentences is that both spouses feel affirmed at the level of deepest need. What usually happens is this: Sarah says, "Yes, I felt unloved. I am sorry for coming across so disrespectfully. Will you forgive me?"

I reply, "Yes. Will you forgive me for coming across as unloving?" She answers, "Of course." And it's over. Just that quickly.

IT WORKS—EVEN ON OUR BAD DAYS

Having said that, on any given day Sarah and I can get nasty with each other. We can get stubborn and pout. We can even raise our voices! I can give an evil glare. I can shut down, refusing to talk. Sarah can stomp out of the room. We step on each other's air hose—sometimes with gusto!

But no matter what happens, we both have a firm commitment that we will get to our Love and Respect sentences before we go to

It is always wise for a husband to be "humble in spirit" (1 Peter 3:8).

bed. If I'm feeling disrespected, I tell her so and then ask if I've been unloving. If she's feeling unloved, she tells me so and asks if she's been disrespectful. The biblical teaching is: "Be angry, and yet do not sin; do not let the sun go down on your anger" (Ephesians 4:26). This works, and it works well.

The struggle is in humbling yourself, authentically making these two brief statements, and then letting them lead to an honest discussion. If you don't want to see positive change in your marriage, you won't go there. But for me as a man, talking about feeling disrespected is in keeping with who I am. The Love and Respect message provides me an incentive to "go there." And when I say to Sarah, "Did I come across as unloving?" she is invigorated to engage me in response. It works.

If I Can Do It, So Can You

As mature men, we need to take leadership and put this out on the table. We must acknowledge our feelings—we need to feel respected. However, as we do this we must acknowledge our wife's feelings—she needs to feel loved! This is a fair and balanced approach that allows the two of you to unpack what really happened. Avoiding the whole thing time and again (or blowing up each time) remedies nothing. A spouse wrote:

> We were able to talk about "sticky" situations without the discussion ending in a heated argument. THAT was the phenomenal part! And we both were laying it on the line as far as admitting to one another, "Yes! That is how I've felt all these years!" . . . So we've begun this new level of learning together. I'm very excited. I already see my marriage improving dramatically. It was like a weight had been lifted from our very countenances when we conversed and came to all the realizations we had!

Admittedly, this takes guts. One man told me:

> I see my wife's anger and hate for me, and at times I just don't know how to deal with this. . . . I know that she is not asking for a lot, but I have never really been good at communicating with her and don't know how to start and then continue doing it. I am tired of fighting with her, and many times I avoid communicating so that it does not escalate into an argument. She perceives my lack of communication as not caring or being dishonest with her. I just don't know why it comes so hard for me to do.

Another husband put it this way:

> Our disagreements are centered on her emotional outbursts and
> my lack of emotion. I love my wife and consider myself emo-
> tional about her. However, I try not to allow emotion to con-
> trol me. I believe love is expressed with actions and not with
> reactions. . . . I do love the emotion my wife has, and I know
> God has us together to love and respect each other as we seek
> to glorify Him, but I struggle when my wife justifies her behav-
> ior as an uncontrollable emotional reaction. I'm not looking
> for something to condemn her with; instead, I would like to
> handle this.

To both these husbands I say, "Gentlemen, it is true you are not
designed by God to enjoy contempt, but He does call you to take
the hit."

In his extensive research on marriages, Dr. John Gottman concluded that it was very effective when a husband could embrace his
wife's anger. He advised men *not* to avoid conflict if they want to make
their marriages work. To sidestep the problem, to leave the conflict
unresolved, would only upset the wife more. The husband must always
remember that the wife must talk about what's eating her. As she vents
her feelings, she believes she is keeping the marriage healthy and helping the relationship work more smoothly. She is not trying to attack
her husband personally. "If you stay with her through this discomfort,
and listen to her criticisms," says Gottman, "she will calm down. If you
stonewall, she'll be edgy and may escalate the conflict."[1]

My suggestion to fellow husbands is: instead of running from your
wife, will you move toward her or let her move toward you, firing her
venomous little darts as she comes? If you're ready to take the hit, you
can stop the craziness. After she vents, you can lovingly say, "Honey, I

love you. I don't want this. When you talk this way, I know you're feeling unloved. Let's work on this. I want to come across more lovingly, and I hope you would like to come across more respectfully." (For more ideas, see appendices A, B, and C.)

The Husband Who Never Stopped Loving

One of the most striking examples of a husband who never stopped engaging his wife, even as she tried to deal their marriage a deathblow, came to me in an e-mail written by the wife after she and her husband had traveled six hundred miles to attend one of our conferences. When they arrived at the conference, their marriage was held together by a tattered thread. They both agreed it was the best conference they had ever attended, but they went back home with the wife still feeling very negative about the marriage. She was still tired of her life and her husband. But her husband wouldn't give up, and the rest of her e-mail tells the story:

> *"Suppose you love those who love you. Should anyone praise you for that? Even 'sinners' love those who love them"* (Luke 6:32 NIRV).

> We are still together today because, for the past few months, he has done exactly what you talked about at your conference concerning "His Love Regardless of Her Respect." He loved me when I was not lovable at all and held on to our marriage and his family, when there was absolutely NOTHING to hold on to.
>
> This past October I asked him to please leave the house. I wanted to be alone, I wanted space, and I just felt like I didn't love him anymore. Reluctantly, he left for a couple of weeks. . . . I knew that my life and the life of the girls would drastically change with a divorce. I thought about the shared visitation and how we would also have to sell our home, which we recently finished

remodeling, but I didn't care, I just wanted out! [Meanwhile] he prayed, studied marriage books and tapes, and made a decision to love me no matter what.

The girls were really starting to miss him not being around, so we decided he would return home "until further notice." Well, he would hold my hand every night and pray for me and for our marriage, as I stared up at the ceiling anxiously waiting for him to finish. He would leave little notes, or a little flower on the bathroom mirror or in my car. So many little things he would do to show me that he loved me and wasn't going to let this marriage end easily.

It just irritated me. I thought, *Can't he understand that I don't love him, that I don't want to be with him anymore? Why is he trying so hard?* I didn't feel that high "in love" feeling for him anymore. My needs weren't being met so I wanted out—very selfish and immature. . . .

I was emotionally going through something that neither of us really understood, but he stayed there and loved me through it. I'll spare you all the little extra details, but I eventually broke. No woman in her right mind could let go of that much love and commitment.

[Now] I am very much in love with my husband. I've learned that love is not a feeling, it's a choice, a commitment. We didn't become a statistic because my husband chose to love me no matter what my reaction toward him would be. It's really humbling to look back and see how loving and patient he was with me (trust me, it wasn't easy) and how he, only through the strength of Christ, saved our marriage. I can't say we're completely out of the tunnel yet, but we are certainly very close.

There is really little to add to this woman's story except, "Amen." Her husband understood, even when it seemed there was no way to understand. Her husband engaged her even when she would roll her eyes to the ceiling as he prayed (talk about disrespect, not to mention irreverence). The bottom line is, he won the game—*they* won the game—and they are together today because he was willing to do whatever it took to stop the Crazy Cycle. Then she finally got the message and wanted to stop it too.

No matter how desperate or hopeless a marriage may seem, if husband and wife both have basic goodwill in their hearts, they can stop the Crazy Cycle. But like the husband who never gave up, they have to be willing to do whatever it takes. In saying "do whatever it takes," I mean winning within the boundaries of "the law of Christ" (1 Corinthians 9:21). Christ's law may mean constant giving and forgiving: "Love covers a multitude of sins" (1 Peter 4:8; Matthew 5:38-46). But Christ's law may also mean turning someone away from "a multitude of sins" (James 5:20; Matthew 18:15). Love must be tough. To know which approach to take in your marriage, seek godly, wise counsel.

Of course, doing whatever it takes can take you where you may not want to go. As I counsel couples and conduct seminars, I continually find wives who have been so hurt and even abused that they don't think they can forgive their husbands. And I find husbands who just don't know what to do when she won't forgive. They keep saying to themselves that they've blown it again. And they eventually start thinking, *Could anybody live with this woman? I'm certainly not having much luck.* We'll look at these two concerns in chapter 7.

CHAPTER SEVEN

SHE THINKS SHE CAN'T FORGIVE HIM; HE SAYS, "NOBODY CAN LOVE THAT WOMAN!"

Many a wife is so beaten down by the unloving harshness of her husband that she simply has no hope. She has tried to forgive him again and again, and he only gets worse. Getting in his face—disrespecting him—seems to be the only way she can survive at all. She would like to stop the Crazy Cycle, but she will forgive him when he asks her for forgiveness and not before! The problem here is that few husbands will ask for forgiveness, particularly if the wife keeps going with her disrespect. The Crazy Cycle will spin and spin some more.

The Bible condemns a husband who is "harsh and evil in his dealings" (1 Samuel 25:3).

There are many books on forgiveness and quite a few Bible verses too. Jesus taught forgiveness, and so did Paul. When Peter asked Jesus if seven times was enough to forgive someone, Jesus replied, "[Not seven times], but up to seventy times seven" (Matthew 18:22). In other words, without limit.

Paul may have had Jesus's words in mind when he wrote, "Be kind to one another, tender-hearted, forgiving each other, just as God in Christ also has forgiven you" (Ephesians 4:32).

I freely admit that it's really not "fair" to ask wives to forgive their unloving husbands. But this isn't about fairness; it's about touching his *spirit,* and possibly God will touch him as well. The wife may have been mistreated, but she can influence the situation to take a new course. Can she overlook another unloving remark or thoughtless act? It is easier to forgive when you let go of the belief that your spouse intended evil. The Love and Respect Connection teaches that when the two of you wind up spinning on the Crazy Cycle, your husband did not intend to be unloving any more than you intended to be disrespectful. You reacted because you felt unloved!

If a wife is experiencing marital problems, she is no fool in God's eyes for trying to "be reconciled to her husband" (1 Corinthians 7:11).

Should a husband be unforgiving of your disrespect when your deepest cry was for love? Ideally, the answer is no. But, because he is human, your husband may react in ways that may be unloving when he feels you are disrespecting him. Why be unforgiving when all he wanted was to feel that you still respected who he is as a human being? He may have been harsh, uncaring, even uncouth, but he did not intend evil.

Some wives may be a bit cynical about what I am saying. From all your past history you just *know* your spouse intended evil—at least a little. But do you really think your husband's mission is to treat you unlovingly out of an evil heart? Your husband doesn't get up in the morning thinking, *What can I do to upset her today?* Nor do you awaken with the goal of offending him. Yet we do step on each other's air hose.

Yes, your husband's unloving actions or reactions hurt you. But as Paul put it, "Bear with each other and forgive whatever grievances you may have against one another. Forgive as the Lord forgave you" (Colossians 3:13 NIV). Surely, "forgive" includes your husband, so why not move first and be the mature one? When you forgive him for being unloving, you give up your right to hold a grudge and be disrespectful in return. By forgiving, you gain strength and freedom, and, amazingly, in many instances you halt the Crazy Cycle. A wife writes:

> I didn't respect my husband because I came from a family where my mom had divorced twice and my stepdad who raised me was an alcoholic and neither my mother nor my sisters had respect for him. I also didn't understand that respect was something that my husband needed. He is a very loving person, but he has done some things that have really hurt our marriage and me, and it has been difficult for me to forgive him. . . . I realize now that God focuses on the heart and not on the behavior. Because of this, I have found it easier to forgive my husband. This has set me free.

Jesus said, "He who is without sin among you, let him be the first to throw a stone at her" (John 8:7). Do you know why Sarah can readily forgive me for being unloving? My mature wife has accepted by faith that, in the eyes of God, her disrespect is equal to my lack of love. That is what Ephesians 5:33 loudly implies, so she has laid down her stones. She does not feel she has a right to judge me too severely. In turn, her example has profoundly affected me. When she is disrespectful toward me, I don't hold it against her. Who am I to judge her and overlook my unloving tendencies of anger and lack of servanthood? Forgiveness comes when we see our own unrighteousness. How can we refuse to forgive an offense when we, too, have offended?

Jesus's words of warning ring loud: "Do not judge so that you will not be judged. For in the way you judge, you will be judged. . . . Why do you look at the speck that is in your brother's eye, but do not notice the log that is in your own eye?" (Matthew 7:1–3).

As a wife, if you pass judgment on your husband for being unloving, ask yourself: *Am I guilty of being disrespectful?* One wife heard our Love and Respect message and wrote to tell us:

> My problem is this . . . I was really getting fired up about changing the way I treat and motivate my husband. But my husband stopped me dead in my tracks with news that he is having an affair and has been thinking of leaving me. My world is shattered. He is unsure if he loves me, but he is unready to decide which direction he is going. I want to embrace God's principles, but am unsure if it applies to me in this situation. I am looking for some advice on whether a cheating man is in the position to respond and whether I should be trying such a hard thing at this moment.

I replied to the woman's heart-wrenching situation by pointing out that using Love and Respect principles can and does work with a husband who has done what hers did. "He is in sin," I said. "He is offending both God and you. There is no question about this, but wives are winning their husbands in exactly this situation. We just met with a couple two weeks ago. She won him back. It can happen and it does happen, and it is worth it."

Several months later I e-mailed the woman to see how she was doing. She replied:

> Emerson, I listened hard to what you said to me. I listened even harder to what the Lord was saying, too. I spent months on my knees just getting through it all. . . .
>
> It is hard to explain the way my heart changed through this experience. I remain profoundly amazed that I have the ability to forgive something so unforgivable. I am astounded at the poise and control God provided me with when I was in the midst of my

struggles. . . . I would pray daily and really search my mind for ONE thing to respect about my husband. I despised him. I didn't think I would be able to find one thing. You gave me ideas, and places to start. So that is where I started. Then as we progressed in counseling, he did his part to reassure me she was gone and there was no further contact between them. . . .

It is funny, I feel as though I should have done more work to pick up the pieces of my heart and forgive him. God just did it all, and we never feel worthy of those kinds of miracles. . . . My husband is in love with me again, and has truly had a repentant heart. His affair is long over, and she is history completely, period. We are still in counseling, because there is so much we still need to do to repair a marriage that was never the best it could be. I would say our marriage is better now than it ever has been, and yet we still have a long way to go. God has helped me with my pain, and He has healed me so well.

It worked. I did win him back. When you told me I could, I really wondered if that was possible [but] God has changed my husband more than I have ever expected and I hope it continues. I have changed, too. I am finally seeing in me the wife that I always wanted to be.

There are two things in this lady's letter that are well worth noting. One is that she is amazed at how God put forgiveness in her heart as she committed to obeying His Word. She did not have to work at forgiving her husband; she only had to work on obeying the Lord, and then the forgiveness flowed into her heart. Second, she sees that she is now becoming the wife she "always wanted to be." She realizes that, while he had logs in his eye, she had her own to contend with. Forgiving is the direct opposite of judging. Nothing is easier than judging, nothing is harder than forgiving, and nothing can reap more blessings.

While wives may have trouble with forgiving unloving husbands, these same husbands may be tempted to think there is no way they can ever win—that nobody could love the woman they are married to. But that kind of thinking is a dead end. There is a way to win and to "love that woman" after all, as we will see below.

IF YOU FAIL TO LOVE HER, REBOUND!

Many basketball coaches put almost as much emphasis on rebounding as they do on shooting. Great players always chase down rebounds at both ends of the court. They pick up on the angle of the missed shot and position themselves to be in the right spot when the ball comes down off the rim. In many cases, after recovering the ball, they score a basket and get fouled in the process. Any coach will tell you good rebounding will keep his team in the game.

The analogy is obvious. The husband who is starting to "get it" about the Love and Respect Connection, and who seeks his wife's forgiveness, can't let a few misses stop him. Perhaps you have failed again to decode her deeper cry. You have failed again by reacting unlovingly to her contempt. In fact, you got tired of all the verbal blows and you stonewalled, withdrawing from her constant criticism.

To rebound after being unloving, "confess your sins to one another" (James 5:16).

Never give up. When you miss, rebound! Go after it again. You can and will win your wife's heart, even on the heels of a miserable first performance, or a second, or a third. Whenever you forget and react in an unloving way, rebound. Tell her, "I'm sorry. Will you forgive me for reacting so unlovingly?"

Right now husbands reading this may be thinking, *Emerson, that's okay for you, but you've never had to face what I face.* Well, let's look at my record. I'm supposed to be the Love and Respect poster child. I have preached the Love and Respect message for more than five years, but I still have moments when I get angry and withdraw. I am still only a man, and the flesh can be weak no matter how much experience you think you have.

And through the years I have had more pressure than some men. There were times when, despite all of what I had been telling seminar goers about the Love and Respect Connection, I would become angry when Sarah would criticize me, and I would try to stonewall her. She would simply follow me through the house, saying, "What would you say to a husband who was acting like you? How would you counsel *him* to treat me?"

Good grief! Stop the planet, I want to get off! How embarrassing! How awkward! How unfair!

At some point, however, I have to calm myself down. I have to grow up—be mature! Like the Fonz in *Happy Days,* I try to mouth, "I was wrrooo . . . I was wrrroooo . . . I was *wrong.*"

I don't like to be disrespected and then have to apologize for being unloving any more than the next guy. It's not normal! But I know from personal experience that it is possible to fail, even as a so-called expert, and still recover. I know what it is like to rebound when you seem unable to "make any shots" on a certain day. As I prayed and sought answers to my own weaknesses, I found help in the Scriptures. Malachi tells us, "Take heed then to your spirit, and let no one deal treacherously against the wife of your youth" (2:15). I also found real solace in Proverbs 24:16: "For a righteous man falls seven times, and rises again."

None of us is perfect. We all blow it. As a man takes baby steps toward a better marriage through the Love and Respect Connection, he may find himself falling seven times and possibly more. But he should take a lesson from one of his own children when that child was learning to walk. No toddler falls the first time and stays on his bottom. He gets up and falls down, gets up and falls down, gets up and falls down, gets up and . . . keeps walking. Eventually, he figures it out.

Husbands, some of you have stuff from the past. Bad habits exist. The sins of your fathers are visited upon you (see Exodus 20:5). You will slip and not think about decoding her message at the moment because she feels so offensive. You might even say, "Drop it," and then you will try to move on without thinking more about it.

While God is gracious and kind, He knows that old habits don't

If she has something against you, "go and be reconciled" (Matthew 5:24 NIV).

die unless they are dealt with. It is in moments like these that He will speak to you, saying, "Go back. You honestly forgot to decode her message. You responded like a male. You thought you were doing the honorable thing by refusing to engage her. But that isn't going to work now. It won't stop the craziness. I want you to hear her deeper cry and move toward her. Allow her to vent. Embrace her negativity and anger."

If you can do that—if you can take the hit and keep coming—then you'll be able to say something like this: "Honey, I'm sorry for coming across so unlovingly. When you come at me like that, it makes me angry because I feel you don't respect me. But I want to change. Please help me."

When his wife comes at him with disrespect flashing in her eyes and venom shooting from her tongue, every husband has two choices: (1) defend his pride by firing back venom of his own or stonewalling her, or (2) try to hear his wife's cry and respond with unconditional love.

I have made the decision that, with God's help, I will always choose option 2: try to hear Sarah's cry and respond with unconditional love. But even though our marriage is much better and stronger than ever, I still miss the loving mark now and then. And when I miss—even ever so slightly—I rebound. After calming down (usually in a few minutes), I say, "I'm sorry. I know I've been unloving." And, of course, from the other side of our marriage, that wonderful woman who I always knew would be my friend, responds and says she's sorry for her disrespect. (Best of all, she no longer follows me around the house wanting to know how I would advise a husband who was acting like an unloving schmuck!)

MARRIAGE—A TWO-BECOME-ONE PROPOSITION

It is my hope that husbands and wives will use the insights in this chapter, as well as in chapters 3 through 6, to find the courage and motivation to try the Love and Respect Connection to stop the Crazy Cycle. It is true that unconditional respect by wives for husbands is the part of our message that is seen as new and even revolutionary. Respect for husbands has been there all the time, nestled in a short phrase in Ephesians 5:33, and for some reason we in the church have missed it over all these years. But now the secret seems to be out. As the wife sees her husband's goodwill and forgives the past, many of her disrespectful feelings can leave her. Even if some remain, her respectful actions can empower her to influence the marriage in the direction she longs for it to go.

In these several chapters I have tried to balance the scales and make husbands aware of the tremendous power that can be theirs if they decide to reach out with understanding, engage their wives even when being dealt verbal deathblows, and rebound when they fail to unconditionally love as God directs. Yes, a marriage can survive, and even improve somewhat, with one spouse carrying most of the load, but God's design is that marriage be a "two-become-one" proposition. As husbands and wives learn to respect each other and love each other, miracles do, indeed, happen. Bad marriages become good, boring marriages become exciting, and good marriages become better and better.

One husband whose "great marriage" became much better wrote to tell us of being married for twenty-three years, having wonderful children, and being able to start a television and radio ministry to families. But something was missing, and he shared with his wife that God had been moving in his heart to take a different approach to working with couples in crisis. He could see that the very real differences between men and women were not being recognized in a society that was out of balance in the ways it was training men and women to think from an early age. He and his wife discussed his greatest need (respect) and her greatest need (love). Then, a few days later, they heard about the Love and Respect Connection on the radio! They ordered some of our materials, and after going over them, they realized that God was doing some big things in their lives by "divine appointment." His letter went on to say:

> Even though, on the outside to many, it looked as if we had a great marriage (we do), there were several areas in our marriage that I had secretly given up on. On a scale of 1-10 we were living with a 5-6 marriage most of the time. We both wanted a marriage that was characterized by being in the 9-10 (at least some of the time). After reading your book, my wife and I left for several days, and the best I can describe it, God brought the greatest breakthrough I have seen in my relationship with my wife. Somehow God softened our hearts as we began to really look at this Love and Respect issue with more priority. This should come as no surprise, but it is so much easier to teach what is right and true than to completely live it for yourself. Now my wife and I continue to grow even closer and I think our effectiveness in administering to couples in need is being greatly impacted.

We also get many letters from couples whose bad marriages have become good. For example, we heard from a wife who admitted that both she and her husband were on marriage number three. In addition, they were in recovery for alcoholism, and she had come from a broken home and had very little respect for men. After two years of this third marriage, she wasn't sure it would last either. She had been reluctant to marry again after two failures, but after meeting with a counselor, she wanted to "do it God's way this time." Then her husband was injured and needed surgeries that kept him out of work for two years. The financial strain was terrific in trying to care for a blended family of five teenage boys. Her husband seemed to have no self-respect and wasn't acting respectful or loving toward her. She felt if she just loved him more it would work, but it didn't. They tried studying videos and workbooks on marriage, as well as counseling, but they couldn't turn around their Crazy Cycle. Feeling trapped and helpless, this wife cried herself to sleep at least two times a week and could not imagine going on like this much longer, when she heard about our book, *Motivating Your Man God's Way*. Her letter continues:

To stop the Crazy Cycle, obey God's Word, "which also performs its work in you who believe" (1 Thessalonians 2:13).

> After reading your book, I apologized to my husband and told him I had not been respectful of him and that I truly wanted to, and then I started doing just that. And, Ta Dah! It works. My gratefulness cannot be expressed. I finally "get it." . . . Thank you for revealing to me how to respect my husband as God has commanded. I have been using respectful phrases and my attitude (and most importantly his attitude and behavior) has done a 180-degree turn. I have peace and hope that this will be our last marriage and that it will honor our God.

I especially like a letter we received from a daughter who reported on the difference that the Love and Respect message made in her parents' marriage. Her mother told her that she just asks the Lord to change the look on her face and the feelings she has. That always works (if she keeps her mouth shut!). The daughter's letter continued:

> Anyway, my mother is doing that and my dad is confessing things from the past. She is seeing a big change in the way he is thinking and acting and it has given her hope for the future. She also says she is using the respect words and is seeing immediate results in the way my dad responds back. . . . This is awesome because they have never been able to talk serious without anger or at least volume. . . . Thank you for bringing hope to my mother and ultimately to me and my sisters.

From the Crazy Cycle to the Energizing Cycle

Letters like these just keep coming. The Love and Respect Connection is stopping the Crazy Cycle in marriages all over the country. If husband and wife can commit to meeting each other's primary needs—unconditional love for her and unconditional respect for him—they will take a giant step toward keeping the Crazy Cycle under control. Note that I did not say "getting rid of the Crazy Cycle once and for all." As much as I wish I could give you a surefire way to do this, I can't. All of us get on the Crazy Cycle from time to time because nobody is perfect. Sarah and I still work at controlling the Crazy Cycle because we can react negatively to each other in small and seemingly insignificant ways. She sees pink and I see blue; she hears pink and I hear blue, so conflict is bound to happen. Keeping that conflict contained and not letting it escalate is what controlling the Crazy Cycle is all about. (For ways to control the Crazy Cycle, see appendices A and B.)

Sarah and I have learned to recognize the signs of when the Crazy Cycle is even threatening to spin. And we know how to slow it down and stop it when it does start making a revolution or two. Best of all, we have a secret weapon that usually keeps the Crazy Cycle in its cage. It's called the Energizing Cycle, which is driven by a simple mechanism:

HIS LOVE MOTIVATES HER RESPECT;

HER RESPECT MOTIVATES HIS LOVE.

In part 2 of this book I will give you literally dozens of ideas, principles, and strategies that will put your marriage in the Energizing Cycle. And, if you commit to working at it, you will stay there!

PART TWO

THE ENERGIZING CYCLE

Because the Crazy Cycle is always ready to spin, you and your spouse need to get on the Energizing Cycle and stay there. The following chapters contain important scriptures that apply to the Love and Respect Connection in marriage. I also share principles, techniques, and common sense to help husbands and wives learn how to practice the Love and Respect message on a daily basis. As we learned in part 1, husbands need particular help with love, and wives need particular help with respect.

To simplify matters, I use two acronyms containing six areas of key importance for each spouse: **C-O-U-P-L-E** is advice for husbands with separate chapters on **C**loseness, **O**penness, **U**nderstanding, **P**eacemaking, **L**oyalty, and **E**steem. **C-H-A-I-R-S** covers advice for wives and includes separate chapters on **C**onquest, **H**ierarchy, **A**uthority, **I**nsight, **R**elationship, and **S**exuality.

It takes constant work to stay on the Energizing Cycle. These brief chapters are full of biblical help and practical tips that will help you build a better and stronger marriage.

CHAPTER EIGHT

C-O-U-P-L-E: How to Spell Love to Your Wife

(Note to wives: This chapter and the six to follow are
"for husbands only," but wives are invited to read along.)

Gentlemen, we have spent quite a quite a bit of time learning how to stop the Crazy Cycle. In the following chapters, we want to focus on getting on the Energizing Cycle and staying there. The Energizing Cycle is proactive. It is positive. And it is preventative. Stay on the Energizing Cycle and the Crazy Cycle will not spin.

Because you and your wife are human, however, the Crazy Cycle may start to make a revolution or two. It still does for Sarah and me, *but only when we forget to use the tools and techniques in the Energizing Cycle.* What I will cover in chapters 9 through 14 may not seem to be "natural" for you, and that's okay. As we have already seen, love is not a husband's mother tongue. But as you live out the several simple truths for husbands set forth in Scripture, which are presented in the acronym C-O-U-P-L-E, it will energize your wife. She will respond with respect, and that *is* your mother tongue.

Since wisdom "will honor you if you embrace her" (Proverbs 4:8), I believe a good-willed wife will honor you when you love her.

Before we get into the details in **C**loseness, **O**penness, **U**nderstanding, **P**eacemaking, **L**oyalty, and **E**steem, we need to look at the word *C-O-U-P-L-E* itself. It means two people connected together, and this is the key to how women view relationships. Wives want connectivity.

Think of a photograph of the two of you, which symbolizes your relationship. As troubles, big or small, hit your marriage, imagine that photo being ripped straight down the middle, or at least torn a bit. Your wife sees it as her mission to tape the relationship back together. She wants to connect with you, and she approaches you with that intention in mind.

Here is where couples often run into trouble as they try to work out their problems, even small ones. Women confront to connect. The typical response from a man, however, is that he thinks his wife is confronting to control. If another man talked to this man like that, he would sound intentionally provocative. Is that not why some men feel their wives are picking a fight?

Even the simplest and mildest "confrontation" between you and your wife is an excellent illustration of this basic difference between the deepest needs of a man and a woman in a relationship. It is a clear picture of how the codes you send one another can be misinterpreted because of your very different needs. In part 1 we looked at the need to learn how to decode. When your good-willed wife appears negative and offensive, she is crying out for C-O-U-P-L-E. At such moments your feelings may tell you she's just being critical and disrespectful. Take it by faith, however—what she really wants is to connect. She wants your love.

THIS HUSBAND WOULDN'T BELIEVE ME UNTIL . . .

One couple who came to me for counseling had the very problem I am speaking of. She had been confronting him and he felt suffocated, frustrated with her controlling attitude and her seeming "lack of respect" for him. I told the husband, "Sir, your wife is confronting you to connect."

"No," he answered quickly. "She tries to control me."

I turned to the wife and asked, "Are you really confronting him to try to control him?"

"Of course not," she replied. "It's just what you said. I'm trying to connect with him."

I turned back to the husband. "You see?"

He did not see. He insisted, "She's a controlling person."

In that session and several others, that husband would not let go of his interpretation of his wife's "confronting ways." He was convinced he knew what she meant and he knew why she was doing what she was doing. He had received her code, translated it, and thought he understood the message: "She is a controlling person."

When on the Crazy Cycle: "the way of a fool is right in his own eyes" (Proverbs 12:15).

Obviously, he was wrong, but at that point he wasn't willing to try to decode his wife more accurately.

As it so happened, they later attended one of our Love and Respect Conferences and sent me a note afterward: "We are now a Love and Respect couple. We realize that we misinterpret the codes we receive and when we try to communicate what we feel, it can come across in different ways than we intend."

This couple "got it," particularly the husband. He figured out that if his wife came across to him as controlling or too negative or too complaining or too disrespectful, he had to realize he could easily misinterpret her code. Her cry was, "Love me!" When he withdrew, she would simply try even harder to access his heart. He saw that as she tried to pull him closer, he had mistakenly assumed she was trying to put him even more firmly under her thumb. Once he learned to decode her correctly, he started to make progress in getting off the Crazy Cycle and on the Energizing Cycle (see page 115). She was not scolding him as a "bad boy." She longed to be his lover, not his mother.

LEARN TO TRUST YOUR INSTRUMENTS

Vertigo is defined as a sensation of dizziness and the feeling that you are being whirled about in your environment. The term *vertigo* is sometimes used when training people to fly, especially when they learn to fly on instruments without being able to see where they are going. Unless

> To decode correctly, be *"a wise man…who listens to counsel"* (Proverbs 12:15).

a pilot learns to pay attention to his instruments, he will feel as if he is being whirled about, quickly get disoriented, and crash. He learns that if his instrument panel tells him he's upside down, even if he feels he's right side up, he should listen to the instrument panel and turn the plane right side up, no matter how he feels. The instrument panel is not hampered by "feelings," nor is it blinded by an impassable bank of clouds or fog enveloping the plane. In short, the instrument panel cannot be fooled and it does not lie.

As we go through all of the secrets in C-O-U-P-L-E and the various aspects of connectivity, I want you to treat the following six short chapters as your instrument panel. Don't always let what you see, hear, and seem to feel determine how you will interpret a situation. Instead, keep in mind that you are the one who wears blue sunglasses and has blue hearing aids. They color and influence what you see and hear, and they form your understanding of the code you may be receiving from your wife.

You may think, *Maybe some men's wives are trying to connect with them, but not mine. She is trying to control me.* You have to set all that aside. You have to trust your instrument panel, which is labeled C-O-U-P-L-E. Do this and you won't get disoriented and dizzy, sure signs of the Crazy

Cycle. Instead, you will energize your wife. C-O-U-P-L-E is based on foundational biblical passages related to husbands in marriage. You cannot go wrong trusting and obeying God's revelation. You will learn how to show love in your tone, words, and face, even in the middle of a conflict that would normally send you into some state of stonewalling or irritation. And you will see her melt. Trust me, the Energizing Cycle is truly powerful—when you trust your instrument panel.

You cannot go wrong when you say, "I trust in Your Word" (Psalm 119:42).

In the Ocean of Conflict, Men Sink Unless . . .

As we saw in part 1, a man's tendency is to pull back from conflict. When the ocean of marriage emotions becomes turbulent, a husband can feel as if he is drowning. A wife, on the other hand, stays afloat quite naturally and comfortably. But if a husband will use biblical principles—God's techniques, if you will—I believe that he can learn to swim through the conflict.

A man voiced his discontent to me about the way his wife would verbally emasculate him. He was a man's man, "blue" to the core. His tendency during her flareups was to stonewall, which sent her through the roof. I coached him to approach her differently to discover the benevolent power he possessed over the spirit of his wife, a power every woman readily defers to when loved.

He reported back to me his shock when he tried what I suggested. As usual, she became disgruntled and vexed with him about something trivial. He stopped her and said gently but firmly, "Look, you can continue to emasculate me or you can join me on the couch where we can sit down and pray over this."

Like air out of a balloon, all the negativity drained from her. She stopped her ranting, turned, headed for the couch, sat down, bowed her head, and put her hand out for him to hold. He was in utter disbelief. He had never seen such a sight. I told him, "Look, women may seem to be out of control or it may appear they are trying to control you, but their real motive is to connect in love. When she feels true love coming toward her, she immediately and respectfully aligns herself with the spirit of her husband. Her goal is accomplished. That was her purpose all along!"

Using the Love and Respect Connection proves that "a man of knowledge increases power" (Proverbs 24:5).

This husband saw my point. He admitted that trying my suggestions went against his natural grain, but when he saw the results, he became a believer. He had learned to trust his instrument panel. (For examples of how to tell your wife your needs and to gain insight into her needs, see appendix C.)

TO LOVE HER DOESN'T MEAN BECOMING "PINK"

Note that when I ask you to trust your instrument panel and pursue a course of love with your wife, I am not calling on you to become a woman. We make a huge mistake in the church, particularly among evangelicals. We tell men to "get in tune with their feminine side," yet we don't tell women in get in tune with their masculine side.

Men are not to be effeminate (see 1 Corinthians 6:9). When I challenge a husband to love, I am not calling on him to become pink. Instead, I call on him to be a man of honor—to adjust his blue sunglasses and blue hearing aids a bit and put on love.

The truth is, it is easier for many a man to die for honor than to move toward a contemptuous wife in a loving way, saying, "I believe I was wrong. Can we talk about this?" To turn to your wife in the middle of a conflict and say, "I am sorry. Will you forgive me?" takes guts. I know because I have been there. It isn't pleasant, but it works powerfully. Over time it becomes easier, but it is never natural. Even so, this response gives you the power to drain the negativity out of your wife in conflict after conflict.

And the best part of it is that you, the male who tends to see and hear life through blue, will touch your pink wife in the tender and loving way she desires. Some wives simply melt. Others warm up considerably. At the very least, she will soften and you can talk through whatever the situation may be. You will gain the right to appeal to her to understand your need for respect and to join you on the Energizing Cycle.

When you act on C-O-U-P-L-E, you will "enjoy life with your wife, whom you love" (Ecclesiastes 9:9 NIV).

As we study C-O-U-P-L-E, my prayer is that you will discover how Scripture describes God's heart and will learn what it means to be a husband. You won't have to become a Bible scholar and study dozens of passages. I'll show you only a small number of verses but they will all be significant because they spell love to a wife. As one husband told me, "The information is working. I have seen the glow in my wife's eyes when I apply it and defeat and despair in her eyes when I fail to practice the principles you are trying to teach me through your material and God's Word."

To keep that glow in your wife's eyes, act on the biblical principles I will describe in the following chapters and your wife will feel loved. That's connectivity—that's coupling. You will energize your wife God's way and see how His way works in the heart of a good-willed woman!

Still a bit dubious? Let's take a closer look at C-O-U-P-L-E and see. We'll start with **C**loseness.

CHAPTER NINE

CLOSENESS—SHE WANTS YOU TO BE CLOSE

It is no coincidence that early on in the Bible—in describing the first marriage in human history—there is a living definition of the meaning of closeness. "Therefore shall a man leave his father and his mother, and shall cleave unto his wife: and they shall be one flesh" (Genesis 2:24 KJV).

When Scripture speaks of "cleaving," the idea in the Hebrew is to cling, hold, or keep close. Two are joined together face to face, becoming one flesh. Did you know that in all of God's creation only human beings are sexually intimate face to face? Cleaving, however, is more than sexual. Cleaving also means spiritual and emotional closeness. This is a salient passage for husbands—full of insight. Your wife will feel loved when you move toward her and let her know you want to be close with a look, a touch, or a smile.

In the book of Deuteronomy we find still more about what it means to be close. "When a man takes a new wife, he shall not go out with the army nor be charged with any duty; he shall be free at home one year and shall give happiness to his wife whom he has taken" (Deuteronomy 24:5). This is a fascinating passage because it shows how well the Israelites understood marriage. Why the whole first year?

They knew that the first year of marriage is fundamental. It is important to set the tone for the closeness of the relationship, before the wear and tear of life takes the husband away for periods of time, before they face other problems.

THE FIRST FEW SECONDS SET THE TONE

Spending all of the first year together and never being apart is not feasible for the modern marriage, but you can still set a positive tone each day. When you come home after you have been apart, the first few moments of reconnecting will set the tone for the rest of the evening. In today's culture, economics often dictate that husband and wife both work. Your wife may arrive home after you do, but the basic dynamics of closeness still apply.

Remember that she wants to connect. She wants face-to-face involvement. You both have had a long and possibly tough day. If all you want to do is flop on the couch and watch TV while she fixes you a nice dinner, you are missing it big time. This kind of uninvolved behavior will not make your wife feel loved. She will feel loved if you come into the kitchen and help her prepare dinner (even if it's nothing more than setting the table). Or you could possibly even start dinner before she gets home (what a concept!).

The heart focus of a husband is to be a lover "who sticks closer than a brother" (Proverbs 18:24).

Yet another idea is to sit and talk with her as she gets the meal together. Tell her about your day, and be sure to ask her about hers. She may be busy with children or other duties, but she will be listening, I assure you. What she tends to look for is your desire to "dwell" with her for a short period to discover where her heart is. If she senses you authentically want to connect, this can do more for her than a one-hour discussion. For your wife, face-to-face time is heart-to-heart time. (This is especially true if she is deeply burdened, and the wise husband tries to pick up clues that suggest this might be the case.)

Some husbands might think that spending all of this time in the kitchen is unmanly, but as we have seen in Deuteronomy 24:5, the Hebrew generals did not mock a warrior for being home. In fact, as a man of honor, he was ordered to spend his first year of marriage with his wife. Undoubtedly, a young bridegroom wanted to be out with his comrades fighting the enemy, but as a man of honor he learned to do two things: in the field he did what was respectable, and in the family he did what was loving. He wore his two hats interchangeably and wore them well.

What My Four-Year-Old Taught Me about Connecting

If a husband will adjust his blue sunglasses and blue hearing aids, he will understand that his wife has a need to feel close and connect face to face in a way that he does not. Think about coffee shops across the land where cappuccinos and lattes are sipped and savored. Many of these shops have little round tables with two chairs facing each other. Usually two people are seated at these small tables, leaning forward, face to face, hand under chin, and they are talking. Are these talking people men or women? As a rule, they are women. Women like round tables that place no one at the head in a position of leadership. They like to see eye to eye and connect on a personal level.

I learned about this female need for face-to-face connection from my daughter, Joy, when she was just four years old. One evening I put her to bed, and I lay there with her for a few moments to help her get to sleep. The room was pitch black, and Joy was talking as usual—little Miss Motor-Mouth. Neither of us could see the other in the darkness. As she was talking, suddenly she said, "Daddy, look at me!" Then her little hands reached over and grabbed my face, forcing me to look toward her. Already at this age, even in the dark, she sensed that Daddy wasn't looking, and if he wasn't looking, then he wasn't listening! I cannot recall my sons, Jonathan and David, ever grabbing my face like that and demanding, "Look at me!"

This connectivity is what women look for in any relationship, and especially marriage. When she married you, she thought you would be like her best girlfriend—you would figuratively sit with her at the little round table to talk eye to eye. But that probably didn't happen. With many husbands, it seldom or never happens.

INVOLVEMENT OR INDEPENDENCE?

Before you take a guilt trip, realize that no man can meet all the emotional needs of a woman. At the same time, perhaps you can start to try to meet some of your wife's needs by forgoing your tall, cool one, your newspaper, your *SportsCenter.* You can understand what she is doing when she moves toward you, which she normally will do. That's why she follows you around in the evening (or did when you were first married). It's her way of showing you she loves you.

A woman in love longs for closeness: "When I found him whom my soul loves; I held on to him and would not let him go" (Song of Solomon 3:4).

One way to picture your marriage is with a line that has the word *Involvement* at one end and the word *Independence* at the other, as shown below:

Involvement_____Independence

In the typical marriage relationship, she leans more toward the "Involvement" side while he leans more toward the "Independence" side. When you get too independent (especially when you stonewall), she does not feel close to you and begins to feel you don't love her. When she doesn't give you the space you need, you begin to feel that she's trying to get too involved and doesn't respect you. The line illustrates the tension that exists between your basic needs for involvement and independence. Tension is not bad; it is simply there. In fact, it is a necessary part of your relationship. A degree of tension in a marriage is actually one of the things that makes the relationship good (more on that in chapter 12).

ONLY CHICKENS GET HENPECKED

The tension between involvement and independence is another illustration of the difference between pink and blue. As a man, you will probably not be able to be as involved with your wife as much as she may like. I am not asking men to become women who sit at tiny tables at cappuccino shops and sip coffee as they share life face to face. You are a man, and your wife loves you for being a man, not a woman. She doesn't expect you to become feminine, just like her girlfriend. But when you move toward her, when you show her you want to connect in even small ways, watch what happens. This will motivate her. It will energize her—and it will keep your marriage off the Crazy Cycle and on the Energizing Cycle.

Of course, you can always grab tightly onto your brass ring called "Independence." You can insist on having "your space." After all, you work hard all week and you deserve a little golf (or fishing or watching a good game on TV). You aren't going to be the henpecked husband who can never get out with the guys because his wife always has chores or errands she wants him to do.

And besides, you're not going to move toward her until you get a little more respect, a little more awareness of your need for space and independence. This, of course, does not work, never has worked, never will work. You cannot motivate your spouse to give you what you need by withholding what she really needs. If you do, you are only jumping on the Crazy Cycle. Without love, she'll react without respect; without respect, you'll react without love.

One of the biggest stumbling blocks to drawing closer to your wife may be the classic male fear of being so con-

A husband is to recognize that "in the Lord, neither is woman independent of man, nor is man independent of woman" (1 Corinthians 11:11).

trolled you feel you can't make a move without checking with her. If you have committed to being a Love and Respect husband, fears that you will be "henpecked" are childish. Genesis 2:24 talks about cleaving and becoming one flesh with your wife. There isn't a word about being henpecked. Obviously, both of you need some space now and then, and working that out is part of becoming mature adults who communicate and who try to decode each other's needs. (See appendix A, page 305.)

CRAZY CYCLE VERSUS ENERGIZING CYCLE— BATTLE TO THE DEATH

So choose to be an adult. I did, and it worked. I finally understood that to stop the Crazy Cycle and stay on the Energizing Cycle, I had to give Sarah what she really needs. When I did that, a funny thing happened: she became motivated to give me what I really need. To paraphrase the golden rule: "Just as you want your spouse to treat you, treat your spouse in the same way" (see Luke 6:31). There is no neutrality here. In a way, this is war—a battle to the death between the Crazy Cycle and the Energizing Cycle. You can either motivate your wife rightly or you can demoralize her. It's your choice.

There is an old story about an older couple having dinner in a restaurant. The wife sees another couple about their age sitting in a booth nearby. She sees the husband sitting close to his wife, with his arm around her. He is whispering things in her ear, and she is smiling and blushing. He's gently rubbing her shoulder and touching her hair.

The woman turns to her husband and says, "Look at the couple over there. Look how close that man is to his wife, how he's talking to her. Look at how sweet he is. Why don't you ever do that?"

Her husband looks up from his Caesar salad and glances over at the next booth. Then he turns to his wife and says, "Honey, I don't even know that woman."

A wife is always hoping, "Now . . . my husband will be attached to me" (Genesis 29:34 ESV).

An old joke—perhaps even a corny one— but it makes a point about pink and blue. Pink wants closeness; blue is busy with his Caesar salad, anticipating the prime rib to come. Until both adjust their sunglasses and hearing aids, there will be continued tension that will not make a great marriage. A great marriage happens when the tension is dealt with creatively—or when tension is avoided completely by doing a few positive, loving things. This can pay off big time, especially for wives. One woman reported, "My husband has been talking more to me, been more affectionate, and I feel like we have been closer in the past few weeks than we have in years."

BEING CLOSE COSTS NOTHING—BUT YOUR TIME AND LOVE

Many of the following tips and techniques are the courtesy of my wife, Sarah, who speaks on the Energizing Cycle during one session of every conference we do together. As she compiled her list of ideas to help husbands, Sarah put down things that appealed to her, and she also asked a large number of other women what would make them feel closer to their man. They came up with simple but effective ideas. For example, do you realize the power in just holding her hand? Just the other day I was walking with Sarah and she said, "A woman feels close to her husband and, therefore, feels loved when he holds her hand." Of course, I immediately took her hand. I'm a quick study.

Or consider the power of a hug. A few years ago, Sarah's mother and mine died very suddenly within an eleven-month period. She was close to both of these women, and I would often find her standing at the kitchen sink sobbing. All I would do was go up to her and hug her. I said nothing, but I held Sarah until she quit crying. She told me later, "I felt so close to you when you did that."

Or consider being affectionate without wanting sex. That may sound a little bit like an oxymoron, but it's true. It's been said that sexual intimacy often begins at breakfast—or at some other time during the day. Hug her, hold her hand, tell her you love her, tell her how pretty she is. Be affectionate but not sexually aggressive. Touching her and kissing her only when you want sex is usually a turn-off to your wife. She builds up to sex much slower than you do, so through the day keep your advances in the affectionate zone only. When you set the right tone with little encounters during the day or evening, it leads much more naturally and easily to sexual intimacy later.

Remember: be affectionate and attentive every day, not just on days you want sex. Affection should be an end, not a means. Hear what this wife is saying:

> He watches *SportsCenter*, but I slow down at 10:00. I want to quiet down and cuddle like we did when first married. However, without the kids, we are two strangers who are not on the same path. This is causing a problem with me being sexually intimate. That is the only time we are close. I need something apart from that.

I've just touched on a few examples. See the list below, as well as lists at the end of other chapters in C-O-U-P-L-E. Note that all these suggestions are simple and cost nothing but your time and willingness to be close.

YOUR WIFE FEELS CLOSE TO YOU WHEN . . .

- you hold her hand.
- you hug her.
- you are affectionate without sexual intentions.
- you are with her alone so you can focus on each other and laugh together.
- you go for a walk or jog . . . anything that results in togetherness.
- you seek her out . . . set up a date night . . . eat by candlelight.
- you go out of your way to do something for her, like run an errand.
- you make it a priority to spend time with her.
- you are aware of her as a person with a mind and opinions . . . let her know you enjoy discussing things with her and getting her insights.
- you suggest the unexpected . . . get takeout and eat on the beach . . . take a walk to see the full moon . . . park on the bluff and watch the sunset.
- you pillow talk after making love . . . lie close with your arm around her and share feelings and intimate ideas . . . and never turn on *SportsCenter* or *Nightline*.

Chapter Ten

Openness—She Wants You to Open Up to Her

While doing marriage counseling, I have noticed a distinctive trend among the couples who come in to see me. As they enter my office and sit down, the husband will position himself so that he can see me. He will occasionally look up or down or to the opposite side, but he seldom looks directly at his wife except with quick glances. The wife will position herself so she can see her husband and me. She will watch us both because she is trying to figure out what is going on inside of her husband—what he is thinking. Remember, as a woman, she is expressive-responsive. She wants to talk about things. She wants to have her problems out in the open for discussion in order to solve them.

Her husband, however, plays it close to the vest. He is the opposite of expressive-responsive—what psychologists consider "compartmentalized." His wife senses something is going on inside, but he won't talk about it. "Nothing is wrong," he says. Yet her intuition tells her he is definitely upset. So the wife is confused, and she says, "I sometimes don't know which to believe." But she never quits. She keeps coming at the problem, trying to figure it out. She longs for his love, which is experienced in her world by connecting openly with his heart.

Smash One of Her Lights and All of Them Go Out

To fully understand the dynamics that are going on when a couple sits in my office for counseling, it's helpful to define the terms *expressive-responsive* and *compartmentalized* with a simple illustration. We have already seen that men and women are very different—pink and blue see and hear things differently at the level of marital intimacy. Think of this difference as two types of electrical circuits. On one circuit there are three thousand lights, and the circuit is so designed that if one light gets smashed the whole string goes out. On the other circuit there are

three thousand lights, and it is designed so that if you smash two thousand of these lights, the other thousand will still work.

A closed husband seems to his wife to be so ill-tempered "that no one can even talk to him" (1 Samuel 25:17 NIRV).

At the level of intimacy, the wife is like the first circuit. If a serious marital conflict exists, this affects her whole being. All of her "lights" go out, and she shuts down totally. This is because she is an integrated personality. Her mind, body, and soul are connected and her entire system reacts to feelings of hurt. Let her husband make one small, unkind remark that feels unloving to her and she is totally upset with him until things are repaired. As one wife told me, "If I'm battling with him in one area, I am at war with him in all areas."

Sometimes a woman can feel at war with her husband because he leaves her feeling lonely. Following is the kind of letter I receive from many wives:

> So many nights he would come home, watch TV till late, come to bed wanting sex, and I would feel used and unloved. Those feelings of loneliness, I guess, came back to me last night and I didn't like the way I was feeling. . . . I felt like the TV was more important than me. I realize it isn't true, but that is how I feel.

He gets very upset with me when he reads my body language.
He will hardly talk to me for days.

Let every husband heed what this woman is saying. When she believes there is a problem, when she feels hurt, lonely, or neglected, she definitely has no interest in responding to you sexually. When her spirit is crushed, her body is unavailable.

The wife's crushed spirit is not hard to see. Her face tells it all. While women are expressive, men are more poker-faced. The wife may complain that her husband seems to be able to operate as if there is no problem between them when she clearly is still upset and feeling crushed. He goes to work, and when he returns home, he cannot believe she is fully charged to talk about an earlier tension. Usually he has to be reminded of what exactly happened because he has forgotten. For her, the whole day has been interwoven with the spat they had at breakfast. She has replayed and rehearsed the episode a dozen times. But he says, "Oh well . . . let's just forget it, okay? Let's move on."

She cannot imagine how he could make such a remark. Why is he not upset the way she is upset? The answer is easy. Remember the two electrical circuits? Her husband is the one where you can smash two thousand of his lights and the other thousand will still work. That is what is meant by "compartmentalizing" his problems. A man has much more ability to control his reactions. His blood pressure may be going through the roof, but he can keep it under wraps. He may be deeply pained, but he shoves it into a "compartment" in his mind, saying to himself, *What's the point in trying to talk about this if that's the way she feels?*[1]

WIVES SEE HUSBANDS AS MYSTERIOUS ISLANDS

What I have just covered is a powerful piece of information for all husbands. Understanding that she is integrated, that she is expressive-responsive, gives you a huge insight into knowing how to respond when she probes to get you to open up. When a couple sits in my office, the wife is trying to figure him out. She cannot understand why her husband is not as expressive as he was during courtship.

During those first months of dating, both of them had been totally open, sharing inner dreams, yearnings, fears, and failures. They spoke heart to heart, and their openness was something they could literally feel, much like the lovers described in Song of Solomon: "The one I love was at the door, knocking and saying, 'My darling, my very own, my flawless dove, open the door for me!'" (5:2 CEV). The imagery of the opening door symbolizes two people drawing close and sharing their hearts. They are attracted to each other sexually, emotionally, and spiritually.

So what happens to the typical male's "openness" once he is married? During courtship the man was seeking to discover the woman of his dreams. It was an exhilarating adventure. Once he concluded that she was his dream come true, contentment set in. He no longer felt the need to share and be open. In fact, he preferred simply being together, shoulder to shoulder, and saying little (more on this in chapter 20). He didn't understand that his openness during courtship was spelling love to her in big letters, and that she was being energized beyond words by his transparent talk. Now that he is married, he doesn't understand her need for him to be open—to simply talk to her, share with her.

Every wife dreams of narrating to others, "My beloved speaks . . . to me" (Song of Solomon 2:10 ESV), as she reports in detail their romantic conversations and adventures.

To wives, husbands often appear as mysterious islands. Wives keep paddling around their husbands, looking for a place to come ashore, but there is a fog holding them back. There is no place to land. He appears to refuse her access. As one wife wrote to me:

He is completely disengaged. It is really difficult being around him. He NEVER talks. I have no idea what would touch his heart and I really would like to know. It seems as though I am stumbling around in a dark room and the light switch is not where it is supposed to be.

Of course, there are always exceptions. I have counseled couples in which the woman holds in her problems and the man wears his heart on his sleeve, but down through the years these couples have been in the minority. Generally speaking, men and women follow the pattern I lay out above. (See appendix D.)

SARAH PREFERS TO BE UP-TO-DATE ON A DAILY BASIS

Most wives are like Sarah. She prefers to talk about marital problems on a daily basis to keep the relationship "up-to-date." Sarah feels this prevents any major problems from developing. Throughout our early years of marriage, I really didn't understand what she meant by keeping things up-to-date to prevent problems. In fact, I often thought that talking about potential problems on a daily basis had to mean we really did have some kind of major marital problem!

Through the years I misinterpreted Sarah's purpose behind the talks. I often felt they were another rebuke for my failure to be loving, so I'd pull back to prevent feeling disrespected. When I responded to her questions with silence, she would move toward me even more, trying to find out what the difficulty was. And that only made me withdraw all the more. I finally learned what was going on, but until I did, the Crazy Cycle spun more than it needed to.

I, Emerson, needed to be reminded of the Scriptures: "The heart of her husband trusts in her" (Proverbs 31:11).

Now, to keep us on the Energizing Cycle, I work hard at decoding

Sarah's messages when she starts asking questions or pressing me for information. I still have that natural male inclination to think she may be snooping, prying, criticizing, or even trying to control me. I am tempted to feel like the husband who told me, "My wife is always prying. I feel like she has these giant claws, you know the kind they use to open up automobiles to rescue people inside, and she is meddling to get inside me. I need my space. I need my independence."

I know how this man feels, but I put those kinds of thoughts aside. I know Sarah is not trying to control me; she is a good-willed woman. I know she just wants to connect with me and feel an openness and closeness between us. This is a powerful part of her femininity—why I fell in love with her in the first place.

> *"She does him good and not evil all the days of her life" (Proverbs 31:12).*

As a husband you must understand that those feelings of being interrogated and thinking your wife is snooping or asking a lot of unnecessary questions are going to come over you. It will happen, and you must stop yourself before you get upset. Think about *why* your wife is doing this. She wants to keep things up-to-date. She's moving toward you because she loves you—*you matter to her*!

BEWARE OF BECOMING EMBITTERED

Unfortunately, some husbands can't or won't try to deal with their verbal wives because they fear feeling inadequate and disrespected. One woman acknowledged, "Through the years I came off as the heavy in the relationship and he always felt when we discussed things it was to fix him and he avoided our so-called discussions."

One man who along with his wife was struggling to spend more time on the Energizing Cycle wrote to admit that at one time his fear of openness had been a major problem. He said:

I did not reveal myself to her. I stuffed many of my thoughts, emotions and needs that I feared would lead to rejection if I voiced them. . . . This was cutting her off. . . . I believe this was an abdication of my responsibility. I have known for many, many years that honesty and openness is God's way but had not really come to terms with it until recently.

Over the years I have dealt with many bitter husbands whose anger simmers just below the surface. This kind of husband is not sweetly and gently open with his wife. Instead, he is suspicious of her and feels she has an agenda to irritate and provoke him. His wife intuitively knows, or strongly suspects, he is secretly and constantly mad at her. Paul may well have had this kind of man in mind when he wrote the only negative admonition in the entire New Testament to husbands about how they should treat their wives: "Husbands, love your wives and do not be embittered against them" (Colossians 3:19).

The concept conveyed in the Greek is the idea of a bitter taste in the mouth. To be embittered means that you are upset and irritated, exasperated, indignant, and angry. When we talk about a person being bitter, we usually think he is churning angrily inside over some past disappointment. The embittered husband can be harsh, cynical, or resentful. Instead of being open to his wife, he closes off his deepest heart, giving the impression there is very little he finds tasteful about her.

The bitter husband has no hope for openness with his wife. Perhaps some degree of bitterness is still a problem for you in your marriage, even though you and your wife have vowed to get off the Crazy Cycle and start energizing each other. The answer to bitterness is to listen to the gentle prodding of the Holy Spirit (see John 14:17, 26; Romans 8:9). That can work wonders, as one wife's letter clearly shows. She and her husband attended one of our Love and Respect Conferences. Afterward, she still felt emotionally raw and vulnerable. The next day he sharply criticized her driving. Sensing she was hurt, he later asked if everything was okay. She told him how she felt—she couldn't please him when she drove—and he argued, saying that her feelings were wrong, making her feel worse. The letter continues:

> But about five minutes later, he came to find me, to tell me he was sorry, and that if what he was doing [to be] helpful was, in fact, harmful, he would stop immediately. Then we hugged and it was over. How wonderful! Just a little thing but great!

"So guard yourself in spirit. Don't break your promise to the wife you married when you were young" (Malachi 2:15 NIRV).

This husband decided to concentrate on his inner man. Instead of rationalizing his negative attitudes and criticisms, he reconsidered. He listened to that still, small voice within. As he opened up to his wife, she felt his love! If only husbands could recognize the power of their love and how badly their wives want it.

Here are quotes from different wives who long for openness and a little tenderness:

> I need him to dig deep and shoot straight and be willing to answer from his heart and not from the emotion of anger. It doesn't work.

> Rather than being withdrawn and aloof, my husband has begun to do things I only wished he would have done in the past (i.e., share his heart with me).

> Amazing things began to occur. He began to reveal his heart. We actually have conversations rather than monologues.

How Will You Then Live with This Sensitive Creature?

At this point many a husband might be saying, "Good grief! I had no idea what I was getting into when I married this sensitive creature." That's right, you didn't; but you should be thankful for your wife's sensitivity and its many facets. Her sensitivity enables her to stay up all night with the kids when they are sick. Her sensitivity is what drives her to wait on you hand and foot when you're down with the flu, moaning, groaning, and wanting another Excedrin. Yes, her sensitivity sometimes causes her to feel that you're closing yourself off from her, that you're angry with her. You may be tempted to say, "Oh, please don't be so sensitive," but better to realize you must take her weaknesses with her strengths.

Every husband must make a decision about his wife's sensitivity and needs. He can close himself off and refuse to be open, or he can move toward her and connect with her at new levels of openness. One of the simplest yet most effective steps you can take is simply to share your day with her. If you don't want to talk at that moment, say something like, "Something happened at work today, and maybe we can talk about it later, but right now I would rather not. There is nothing wrong between us." That last phrase is what she will be looking for. She needs reassurance that your mood has nothing to do with her.

When you do talk, be especially wary of sounding harsh. A man is typically quite forceful in expressing his opinions. You can sound harsh without realizing it. You may not have meant to be harsh, but your wife deflates right before your eyes. As you simply stated the facts and firmly gave your opinion, you clamped down on her air hose.

A few years ago, one of our teenage sons was talking to Sarah in what she considered a very harsh way. She said firmly, "David, please don't speak to me that way." According to Sarah, he looked at her as if she were from another planet.

He said, "What do you mean? That's how I talk to my friends."

"Guess what?" Sarah replied. "I'm not one of your friends. I'm your mother, and I'm a woman." So David got a good lesson that day entitled "Why You Shouldn't Be Harsh 101." (For more instructions, see appendices A, B, and C.)

And one more thing. At the risk of sounding like a broken record, remember that if you are good-willed and open to your wife emotionally, she will feel close to you and open with you sexually. To put it another way, you must not be open to "get sex." A wife sees through that and is turned off sexually. But when you authentically meet her emotional needs, she'll be empathetic to your sexual needs. God has designed marriage to be symbiotic.

You will find more ideas in the list of tips below. But the main thing is to trust your wife's heart. Open yourself to her, and you will stay off the Crazy Cycle as the Energizing Cycle hums along nicely.

YOUR WIFE FEELS YOU ARE OPEN TO HER WHEN . . .

- you share your feelings, telling about your day and difficulties.
- you say, "Let's talk," ask her what she's feeling, and ask for her opinions.
- your face shows you want to talk—relaxed body language, good eye contact.
- you take her for a walk to talk and reminisce about how you met or perhaps you talk about the kids and problems she may be having with them.
- you pray with her.
- you give her your full attention . . . no grunting responses while trying to watch TV, read the newspaper, or write e-mails.
- you discuss financial concerns, possible job changes, or ideas for your future.

CHAPTER ELEVEN

UNDERSTANDING—DON'T TRY TO "FIX" HER; JUST LISTEN

We have already touched on 1 Peter 3:7 in chapters 2 and 3, but now we want to look at this verse through a lens labeled "How to Have Empathy for Your Wife." Peter advises husbands, "Live with your wives in an understanding way." I love this verse because Peter doesn't say that I have to understand Sarah. Like every other male, I know that I cannot totally understand any woman, even the one I love with all my heart. The key is for me to come across as wanting to live with Sarah in an understanding way, and, even more, I want her to know that I trust her heart.

I realize that 1 Peter 3:7 is a controversial verse for some because the complete passage says that husbands should live with their wives in an understanding way " . . . as unto the weaker vessel" (KJV). Feminists bristle at that one and claim, "The man is not the stronger sex. We're equal!" What we must remember, however, is that Peter makes a comparative statement, not a qualitative one. He is not saying that women are weak. He is saying that a wife is a "weaker vessel" because of her vulnerability to her husband within the marriage relationship.

Your wife is vulnerable to you in at least two areas: (1) when you say things such as, "I just don't understand you . . . I wonder if it's worth it to try?" and (2) when you dishonor her by treating her as less than an equal "fellow heir of the grace of life" (see 1 Peter 3:7). Feminists try to use this verse to say the Bible declares women are the weaker sex. What Peter is saying is that a wife is vulnerable to her husband (not that all women are weaker than all men); and when you, her husband, do not seek to understand her, she is very vulnerable, indeed.

One grateful wife of an understanding husband wrote to tell me, "Even when I have rebelled against his leading, he understands and accepts me, and does not hold a grudge against me."

Always Handle Porcelain with Care

One way to look at the phrase "weaker vessel" is to think of two bowls: one made of porcelain; the other made of copper. The husband is copper; the wife is porcelain. It's not that she is of less value—in fact, a porcelain bowl can sometimes have greater value than a copper bowl. The bowls are different and have different functions in different settings.

But your wife—the porcelain bowl—is delicate. She can be cracked, even broken if you are not careful. In the heat of frustration, a husband might say, "Nobody can understand women—particularly you." And at this point he might turn around and go off somewhere to stonewall for a while, vowing to himself not to kowtow to her controlling manner until she starts respecting him.

If you've been in a situation like this and then uttered unfortunate words along these lines, you might want to look down and notice the holes in your shoes. You just shot yourself in both feet—again. God has not made your wife to function around that kind of attitude. God is calling husbands to realize that their wives are porcelain bowls on which He has placed a clearly legible sign, "Handle with Care."

One husband finally realized his wife was his ally, not his enemy. He saw her as the kind of woman Peter describes, delicate and worthy of honor. In accepting her and appreciating her, the whole relationship began to shift. He said:

> We are on a new plateau of understanding each other. I used
> to pray over and over, "God, please heal our marriage, the pain
> is too much. Why did You ever put us together?" Now I am
> VERY thankful He did! My wife is my match in every way,
> before I could not see it. A HUGE burden has been lifted . . .
> I am not the same.

The C-O-U-P-L-E Principles Are Connected

Perhaps you have been noticing the connection in the principles that are represented by the letters of the word *C-O-U-P-L-E.* **C**loseness and **O**penness are very similar, and one plays off the other. And **U**nderstanding plays off of closeness and openness. As you draw close to your wife and are open with her, she will sense that you understand or at least you are trying to. Remember, the husband is the Christ figure; the woman is the church figure. And as a church places its burden on Christ, a wife wants to place her burdens on her husband. Even if she can't articulate it in these words, your wife thinks of you as that burden bearer—as having those big shoulders. When she comes to you for understanding, it is a compliment. This is a big part of what love is all about. But when you shut her out, close her down, or don't seem to hear what she is trying to say, it devastates her spirit.

"Husbands, love your wives, just as Christ also loved the church and gave Himself up for her" *(Ephesians 5:25).*

TO UNDERSTAND, JUST LISTEN

How can you be an understanding husband? The most powerful weapons you have are your ears. Just listen to your wife, and she is much more likely to feel understood.

But because his hearing aids are blue, a husband has a major hurdle. To "just listen" is usually not his strong suit. He is better built to analyze, give answers, and "fix" the situation. The unaware husband doesn't readily decode the messages his wife is sending when she comes to him with her problems. One vivid example is when Sarah and I were first dating at Wheaton College. She was taking Spanish and wasn't doing very well. As we sat in the library one day, she started telling me her troubles with her Spanish class. I listened carefully as she poured out her problems, then I said, "Okay, I'll start working on this. The solution is in creating a study calendar. We break your lessons up into little pieces, and each day you study a small chunk."

Then and there at the library study table, I busied myself laying out a study schedule for Sarah. In a few minutes I had the schedule complete. I looked up, and Sarah was nowhere to be found. I glanced across the library and saw her laughing heartily with her girlfriends, having a good time. Unsure of what was going on, I wondered to myself, *Did I somehow solve her problem already?*

So I caught Sarah's eye and motioned her over. She came quickly and sat down with a happy look on her face. "Did I solve your Spanish problem?" I asked.

"Oh, no, not really."

"Then why are you happy?" I asked.

"I just needed somebody to listen to me," Sarah said with a big smile. "Now I feel better."

Somehow I had managed to give Sarah just what she wanted—an

UNDERSTANDING—DON'T TRY TO "FIX" HER ✤ 149

understanding ear. Of course, I went on to try to "fix her problem," but by the time I had started on that she already felt better. You might say I lucked out on that one. Later there were other situations after we were engaged and then married where I was guilty of wanting to fix more than listen, and I heard about it.

The dynamic that was at work that day in the library when I listened to Sarah pour out her Spanish problems is a very powerful one. The truth is, I really didn't have to fix her problem; all she really wanted was my listening ear. (I learned that Sarah has needs that I do not have, and that is okay. Also, she has learned that I have needs she does not have, and that is okay with her!) As a husband, if you can grasp that you don't always have to solve your wife's problems, you will take a giant step toward showing her empathy and understanding. Not only that, but it will save a lot of time, trouble, and turns on the Crazy Cycle.

"Do You Need a Solution . . . or My Ear?"

Over the years I have had my ups and downs with being a good listener, but I have learned when Sarah comes to me with a burden, I ask two questions. The first question is, "Am I in trouble?" The answer to this is usually, "No, no, no."

My second question is really the more important one. "Do you need a solution or a listening ear?"

Then Sarah can say, and she usually does, "I just need you to listen."

So I listen. After Sarah has shared her problem, big or small, she feels better. She goes away feeling understood and loved. The Energizing Cycle is humming.

But in counseling situations and at our conferences, I meet many husbands who don't "get it." In fact, trying to fix instead of listen is often a big point of conflict in the marriage. These husbands are still operating with strictly blue sunglasses and blue hearing aids. They are coming at problems like men.

At times one man comes to another with his problem. Instinctively, Harry knows that Joe is not approaching him so he can "release his emotions." He knows Joe isn't hoping that he will just "listen to him." (Only when a man is in a really major crisis will he want someone to just listen because he is absolutely at the end of his tether.) But 95 to 98 percent of the time one man comes to another to share his problem

> The wise husband is "quick to listen, slow to speak" (James 1:19 NIV).

because he would like some help. So Harry says, "Well, have you tried this?" and he lays out a possible solution.

"That's a good idea," says Joe. "Thanks a lot."

Men, you see, believe they help others by solving their problems. It is well known that men and women score differently on tests. He is high in analytical aptitude; she is high on verbal aptitude. He tends to think in terms of analysis, and that is the way he processes things. (More on this in chapter 19, covering the husband's Insight.)

And so, after helping Joe out, Harry might go home, where his wife approaches him with a problem. Because he had such good luck with Joe, Harry tries to solve her problem, only to hear, "Will you quit trying to fix me and just try to listen?" Being a typical male, Harry doesn't like this response much. He can't believe his wife can be so disrespectful and ungrateful. After all, he was only trying to help. But it's at this point that Harry needs to pull back. He needs to learn the line: "Honey, do you need a solution or do you just want me to listen?"

This isn't natural, but I guarantee it is effective. One thing to remember is that when a wife comes to a husband with her problem, she isn't coming because she wants him to solve it. In fact, in many cases she knows exactly what she needs to do. But she's coming to share, to feel understood, to communicate at an entirely different level. Men tend to communicate for one reason only: to exchange information. They wonder, "Why else would you want to communicate? Get to the facts. Share opinions. Come to some conclusions. What else is there?"

So when a wife comes up and says, "Can we talk?" the husband responds, "What about?" He is ready to exchange information, to give solutions. But then she says, "Oh, I don't know. I just need to talk." This is not a comforting line for the average husband. This throws his information exchange system totally out of whack. He begins to get suspicious. She must be setting him up to bawl him out about something.

Hannah is barren, so her husband tries analytically to solve her problem: "Why is your heart sad? Am I not better to you than ten sons?" (1 Samuel 1:8).

"Just Talking" Is a Key to Understanding

In chapters 9 and 10 I stressed the importance of setting aside time to talk to your wife. This is not an option. This is a must. Talking is when women report to build rapport. This may sound like "small talk" to you. You may or may not be ready for it at all times, particularly after getting home from a hard day at work, but take time to talk to her if at all possible. Understand the importance she puts on sharing her report and having you share yours. You don't have to give every detail of the day. Try, however, to go over a few highlights, a certain happening, something that will make her feel loved because she will be building rapport with the most important person in her life.

Remember, too, that wives love to talk to release their emotions. Because a woman is an integrated personality, she is like a teakettle— she collects all the things that have happened to her over the day, and there is a buildup. She needs to release some of these feelings, and it really can't wait until tomorrow or the next day. As we discussed in chapter 10, men are compartmentalized. You can stuff things away and not have to talk about them; you don't have pressure building inside the way your wife does. When you let her share her small talk and give her a chance to "let off steam," she will feel good. She will feel connected to you.

"Since she is a woman" (1 Peter 3:7), God made your wife with different needs and vulnerabilities from your own; so don't pass judgment on her.

Women also need to talk to realize their feelings. Men usually know what they are feeling, and they will talk about it if they think it is necessary. Women, on the other hand, can be feeling a lot of things but not know exactly what they are. As they begin to talk about what happened through the day, they can work back to the problem that they can't seem to put their finger on. That's why a wife sometimes says, "Can we talk?" When asked, "Why?" she doesn't really know—she just had a bad day and, "I just need to talk." As a husband, you must realize your wife needs to process her feelings—to realize exactly how she is feeling. As she talks to you, it clarifies things for her; then she feels better and she feels understood.

UNDERSTANDING TAKES SCHEDULED TIME

Sarah and I came to a point in our marriage where our kids were young and the demands of the day were heavy on both of us. So, after dinner, we told our oldest son to watch the other two, and we locked ourselves in our bedroom. This fifteen-minute period was Mom and Dad's time, and the rule was "Don't interrupt until we're done."

The best thing about those fifteen minutes after dinner was that they were predictable. Sarah knew this would be her time to talk to me, to share her feelings. At another stage in our marriage, we were having some tension because Sarah was always seeing me either coming or going. She wanted more than transitional moments to tell me all the things that she was feeling, so we set up a date night. The tension disappeared because now Sarah had a predictable time with me: Thursday nights. And so she'd save up what she had on her mind and heart. She would literally make lists, and after we had dinner somewhere, she would go down her list and we would talk.

Some husbands might be wondering, "Okay, you and Sarah talk—about *what?*" If your wife is typical, you don't have to carry the conversation; just be sure to listen. Don't be thinking of tomorrow's appointment or getting the car serviced, etc. And every now and then repeat back what she is saying. For example, "That's interesting. What I hear you saying is . . ." This way she will know you are listening and that you care about what she is saying.

As an understanding husband, always be "making the most of your time" (Ephesians 5:16).

There are many ways to let your wife know that you are trying to understand her and what she faces each day as the emotional center of your home. At every opportunity express appreciation for all she does. We know of one husband who gave his wife a special card, thanking her for every menial task she does around their home: from washing the clothes to doing the cooking, from taking the kids to school with lunches packed to helping them with their homework. There was a list of ten or fifteen items. The wife was so touched by this card that she said, "I'm sticking this in my Bible and I'm going to reread it often."

That wife felt understood—at least in part. Be aware, however, that a woman's need to feel you understand is insatiable. It will take constant effort on your part, and while you can never do it perfectly, every effort you make will tell her, "I love you."

This husband's letter sums it up beautifully:

It has always been one of my goals to provide my wife with a safe environment in which she can be free to be the person God made her to be, and I hope that this is happening. She now freely identifies herself as someone who, just a couple of years ago, was "not happy," but has put that behind her. I hope that I am understanding her better and being a better friend to her. We have a lot of challenges each week raising four kids, but we are a team, and I feel like we are working through all of it together, with God's active presence and help.

She'll Feel You're Trying to Understand Her When . . .

- you listen and can repeat back what she said.
- you don't try to "fix her problems" unless she specifically asks for a solution.
- you try to identify her feelings.
- you never dismiss her feelings, no matter how illogical they may seem to you.
- you say, "I appreciate your sharing that with me."
- you don't interrupt her when she's trying to tell you how she feels.
- you apologize and admit you were wrong.
- you cut her some slack during her monthly cycle.
- you see something that needs to be done and you do it without a lot of hassle.
- you express appreciation for all she does: "Honey, I could never do your job."
- you pray with her and for her.

CHAPTER TWELVE

PEACEMAKING—SHE WANTS YOU TO SAY, "I'M SORRY"

While in graduate school, I took a class that involved quite a bit of discussion of conceptual frameworks for certain ideas. There were only two or three of us men in the class—the rest were women, and all of them were feminists. One day the word *connectivity* came up for discussion. I noticed that the women literally brightened up, and a surge of energy seemed to run through the room. I addressed a question to the ladies: "What is connectivity to you?" They paused. They rummaged about a bit and then said things like, "Well, it's to connect . . . to be one . . . to be soul mates."

That was good for a start, but I wanted to know more. "Could you give me a working definition of this? After all, we're all working on PhDs here. We need to be able to discuss and define this in specific terms."

None of the women could. They admitted, "We can't. We just know when it is present and we know when it's not."

"I see," I said. Of course, I didn't see but we had to move on to the next concept.

I never forgot that discussion, and I continued to work on defining *connectivity* as I entered the pastorate and especially as I began counseling married couples. Eventually, I came to a much better understanding of connectivity as I created the C-O-U-P-L-E acronym. As we have already seen in these chapters, there are many sides to connectivity. We have already looked at closeness, openness, and understanding. Obviously, all of these have a bearing on how connected a wife feels with her husband.

There is a fourth side to connectivity that we need to look at very carefully—**P**eacemaking. In some ways, it might be most important. If there is a rift, a conflict, even a sense of tension, you and your wife are not fully at peace, and, therefore, you can't really feel connected. Without peace in your relationship, she doesn't feel close, she doesn't feel you're open, and she certainly thinks you don't understand. All this can be traced back to the tension or rift that has come between you.

Along with research done by academics on connectivity, I also studied the Scriptures and came upon a paradox. I learned that God intended for some conflict to exist in a marriage (see 1 Corinthians 7:3–4). Even secular research showed that the best marriage relationships have some conflict. It's almost as if you need a degree of conflict to keep the passion there. The sequence seems to have the couple experience a misunderstanding; they have a minor argument, a bump of some kind. But as they work through this conflict, they deepen their understanding of each other and value and appreciate one another all the more as they reconcile the conflict.

> *If you are angry with your wife, even for "a brief moment," she is "grieved in spirit" and "rejected," and needs reassurance that you love her (Isaiah 54:5–8).*

Obviously, when the sparks fly and a couple has a conflict, serious or minor, there is a risk. It can go one of two ways. Sparks can cause a controllable fire that heats the house and makes things warm and comfortable. Or sparks can set a wildfire that burns the house down. All married couples must realize that the sparks are going to be there. The question is, how will you control them?

I talked with one husband who confessed that he tried to motivate his wife to show him some respect by acting very unlovingly. He distanced himself from her. He closed off his spirit in anger. He disregarded her feelings. He argued his points to win and never reconciled. In short, he never made peace with her. He admitted to me, "I thought if I did all that, she'd start showing me a little more respect." Then he put his head down on the table in despair and said, "But she divorced me. Until now I didn't know why."

HUSBAND AND WIFE CAN "WORK IT OUT"

As you have conflict, your wife will probably recognize it much sooner than you do. She can feel rejected by you in a way that you do not feel rejected by her (see Isaiah 54:6)[1]; consequently, she wants to have things resolved between the two of you, and she will move toward you to get this done. As you go head to head and solve the problem, you become heart to heart. This is very precious to her. It's a very powerful thing for your wife when she knows that the two of you are at peace.

Don't refuse to make peace by running from conflict with your spouse. Conflict is not a sign you have a bad marriage. In fact, the Bible says that those who marry "will have trouble" (1 Corinthians 7:28). What kind of trouble did Paul have in mind? Earlier in the chapter, he lays down an excellent principle for dealing with conflict in marriage: "The husband must fulfill his duty to his wife, and likewise also the wife to her husband. The wife does not have authority over her own body, but the husband does; and likewise also the husband does not have authority over his own body, but the wife does" (1 Corinthians 7:3–4).

In this passage Paul is giving advice to married couples in the church at Corinth. It was not uncommon in the first century for some believers to get the idea that a good Christian would abstain from sex completely, and apparently that was what was going on at Corinth. To correct this error, Paul encourages sexual relations between husband and wife, because this is the way not to fall into temptation and immorality outside of marriage (see v. 5).

It seems a little odd, however, when Paul says that the wife doesn't have authority over her body and the husband does, and the husband doesn't have authority over his body and the wife does. What does Paul mean? I believe he is laying out one of the great principles of the New Testament: because you have equal but differing needs, you will experience conflict. But you can work this out as partners. The husband should not act independently from his wife, and the wife should not act independently from her husband. A husband and wife should and can act together.[2]

"Submit to one another out of reverence for Christ" (Ephesians 5:21 NIV).

It is as if God said, "I'm going to allow for tension to exist in your marriage. I intend for you to work this out, because as you work out your tensions, your relationship is going to deepen and then deepen some more, and you're going to continue to go through life working it out—back and forth, back and forth."

"My Wife Is Always Getting Historical"

As I talked with one man about his marriage, he told me that every time he and his wife got into a fight, she would get "historical." To be sure I understood, I asked him if he actually meant "hysterical." He said, "No, historical. She keeps dredging everything up from the past."

Many wives are very good at getting historical. That's why it doesn't do a husband a lot of good to try to end a conflict by saying, "Let's just drop it." That is not how she thinks, and she will not drop it. She may let it go for the moment, but she will remember, and eventually she will start "rehearsing history" for her husband again.

Almost every husband I have ever talked with can share stories about his wife's seemingly limitless capacity to remember who said what, where it happened, who was wearing what, etc. Your wife is wired to get historical, to bring things up that you've totally forgotten, to go full circle and get them resolved. She's dredging them up so she can clear the air and feel love in the relationship. And you, the hapless husband who stands bewildered before her seemingly superhuman memory, will have to come to the point where you accept that this is her integrated personality in action and that she can't "just drop it."

Whenever she gets historical, she is trying to reconcile with you. She wants you to be open with her, and she's trying to encourage understanding and peace between you. She wants to be sure you aren't angry with her so that she can feel loved. She is not trying to provoke you, although it may sound that way as she delivers her historical diatribe. Husbands have a hard time believing this. The fellow who told me his wife often got historical was more than skeptical when I tried to explain that she was just trying to increase feelings of love between them.

"No way," he said in bewilderment. But it's true because this is how a woman's mind works. During a conflict, the woman's approach to solving that conflict is very different from how the man resolves conflict. As discussed in chapter 4, two women who are good friends will get into a serious disagreement, but later—perhaps the next day or perhaps in half an hour—they will resolve it as each one states her side. They get it all out on the table and finally ask each other for forgiveness. The problem is that the typical wife will go home and try to use this same approach to resolving conflict with her husband. But it doesn't work. Why? Because the typical male resolves conflict without a lot of discussion, sharing of feelings, or apologies.

Some men might apologize to one another, but as a rule it's just sort of taken for granted that they will "just drop it," and they do. So when a husband is approached by a wife who wants to resolve a conflict by sharing feelings and coming "full circle" to a resolution, he balks. Halfway around her circle the husband says, "Drop it. Just forget it. It's over with." But the problem with that is, she won't believe him. In her mind, she knows it's not over. She knows she will bring it up again because she's still sitting on the whole thing. She is so dominated by the drive to love that it is difficult for her to believe that her husband could process it any other way than she processes it.

Here's what happens. When you shut down a discussion by saying, "Just drop it," your wife is likely to think you're still secretly angry with her and that this thing is really unresolved. Without any resolution, it will be very difficult for her to be happy. This letter catches the frustration a wife can have:

> Inside I continue to die, because I am so unaware of how to let the Lord restore this relationship. My husband has told me on more than one occasion that we are unusual in our love for each other. Most people do not know the intimacy we have at times. But the patterns of arguments . . . and not ever really feeling reconciled are taking a toll on me.

For any husband who wants fewer ongoing arguments, the path to peace is plain. He must learn to simply say, "Honey, I'm sorry. Will you forgive me? I did not mean to do that." Do this, even if in your mind most of the guilt or blame is hers. The percentage of guilt is not the issue. As always, the real issue is love and respect.

Why It's Hard for a Man to Say, "I'm Sorry"

As a husband, I want to share with all husbands that I understand why it's hard to say, "I'm sorry." When a woman says, "I'm sorry," to her it's an increase of love. But when a man says, "I'm sorry," he fears that he will lose respect. This is especially true if he says he's sorry for something and then his wife brings it up again because she isn't convinced he means it. She simply thinks the issue is not resolved and it must be discussed some more; but he thinks she has just violated his honor code. For him, going over it again is a lot more serious.

> *"To sum up, all of you be harmonious, sympathetic, brotherly, kindhearted, and humble in spirit"* (1 Peter 3:8).

It is easy enough, of course, to just accuse the male of being "proud." I am not saying that there is not some element of pride involved here. But mixed in with male pride is a deep sense of honor and wanting respect. To all husbands I want to say, I've been there. I have had to push through and say to Sarah, "I'm sorry. I was wrong." And when I finally convinced her that I meant it, it healed her spirit. Those simple words put her at peace.

A wife can be extremely upset, but if a husband humbly expresses sorrow for what he did, she melts. I don't think very many men grasp this. A wife wrote me about a fight she had with her husband earlier in the evening. It was silly. In fact, at one point they had talked about kissing and they ended up fighting. She went to bed, and he came later: "I laid there for a while and then out of the blue he said (facing the wall), 'I'm sorry, and if you still want that kiss, you can have it.' And I fell in love with him all over again. Needless to say, we weren't fighting any more."

As a husband, hear this woman's language: "I fell in love with him all over again." A wife has a wide range of emotions—highs and lows.

You can energize her toward the high end of the spectrum by doing just what this husband did.

A SHORT COURSE ON PEACEMAKING

Still not sure about how to make peace with your wife? Following are some good techniques and principles, which correlate with Scripture.

First, have absolute confidence in the power of your loving demeanor. To paraphrase Proverbs 15:1: "A gentle, loving answer turns away wrath, especially your wife's." When you show a loving demeanor during a conflict of any kind, you are likely to touch the deepest part of her heart. Your loving attitude triggers something within her heart as a woman. God made her this way. Bottom line, she reciprocates. A husband cannot outgive a good-willed wife. But when you "give in," be sure you mean it. If she detects insincerity on your part, you're probably due for another spin on the Crazy Cycle (see page 5).

"If possible, so far as it depends on you, be at peace with all men" (Romans 12:18).

Granted, a husband can ask, "What if I keep loving and keep giving in and still feel disrespected? What should I do?" At this point you have earned the right to say, "I am seeking to give in to you and to be loving, but I am feeling disrespected. What am I saying to you that is unloving?" Good-willed women tend to respond to reasonable, loving, honest requests and will seek ways to be more deferential. If your wife did not "see it" the first time, she will very likely see it the second time.

Second, you will make peace with her when you don't blame her but, instead, confess your part of the blame (see James 5:16). I have said it already, but I repeat for emphasis: admit when you are wrong and apologize by saying, "I'm sorry." That is a big turn-on for a woman, but an even bigger turn-on is to add, "I think I really understand your feelings and why you react as you do. Will you forgive me?"

One more thing about confessing: Your motive should never be to confess so she will admit she was wrong, too, but often that is exactly what happens. Women are wired for "equality." For example, she doesn't like feeling inferior or in the wrong, but neither does she want you to feel you're inferior or in the wrong. After you confess, my prediction is that she will quickly say, "It's not all your fault. Actually, it's me too. In fact, it may be more me. I am sorry for what I did. Will you forgive me?" She will meet you halfway almost every time. This is peacemaking in a woman's world.

"Put yourselves under God's mighty hand. Then he will honor you at the right time" (1 Peter 5:6 NIRV).

Some men think, *Why bother with all this "I'm sorry" stuff? They're just words.* You must understand that words are very powerful to your wife. Remember, although she may not be consciously thinking it, you are the Christ figure to her. God has instilled that in her. If you utter sincere words of apology, forgiveness, and love, she will trust those words and trust you. It can heal the whole thing, and you will be joined together, in a sense, as soul mates, "no longer two, but one" (see Matthew 19:6). You will experience the harmony and connectivity that God intended for marriage.[3] (Also see appendix A and B.)

Peacemaking can be difficult, but it is always worth it. It's ironic that a lot of men work out in the weight room, trying to make themselves look like Mr. Universe because they think that women get turned on to a hard body the way men are turned on to a female in a bikini. But it doesn't work that way. What turns her on is personality. Oddly enough, one of the things that really turns her on is saying in genuine humility, "I am sorry. Please forgive me." This touches her spirit so much that she may want to grab your hand and drag you to the bedroom. Now that seems like a pretty good deal worth any possible loss of respect. I'm not saying it works for every husband, but it has been known to work for many. I had a man come up to me after one of our marriage conference sessions and say, "You know, this saying 'I'm sorry' really works. This week I've said 'I'm sorry' eighty-four times!"

She'll Feel at Peace with You When . . .

- you let her vent her frustrations and hurts and don't get angry and close her off.
- you admit you are wrong and apologize by saying, "I'm sorry. Will you forgive me?"
- you understand her natural desire to negotiate, compromise, and defer, and you meet her halfway.
- you try to keep your relationship "up-to-date," resolving the unresolved and never saying, "Forget it."
- you forgive her for any wrongs she confesses.
- you never nurse bitterness and always reassure her of your love.
- you pray with her after a hurtful time.

CHAPTER THIRTEEN

LOYALTY—SHE NEEDS TO KNOW YOU'RE COMMITTED

It happens in almost every marriage. Wanting reassurance about his love, she asks, "How much do you love me? Will you love me when I'm old and gray? If I'm an invalid? What if I get Alzheimer's?"

There are two ways a husband can go with this question. The wrong way leads straight back to the Crazy Cycle, and it involves having a little fun at your wife's expense. You're just kidding, of course, so you say, "What's the matter? Afraid I'll trade you in for a new model? Don't be silly, I plan to keep you around . . . at least for a while."

A wife may know that her husband is just kidding when he says things like this, but the big, dumb buck is stepping on her air hose, nonetheless. When she asks, "Do you love me?" she's not asking for information; she's asking for reassurance.

The much smarter and wiser answer to her question is, "Of course I love you, and we're going to get old and gray together." Then she'll probably ask, "Why?" or "What is it that you love about me?" She wants to draw this out of you because reassurance of your love energizes her.

> *A woman always likes to hear her husband exclaim, "You alone are 'my love'" (Song of Solomon 2:10 KJV).*

A wife *must* have reassurance. As one wife writes:

We have a wonderful marriage and friendship, yet we find ourselves on the Crazy Cycle in our hectic lives, and the info we
gained at your conference has given us a new understanding of
one another. I had been trying to explain the times when I felt
"emotionally disconnected" from him. Now he finally understands. . . . We are able to talk now, and when I say I feel disconnected he says, "I am sorry and I don't want you to feel that
way." We both walked away with a feeling of confidence knowing that we both have a commitment to the Lord first [and then
to each other]. We feel very lucky and blessed. . . . I guess I just
feel like I have a renewed relationship with my husband.

She's a One-Man Woman, and He's . . . ?

Your wife knows she's a one-man woman, that she's committed to you,
but she may wonder at times if you are a one-woman man. It's perfectly
natural for a wife to think this, particularly when she sees her husband
being attracted by some beautiful female walking by or on TV. She
takes this as a possibility that he might be unfaithful to her. To be can-
did, she is insecure in this area and she needs reassurance, not jokes and teasing.

*Every woman wants
her husband to be
"faithful to his wife"
(Titus 1:6 NIRV).*

Let's look at the other side of the coin.
Suppose your wife came home and said, "Do
you know that Dave Smith down the street
just got his third promotion? Well, my good
friend, Marge, works in his office and she says people stop at his desk
all the time to get counsel. The word is that he's a real man's man. You
know he runs marathons—and lifts weights at his health club. He's
making excellent money and spends a lot of it on his wife and kids.

When are you going to start working out and getting rid of that pot-belly? And when is your next promotion coming up? We could sure use some more money around here."

Now, that speech is more than overstated, but you get the idea. If your wife said anything along those lines, it wouldn't make you feel good. In fact, depending on the kind of day or week you've had, you might be devastated.

IT'S A "SWIMSUIT ISSUE" WORLD

Have you ever thought about how difficult it is for a wife in today's sex-happy, pornography-riddled, "swimsuit issue" world? The way in which she looks at that world through her pink sunglasses is much different than the way you look at it through your blue ones. That is why Job had the right idea: "I made an agreement with my eyes. I promised not to look at another woman with sexual longing (Job 3:11 NIRV). Job recognized that "sinful people are destroyed. Trouble comes to those who do what is wrong" (Job 31:3 NIRV). Job understood the impact of his actions, not only on his spiritual life but also on his relationship to his wife.

The phrase "Drink water from your own well" (Proverbs 5:15 NIRV) means be faithful to your own wife.

All husbands might learn from Job at this point. When a woman senses that her husband has made a covenant with God and that he's trying to make Jesus the Lord of his life in every area, including his marriage, she feels more secure. When she is assured of her husband's love and loyalty, she is energized and motivated. This is the way God has made her, and this is why the covenant of marriage is based upon loyalty—until death do you part.

Your wife feels so deeply what the lover in Song of Solomon expressed: "Keep me close to yourself like the ring on your finger" (8:6

NIRV). The custom of giving each other a ring during your wedding ceremony captures the idea behind this verse. And, oh, the symbolism of that ring to a woman! The ring tells her she is loved and no longer alone! There is one person in the world who will be loyal to her—for life, not "until divorce do you part."

Many men do not wear wedding rings because of the kind of job they do, because they engage in sports, or because they have put on a few pounds through the years and the ring no longer fits. But a ring that no longer fits can be enlarged, or you can purchase another one for a few dollars. Rings don't cost that much, and even if you have to take it off now and then while at work or playing a game, you can always slip it right back on. A wedding ring is a sign of loyalty. No husband should leave home without one.

And while you are sure to wear a wedding ring, also be sure to never bring up the "D" word, even in jest. The word *divorce* does not make your wife feel secure, no matter what the context. Why start slipping back toward the Crazy Cycle? Do everything you can to let your wife know you are committed to her for as long as you both shall live.

Are You Being As Loyal As You Could Be?

"Don't break your promise to the wife you marrried when you were young. 'I hate divorce,' says the LORD God of Israel" (Malachi 2:15–16 NIRV).

Malachi 2:14–15 is a helpful reminder of how God feels about marital loyalty. In this passage the prophet is confronting the Israelites for breaking their marriage bonds rather freely. Divorce was rampant, and that's why Malachi said that "the LORD has been a witness between you and the wife of your youth, against whom you have dealt treacherously, though she is your companion and wife by covenant. . . . Take heed then to your spirit, and let no one deal treacherously against the wife of your youth."

At this point you may be saying, "Emerson, aren't you pushing it a little bit? I may need some help with being as loving as I should be, but I'm not 'dealing treacherously with my wife.'"

I'm not saying that you or any other good-willed husband are being treacherous toward your wife. This passage from Malachi, however, is a good reminder to do some self-evaluation. What is going on in your spirit? What are you feeling for your wife? Are you being open and understanding? Are you being as loyal to her as you could be?

It's no coincidence that the very first words Malachi uses as he goes on to verse 16 are: "'For I hate divorce!' says the LORD, the God of Israel." Malachi is describing a situation that began with the Crazy Cycle. The Israelites knew nothing about that term, but they were on the Crazy Cycle nonetheless. That's why I'm urging you to stay open and on the Energizing Cycle (see page 115) in order to avoid all the craziness you can. Remember, without love, she reacts. And a big part of being loving is to be loyal in every way.

ROBERTSON MCQUILKIN KEPT HIS PROMISE

One of the finest examples of a loyal husband I have found is the story of Robertson McQuilkin, who left his position as president of Columbia Bible College and Seminary[1] after twenty-two years because his wife had developed Alzheimer's disease. The disease had progressed to the point where his wife simply could not stand having him gone, even for a few hours. She would actually think he was "lost" and would go in search of him after he left home for work.

"Many claim to have love that never fails. But who can find a faithful man?"
(Proverbs 20:6 NIRV).

It was clear to McQuilkin that his wife now needed him full time. His decision was difficult, but in a way it was simple. He said, "The decision was made in a way forty-two years ago when I promised to care for Muriel in sickness and in health 'til death do us part.' "[2] McQuilkin went on to say that he wanted to be a man of his word, and he also wanted to be fair. His wife had cared for him sacrificially during all of those forty-two years, and if he cared for her for the next forty years, he still would not be out of her debt.

"All of you should honor marriage. You should keep the marriage bed pure" (Hebrews 13:4 NIRV).

For McQuilkin, this simple decision was the only option for him, but there was more to it than just keeping a promise and being fair. "As I watch her brave descent into oblivion, Muriel is the joy of my life," he said. "Daily I discern new manifestations of the kind of person she is; the wife I always loved."[3]

McQuilkin wrote a book about his experience, *A Promise Kept*, and in it he mentioned how startled he was by the response to his resignation as president of Columbia Bible College and Seminary to care for his wife. Husbands and wives renewed marriage vows. Pastors told his story during sermons. It was all a mystery to him until a distinguished oncologist, who dealt constantly with dying people, told him, "Almost all women stand by their men; very few men stand by their women."

WHY YOU SHOULD BE ESPECIALLY GOOD TO YOUR DAUGHTERS

That all women stand by their men and few men stand by their women is obviously a generalization. There are always exceptions, and Robertson McQuilkin is an incredible example. But the reasoning behind this rule of thumb is that women are much more the natural caretakers than men. There is an old saying, "Be good to your sons, but be especially good to your daughters." Why? Because if you become a widower and infirm in your old age, it is your daughter who will do everything in her power to convince her own husband to move into the area where you live so she can be near you to take care of you. This kind of loyalty is part of a woman's spirit.

When your wife becomes a bit insecure and moves toward you with questions about how much you love her or why you love her or if you will ever leave her, you might feel it's some kind of trap. You may think you're being set up so she can condemn you and show you disrespect if you hesitate with your answer. But that's not it at all. She moves toward you in that fashion because she is loyal to you and needs reassurance of your loyalty to her.

You may have heard this old joke. A group of men were golfing one day and four of them were on the eighteenth tee, ready to tee off. Just then a funeral procession went by, and one of the men stood up straight, took off his hat, and put it over his heart. His golf buddies were stunned. Someone said, "We've never seen anyone ready to tee off and then stop to put his hat over his heart to honor a funeral procession. That's amazing."

The man answered, "Yeah, she was a great woman. We were married forty-three years."

Play golf or attend your wife's funeral? Absurd, of course, and possibly funny to a group of men. But I guarantee that your wife will not think this joke is any funnier than being teased about "being turned in for a new model." She is not built to appreciate that kind of humor. She is so constructed that she appreciates loyalty and commitment. Assuring her of that will keep you both on the Energizing Cycle.

SHE IS ASSURED OF YOUR LOYALTY WHEN . . .

- you speak highly of her in front of others.
- you are involved in things important to her.
- you help her make decisions, such as ones regarding the children.

- you don't correct her in front of the children.
- you don't look lustfully at other women.
- you make her and your marriage a priority.
- you are never critical of her or your children in front of others.
- you include her in social gatherings when others may leave their spouses home.
- you tell the kids, "Don't speak to your mother that way!"
- you call and let her know your plans.
- you keep commitments.
- you speak positively of her and the children at all times.

CHAPTER FOURTEEN

ESTEEM—SHE WANTS YOU TO HONOR AND CHERISH HER

Over the years, many men have come to me and said, "You know, Pastor, my prayer life isn't what it should be."

I respond, "How are you treating your wife?"

"No, no," the husband hastens to explain. "My prayer life isn't where it ought to be."

"How are you treating your wife?"

"No, no, Pastor, I'm saying my prayer life; I'm not talking about my wife."

I smile and say, "I *am* talking about your wife."

In part 1, we talked about scriptural reasons that husbands are to value their wives as equals. The major passage we looked at was 1 Peter 3:7, which tells husbands to live in an understanding way with their wives, " . . . and show her honor as a fellow heir of the grace of life." Tucked into 1 Peter 3:7 is one more phrase that every husband should heed. Peter adds that the reason the husband should treat his wife in an understanding way, as a fellow heir in Christ, is so that his "prayers will not be hindered." That is why I would often tell men who came to see

> "The LORD looks with favor on those who are godly. His ears are open to their cry" (Psalm 34:15 NIRV).

me for counsel that, if heaven seemed silent to their prayers, perhaps they were not honoring their wives as God intended.

These men were sure they were doing all the right things, walking in integrity, and serving the Lord, but when they prayed, the heavens seemed as brass. They kept wondering, "God, why aren't You hearing me?" And as we probed a little deeper, we often saw that the answer for these men was that they weren't living with their wives in an understanding way that honored and esteemed them. As soon as these men started obeying Scripture, their prayer life improved.

THE C-O-U-P-L-E PRINCIPLES ARE CONNECTED

In a very real sense, the C-O-U-P-L-E acronym is a commentary on the best way to show respect to a wife. The best way to respect or honor a wife is through your **C**loseness, **O**penness, **U**nderstanding, **P**eacemaking, **L**oyalty, and now **E**—for **E**steem. A wife who is esteemed will not sing Aretha Franklin's refrain, "R-E-S-P-E-C-T." Scripture speaks of how a man should esteem and cherish his beloved. "How beautiful and how delightful you are, My love, with all your charms!" (Song of Solomon 7:6). A husband is to be one who "cherishes" his wife (Ephesians 5:29).

In the well-known passage of Proverbs 31, verses 28-29 say, "Her children stand up and call her blessed. Her husband also rises up, and he praises her. He says, 'Many women do noble things. But you are better than all the others'" (NIRV).

God has made women so that they want to be esteemed, honored, and respected. The way to honor your wife, as well as to honor your covenant with God, is to treasure her. When I say your wife wants "honor" (respect), it is a different kind of honor from what you seek as a man. For her, respect is a part of love. Probably the only time you will ever hear her say, "You don't respect me!" is when you dismiss her opinion. Actually, her exact words might be: "I know you don't love me because you don't even respect me!"

Respect, honor, and esteem are not qualities in and of themselves for your wife; they are components of the love she wants from you. To put it another way, love has many parts, and we are looking at six of them here with the acronym C-O-U-P-L-E. In chapters 15 and following, we will talk about how a wife spells respect to her husband with the acronym C-H-A-I-R-S. Something in his nature feels called to "chair" the relationship. He does not feel this in the sense of "being superior." He simply feels responsible to protect her and to die for her. God has made husbands this way, and they feel this responsibility equally.

The biblical view is that a wife does not feel called to die for her husband as he feels called to die for her. In Ephesians 5, the husband is the Christ figure; Christ died for the church. The wife is the church figure, and her husband is to die for her. Your wife does not want to chair the relationship, but she does want to be first in importance to you. This is what Peter means by "show her honor" (1 Peter 3:7). Your wife wants to know that you have her on your mind and heart *first and foremost*. This is what I mean by "esteem"; when it's there, your wife will feel treasured as if she's the most loved woman on earth. Also, she will want to respect you in a similar way that the church reverences Christ. Remember that your love motivates her respect, and her respect motivates your love!

OUR KIDS OFTEN MADE SARAH FEEL LIKE A FAILURE

On many occasions while our children were growing up, Sarah would get discouraged with her mothering role. When the kids got into trouble, caused trouble, or were just plain trouble, as kids can be, she felt inadequate, and that flowed into self-depreciation. She would say,

"I feel like such a failure." When our kids were very young, I used to ignore Sarah's complaints or play them down as "no big deal."

But as our two sons and daughter got into the teenage years, I began understanding what Sarah wanted when she came to me to say she felt like a failure or that she was "no good" as a mom. She wanted reassurance that I believed in her and the course she was taking in her role as a mother. She just wanted to know if I had confidence in the decisions she was making or was I second-guessing her. I continually let her know that I valued her efforts and commitment and that I prized her and the part she played in my life as well as in the lives of the children. I knew I could not do her job, and I often told her so.

The Love and Respect Connection can help you have an enjoyable, healthy, meaningful marriage relationship. Life, however, will never be totally perfect. When Adam and Eve fell in the Garden, sin became the universal problem for all of us (see Genesis 3; Romans 5:12–20). Tension, conflict, and problems will occur, and you must be prepared to deal with all of it. As the husband, you tie your self-image into who you are in the field—that is, in work, in accomplishments, in conquests (see chapter 16). Your wife, however, ties her self-worth into who she is in the family. Yes, it is true that today many women have careers and important positions outside of the home, but one woman who was the vice president of a major airline said it well: "At the end of the day, all that's important is that I know he loves me and values me. That's what I want more than anything else."

USE SYMBOLS TO SHOW YOUR WIFE ESTEEM

After getting out of military school and entering Wheaton College, I began asking, "Who are these people called women?" I had been withdrawn from them in military school from age thirteen to eighteen. I had a lot of questions that most guys weren't asking. I can recall being in the dining hall with a bunch of the guys and asking, "Why do you give a girl a rose after a fight?" They all gave me a blank look, and finally one of them said, "I don't know, it just works. Pass the bread." But I wouldn't give it up. I knew there was a symbolism here that I did not understand. Giving roses to a man typically doesn't cause him to tear up and need a handkerchief.

Later, after meeting and marrying Sarah, I learned a lot more about the power of symbolism and how it conveys to a woman that you value her and love her. You will never be able to show her the amount of emotional openness and esteem that she really wants—no man could—but symbolic things can do a great deal to bridge the gap. I am talking particularly about anniversaries and birthdays. Women put great store in these occasions (remember my magnificent goof by forgetting Sarah's birthday?).

> *"Keep me close to yourself like the ring on your finger"* (Song of Solomon 8:6 NIRV).

Women are the ones who have babies, and that's one reason that birthdays are a big deal to them. For nine months she is asked, "When is the due date?" Birth is part of the culture of women. Only women give birth. As Jeremiah observed, "Ask now, and see, if a male can give birth" (Jeremiah 30:6). In a woman's mind, who could possibly forget a birthday? She never would.

Much the same way, a marriage date is etched in the woman's soul. Since childhood, your wife dreamed of the wedding day as she played dress-up and sang, "Here Comes the Bride!" Even today, your wife will show wedding pictures to her friends. They will talk about her dress, her hairdo back then, etc. Husbands, however, never played dress-up in tuxes. Husbands do not say, "Hey, Harry, let me show you what the guys wore in my wedding." This is a graphic illustration of pink and blue, and you should be aware of it. For your wife, there are no more important dates than your wedding anniversary and her birthday, as

well as the birthdays of others in the family. All of these dates are oppor-
tunities for you to show her that you love and esteem her by remembering them and celebrating them with her.

"Does a young woman forget all about her jewelry? Does a bride forget her wedding jewels?" *(Jeremiah 2:32 NIRV).*

How you celebrate her birthday or your anniversary is an art, not a science. The scientific approach puts a lot of stock in the material, the expensive. Suppose one man buys his wife a Mercedes for her birthday (I can think of three men I know who did just that). The other man takes his wife out to the park and they go for a nice walk and share feelings of love and closeness as he tells her how much she means to him. On the way back to the car, he finds a small, flat rock, picks it up, and brings it home. Then he writes a little poem or some other notation on it and presents it to her as a memento of the walk they took that day. Whose wife will appreciate her gift the most?

The natural male (blue) inclination is to think that the expensive gift would be far more meaningful to a wife. After all, if you bought another man a Mercedes, he'd go around telling all of his friends, "Wow! What a great guy Joe is. I can't believe it. He gave me this wonderful car!"

But when you buy a woman a Mercedes, she is much more likely to say to her girlfriends, "Look, he got me a Mercedes. I wonder if he is trying to buy me off or something."

Let's get back to that little rock. When she's ninety-three and you've been dead for a decade, what is she going to keep on her mantel? A picture of the Mercedes? Absolutely not! She's going to keep that rock, because it is symbolic of a time when her husband gave her special attention, devotion, and esteem.

One husband attended our conference with his wife of twenty-four years and quickly grasped the power of "little, thoughtful things." His wife wrote:

Valentine's Day was very unique. . . . I woke up to a candy scavenger hunt. My husband had taken the time to write four short poems and attached each to a baggie filled with four different kinds of Valentine candy. . . . It started in the bathroom . . . and had clues of where to find the next. I just giggled around the house, it was so fun. . . . That night my husband made reservations to go to a Valentine supper. A classic guitarist played; they took our picture and put it in a special "thank you" frame from the restaurant. We feasted on wonderful food in a very relaxed atmosphere. It was absolutely one of the most memorable evenings! Thank you for encouraging my husband to love me.

This woman's words illustrate a key truth: the expense of a gift is secondary to the thought your wife senses you put into the gift, card, or activity. God designed your wife to be touched by things that symbolize your love and show that you treasure her. She wants to know you think about her. She wants that to come from your heart without any prompting. Truly, it is the thought that counts!

Does Your Wife Ever Want You to Read Her Mind?

The Valentine story above is what can happen when all goes well. Sometimes, however, Murphy's Law kicks in—at least a little bit. To illustrate, I'll stay with the theme of taking your wife out to dinner. Suppose it's your fifth anniversary and you come home and say, "Honey, I want to take you out for dinner for our anniversary. Where do you want to go?"

She says, "Oh, I don't know."

You respond, "No, I really want to take you wherever you want. Where would you like to go?"

She says again, "I don't know; why don't you decide?"

"You want me to decide?"

"Yes, I do."

"But I don't want to decide. I want to take you where *you* want to go."

"No, I want you to decide," your wife insists.

Okay, you decide: "Well, I just read that the Freeway Steak House has the best beef in town. Why don't we try it?"

And she says, "I don't want to go there."

A lot of husbands—maybe most husbands—have been in situations similar to this. At this point you can go in one of two directions: You can process your wife's seemingly maddening response by getting irritated and even angry. Equipped to see and hear in blue, you can think that your wife should *know* she can't be so unreasonable, illogical, and provoking. If she wants to ruin the evening, she has both of you halfway to the Crazy Cycle already.

But there is another choice. You can weight the scales in favor of the Energizing Cycle. You can remember that your wife sees and hears in pink. You can adjust your blue sunglasses and blue hearing aids and be patient. Instead of getting irritated, you seek a little more information.

Now in truth, your wife really wants you to sort of "read her mind." She is thinking, *If he loved me as much as I love him, he'd figure out where I want to go without my having to tell him. That's what I'd do for him. Why can't he do that for me? I want to know he really thinks about me as I think about him and feels about me as I feel about him.*

Every husband has been expected to read his wife's mind. Though mind reading seldom is possible, there are ways to make good guesses. You can say, "Okay, the Freeway Steak House is pretty limited, just steak and ribs. How about . . . ?" and then you name two or three other restaurants that have ambience and atmosphere, as well as a broader menu. Chances are you'll hit the jackpot with one of these and she'll say, "Okay, that sounds good." Your fifth anniversary is saved from disaster and, even more important, your wife feels that you hold her in high esteem—that you really treasure her and want her to be happy.

There are other situations, however, where your wife doesn't want you to read her mind, but she still strongly disagrees with you. This can get a little sticky. How do you treat her with esteem if her opinion conflicts with yours (or possibly even sounds a little wacky)? Because males tend to be so bottom-line, it would be easy to sound harsh without even realizing it. Actually, there are three ways you can answer a wife when you don't agree with her, and they can all keep her esteem intact. First, you can simply say, "Honey, thanks for sharing your opinion." Second, you might say, "Honey, let me think about that." That tells her you are processing her ideas. Third, and possibly best, you say, "Sweetheart, even though I don't feel the same way you do about this, I value your opinion and I trust your heart."

THANK HER FOR ALL SHE DOES

One other way to esteem your wife is to let her know you really appreciate all she does. You may have heard the story of the husband who came home from work to find bikes and scooters blocking the driveway, the house in shambles, dirty dishes stacked in the sink, dirty laundry piled up, pieces of clothing scattered everywhere, and his two preschool children drawing on the walls. He finally found his wife, asleep in bed. He woke her up and asked, "Honey, the place is a disaster, the kids are running wild—what is going on?!"

She looked at him with a wan, tired smile. "Well, you know how you always come home and you ask me what I did all day?"

He says, "Yeah . . . "

"Well, today I didn't do it."

Esteem your wife for what she does, but don't overlook cherishing her simply for who she is. One woman said to her husband, "I just got off the phone with my sister. She's incredible. She tells me that she helped her husband build a back porch on their house this summer.

"Rejoice in the wife of your youth" (Proverbs 5:18b).

She also made a rocking chair, and she's in an exotic foods cooking class. She's always doing something, making something. I feel so inadequate when I talk with her. What do *I* make?"

Her husband turned to her and said, "You make me happy."

Bingo! Bonus points for that husband! He knows how to esteem his wife. Following are more ideas on how to esteem, cherish, and honor the most important person in your life.

YOUR WIFE WILL FEEL ESTEEMED WHEN . . .

- you say, "I'm so proud of the way you handled that."
- you speak highly of her in front of others.
- you open the door for her.
- you try something new with her.
- you give her encouragement or praise with kindness and enthusiasm.
- you notice something different about her hair or clothes.
- you are physically affectionate with her in public.
- you teach the children to show her and others respect.
- you value her opinion in the gray areas as not wrong but just different—and valid.
- you choose family outings over "guy things."
- you make her feel first in importance.
- you are proud of her and all she does.

CHAPTER FIFTEEN

C-H-A-I-R-S: How to Spell Respect to Your Husband

(Note to husbands: This chapter and the six to follow are "for wives only," but husbands are invited to read along.)

Ladies, we have taken your husbands through C-O-U-P-L-E to help them become more loving men. Now it's your turn. In the next six chapters, we will take you through the acronym C-H-A-I-R-S to give you practical, biblical ways that will help you become more respectful women.

Wives do not need a lot of coaching on being loving. It is something God built into them, and they do it naturally. However, they do need help with respect. Part 1 contained many letters from wives who discovered the tremendous power in giving their husbands unconditional respect. Admittedly, this is a foreign term to many women, and even though you have bought into the idea that your husband wants and needs respect, it is still a difficult concept to practice.

> *"A wise woman builds her house. But a foolish woman tears hers down"* (Proverbs 14:1 NIRV).

This wife's letter represents how many women feel as they attempt to get off the Crazy Cycle and on the Energizing Cycle:

Applying respect in my marriage is quite foreign and I have really had to work at it. I always thought I just needed to love more. What a revelation for me, because loving more wasn't helping. Thank you again! I am so excited about where our marriage will go from here as we apply what we have learned. I have a new energy for our relationship.

Providing more energy for your marriage is exactly what the C-H-A-I-R-S chapters are all about. C-H-A-I-R-S is an acronym that stands for six major values that your husband holds: **C**onquest, **H**ierarchy, **A**uthority, **I**nsight, **R**elationship, and **S**exuality. Each of these values will be covered in a brief chapter. In **C**onquest, you will learn to appreciate his desire to work and achieve. **H**ierarchy deals with appreciating his desire to protect and provide. **A**uthority covers appreciating his desire to serve and to lead. **I**nsight touches on appreciating his desire to analyze and counsel. **R**elationship helps you understand his desire for shoulder-to-shoulder friendship. **S**exuality explains his desire for sexual intimacy. In these six areas, you will learn how to spell "respect" to your husband. (For how to share your needs with each other, see appendix C.)

When a wife "is clothed with . . . dignity," she carries herself honorably and comes across respectfully (Proverbs 31:25 NIV).

Granted, "unconditional respect" almost sounds to some women like an oxymoron. After all, he should *earn* respect, not be given respect unconditionally, or so many women seem to think. Ever since I have started teaching the Love and Respect Connection, I have struggled with helping wives see what unconditional respect can do for their husbands—and their marriages. Giving your husband unconditional respect is the clear path to receiving unconditional love from him, but it is still hard for women to grasp. Here are reports from two wives who are reaping the benefits:

I kept trying to get some attention and affection. . . . One night a few weeks ago, he said to me for the hundredth time, "You never listen to me" as an explanation for that month's ice cold treatment. That night I relistened to your "man" talk and I finally understood what he meant . . . what he was getting was a whole lot of badgering in [my] attempt to get closer to him. I immediately changed my approach [and] got very conscious of my choices and outcomes and the result has been wonderful . . . he has been very loving.

———

I am thankful for this concept of unconditional respect, because now I feel I can return, in a way that is meaningful to him, all the love he gives to me. . . . As a martial artist, I have learned a lot about respect, just didn't realize it was a language. . . . I never knew it was a need, let alone a language. . . . I am learning to communicate more effectively with my teenage son as well, thanks to this new awareness of respect.

How to Use the "Respect Test" with Your Husband

When I began teaching the Love and Respect Connection, I would talk to various groups and quote them the key passages: Ephesians 5:33 ("The wife must respect her husband" NIV) and 1 Peter 3:1–2 ("Wives, be submissive to your own husbands . . . as they observe your chaste and respectful behavior"). But, frankly, many women would dismiss these verses almost flippantly by pointing out that Paul was a male and so was Peter. How could they know how a woman felt?

Instead of preaching sermons about not rebelling against inspired Scripture, I devised a way they could test the concept of unconditional respect with their husbands. Not surprisingly, I called it the "Respect Test." I asked a group of wives to spend a bit of time thinking of some things they respected about their husbands. It took some of them quite awhile, but they all finally did it. Then I told them to go home, wait until their husbands weren't busy or distracted, and say: "I was thinking about you today and several things about you that I respect, and I just want you to know that I respect you."

After saying this, they were to not wait for any response—just mention something they needed to do and quietly start to leave the room. Then they were to see what would happen. One woman reported back to me that after telling her husband she respected him, she turned to leave but she never even made it to the door. He practically screamed, "Wait! Come back. *What* things?"

Fortunately (and this is very important), she was ready to tell him what she respected about him and she proceeded to do so. After she was finished, he said, "Wow! Hey, can I take the family out to dinner?"

The wife was aghast. Her husband had seldom if ever taken the family out to dinner. What was going on here? I explained to her that

When doing the Respect Test, you ". . . walk by faith, not by sight—" (2 Corinthians 5:7).

a man's first and fundamental impulse is to serve, especially in response to being honored. She had honored him, and he wanted to do something about it. The wife had to ask for a rain check because the kids had commitments that evening, and he agreed. About fifteen minutes later, however, she heard pots and pans banging in the kitchen. She went to look and found her husband fixing dinner. Her husband had *never* fixed dinner. *Never*—this was a first! Again, he was serving.

A few days later, this wife wrote to us again and said, "You won't believe it. He's in the laundry room! Do you have any other 'respect tests'? I think I might get a cruise out of this."

Could a wife use the Respect Test to manipulate her husband to take her on a cruise? That's possible, but this wife was not guilty of manipulation. She sincerely tried expressing respect for her husband,

and it worked far beyond her expectations. To repeat what I said earlier, a husband who has basic goodwill will serve his wife when she respects him for who he is. I am convinced that the key to motivating another person is meeting his or her deepest need.

Granted, not every wife may get the same response that this woman received. Some husbands might mull over the Respect Test for a while and say something later. Or they might say nothing at all. The point is, using the Respect Test means taking a step of faith. It is admitting that you understand what God's Word says about unconditional respect for your husband. You show him respect *regardless of his response.*

BE READY WITH REASONS THAT YOU RESPECT HIM

When a wife tells her husband that there are several things that she respects about him, most husbands—after regaining consciousness—will instantly ask, "What were you thinking? What do you mean? What do you respect about me?" A wife needs to be prepared to answer these questions honestly and genuinely. Don't expect to make your respect statement, head for the hills, and hope he never mentions it again. Trust me—that won't happen.

But what if a wife just doesn't know what to say? We have talked with many wives who admit there just isn't anything they really respect about their husbands. But a wife who says this is usually too angry or perhaps too discouraged to think about what she can respect in her husband. First, this kind of wife must ask herself, "Is my husband, as unaware and unloving as he is, a man of basic goodwill?" If the answer to this question is yes in any degree at all, then this wife can start making her list. It will help her to realize that her husband is made in the image of God, and he has God-given attributes that are worthy of respect. For example, he desires to work and achieve and to protect and provide for this family. He desires to be strong and to lead in the good sense of the word. We'll look at these and other God-given male attributes in following chapters. The point is this: *look at his desires and not his performance.* Here are some thoughts to get you started. You can frame them in your own particular words.

"Honey, I respect how you get up every day and go to work to provide for our family. This isn't an option; you have to do it and you do."

"Honey, I respect you for your desire to protect me and provide for me and the family. I think of all the insurance you have for us. I know the bills weigh on you at times, and I admire you for your commitment."

The key is to focus on the positive instead of always going back to the negative. A wife must try to see what God sees. Is your husband basically a man of goodwill? Get in touch with that fact and express respect for it. A Scripture passage I often reference regarding goodwill in marriage is 1 Corinthians 7:33–34. Paul assumes that married couples in Corinth have goodwill toward each other. He points out that an unmarried man has more time for doing the Lord's work but that a married man "is concerned about . . . how he may please his wife" (v. 33). Paul goes on to say that it is the same for a wife who "is concerned about . . . how she may please her husband" (v. 34).[1]

A good-willed husband does not try to displease his wife but to please her, as Paul clearly states in 1 Corinthians 7:33. I always urge a wife who is feeling unloved to be slow in asserting that her husband is unloving or does not want to love her. That is impugning an evil motive upon her husband, which is too drastic a judgment. True, a husband may not be as loving as he ought to be, but he is not consciously, willfully, and habitually trying to be unloving and displeasing. During those moments when a husband displeases a wife or a wife displeases her husband, it helps to keep certain scriptures in mind: "The spirit is willing, but the flesh is weak (Matthew 26:41) and "Indeed, there is not a righteous man [*or woman*] on earth who continually does good and who never sins" (Ecclesiastes 7:20; italics mine).[2]

When a husband gets angry or stubborn, his wife must realize he is not set on a course to hurt her. He tries to be well-meaning. He wants a happy marriage. And because he wants that happy marriage, wives who try the Respect Test can be amazed at what will happen. Men are starving for respect. One wife who attended one of our conferences wrote to me and reported what happened when she used the Respect Test. Instead of talking to him, she typed up a card that told her husband how much she respected him for working so hard to provide for the family and letting her be a stay-at-home mom for their three daughters. She tucked it in his briefcase, and he found it the next day by midmorning. Immediately, he called her on his cell phone and thanked her for making his whole day.

When a wife wisely applies respect, she is "a wise wife . . . given by the LORD" (Proverbs 19:14 NIRV).

I could give you many other reports from wives who tried the Respect Test and passed with flying colors. Some have done it face to face, others have written notes, and others have called their husband at work and left a respect message on his voicemail. It doesn't matter how a wife uses the Respect Test, but when she does, it can be the first step toward a real breakthrough in the marriage. One wife wrote:

> Just a few days ago, I decided to tell my husband that I respect him. It felt so awkward to say the words, but I went for it and the reaction was unbelievable! He asked me why I respected him. I listed off a few things, although I could have said many more, and I watched his demeanor change right before my very eyes!

If your relationship has been unfulfilling, try to think back to the point where it lost its intimacy. You may remember feeling wounded in spirit because you did not feel your husband loved you in a meaning-ful way, and you reacted. Ever since, the Crazy Cycle has spun for you to one degree or another. This wife admitted:

> We've been living in the Crazy Cycle for more years than you
> can imagine. I've already respected him; I just wasn't showing
> it because I felt so unloved. I guess it was my way of retaliat-
> ing, but I honestly didn't know it. As I [started] really looking
> at him during some interactions I was shocked at the look on
> his face. I saw that he felt disrespected! How could I never see
> it before? The best way I can describe what I see happening
> now is that he is melting, and I feel hope for the first time
> in years.

This wife found the way off the Crazy Cycle! The following chapters are designed to help you start practicing respect for your husband in ways that will energize him and your marriage. The word *C-H-A-I-R-S* describes the typical man. Yes, I know there are exceptions, but men, in general, see themselves as the ones who should "chair" the relation-

A husband wants to be seen as one "who man-ages his own household well" (1 Timothy 3:4).

ship. That may not be politically correct, but we're not here to discuss political correctness. We're here to discuss the way things are—the way men and women feel in their souls. We've looked at how women feel in their souls, and now we must consider how men feel. Neither is wrong; they're just as different as pink and blue.

In most cases, men see themselves in the driver's seat. Whether they are any good at chairing the relationship and being in the driver's seat can be debated. But in terms of a man's self-image, he needs to be the chairman; he needs to drive. He needs to be first among equals, not to be superior or dominating but because this is how God has made him and he wants to take on that responsibility. Keep this vital fact in mind as you read through the six concepts that follow, which will explain how to spell respect to a man and get you both on the Energizing Cycle. As these concepts unfold, you will get a clearer picture of who your husband is and how God has made him (and your son if you have one). And, as you practice these concepts, you may well enjoy what many wives have experienced. For example:

> We have never had a marriage that was close and intimate [and loving] until I began practicing respect. I always knew that something was lacking, but figured it was him [being unloving] and not me [being disrespectful]. Now I feel loved and I know he feels respected and a tremendous void has been filled in our lives.

> ———

> Your comment [was] that it is easier for men to respect their wives than to love them, and easier for wives to love their husbands than to respect them. I have never come across that thought, ever before. It was really striking to me. This was really, really important.

> ———

> My husband and I are enjoying such a sweeter relationship these days. I have learned to be keenly aware of what I am communicating (including facial expressions and tone of voice) and my husband has responded by allowing me to tell him when I am feeling unloved. We have avoided the Crazy Cycle completely since I committed to be obedient to God in this. Thank you from the bottom of my heart!

Those are just a few of dozens of such comments that we have received. As Dale Carnegie once said, "Truly respecting others is the bedrock of motivation." It is also the key to getting off the Crazy Cycle and on the Energizing Cycle. Read on and learn specific ways to motivate your husband to love you as never before.

CHAPTER SIXTEEN

CONQUEST—APPRECIATE HIS DESIRE TO WORK AND ACHIEVE

As we begin to unpack the acronym C-H-A-I-R-S, our first letter is C, standing for Conquest. Because I am talking primarily to wives, many of you may be wondering why I picked such an unromantic word. "Conquest" sounds like something out of the dark ages of chauvinism when men believed it was their right to conquer women —physically, sexually, mentally, and emotionally. That kind of conquest is not at all what I have in mind.

By "conquest," I mean the natural, inborn desire of the man to go out and "conquer" the challenges of his world—to work and achieve. As a wife, if you can start to understand how important your husband's work is to him, you will take a giant step toward communicating respect and honor, two things that he values even more than your love.

That a husband values respect more than love is very difficult for many women to grasp. God has made you to love, and you see life through pink lenses that are focused on love. You give love, you want love, and you may not quite understand why your husband does not operate the same way. When I say a husband values respect more than love, do I mean that your husband does not value love at all? Of course he values your love—more than words can describe—but he spells love R-E-S-P-E-C-T.

Let's create a scene that might illustrate how a man feels about conquest. Suppose a husband has just lost his job. He comes home and tells his wife. He looks shattered, dazed, defeated. To help her husband, the wife says, "It doesn't matter. All that matters is that we love one another." Does this seem to help? He looks at her blankly, shrugs, and plunks down in front of the TV. For the rest of the evening he is withdrawn, not wanting to talk. His wife is baffled. She tried to comfort him, and now he has withdrawn from her.

Actually, the answer is quite simple. Pink and blue are at it again. Pink tried to comfort; blue was offended by her overtures. To help you understand, let's create another scene where the wife has a miscarriage. Her husband comes to her and says, "Honey, it doesn't matter as long as we love one another."

Some women might say I'm talking about apples and oranges. How can I compare losing a job to losing a baby? I'm not arguing the value of what is lost here; I'm explaining how important your husband's job is to him. In his eyes, he has lost something that is extremely important—it is part of the very warp and woof of his being.

This is why, in all likelihood, if you try to comfort your husband after he loses his job by saying, "It's okay, honey; we have each other," it may not help much. He knows he has you. He is secure in your love, but he also identifies strongly with the fact that he is someone who works, who has a position, who has responsibilities. Where did he get this deep-seated feeling about his work?

From the Start, Adam Enjoyed His Work

To learn where husbands got this tremendous drive to work and achieve, we must go back to Genesis and the first career assignment in history. "Then the LORD God took the man and put him into the garden of Eden to cultivate it and keep it" (Genesis 2:15). Before Eve was created, God made Adam, and God made him to work. It's interesting to note that Eden was not a place with free handouts wherever Adam turned. The trees provided food, but Adam was to cultivate and keep them. God set Adam up with almost everything he needed: a beautiful place, plenty of food, and a good water supply (see Genesis 2:10).[1]

With a great job and perfect working conditions, Adam seemed to have it all. But the Lord knew something was missing. To fulfill his vocation, his call, Adam needed a woman to be his counterpart. So God made "a helper suitable for him" (Genesis 2:18). The Hebrew word for "helper" (or "helpmeet") means literally "a help answering to him," or "one who answers." In 1 Corinthians 11:9, Paul takes this thought further: "For indeed man was not created for the woman's sake, but woman for the man's sake."

My observation is that during courtship a woman glows with a message to her man: "I love you and am here for you. I respect what you want to do and who you want to be. I long to help you. That's what love is all about." After marriage, however, things change. Her way of helping can feel anything but respectful to her husband. For example, one wife of almost sixteen years and a homeschooling mother of three, thought she had the right motives to be a helpmeet, but she could see she wasn't being received as such. She writes:

> He received what I thought were well-meaning ways of helping as intentions with wrong motives. . . . I am finding out I have come across in a complaining negative attitude more than I care to realize. . . . Since I have been purposing to show respect, I have definitely seen the blessing, my husband has been talking more to me, been more affectionate, and I feel like we have been closer in the past few weeks than we have in years.

Obviously, passages like Genesis 2:18 and 1 Corinthians 11:9 are not favorites with the feminist movement.[2] To feminists this is politi-

From Jacob's day until now, a man asks, "When shall I provide for my own household?" (Genesis 30:30).

cally incorrect—something written by a man, making God to appear to be sexist. But Scripture is not so easily dismissed. From the very beginning, man was called upon to "work in the field" and to provide for his family. The male feels a deep need to be involved in adventure and conquest. This is not an option for him; it is a deep-seated trait.

A Man's First Question: "What Do You Do?"

The first question a man usually asks another man when they meet for the first time is, "What do you do?" Right or wrong, most men identify themselves by their work. God created men to "do" something in the field. Watch young boys as they pick up sticks and turn them into imaginary guns or tools. Recently a mother told us she had prevented her son from having any toy guns or using sticks as pretend rifles, but when he made his cheese sandwich into the form of a pistol and was shooting at a friend, she cried out in exasperation, "I give up!"

Mothers should never give up because this is simply part of a boy's nature. He is called to be a hunter, a worker, a doer. He wants to make his conquest in the field of life. The academic term for this is the "instrumentality of the male."[3] From childhood, there is something in a male that makes him like adventure and conquest. He wants to go into the field to hunt or to work in some way.

During a Love and Respect Conference, when we talk about this male drive for conquest that starts very young, I ask the wives, "How do you want your future daughter-in-law to treat your son? He's going to have this same need to achieve and to work. I'm sure that you will want his wife to support him, just as your husband wants you to support him." When I mention their sons and what might happen when they marry, the light goes on for many women who are struggling with the concept of unconditional respect. One wife told me, "When you put it this way, it changes the whole focus. I feel differently about how I treat my husband than how I want my son treated by his future wife. That shouldn't be."

How deeply men value their inborn desire to work and achieve is graphically illustrated in two friends of mine who faced the threat of cancer. Both men calmly faced death and accepted what they thought would be their end. Through all the chemotherapy and accompanying problems, their optimism and faith remained strong. In the end, both men survived, but both still suffered terribly from a common foe. One of the men chose to sell his company to allow himself to serve God with whatever time he had left. However, for a period of time after the sale, he found he did not know who he was without his work. He told me, "I was never depressed when dealing with cancer and possibly dying, but when I left my work, which was my identity, I went into a depression that was like nothing I had ever experienced before."

The other man suffered horribly and was at death's door, but somehow he, too, recovered. He returned to work, and life was wonderful, but then he lost his job. He came to see me, depressed and defeated. He told me that being out of work was harder than dying. Ironically, both of these men were more deeply affected by losing their careers than they were with facing death due to cancer.

Many women have no idea of the importance men put on their work. If a wife even implies, unknowingly, that her husband's work is not that important, she has just called him a loser. I can recall a friend of mine who built a very profitable business and was then approached by someone who wanted to buy him out. In his mind, there was no greater compliment because this buyout meant he would be financially secure and socially honored. To him, this meant success. The buyout finally happened, and he came home to announce the good news to his wife. She, however, was preoccupied with home and family issues. Distracted, she said, "That's nice, dear" and then went on accomplishing one of her to-do list items.

This man told me later that he was crushed. He said, "I was so hurt I made a decision never to share things with her again." I don't endorse his decision, but I can empathize. A woman would probably be able to empathize if she could picture a reverse situation. She announces she is pregnant and her husband, distracted by his television program, says, "That's nice, dear." By way of stark contrast, here is a letter from a wife who chose to stand by her man:

> My husband has been going through a big struggle and has been the target of a lot of criticism and rumor. I have chosen to stand next to him . . . and show respect and commitment in the face of the criticism and rumors. He and I have lost friendships spanning fifteen to thirty years because of this struggle but have grown closer in the process. He tells me what's going on now, shares the e-mails with me, etc., instead of being all closed up and quiet. God is so good to me, giving me the knowledge I need at the time I need it.

Do Women Want to Have It All?

When I speak of a man's deep-seated desire to work, I am not saying women have no desire to work. Women have always worked, but generally they did so in the home with children nearby. In recent decades, women have discovered they are quite capable of going out into the workaday world and holding significant positions and making tremendous achievements. But when a wife goes out to work, the question remains: who will remain at home to care for the kids? The answer is day care, a solution that at best is hardly ideal and, at worst, is severely harmful to the children.

It is interesting that in the Western world at least, women see careers as a freedom-of-choice issue. Women don't want to be told they have to work. They want the freedom to choose full-time mothering and/or a career.

Most men feel that work is not an option. Comedian Tim Allen has observed that women have all kinds of choices. Men have one: "Work or go to jail." Yes, it is true that in some homes the woman works and the man takes care of the kids. Generally speaking, however, our sons will feel they have to work in some field, but our daughters will want the freedom to choose between pregnancies and promotions.

My counseling experience leads me to conclude that the typical woman is looking for a husband who is capable enough to enable her to leave the workforce if she so desires. As she evaluates her future with a man, she instinctively considers his ability to take care of her and the children. The good-willed woman marries for love, not for money; nonetheless, she is very aware of the need to make a "nest." She asks herself, "Can he provide sufficiently to make it possible for me to stay home with my little chicks if that's what I want to do full time?" The woman who asks this question is being wise. I hope my daughter weighs her options in this way.

There is also the question of just how much a wife who is the main breadwinner enjoys her role. Remember the basic question that all wives have: "Does he love me as much as I love him?" Women are basically insecure about this, and if a wife is out there doing the providing, bringing home the money while he stays home, her insecurity goes up, not down. She wonders, "Would he even be here if it weren't for the money I make?" Becoming the main provider for the family can result in the woman being attacked at her level of deepest fear.

A man always feels the call to the field, while the natural instinct of a woman is the call to the family. The husband instinctively knows he needs to be out there performing, no matter what other pressures he may be facing. I believe that most men reflect Adam and most women reflect Eve deep within their core. Like Adam, he feels a call to work in the field on behalf of the family. Most women feel like Eve. She alone can have a baby and, if she has a baby, she wants the option of having her Adam work in the field on her behalf.

Adam does not expect Eve to have a baby and hand the baby to him so she can go back to work. Those who advocate domestic equality promote this idea, but after doing my PhD dissertation on effec-

> *Despite feminism's cries, a wife best qualifies as the one who "tenderly cares for her own children" (1 Thessalonians 2:7).*

tive fathers, I would not agree. This is not to downplay a woman's abilities and her desire for a career. Women can be called to positions of important leadership (see Judges 4:4), but I want to emphasize her incomparable worth as mother to an infant. A father with an infant does not compare to a mother with an infant.

I do not believe any social engineering will make Daddy "a natural mother." Typically, the woman leans toward having the baby and caring for the baby; the man leans toward working in the field for her and the baby. Yes, I know there are exceptions in today's culture, but for the typical woman, her first desire is not for a career; it is for home and family.[4]

HAVE YOU EVER SAID, "THANKS FOR WORKING"?

For those women who would like to do one simple thing that would encourage their husbands and show them respect concerning this whole area of conquest, just try writing him a note. It doesn't have to be long or profound. All it has to say is, "Honey, thank you for getting out there and working." If you want to elaborate, tell him that you are grateful that he has given you the opportunity to choose to go out and work or to be home with the children, and you just want to thank him for that.

I talk to women who tell me that they thought about thanking their husbands for working—in fact, they've thought a lot about it but have never told them. I asked them how they would feel about a man who says he thinks a lot about how much he loves his wife but never tells her. The usual response is shock or anger. "What do you mean, a man could live with his wife and never tell her he loves her?" They can't believe it.

The point is easily made. Relationships go both ways. Of course, he should tell you he loves you. But you should turn to him and say, "Honey, thank you. You have to get out there and work every day. I don't know if I totally understand it, but I appreciate this. I really respect you." Watch what your husband does with that. See how he reacts. I guarantee you it will make a tremendous difference. (Also see appendix A and C.)

He Wants a Woman Who Believes in Him

In one of my Christian education classes in college, the question was asked, "What do you want in a spouse?" I remember saying, "I want a woman who will believe in me." There is a parallel here between Christ and the church. Christ wants us to believe in Him, and we do that to the glory of God. But in the human sense, in the marriage relationship, men do *"A wife of noble character is her husband's crown" (Proverbs 12:4 NIV).* what they do for the admiration of one woman. When you fell in love and he married you, he felt that you believed in him and he appreciated that—perhaps far more than you have ever realized. It touched his spirit, because this is something huge within the male. He married you, and he thought that your "cheerleading" would last forever. But years later, his work appears to compete with the marriage and the family. Instead of admiring him for his work efforts, you may be feeling neglected.

It's possible your husband may be in the "workaholic" category and you have every reason to feel neglected. You may be tempted to feel like one wife who wrote to us to say, "I have come out and said in the past that his work is more important than I am and that it's all about him. I have said that his laptop is the 'other woman' in our house and I can't compete with it." Workaholism is a very real and serious problem, but I believe that if you and your husband are trying to be a Love and Respect couple, what he needs is support and respect for his work efforts. If he is a good-willed man who is neglecting the family by working too much, he will realize it, and you can talk it through and work it out. (For more on workaholism, see appendix E, p. 315.)

When you support and appreciate your husband, he will say that he has received "favor from the LORD" (Proverbs 18:22 NIRV).

Your first job is to be sure that you support his efforts for conquest—to get out there to work and achieve. Never let him feel unappreciated and that he's just a meal ticket. Always be aware that, because of your pink sunglasses and pink hearing aids, the messages you send can misrepresent you. His blue sunglasses and blue hearing aids can decode you all wrong, and he mistakenly feels that you see him as just your bread and butter. That is why it is so important that you thank him and let him know you admire and support him. If you say those words, it will do a lot to help his blue hearing aids pick up the right message, and your support of his work efforts will motivate his love for you. One wife's brief note says it all:

One day I put a note in his lunchbox, thanking him for some
things. He told me thanks that night, and on Valentine's Day
I wrote another note about his dedication to his job and family
and how I appreciated that. I could tell by the look in his eyes
it meant a lot.

YOUR HUSBAND WILL FEEL YOU APPRECIATE HIS DESIRE TO WORK AND ACHIEVE WHEN . . .

- you tell him verbally or in writing that you value his work efforts.
- you express your faith in him related to his chosen field.
- you listen to his work stories as closely as you expect him to listen to your accounts of what happens in the family.
- you see yourself as his helpmate and counterpart and talk with him about this whenever possible.
- you allow him to dream as you did when you were courting.
- you don't dishonor or subtly criticize his work "in the field" to get him to show more love "in the family."

CHAPTER SEVENTEEN

HIERARCHY—APPRECIATE HIS DESIRE TO PROTECT AND PROVIDE

An old saying observes, "Fools rush in where angels fear to tread." Ever since I have been sharing the Love and Respect Connection around the country, I have been willing to be fool enough to use terms that are just not politically correct. One of these words is *hierarchy*. In some groups, women hear it and think immediately of the chauvinist mind-set: "The male dominates the female" . . . "It's a man's world" . . . "Men are superior and women are inferior" . . . and on and on.

I can't really blame these women, because over the centuries, men have used Scripture in ignorant, abusive, and even evil ways. They have justified all kinds of terrible treatment of women, all in the name of "the Bible says so."

But the Bible *doesn't* say so. It says something much different from what is claimed by chauvinists. It also says something much different from what feminists purport.

In chapter 16, we mentioned the deep desire God built into man to go out into the field to work and achieve. Another desire God built into the man is to protect and provide for his wife and family and, if necessary, to die for them. This desire to protect and provide is part of the warp and woof of a man. An obvious example is life insurance. In the United States alone, billions upon billions are spent on life insurance premiums, bought mostly by men. Why? Because of their instinct to provide. They feel a sense of security and restfulness knowing their families will be taken care of if they die.

What Is the Real Meaning of "Biblical Hierarchy"?

"All that may be well and good," some women tell me, "but how does a man's willingness to protect and provide for me place him above me in some kind of hierarchy?" Over the years I have talked to many a wife who is so controlled by her fear of her husband's headship that she overreacts by habitually showing contempt and verbally abusing him. I believe, however, that when a woman understands hierarchy from a true biblical point of view, it relieves most, if not all, of her fears.

The passage that spells out biblical hierarchy is Ephesians 5:22–24: "Wives, be subject to your own husbands, as to the Lord. For the husband is the head of the wife, as Christ also is the head of the church, He Himself being the Savior of the body. But as the church is subject to Christ, so also the wives ought to be to their husbands in everything."

"But if anyone does not provide for his own...he has denied the faith and is worse than an unbeliever" (1 Timothy 5:8).

In some translations, the words "be subject to" are translated "submit." The Greek word here is *hupotasso*, a compound word that means to rank under or place under. God is not giving husbands some carte blanche label of "superior"; He is giving husbands a tremendous responsibility, as Paul clearly points out in the next few verses: "Husbands, love your wives, just as Christ also loved the church and gave Himself up for her, so that He might sanctify her, having cleansed her by the washing of water with the word, that He might present to Himself the church in all her glory, having no spot or wrinkle or any such thing; but that she would be holy and blameless" (vv. 25–27).

Here the responsibilities of being "head" are clearly spelled out. The husband is given the awesome responsibility to love his wife just as Christ loved the church and gave Himself up for her. That is why the good-willed husband who understands this passage sees it as his duty to protect his wife. At the same time, the wife is called upon to place herself under that protection. This is the biblical definition of hierarchy. It is not male superiority for the sake of putting down the female. It is the male's responsibility to place himself over the female and protect her. How this works out in the interplay between husband and wife in a marriage can take some interesting turns. One wife wrote:

> Over the years when I would drive on ice and start to slide, I'd slam on the brakes. He'd tell me to let off the brakes. The other day I was driving alone and hit ice. Starting to slide, I hit the brakes and in my mind I heard his voice, "Let off the brakes." It saved my life. I realized from your conference that his counsel to me was for my protection. His firmness with me was rooted in his protective role. So I came home and told him, "You saved my life." I praised him and sought to honor him. Before, I just felt it was a put-down, and that wasn't his motive at all.

Will the concept of biblical hierarchy lead to abuse? Will a man take advantage of being head of the family by putting down and even abusing his wife and children? Yes, this is possible, but because it is possible does not mean a woman should refuse to allow her husband to be the head. If a husband is evil-willed, the abuse will happen anyway, no matter what the family structure is. Any hierarchical role given

"The evil man brings evil things out of the evil . . . in his heart" (Luke 6:45 NIV).

to him has nothing to do with the abuse. The evil-willed man always treats those around him abusively. If a man is good-willed, his wife's respect and his hierarchical position will not cause him to abuse, because that is not in his nature. He will not use his position as "chair" of the family against those he is to love and protect.[1]

PAUL VERSUS TODAY'S CULTURE

In Ephesians 5, Paul lays out the ideal marriage relationship. The wife is subject to her husband and under his protection. The husband loves his wife and would be willing to die for her. The last thing he would ever want to do is take advantage of her, put her down, or treat her as an inferior of any kind. Most of the wives I have counseled agree with this "ideal picture"—to a point. As one wife said, "I want him to be the head; I just want to know he has my needs in his heart."

When most wives say they want their husbands to be the head, they mean not too much, not too little—but just right. The evangelical wife doesn't balk at the biblical teaching; she balks at the extremes to which a husband might take it. She does not want him to dominate her, and at the same time, she doesn't want her husband to have to depend on her either.

As usual, however, the pressures of the secular culture in which Christian families live often cause confusion and contradiction. Often both spouses have to work just to keep the bills paid. In many cases, the wife makes as much as the husband and sometimes more. This is a tremendous bargaining chip that tempts her to think she isn't being treated as "equal enough." In today's fast-moving, dual-income households, it's easy for the concept of headship and wifely submission to start feeling old-fashioned and out-of-date.

The problem many women have today—including Christian wives —is that they want to be treated like a princess, but deep down they resist treating their husbands like the king. They aren't willing to recognize that in the depth of his very soul a husband wants to be the one who provides and protects—he wants to be an umbrella of protection who would willingly die for his wife if need be.

When we got married, Sarah expressed her fear that we would not have enough financially. She was raised by a single parent and had known what it was like to be short of money a lot of the time. I told Sarah, "I am responsible. I will provide. That is not for you to worry about." She shares that this took a weight off her back, and she let go *Men of goodwill understand the rallying call to "fight for . . . your wives" (Nehemiah 4:14).* of her concern. She chose to trust me. If she had stayed concerned and worried and kept after me about, "Will we always have enough?" it would have stressed me like few things could have.

How to Deflate a Husband with Seven Words

The desire to provide for my wife is something God put deep within my soul—and every man's soul, for that matter. Admittedly, men are very sensitive to put-downs in this area of providing for the family. Sarah and I had just finished a Love and Respect Conference when a couple came up and told us a story. It seems they had just built a brand-new home, and another couple asked if they could take a tour. The new homeowners said, "Of course; come on over." Soon they were taking the couple through the beautiful new home which had every feature imaginable—lovely fixtures, granite countertops. They had spared no expense.

Halfway through the tour, as they were coming down the steps from looking at all the upstairs bedrooms and the many adjoining baths, the wife in the visiting couple turned to her husband and said, "You need to get a second job." The couple giving the tour of their home were stunned by the woman's remark. They both could see the spirit of the husband sink before their very eyes. The visiting couple left a few minutes later.

What is doubly sad about this story is that the wife who made the remark to her husband about needing a second job probably didn't even realize what she had done. She was simply commenting on the grandeur of the home they were touring and never thought that what she was saying would hurt her husband's feelings. But hurt them she did because she just didn't understand her husband or the need to show him respect. It's not a bad rule for a wife

"Those who talk a lot are likely to sin. But those who control their tongues are wise" (Proverbs 10:19 NIRV).

to always ask herself, *Is what I'm about to say or do going to come across to him as respectful or disrespectful?* (Also see appendix A, page 305.)

SHOWING RESPECT BY CANDLELIGHT

There are many ways to show your husband respect. Just look for ways to appreciate his desire to protect and provide, especially when things aren't going too well for him.

Dr. E. V. Hill, a dynamic minister who served as senior pastor of Mt. Zion Missionary Baptist Church in Los Angeles, lost his wife, Jane, to cancer a few years ago. At her funeral, Dr. Hill described some of the ways she had made him a better man. As a struggling young preacher, E. V. had trouble earning a living. E. V. came home one night and found the house dark. When he opened the door, he saw that Jane had prepared a candlelight dinner for two. He thought that was a great idea and went in to the bathroom to wash his hands. He tried unsuccessfully to turn on the light. Then he felt his way into the bedroom and flipped another switch. Darkness prevailed. The young pastor went back to the dining room and asked Jane why the electricity was off. She began to cry.

"You work so hard, and we're trying," said Jane, "but it's pretty rough. I didn't have enough money to pay the light bill. I didn't want you to know about it, so I thought we would just eat by candlelight."

Dr. Hill described his wife's words with intense emotion. "She could have said, 'I've never been in this situation before. I was reared in the home of Dr. Caruthers, and we never had our lights cut off.' She could have broken my spirit; she could have ruined me; she could have demoralized me. But instead she said, 'Somehow or other we'll get these lights back on. But tonight let's eat by candlelight.' "[2]

This poignant story is a case study on how a wife should appreciate her husband's desire to protect and provide. It is likely Mrs. Hill didn't have a complete definition of biblical hierarchy in mind when she lit those candles, but she instinctively knew how to support her husband and appreciate his desire to protect and provide. As Dr. Hill admitted, she could have broken his spirit with words of criticism or sarcasm. Men see themselves as "over" their families. This is why a husband is extra sensitive during conflicts when he hears what sounds like put-downs. The pink wife may not see herself as putting down her husband during a heated discussion over finances. She is only letting him know how she feels so he can respond with love and understanding. However, because her blue husband has a hierarchical mind-set, her comments sound belittling to him. Mark it down. Men are more vulnerable to criticism when it is related to "headship" issues.[3]

THE CARD HE'LL KEEP FOREVER

Suppose you are a wife who trusts her husband. He may not be perfect as the head of the family, but you are quite willing to allow him to live that role as you submit to his leadership. How can you apply what I've been saying? Can you show him respect in his role as the head and the leader? One of the simplest methods that I suggest for wives is to send their husbands what I call a "respect card." According to my research, men seldom keep love cards their wives send them with all the little hearts, *X*s, and *O*s. But I will guarantee you he will keep a card you send him that says, "I was thinking about you the other day, that you would die for me. That is an overwhelming thought to me." Sign it, "With all my respect, the one who still admires you."

"The right word at the right time is like golden apples in silver jewelry" (Proverbs 25:11 NIRV).

Remember, do not sign it, "With all my love." He knows you love him. Sign it, "With all my respect." Your husband will keep that card forever. You will walk in on him years from now and find him re-reading that card. Why? Because you said it his way—in his mother tongue. To speak in a husband's mother tongue of respect is very powerful, indeed. One man wrote:

> I had received a "respect letter" from my wife. I was so amazed by this letter I saved it . . . it clearly had a powerful effect on me. Not only did I save it, I read and re-read it. I guess if there's one fan I want in the world, it would be my wife. And this letter seemed to fit the bill nicely. I was pleased that she did recognize some of my sacrifices, not that I'm looking to be a martyr . . . but the respect/love cycle that you talked about is right on the money.

The respect this husband felt when he wrote me is light-years from what happened to the man in the following story. It seems that Joe was ninety and dying. All his adult children were gathered around the bed, and suddenly he smelled the aroma of his wife's apple strudel baking out in the kitchen. He said weakly, "Oh, Mary, I smell your mother's strudel. What a woman! For seventy years I've been married to her. Mary, would you tell your mother I'd like just a little bit of that strudel?" Mary left but returned almost immediately without the strudel. Old Joe asked, "Mary, my daughter, where is the strudel?" Mary answered, "Mom said you can't have any. It's for after your funeral."

A ridiculous story, true, but it does make a point about respecting a man in his home right up to the last. If you want a Love and Respect marriage, do not argue or fight against hierarchy. Also, guard against slowly "taking over." Joe's wife was so focused on the needs of others that she took over the family, and in the process her husband was once again put down, belittled, overlooked. She is an example of how a woman can be so loving toward her family she doesn't see her disrespect for her husband. This is why I keep calling on wives to awaken to God's revelation concerning a husband's position as provider and protector and his need for respect. Perhaps this wife's letter says it as well as any:

> I can't believe I've never heard [unconditional respect] before. My father was a pastor. We did premarital counseling, I was on staff at a major church, and I teach women's studies at the church. I've sought counsel from older, wiser women, and we've been to marriage counseling . . . all to have my eyes opened up now through your book. I realize now that my husband is not being arrogant when he talks of feeling disrespected. That's his love language. I also realize I must learn to respect him because of the position God gave him in our family, not because I feel he deserves or doesn't deserve it, but because God wants me to be obedient to Scripture. He knows what's best for me—HIS way is always best.

YOUR HUSBAND WILL FEEL YOU APPRECIATE HIS DESIRE TO PROTECT AND PROVIDE WHEN . . .

- you verbalize your admiration of him for protecting you and being willing to die for you.

- you praise his commitment to provide for and protect you and the family (he needs to know you don't take this for granted).
- you empathize when he reveals his male mind-set about position, status, rank, or being one-up or one-down, particularly at work.
- you never mock the idea of "looking up to him" as your protector to prevent him from "looking down on you."
- you never, in word or body language, put down his job or how much he makes.
- you are always ready to figuratively "light the candles," as E. V. Hill's wife did when they couldn't afford to pay the light bill.
- you quietly and respectfully voice concerns about finances and try to offer solutions on where you might be able to cut spending.

CHAPTER EIGHTEEN

AUTHORITY—APPRECIATE HIS DESIRE TO SERVE AND TO LEAD

It was question-and-answer time in one of our Love and Respect Conferences, and the topic was, "The Husband's Authority in the Home." An eager young wife said, "I want him to be the head; I want him to be the leader. I just want to make sure that he makes decisions in keeping with what I want."

The room broke into laughter—men as well as women (perhaps a lot of the men present knew exactly what she was talking about). The gal turned beet red. She had made the comment in all innocence. She wasn't being belligerent or malicious or trying to demand her rights. She was just being honest. I had to chuckle a little myself. Her innocent remark reminded me of a story I chose not to share at that moment because I wanted to spare her more embarrassment. It seems a couple got married and decided that he would make all the major decisions and she would make all the minor decisions. After twenty years, he realized that there had not been one major decision yet.

WHO'S THE BOSS AT YOUR HOUSE?

In today's feminist-dominated culture, the question of, "Who's the boss?" can be a source of humor or of conflict. Many men have been cowed by the feminist argument that men and women are totally equal, and husbands don't have any more authority than their wives do.

But for the Christian couple, the question is, what does the Bible teach about who has authority in the home? We have already seen in chapter 17 that Paul lays out the biblical hierarchy of the home: The man is the head, and the wife is to be subject to him (see Ephesians 5:22–23). And we have seen that the good-willed husband does not try to use his position of head as some kind of club to beat down his wife and his children. He acts responsibly—and lovingly—to be the leader that God has asked him to be.

Nonetheless, the subject of male headship and authority is a sensitive one. The young woman who said her husband is to be the head and make the decisions as long as his decisions met with her approval is not alone. Many wives feel the same way. In fact, many wives would tell you that they are better decision-makers than their husbands, and they often are. They have better judgment than their husbands on many fronts, yet they are stuck with this concept of having to defer to their husbands and let them "be the boss."

A wife's deferential attitude should not undermine her God-given abilities: "She considers a field and buys it; from her earnings she plants a vineyard" (Proverbs 31:16).

A wife who runs her own business and admits she has a strong personality struggles with submitting to a husband who is "not much of an encourager." She realizes the issue is really "between me and God," and she knows that if she could trust the Lord:

. . . it would be so much more peaceful. Wow, why is it so hard to lay it down? I can see it, and I believe it, but I'm not doing it. I hear my daughter, who is fifteen, talk about never getting married because she will never submit to a man, and I feel very ashamed. We are having a lot of good talks about this stuff, but, of course, more is caught than taught, and I want to get it right. So, anyhow, I am going to keep at it, and by God's grace get it right! (And try not to strangle my husband in the process.)

Does Scripture Teach "Mutual Submission"?

Many Christian wives are uneasy with subjects like headship and authority. When Paul pens lines like Ephesians 5:22–23, he sounds hopelessly sexist, especially to women who have domineering husbands. And it doesn't help any when he adds in 1 Timothy 2:12: "I do not allow a woman to . . . exercise authority over a man, but to remain quiet." In recent years there has been a movement in the church among some scholars and teachers to suggest that the Bible talks about "mutual submission"—that is, that men and women are to be equally subject to one another. The text that is used for this position is Ephesians 5:21: "Submit to one another out of reverence for Christ" (NIV).

According to the mutual submission point of view, Ephesians 5:21 means that "every Christian should be subject to every other Christian, and wives and husbands, especially, should be 'subject to one another.'"[1] The idea behind mutual submission in this sense is that the wife does not owe submission of any unique kind to her husband.

When women "follow the lead of their husbands" (Titus 2:5 NIRV), they trust God to guide their decisions.

But if this is true, it is hard to explain Ephesians 5:22, where wives are clearly told to "submit to your husbands *as to the Lord*" (NIV; italics mine). As I mentioned in chapter 17, the Greek word for "submit" is *hupotasso,* which means to rank under or place under. As a wife places herself under her husband's protection and provision, there will come moments when disagreements arise. Honest stalemates can still happen. If a decision must be made, the wife is called upon to defer to her husband, trusting God to guide him to make a decision out of love for her as the responsible head of the marriage.

What, then, did Paul mean when he said Christians should submit to one another? For husbands and wives, I believe the answer is found in Love and Respect. If husband and wife have a conflict over how to spend money, for example, the husband "submits" to his wife by meeting her need to feel that he loves her in spite of the conflict. He submits to her need for love (see Ephesians 5:21, 25). On the other side, the wife "submits" to her husband during a conflict by meeting her husband's need to feel that she respects him in spite of the unresolved issue. She submits to his need for respect (see Ephesians 5:21–22, 33).

Note that Paul and Peter both begin their discussions of marriage by speaking of submission (see Ephesians 5:22 and 1 Peter 3:1), but they end their discussion by speaking of respect (see Ephesians 5:33 and 1 Peter 3:7). The bottom line is that if husband and wife approach each other with the Love and Respect Connection in mind, all will be well in the marriage, even if a decision appears to be stalemated. A wife who attended our Love and Respect Conference wrote:

> I was struck by the "back to basics." There is much talk about communication in marriage, and meeting each other's needs, when the simple solution to our marriage problems is in God's Word. We say that the Word gives us what we need for life and godliness but stray from that into popular psychology. I periodically read the Ephesians passage to remind myself of submission.

Although humbling myself to submit is hard, having a considerate, wise Christian husband makes it easier.

Husbands Are Responsible to "Make the Call"

Obviously, someone can say, "All right, Emerson, suppose love and respect are both present—he wants to love her and she wants to respect him. Which way should the decision go? Who is going to make the call?" I believe that in most cases when love and respect are both present, couples resolve the conflict. Two good-willed people who feel loved and respected almost always discover a creative alternative that resolves the conflict.

When love and respect are present in the marriage, husbands and wives process things far more wisely. They accept the fact that a degree of conflict is inevitable in a marriage relationship. As the conversation progresses, neither one overstates his or her position. No one "loses it" emotionally. Proposals are made to solve the conflict. There are offers and counteroffers. There is give and take. All of this results in a course of action that makes sense to both of them.

There are times when a wife "must obey God rather than men" (Acts 5:29).

We have already seen that Paul clearly teaches that there are times when wives should submit to their husbands as head of the household (see Ephesians 5:22–23). Does this mean that a wife must submit to something illegal, wrong, or evil? Should she go along with being beaten by her husband or watching him beat the children? Should she submit to his plans to do something dishonest or unethical? The clear scriptural answer is, of course not, because that would be preposterous. When a man acts in this way, he is not a good-willed husband, and he forfeits his right to be head and to be followed. A wife's submission to God takes precedence over her submission to her husband. She is not to sin against Christ in order to defer to her husband. (Read the story of Ananias and Sapphira in Acts 5:1–11.) And, sadly, let me add, a wife may need to physically separate from her husband (1 Corinthians 7:11) or divorce him for adultery (Matthew 19:9).

As we have seen so far, there is much a husband and wife can do to "mutually submit" to one another through love and respect. But when somebody has to call the shots, the husband is responsible to do it. How should a wife act if she strongly disagrees with her husband about some issue? First Timothy 2:12 has some advice. Paul writes, "I do not allow a woman to . . . exercise authority over a man, but to remain quiet." Now, if Paul ever penned a sexist line, this would seem to be it. But the Bible is not sexist. The Bible is sharing what the Hebrew mind understood about wisdom and real empowerment. As discussed in part 1, women can win their husbands without a word through their "chaste and respectful behavior" (1 Peter 3:1–2). Is Peter saying that women are insignificant? Of course not. What he is saying is that your quiet and gentle spirit will melt your man's heart.

If you're in a conflict and you remain respectful and quiet as you distance yourself a bit instead of preaching, lecturing, or criticizing, what will he do? Well, it depends. If your quietness is the right kind of quietness—respectful and dignified, not pouty and sour—he will move toward you. He will want to comfort you and take care of you. In essence, he will want to show you love. For the good-willed husband, the wife's quiet and respectful behavior will act as a magnet.

> *"Wives, follow the lead of your husbands. . . . Then let them be won to Christ without words by seeing how their wives behave"*
>
> *(1 Peter 3:1 NIRV).*

Feminists say the Bible puts down women. Actually, the Bible holds up women and gives them advice on how to realize their fondest desires. You don't have to fight. You don't have to push and push and struggle to understand him as you try to move closer only to have him coldly move away. There is another way to get his love, and the Bible tells you what it is. Your quiet and respectful behavior will win him. This is the key to empowerment: *you get what you want by giving him what he wants.*

Authority Must Come with Responsibility

What your husband wants is your acknowledgment that he is the leader, the one in authority. This is not to grind you under or treat you as inferior. It is only to say that because God has made your husband responsible (review Ephesians 5:25–33), he needs the authority to carry out that responsibility. No smoothly running organization can have two heads. To set up a marriage with two equals at the head is to set it up for failure. That is one of the big reasons that people are divorcing right and left today. In essence, these marriages do not have anyone who is in charge. God knew someone had to be in charge, and that is why Scripture clearly teaches that, in order for things to work, the wife is called upon to defer to her husband.

Wives often tell me that if they submit to their husbands, it means burying their brains and becoming a doormat. If you want to work with your husband to reach mutually satisfying decisions most of the time, follow this principle:

Go on record with your husband that you see him
as having 51 percent of the responsibility and,
therefore, 51 percent of the authority.

Tell him that you see him as having more authority because he has more responsibility before God—the responsibility to die for you, if necessary. My prediction is that the nature of your arguments and disagreements will change dramatically. Once you go on record about his authority, he will not feel you are trying to be the boss. As you submit (which simply means recognizing his biblically given authority), you will not be a doormat. In fact, you will get your way far more often than you would if you "stood up for your rights," which usually means being disrespectful.

Many wives are so focused on their own feelings and fears that they ignore their husband's feelings and fears. Ironically, when a wife fears she will bury her brains, she creates fear in him that he'll be called brainless. And fearing she'll become a doormat, she creates fear in him that he'll be walked on. Many husbands get stubborn and resist their wives' requests in order to send a message: "You aren't in charge of me."

Our secular, feminist culture likes to argue that men are dominant in the home—and it's true that some are. More often, however, among good-willed couples, if there are one hundred decisions over a three-month period related to the family, the wife will have a strong opinion on ninety-nine of them, and her opinion will usually be respected and have strong influence. Unfortunately, in many marriages either spouse may have goodwill but not always have good sense. A man can run roughshod; a wife can come across as too forceful and coercive in the home. She isn't this way outside the home, but within the family, with him, she gets aggressive.

Another positive strategy for many a wife would be to defer more to her husband. I often hear many wives complain that their husbands are too disconnected and passive on family matters. But why is he passive? Quite likely in the past, every time he tried to step up to the plate, she had a better idea. After a while, he just let her have her way. If this could be your problem, submission, respect, and quietness will engage your husband and draw him out. This does not put you down or undermine your equality; in fact, it will create real equality.

When you go on record that your husband is 51 percent in charge, this actually gives you more of a platform for sharing the opinions from your deepest heart. Remember, if a husband is acting in a dominating way, he is usually trying to maintain control. His foolish reasoning tells him that if he maintains complete control, he will be respected. Ironically, if his wife gives him the respect he is looking for, he will back off and be less controlling! Trust me. God knows what He is revealing. If you haven't gone on record about his 51 percent, do it now![2] (To check your attitude, see appendix B.)

WHICH MESSAGE DO YOU WANT TO SEND?

Granted, deferring to your husband isn't always easy, especially if you feel he doesn't deserve your respect. One woman wrote to tell me that she acted very disrespectfully in order to send a message to her husband that she felt unloved. She thought this would motivate him to love her and appreciate her, but all the while she was unsupportive of his endeavors, belittling his abilities, undermining his decisions, resistant to his counsel, unfriendly, and disinterested in physical intimacy. She said, "I thought if I did all of this, he'd get the message that I was hurting, frustrated, and angry and that he'd move toward me with understanding and love." But she wept as she realized she had so wounded him that he wouldn't even have sex with her. It took years for him to reopen emotionally to her.

By comparison, I heard from a woman who granted her husband authority in the nitty-gritty area of bedtime. She wrote:

> My husband leaves for work real early. I have never been a real
> stickler on early bedtimes. He now enforces bedtime curfew with
> the kids, and I back him fully, so he can get his undisturbed and
> deserved full night of sleep. . . . I'm now aware that my allowing
> the kids to stay up late not only undermined and disrespected [my
> husband] but his work effort was also disrespected because it
> appeared as if I didn't care that he was tired after working all day.

I now leave decisions to him to administer, and it makes me smile sometimes because he'll ask me in private for my opinion. Then we discuss it and I tell him I respect whatever decision he makes. He even told me last week that I "built him up." . . . Since my respectful attitude, my husband has told me that he loves me more [often] in the last few months than over the last ten years!

Appreciating—and respecting—your husband's desire to serve you and lead the family takes faith, courage, and strength on your part. But I predict it will work. As one wife told me, "The picture-perfect marriage in my mind is not necessarily the one that God has intended for me. I finally realized that when I submit to His control and stop trying to orchestrate my ideas . . . everything falls into place."

Grant your husband authority, as Scripture describes it, and things are much more likely to fall into place. If you try to undermine his authority or subtly rebel against it, the Crazy Cycle will spring to life. A woman who teaches other women in her church on the topic of marriage puts it better than I ever could:

I believe that ultimately a refusal to submit to or respect your husband is a refusal to trust in God. If we as women believe that God is working in our lives and in our husbands' lives, and we can place ourselves under His authority, then we can submit to and respect our husbands.

He Will Feel You Appreciate His Authority and Leadership When . . .

- you tell him you are thankful for his strength and enjoy being able to lean on him at times.
- you support his self-image as a leader.

- you never say, "You're responsible but we're still equal, so don't make a decision I don't agree with."
- you praise his good decisions.
- you are gracious if he makes a bad decision.
- you disagree with him only in private and honor his authority in front of the kids.
- you give your reasons for disagreeing quietly and reasonably, but you never attack his right to lead.
- you do not play "head games" with him to make him back down and be a "loving peacemaker."

CHAPTER NINETEEN

INSIGHT—APPRECIATE HIS DESIRE TO ANALYZE AND COUNSEL

She had little or no respect for her husband. Behind his back she constantly put him down, mocking him and making fun of his ideas and opinions. One day while shopping, she thought it would be interesting to stop at his office just to see where—and how—he worked. She called him on her cell phone and he said, "Well, sure. I'm a little busy, but come on up."

When she got there, he was indeed busy, and she had to wait a few minutes as he dealt with various people. From where she sat, she couldn't help but see that her husband's coworkers gave him high respect. So did his boss—and his attractive young secretary. Then an older man came to her husband's desk, obviously someone who was more experienced with the company but who still worked under him. She didn't exactly know why, but her stomach churned a little when she heard the older man say to her husband, "Yes, sir." Then his secretary came by to give him some papers, and she felt shame—and a little fear—as she saw how this classy young woman looked up to her husband and admired him.

Finally, she had a chance to visit her husband, but she quickly cut it short, said good-bye, and told him she would see him that evening. She made it to the car, got in, and burst into tears. She thought of all the times she had put him down and made fun of him behind his back. And then it hit her: she didn't disrespect him because of his actions toward her or because he was a lousy husband. She realized the real problem was that he wasn't what she wanted him to be.[1]

This woman had been missing at least two things about her husband: (1) he had a lot of ability and insight she was ignoring, to her loss, and (2) he wanted the same kind of respect at home that he received at work.

As Job reveals, wives are not always wise: "You speak as one of the foolish women speaks" (Job 2:10).

This kind of wife is not unique. I have talked to many just like her. She thinks her husband has little to teach her, little wisdom to share about much of anything. After all, she believes she is the one who has to run the house, raise the children, and make the decisions. When this kind of wife attends one of our Love and Respect Conferences or reads some of our materials, it is not unusual for the scales of disrespect to fall from her eyes. Here is one testimony from a wife who finally "got it":

I have longed for a relational intimacy in my marriage for twenty-three years. Little did I know that my lack of respect was sabotaging that desire. I had serious "arrogance" problems, thinking my ways were right and not acknowledging his ideas as worthy of consideration. . . . I thought I was "helping" my "inept" husband. . . . It was quite amazing once the Lord nailed me. . . . Without me spouting my opinion and giving him room to dare to share his, amazing things began to occur. He began to reveal his heart. We actually have conversations rather than monologues. My love and respect for him skyrocketed. In return, he has begun to blossom into the man I always hoped he would be.

I No Longer Believe Totally in Womanly Intuition

In the words of the woman quoted above, I hear something that counters beliefs I used to hold. One belief was that the vast majority of men were opinionated, one-sided, and inattentive. All I heard from the many wives whom I counseled over the years was: "He is unloving, uncaring, and not a good husband." But in the words of the woman you've just read, you find a different story. She admits that she didn't think her husband's ideas were "worthy of consideration." She realizes she was arrogant, not giving him a chance to even give an opinion. And once the Lord "nailed her" and she let her husband talk, their marriage blossomed.

"Don't be wise in your own eyes" *(Proverbs 3:7 NIRV).*

The other belief that I no longer hold is in the exclusive and unique power of womanly intuition. For twenty years I preached, "Men, listen to the intuition of your wives. God will speak to them in a way that He doesn't speak to you because you have blind spots. God will teach you through your wives." Everything I preached was to get men to honor and love their wives. But I began to realize I was tipping the scales too far. It's true that women have intuition and that men should listen to them. It is also true that women have blind spots and need the insight of their husbands. As another wife admitted, "He has lived our whole marriage in fear that he wouldn't say or do something the 'right' way. Since my way was the only right way and whatever he did or thought wasn't good enough, he just shut down."

IT WAS EVE, NOT ADAM, WHO WAS DECEIVED

The wife who thinks she has to provide the answers and do all the thinking should take a careful look at Scripture. We all know the story of the Garden of Eden. God told Adam he could eat of any tree in the Garden but one. Eat of that tree and "you will surely die" (Genesis 2:17). Later, when Eve was created, Adam told her of God's command. But when the serpent found Eve alone and tempted her with, in essence, the subtle question, "Did God really say that?" she couldn't resist. The fruit on that tree looked delightful, and it was guaranteed to make her wise. Totally deceived, Eve ate some of the fruit. Then Adam came up (or perhaps she went and found him). Eve gave Adam some of the fruit, and he ate as well (see Genesis 3:1–6). Was Adam deceived also? Scripture does not say he was deceived, but that he is the one who *disobeyed*—he is the one through whom the whole world fell into sin (see Romans 5:12–19).

Is one automatically chauvinistic for asking a good-willed wife to consider that "it was not Adam who was deceived, but the woman"? (1 Timothy 2:14).

Adam had the insight to realize that he shouldn't eat the fruit, but he went ahead and did so anyway. Was this the first case of a husband being led by his wife with a ring in his nose? Or did Adam simply not want to let Eve get ahead of him by having knowledge that he would not have? No one can say for sure. Paul sums it up in 1 Timothy 2:14 when he discusses the role of women in the church: "It was not Adam who was deceived, but the woman being deceived, fell into transgression."

Apparently, Eve concluded that she knew far more about what was best for her and her husband, and she influenced him to follow her lead. Adam "listened to the voice of [his] wife" and was cursed (see Genesis 3:14–19).

A Marriage Needs Her Intuition and His Insight

When Paul talks about Eve being the one who was "deceived" by the serpent's craftiness (see 1 Timothy 2:14; 2 Corinthians 11:3), he is not spewing chauvinist put-downs of women, as feminists might claim. There is a deep truth here, and we need to reflect on it. Yes, men should listen to their wives, who are naturally intuitive. But wives should not fail to appreciate the insight God has given their husbands and reject their counsel. Instead of listening to Adam's voice, Eve orchestrated things and got Adam to listen to her, even though he knew better.

How does this apply to marriages today? Are wives taking over and becoming the primary voice in the marriage? Not necessarily, but there is always that danger. What I am calling for is a return to the biblical balance. *Husbands and wives need each other.* For wives who are willing to evaluate just where they are on the scale of showing unconditional respect for their husbands, I have two questions: (1) Could you be thinking too highly of your natural discernment and intuition? (2) Is it possible that you might be deceived on certain fronts, and that you could use your husband's insight because you don't see what he sees?

All of us can be deceived, but women need to think about some areas where the serpent is subtly deceiving them even today. One such area involves the criticisms that many wives voice about how their husbands fail to give spiritual leadership to the family. As I have counseled couples over the years, I have listened to many wives share their strong convictions about what their husbands ought to be doing as spiritual leaders. I also receive many letters from women on "his lack of spiritual leadership." Here are some representative examples:

> I want to respect my husband who, while loving me and our children, leaves all the work, planning, teaching, etc., to me without discussing it. He earns money and comes home to play with us. He

leads in family devotions but does not discuss spiritual matters with our children individually, or [with] me. I feel I have five children; one just happens to be an adult. How do I respect him when he makes me the leader by default?

———————

I recognize that after six and a half years of marriage, the biggest ache I have with my husband is his lack of spiritual leadership in our relationship and family. I want so desperately to see my husband making time for the Lord and really pursuing Him. I want to see him praying . . . and seeking God's direction for his life. I want to know that he is fellowshiping with the Lord. I could write more, but I think you get the idea.

If you have such convictions, I cannot say if you are right or wrong, but what I can say is that if you are judging your husband with contempt, you are hurting God's heart. Your convictions can please God, but your contempt can also grieve Him. The Lord loves you and knows the longing of your heart. Abba Father weeps with you about your convictions. But your heavenly Father is also revealing to you that a contemptuous, critical spirit is not the way to win over your "disobedient" husband to your convictions. He gently urges you to maintain "respectful behavior" (1 Peter 3:1–2) even while your heart hurts over unfulfilled convictions. For the wife who isn't happy with her husband's leadership, here are some questions to ask yourself:

- Did my husband ever seek to lead in our marriage, but I differed because I felt it was stupid?
- Do I send him a message that I do not intend to follow him if he makes a decision contrary to what I believe is correct?
- Do I send a message that says, "I want you to lead but only when it bolsters and carries out my desires"?

- Do I want my husband to be responsible, but if he is irresponsible in my opinion, am I exercising veto power?
- Do my words and actions communicate, "You are responsible but I have the authority"?

The above questions can be applied to all areas of leadership in the home. Perhaps they all boil down to this: ask yourself if you may possibly have an attitude of self-righteousness—at least to some degree. I'm not saying you are malicious. You love your husband very much, but you see his faults, foibles, and mistakes. You may well believe, as many women do, that you are a better person than he is and that he needs to change.

What I see happening in some marriages is that the wife believes—or appears to believe—that she does not sin. In many other marriages the only sin that a wife will readily admit to is her negative reaction to her husband's failure to be loving or for losing patience with the children. Beyond these areas, women do not see themselves as sinning, even though they readily admit bad habits and wrong attitudes. They write these off to chemical imbalance, hormonal problems, or dysfunction due to family of origin.

For example, on occasion a husband may venture into that dangerous territory known as "Honey, you're putting on a few pounds." In truth, it is far more than a few pounds—his wife has let herself go, and he feels it is time to be honest. What he usually gets in return is, "You should love me no matter how I look." Or he may be told he knows nothing about her eating disorder and that he should be checking on his own potbelly. If the husband is on the trim side (as many men with very overweight wives often are), she will bring up some other log that he needs to get out of his own eye—that time she caught him viewing Internet pornography or overindulging in alcohol.

The point is, it's easy for a wife to discount or disparage a husband's suggestion that she has some problem that needs correcting. Even if he is gentle and diplomatic in suggesting that she needs to make a correction to avoid hurting herself or others, he is quickly silenced. She is offended, wounded, and angered by his assessment. He is accused of being without understanding and compassion. He has no right to speak. And he will often wind up being shown contempt.

When I speak on this topic in a Love and Respect Conference, I often get feedback, not all of it positive. The medical and psychological model is so engrained in the thinking of some Christians that I have received this question more than once in the mail: "Are you saying that women have no family of origin pressures, hormonal struggles, or chemical imbalances?" My response is simple: I cannot assess every situation. But I can quote John, the Apostle of love: "If we say that we have no sin, we are deceiving ourselves and the truth is not in us" (1 John 1:8).

A stench in God's nostrils are the words, "I am holier than you!" (Isaiah 65:5).

In many marriages it is all too easy for a wife to write off a husband's insight and suggestions because she thinks she doesn't need them or he has no right to give them. But I believe husband and wife *together* need to examine any situation where something is amiss and try to come to a solution or, if needed, seek godly counsel. Through the years, people have readily confessed to me, for instance, that they took medication to escape an unresolved interpersonal issue. They admitted that they knew there was nothing wrong with their biology. To them it was a classic case of avoidance, and medication made it easy for them. A pastor's wife recently approached me in tears to admit that this was precisely her problem.

ARE YOU TRYING TO BE YOUR HUSBAND'S HOLY SPIRIT?

Another thing I share in conferences is that most husbands see themselves as unrighteous and their wives as righteous. This misperception is inaccurate enough, but then there comes that point in the marriage when the wife also sees her husband as unrighteous. Because she is the one who constantly seems to have to be on top of things, such as correcting the children (and him), she slips into an attitude of self-righteousness without realizing it. It is often subconscious, but a subtle judgmental spirit comes over a woman. Many women have admitted to me, "I've got to stop being my husband's Holy Spirit." I agree with them because there is no vacancy in the Trinity. However, I never hear men saying, "I've got to stop being my wife's Holy Spirit."

For a biblical model, let us go to the scene where Jesus visits the home of Martha and Mary. Martha has become overworked and anxious because of all the preparations she's making for dinner. She says to Jesus, "Lord, do You not care that my sister has left me to do all the serving alone? Then tell her to help me" (Luke 10:40). Martha is not asking a question here; she is stating what she believes to be a fact. She is looking into the eyes of Love itself and calling Him unaware and uncaring because He doesn't seem to be interested in what she thinks is important.

Instead of sharply correcting Martha, Jesus lovingly rebukes her for being worried and upset while she missed what was truly important: fellowship with Him. Much more could be said about this account—I have preached many sermons on it—but the point here is that Martha was wrong. She was seeing the world through her particular brand of pink sunglasses, and she was making wrong assessments. The question is, could you be wrong at times for some of the same reasons? And could your husband be trying to help you instead of simply being critical and uncaring?

The bottom line to appreciating a man's desire to analyze and counsel is to realize he does have insight and to beware of any self-righteousness that might undermine his insight. Self-righteousness can deceive you more than any other sin. If you see yourself as far better than your husband, especially in the spiritual realm, he will back away from you spiritually and probably in many other ways. As the years pass, your husband will stop giving advice at almost every level. What can he say to a person who is always right and righteous? What can he say to a wife who views him with contempt? He sees himself with all the problems while she has none. So he grows silent, fearing more censure. Aware of his silence, a wife often says, "Why are you always quiet?" And he winds up thinking, *If I say something, I'm in trouble. If I don't say something, I'm in trouble. But if I don't say something, I'm in less trouble.* That's a sad commentary, but that's what a lot of men are thinking.

> During disagreements with your husband, your beauty should consist of ". . . the unfading beauty of a gentle and quiet spirit, which is of great worth in God's sight" (1 Peter 3:4 NIV).

The old story has it that Gretel says in exasperation to her husband, Hans, "You know ve're fighting and bickering too much, Hans. And I've been tinking, I tink ve need to pray to the dear Lord to take vun of us to heaven, the vun causing the problem. So you pray that He takes vun of us, and I'll pray that He takes vun of us, and then I can move in with my sister."

That's an amusing story—particularly if you're a woman. Guard against the attitude that he is the center of all the problems. Admit that you also have sins, issues, and weaknesses (in areas that he has strengths) and that you don't have perfect judgment in every case. You'll be amazed at how this energizes his soul. As you move toward him, giving him what God has designed him to need—respect—he will feel fondness in his heart for you. As one wife reflected:

> I have stopped offering my opinion unless he asks for it, and his confidence has blossomed. What a load off for me! I don't have to "think" for both of us! Things that I used to consider irritat-

ing (because he wasn't thinking like me) are now a joy and delight because God has opened my eyes to His creative genius in making my husband the way he is. Awesome.

YOUR HUSBAND WILL FEEL YOU APPRECIATE HIS INSIGHT AND COUNSEL WHEN . . .

- you tell him upfront you just need his ear; don't complain to him later that he always tries to "fix" you.
- you thank him for his advice without acting insulted or like he doesn't care about your feelings.
- you recognize his problem-solving approach as his male brand of empathy.
- you realize your vulnerabilities, especially among males, and value his protection.
- you counsel him respectfully when you differ with his ideas (you can be right but wrong at the top of your voice).
- you sometimes let him "fix things" and applaud his solutions.
- you let him know that you believe God has made us male and female for a purpose and that we need each other.
- you admit that you can sin and thank him for his perception and godly counsel.

CHAPTER TWENTY

RELATIONSHIP—APPRECIATE HIS DESIRE FOR SHOULDER-TO-SHOULDER FRIENDSHIP

They had been married for just seven years when they came to me for help because they kept getting into what they called "huge fights."

"How do the fights start?" I asked.

She explained that she would be in the kitchen cleaning or perhaps ironing, and he would call her from the room where he was reading the paper or watching TV: "Honey, why don't you come in here and be with me?"

Thinking this was an opportunity to relate, she would go to her husband and start talking to him.

"No, no," he would tell her. "Don't talk. I just want you in here with me."

Confused, she would say, "But you called me in here. You must want to talk to me."

"No, I just want you in here. I don't want you to talk."

"But you must have something you want to talk about," she would insist. "You called me in here."

At this point, things went downhill fast, and in no time they were in a huge verbal battle. This scenario was happening over and over, and they wanted to know how I could fix it.

Commenting that I don't "fix" marriages but I try to explain what's going on in them, I told the wife (as the husband listened attentively) that he was energized merely by her presence. Then I commented, "If he is reading the paper, watching TV, or even working outside on some chores in the yard, if you will just sit there next to him or pull up a chair and watch while he works, you will see the most amazing energy flow into him."

A woman must consider how to be a companion to a male; after all, God said, "I will make a helper who is just right for him" (Genesis 2:18 NIRV).

I noted the puzzled look on the wife's face. I continued, "This is how men communicate, by sharing experiences. Women share experiences by talking about them to each other, examining and infusing the experiences with their impressions and emotions. Men are different. They share their experiences by sharing an activity. This is what your husband wants to do with you."

As our session ended that day, I told the couple that I was giving a Love and Respect Conference in one of the churches in town and suggested they attend to get the full picture of how the Love and Respect Connection really works. They did so, and when they came to see me again later, the wife had totally "gotten it" about why her husband wanted her to be with him. "You were right," she said. "It almost drove me crazy at first not to talk, but for some strange reason it works. He really wants me to just sit there with him."

How Can "Doing Nothing" Build a Relationship?

When your husband says, "Hey, honey, come in here and watch Discovery Channel with me," what happens? You come in and sit down and he, indeed, does watch Discovery Channel, possibly commenting now and then about "the size of those elk" or "look at the teeth on that crocodile." But most of the time he's fully absorbed in what he's doing: watching TV. If you are a typical wife, you will sit there thinking, *I've got laundry to fold, I have to make dinner, the kids' lunches for tomorrow still aren't packed . . .* Eventually, you will get up and walk away because you need to do all those things, and, besides, you and your husband aren't really "doing anything" anyway. He's just watching TV with you sitting there beside him. You're not communicating, so how could this be building the relationship?

As a wife "you should look not only to your own interests" but also to your husband's shoulder-to-shoulder interests (Philippians 2:4 NIV).

But wives continue to report that that is exactly what happens. One wife decided to go deer hunting with her husband, who uses the bow and arrow. She helped him set up the blind, and they both sat there for hours waiting for a deer to happen by. They saw nothing, they shot at nothing, and they said nothing. Finally, they took down the blind and headed back to the car. To this point she had said not one word the entire time. As they were walking down the trail, her husband turned to her and said, "This was awesome!"

Another wife, despite her reservations about doing something so "kooky," decided to join her husband in his workshop and watch him as he completed one of his projects. She sat down, said nothing, and simply watched. He looked over at her and sort of grinned, and she just grinned back. A few minutes later, he looked at her again and smiled, and she smiled back. This went on for some forty-five minutes. Finally, he said, "I don't know what you're doing, but keep it up!"

Why do men like this shoulder-to-shoulder silence from their wives? I really don't know, but I have to admit it is different. Remember, you're pink; he's blue. If you interpret the world through pink and pink alone, you miss something, just as he misses something if he sees and hears strictly through blue. You need to be lovers, of course, but you also need to be shoulder-to-shoulder friends. (To compare the needs of "pink" and "blue," see appendix C.)

Does Scripture speak of this need for both love and friendship? In Song of Solomon, where the main theme is passionate, ache-all-over-love, the Lord takes time in chapter 5 to say to the couple: "Eat, friends; drink and imbibe deeply, O lovers" (v. 1). Then later, in the same chapter, as the wife recounts how fine and dazzling her husband is ("outstanding among ten thousand," v. 10), she completes her litany of praise by saying, "This is my beloved and this is my *friend*" (v. 16; italics mine).

The New Testament also makes provision for friendship in a marriage relationship. The Greek word *phileo* refers to brotherly or friendship love. In Titus 2:3–4, Paul says older women (who have been "around the block" and are aware of what a husband is like) should teach the younger women to *phileo* their husbands—that is, to be friendly to them.

FOR A WHILE THERE, SARAH WASN'T FRIENDLY

In an earlier chapter I mentioned that I've often asked husbands if their wives loved them, and they quickly reply, "Yes, of course." But when I ask them if their wives *like* them, often the answer is, "No" or, "I'm not sure." I empathize because there was a time in my own marriage when I felt much the same way.

As Sarah will readily admit, she recalls this time of tension between us and realizes that she had grown very negative, trying to change everyone to conform to her standards, particularly of neatness. She complained about every crumb on the counter, every shoe on the floor, every wet towel left on a bed, every candy wrapper that missed the wastebasket. She was trying to help all of us, especially me and my two sons, to realize we would be happier if we were neater and more organized. Frankly, it wasn't working too well.

It so happened that Sarah decided to take a trip to another city to see her mother, and she took along our daughter, Joy. I stayed home with our two sons, Jonathan and David. A week went by, and Sarah and Joy returned from their trip. When I picked them up at the airport, her first question was, "Well, how was your time?"

I replied, "Oh, it was good."

"Did you miss me?" she wanted to know.

I couldn't lie, so I said, "You know, we had a wonderful time. We just ate where we wanted to eat. We made forts when we wanted to make forts. We made the beds when we wanted to make the beds."

> *A husband can be his wife's friend "of her youth" but later be rejected as his wife "[ignores] the covenant she made before God" (Proverbs 2:17 NIV).*

Sarah got my message. She realized that we had made the beds for the first time that week just before coming to the airport. And she also realized that we hadn't really missed her that much. Oh, we still loved her as wife and mother, but we hadn't missed all the badgering and criticizing.

Right there Sarah made a choice that she would like me and our sons despite our sloppiness. She realized we had gotten married because we liked each other. We were *friends*, and she knew she needed to be friendly as well as loving.

Wives, Be Patient with "Just Sit by Me"

The wife who wants to show her husband that she likes him—that she is his friend—will be patient with his strange request to "just come out here and be with me. Watch what I am doing, or just watch TV with me, but let's not talk." When the husband calls the wife in to "just sit by him," he is working on their relationship in a significant way—not significant to her, perhaps, but extremely significant, nonetheless. This is the way a husband communicates. Males prefer shoulder-to-shoulder communication instead of face-to-face communication, and this can occur in the simplest of ways. For example, during our first year of marriage, Sarah and I were in our apartment. I was reading, and she was on the couch. She said, "Shouldn't we be talking?"

I replied, "I'm content just being with you."

Research studies confirm the male preference for shoulder-to-shoulder communication with little or no talking. In one study, researchers performed a series of tests on males and females from four age groups: second graders, sixth graders, tenth graders, and twenty-five-year-olds. Instructions for each pair of females and each pair of males were exactly the same: enter a room, sit down on two chairs, and talk, if you wish.

As the test proceeded, every pair of females, no matter what their ages, reacted the same way. They turned their chairs toward each other, or at least they turned toward each other, so they could be face to face, lean forward, and talk. The males reacted differently. They did not turn toward each other in any way. They sat side by side, shoulder to shoulder, looking straight ahead except for an occasional glance at each other.

The shoulder-to-shoulder wife sees new meaning in "won without a word" (1 Peter 3:1).

Because the females turned toward each other or literally turned their chairs to face one another for direct, face-to-face contact, the researchers assumed they would have the most intimate conversations. Actually, the most open and transparent of all the pairs, male or female, were the tenth-grade boys.[1] This does not surprise me. My observation is that men grow close by doing activities together, shoulder to shoulder. Over time, these common experiences and mutual interests result in a sense of bonding. There is little negativity and few complaints. They don't focus on their relationship, and they rarely talk about how they feel toward each other. As they become friends, one thing is certain—each is there for the other.

Many men can recall being a "blood brother" with his boyhood friend. Two drops of blood blended together symbolized the "forever" bond. The commitment was to be shoulder to shoulder, fighting to the death, if need be. Little girls do not enter this kind of dream world, but little boys do. They build their forts and are ready to do battle and die together. Even now, as I write this, I feel the depth of emotion that every little boy has felt about his "blood brothers."

So what's my point? One day, the little boy grows up, becomes a man, and meets a special young woman. He proposes, and they marry. In his maleness, he assumes the two of them will be together, shoulder to shoulder, just as he has been with his male friends throughout his life. His request is simple: "Hey, let's go do something together." Early on, his wife may cooperate. She is a real friend. However, three children and a ton of laundry later, there are so many more important things to do than fly fish or hang out. Besides, when they do have time to be together, she needs to talk. To her, talking is the way to connect. Being together and never talking, that is absurd!

In most marriages, then, there is a real difference in basic needs. As we saw in chapter 9, she wants to talk, to be close. But in this chapter we see that the natural bent of the male is to be shoulder to shoulder with a lot less talking. Obviously, there must be some give and take at this point as there should be in so many other areas of marriage. Just as sometimes he must make the effort to be with you face to face, you must also make the effort to be with him shoulder to shoulder. When he calls you to be with him and you just do it, with little or no talking, you will see the energy flow into him.

Spend Time Together, Stay Together

Is putting up with this strange male quirk worth it? I can remember that as a boy growing up in Peoria, Illinois, I would often ride my bike up and down the street. I can recall one couple I would see often as I rode by. He'd be working under his car in the driveway and she'd be out there sitting on a stool, smoking a cigarette, doing her nails, or just chewing gum. There was no other woman around. He was under the car, and she was saying nothing while he worked.

For some reason, I always remembered that couple. In fact, years later as I thought about them, I realized something. Many couples on our block divorced, but this couple never did. Somehow, she understood that just sitting there with him and saying nothing while he worked was a positive thing. She bonded with him even though they weren't talking.

If just sitting with your husband, shoulder to shoulder, without talking still seems a bit odd, read the following excerpts from typical letters we receive all the time:

> He likes to have me around on Saturday, just sort of hanging around while he works around the house, either helping or chatting, the side-by-side thing. I have begun to do this and he LOVES it! He actually shares more on what he is thinking these days. . . . This does not come naturally, yet . . . I end up benefiting also by having a spouse who feels loved by being respected [and] he is much more loving.

> When you talked about "shoulder-to-shoulder," I knew exactly what you were talking about. My husband just finally came out

and told me that sometimes all he wanted me to do was just sit with him. He's accepted the fact that there are times when I will be correcting papers as I sit (a teacher's work is never done!), and I have learned that if I'm getting up to check the laundry or do something else, all I have to do is tell him. As long as he knows what I am doing and that I will be back, it's OKAY.

I have counseled many couples who have not had a good heart-to-heart exchange for decades. What can a wife do? Try seeing his need for shoulder-to-shoulder friendship. If he has closed you off and gone quiet, the way to draw him out is by simply being with him during some activity. Don't talk; just be with him. Do this over a twelve-week period and watch what happens. I can almost guarantee he'll start talking. Will he necessarily look at you face to face? Probably not. Will he talk for a long time at first? Probably not. Will *you* be energized by this? Probably not. Will *he* be energized by this? Yes!

In marriage timing is everything: "a time to be silent and a time to speak" (Ecclesiastes 3:7).

Trust me. Your husband has a need you do not have, and that need is met in a way that feels unnatural to you. But as you are just being with him, shoulder to shoulder, his fondness for you will grow inexplicably. It really doesn't make a lot of sense, but the simple truth is he just needs you to be there.

YOUR HUSBAND WILL FEEL YOU VALUE HIS SHOULDER-TO-SHOULDER FRIENDSHIP WHEN . . .

- you tell him you like him and you show it (he knows you love him, but he often wonders if you really like him).

- you respond to his invitation to engage in recreational activities together or you come along to watch him (you don't have to go every time, but just now and then will energize him more than you realize).
- you enable him to open up and talk to you as you do things shoulder to shoulder.
- you encourage him to spend time alone, which energizes him to reconnect with you later.
- you don't denounce his shoulder-to-shoulder activities with his male friends to get him to spend more face-to-face time with you. Respect his friendships, and he will be more likely to want you to join him shoulder to shoulder at other times.

CHAPTER TWENTY-ONE

SEXUALITY—APPRECIATE HIS DESIRE FOR SEXUAL INTIMACY

The doctor and his wife did not have a happy marriage. They were on a Crazy Cycle, and it centered on her ultimatum, which she had laid down several years before. She would not respond to him sexually until he met her emotional needs. She wanted emotional release, she wanted him to talk to her face to face, and until he met her emotional needs, she wouldn't respond to him sexually. After all, that's what love was all about, wasn't it?

Then, through a series of events, the Lord spoke to her and said, "Who is supposed to be the mature one here? He is a new believer and you've been in Christ for many years." She got the message. She decided to minister to her husband sexually, not because she particularly wanted to, but because she wanted to do it as unto Jesus Christ. She didn't have that need for sex. It wasn't within her, but she realized that this was her husband's need, and the Lord had spoken to her about meeting his need first.

So she said, "All right, Lord, I will serve him and I will meet that need gladly." And she proceeded to do so. So what happened? Did her need for emotional release and talking face to face ever get met? She reported back to me, "When we lay there in bed afterward, I couldn't get him to shut up!"

They Kicked the Devil out of Bed

This couple who had been so unhappy for so many years because they had been in a lose-lose standoff suddenly found a win-win situation. As she met his physical need, he reached out to meet her emotional need. Someone has said, just as the devil will do everything he can to bring two people together sexually *before* marriage, he does everything he can to keep them away from each other *after* marriage. This couple defeated the devil soundly. You might say they kicked him out of bed!

If there ever were an issue that isn't really the issue, it is sex. Over the years I've had dozens of couples come to me complaining they weren't getting along. Often the answer to the problem lay in the fact that she wanted intimacy and affection without all the sexual touching, while he wanted sex and was not being too patient with moments of affection only. Sex for him and affection for you is a two-way street. Just as he should minister to your spirit to have access to your body, so, too, you should minister to his body if you want to gain access to his spirit.

"The husband must fulfill his duty to his wife, and likewise also the wife to her husband" (1 Corinthians 7:3).

During counseling a wife told me that she thought sex was man's number one need. I responded that sex is symbolic of his deeper need —respect. By way of analogy, a wife needs emotional release through talking. When that need is met, she feels loved. When a man refuses to talk, that symbolizes to her that he does not love her or care about her need. A husband has a need for physical release through sexual intimacy. When a wife refuses, that symbolizes to him that she does not care about him and does not respect him and his need. A wife also needs to think about how unfair it is to say to her husband, "Have eyes only for me," and continually turn him down when he approaches her sexually. As a wife, you spell respect to your husband when you appreciate his sexual desire for you.

Two Keys to Understanding Your Husband

There are two aspects to understanding your husband sexually. First, realize that his sexuality is much different from yours. Proverbs 5:19 says, "As a loving hind and a graceful doe, let her breasts satisfy you at all times. Be exhilarated always with her love."

It is no coincidence that there is no Bible verse commanding a woman to be satisfied with her husband's breasts at all times. That's a ridiculous statement, but why is it ridiculous? Proverbs 5:19 is speaking to the fact that a man is visually oriented when it comes to sexual desire. He sees a beautiful woman, her face and her figure, and he is stimulated. Women are not visually oriented when it comes to sex, at least not to the degree that men are.

"Your two breasts are like two fawns, . . . which browse among the lilies" (Song of Solomon 4:5 NIV).

Think about when you get out of the shower versus when he gets out of the shower. When you step out of the shower, he is all eyes, oblivious to everything else. But what happens when he steps out of the shower? You probably say something like, "Please stand on the bath mat!" or "Be careful! I just waxed the floor!" You are not visually oriented.

The second aspect of being able to appreciate your husband's sexual desire for you is that he needs sexual release just as you need emotional release (intimacy). In 1 Corinthians 7:5, Paul writes: "Stop depriving one another, except by agreement for a time, so that you may devote yourselves to prayer, and come together again so that Satan will not tempt you because of your lack of self-control." When it comes to our sexuality, both husband and wife need to meet each other's needs. Paul says each is to fulfill his or her duty to the other. Husbands, particularly, can come under satanic attack when deprived of sexual release. Wives might be able to better understand this if they think about how they would feel if their husbands didn't want to talk or listen to them. Being deprived of emotional release would make most women miserable.

A young woman told the following story to Sarah after one of our conference sessions. Every Sunday she and her husband would visit her parents, but one Sunday morning she called her mother and said, "We're not coming." The mother asked, "Why not?"

"Well, because my honey is in a twit," the daughter said.

"Why?" inquired the mother.

"I suppose because we have not been sexually intimate for seven days."

Mom did not hesitate; gently but firmly she let her daughter have it. "You ought to be ashamed of yourself. Why would you deprive him of something that takes such a short amount of time and makes him soooooo happy!?"

Embarrassed, the daughter shouted into the phone, "Mother! I can't believe you said that." But as the young woman finished relating the story to Sarah, she added, "My mom has been married for forty-seven years, and I don't know anyone who has a happier marriage."

This mother gave her daughter good advice, indeed. Sadly, many couples revolve on the Crazy Cycle because without sex he feels disrespected and reacts in an unloving "twit," and she dismisses him as childish. Round and round they go! But it doesn't have to be. Sarah says it best in our marriage conferences: "Wives, what if your husband didn't talk to you for three days . . . three weeks . . . or three months? You would think that abominable. I think you get my point. Some wives want their emotional needs met after marriage but somehow lose sight of their husband's sexual needs. Remember, your son will have the same need. How do you want your daughter-in-law to treat him? Your son didn't ask to be made this way any more than your daughter or daughter-in-law asked to be made with the need to talk intimately on a regular basis!"

THE GOLDEN RULE WORKS WITH SEX TOO

The point here is that your husband's anatomy and design is much different from yours. He needs sexual release as you need emotional release. This is why he loves the act of sex in and of itself. It is a pleasurable act that brings him satisfaction. As a woman, you may feel that the two of you have to feel and be close in order to share sexually. For him, however, it is the reverse: the sexual act is what brings the two of you close!

> *"Do to others as you want them to do to you"*
> *(Luke 6:31 NIRV).*

Remember that sex falls under the same category as everything else described in the Energizing Cycle, be it under C-O-U-P-L-E (what he is supposed to do for you) or C-H-A-I-R-S (what you are supposed to do for him). The rule that never changes is: *you can't get what you need by depriving your partner of what your partner needs.*

There is an old story about a question a man came upon as he filled out a job application form: "Sex: ___." He answered: "Not enough." Men, especially, may smile, but the cold, hard truth is that men are often lured into affairs because they are sexually deprived at home. A man who strays is usually given total blame for his affair, but in many cases he is the victim of temptation that his wife helped bring upon him. The second chapter of Proverbs describes in some detail the benefit in pursuing and acquiring knowledge, wisdom, and discretion. Verse 16 says that discretion will "deliver you from the strange woman, from the adulteress who flatters with her words."

A Dose of Respect Beats a Dose of Viagra Any Day

Being trapped by an adulteress is precisely what happened to the husband of a woman who wrote to me after she figured out why he had an affair. She realized that her husband had been craving admiration just as she craved love from him. He was ripe for having an admiring woman tempt him, and that's exactly what happened in his workplace. Even though they had enjoyed what people thought was a "perfect marriage" for more than twenty years (four teenage children, active in the church, successful business, etc.), he strayed. They separated for a while, but then the wife realized:

> I had become so busy with life, kids, etc., that I had forsaken
> my husband in this area and left him vulnerable to attack from
> the enemy. He said he had been craving something, but he
> didn't know what it was until "she" began to give him what he
> was craving. His need for this was so strong that at one point
> during our separation, he was willing to give up everything—
> marriage, family, business, reputation, even his relationship
> with the Lord—just to continue feeling the respect and admira-
> tion he was receiving from this other woman. He had an
> extremely intense spiritual battle during this time because he
> knew what the right thing to do was, but he did not want to
> give up what he was receiving from her. God is helping me see
> my part in the breakdown of our marriage. My husband is a
> good-willed man and I know that he loves me and he knows
> that I love him.

The letter went on to say that she had tried the Respect Test with amazing results. She started speaking with great respect to her husband, and he immediately responded by telling her how much it "turned him on" to hear her say those respect- ful things. In fact, she relates, "We immedi- ately shared a very intimate sexual experience! It seems that a dose of respect beats a dose of Viagra any day!"

*"With her flattering lips
she seduced him"
(Proverbs 7:21 NKJV).*

Not all affairs end on such a positive note. A husband who had been deprived of sexual release and ultimately strayed wrote to say:

> I don't blame her for [my] immorality, but she doesn't own up to anything. I'm not blaming her, but she is not blameless. She never said she contributed to the problem. I want to forget it but she won't let me forget it. I did wrong, but I didn't just one day decide to go out with another woman. If I had felt she respected me, maybe I wouldn't have done this. I felt at times like she felt I was a failure. So, when someone said, "You're the greatest thing since sliced bread," I went for it. She says I ran to a blonde bimbo. But [the other woman] made me feel really good; it had nothing to do with the sex. Somebody thought I was okay. The more she told me I was a good man, the more I was drawn toward it.

IF HE LOVES ME, HOW CAN HE BE TEMPTED BY OTHER WOMEN?

Sexuality often becomes the reason that couples are not as close as they could be, but it manifests itself in ways you might not suspect. Men may want to be open with their wives, but when they want to be open on topics that threaten rather than increase feelings of love, some women grow uncomfortable if not downright upset. A wife may be wondering why her husband isn't more open when the truth is, she told him many years ago not to be.

As a rule, a wife wants more emotional intimacy only on subjects that increase feelings of love between her and her husband. When the husband shares any kind of "dark side" struggles, let's say with sexual temptation, she grows uncomfortable, or even hurt and angry. She may instruct him to be silent and to change. In other words, be like a woman: "We don't lust for men's bodies, so don't you lust for women's."

It is quite all right for her to share her struggles with body image, weight control, fears, and worries. The husband is to listen and em-pathize with her on all of these subjects. She feels so much better afterward because, in her mind, this increases feelings of love between them. The problem, of course, is that he doesn't struggle with body image, weight control, fears, and worries as she does. He has different struggles. Because his wife does not have those same challenges, however, his male concerns usually don't count when it comes to emotional intimacy.

Every man understands the connotation of this scripture: "David . . . saw a woman bathing (2 Samuel 11:2).

So the husband clams up, especially after being scolded. This, then, contributes to the wife's conclusion that he cannot be emotionally intimate. In actuality, she has told him not to be open. She has a high standard of what emotional intimacy is, but it must entail energizing the love between them and releasing her burdens. If he communicates something that isn't energizing and it creates a burden for her (i.e., sexual temptations he may have when he sees attractive women), he is out of line. She wonders, *How can he be tempted by another woman? Does he love only me or not?*

She cannot comprehend that seeing some well-endowed woman at the office with a plunging neckline would "turn him on." So she assumes that he must be lying. She concludes that the reason he has this sexual attraction toward that woman is because they have already spent a lot of time together (or least he wants to spend time with her), they've been talking, getting to know each other, getting close, etc. She cannot understand the concept that he could be aroused simply by looking at someone he barely knows. She lets him know that it isn't right to be tempted by any other woman in any way, and she doesn't want to hear about that kind of thing again.

She probably doesn't hear about it again, although her husband still struggles with his visual-orientation problem and wishes he could share. Remember the admonition to the husband in Proverbs 5:19? He is to let his wife's breasts satisfy him at all times—and no other. Most of Proverbs 5 is directed at warning husbands of the dangers of adultery. Why? Because the wise teacher who wrote this passage was trying to give men a healthy view of sex. The husband who loves his wife should delight in God-given sex, which means only in the marriage bond.[1]

Remember also, Jesus warned: "Everyone who looks at a woman with lust for her has already committed adultery with her in his heart" (Matthew 5:28). Our Lord understood that men are stimulated visually. Sex is in the forefront of man's consciousness, and whenever he sees someone visually seductive, he can be stimulated.

Simply put, a man is responsive to what he sees. He needs his wife's understanding of his struggles. If he wanted to be untrue to her, he would never allude to this problem at all. A wife longs to receive her husband's closeness, openness, and understanding. You can achieve this in two ways: (1) do your best to give him the sexual release he needs, even if on some occasions you aren't "in the mood," or (2) let him know you are trying to comprehend that he is tempted sexually in ways you don't understand. As you allow him to talk about his struggles, you have all the more opportunity to be his friend as well as his lover.

If your husband is typical, he has a need you don't have. When you shame him, punish him, or deprive him, he feels dishonored for who he is. If your husband feels you do not respect his struggle, his desire for you, and his maleness, he'll pull back from you. But he needs you; you knew that before marriage. As you recognize his need and seek to meet it, you will find him reaching out to meet yours. There is probably no more effective way to give the Crazy Cycle four flat tires and get the Energizing Cycle running on all six cylinders.

He Will Feel You Appreciate His Desire for Sexual Intimacy When . . .

- you respond to him sexually more often and initiate sex periodically.
- you understand he needs sexual release just as you need emotional release.
- you let him acknowledge his sexual temptations without fearing he'll be unfaithful and without shaming him.
- you don't try to make him open up to you verbally by depriving him of sex.

CHAPTER TWENTY-TWO

THE ENERGIZING CYCLE WILL WORK IF YOU DO

I sent him an e-mail one day, letting him know why I respect him. He told me that night he was very touched. . . . I really just prayed and let God lead me in what to say to him and it worked. Also, for some time we have sent SHMILY (**S**ee **H**ow **M**uch **I L**ove **Y**ou) messages to each other. I changed mine to SHMIRY (**S**ee **H**ow **M**uch **I R**espect **Y**ou) and he loved that. The following week, my husband called me in the middle of the day to tell me the reasons he loves me. We've been married almost ten years and he's never done that!

This wife's letter is one of dozens that I could use to sum up the power that can be at work in a marriage when the Energizing Cycle is in high gear. Understanding that a wife's deepest need is for love and a husband's deepest need is for respect is the core in how to make your marriage better. In Energizing Cycle terms, his love motivates her respect; her respect motivates his love. (See page 115.)

How Does a Husband Spell Love to His Wife?

As we have seen, love to wives is spelled C-O-U-P-L-E. Following is a brief review of these six concepts. If a husband memorizes and uses even one or two of them each day, he will do his part in keeping the Energizing Cycle going. Husbands should ask themselves these questions:

1. **C**loseness—Am I always remembering to move toward her and accept her need to talk and connect with me to be reassured of my love?

2. **O**penness—Do I share my thoughts with her, and am I sure I'm not resisting her efforts to draw me out?

3. **U**nderstanding—Am I careful not to try to "fix" her every time she talks about one of her concerns or problems? Am I remembering that she is an integrated personality and whatever happens affects all of her, especially her emotions?

4. **P**eacemaking—Am I always willing to resolve issues, and am I careful to never say, "Let's just drop it and move on"?

5. **L**oyalty—Do I constantly look for ways to tell her that I will be loyal to her forever—that she's the one love of my life, the only woman for me?

6. **E**steem—Do I always let her know that I treasure her and put highest value on her as a person? Do I let her know that what she does and thinks are important to me? Does she know I couldn't possibly do without her?

How Does a Wife Spell Respect For Her Husband?

A wife spells respect for her husband C-H-A-I-R-S and uses these six concepts to let him know how important and vital he is to her. Wives should ask themselves these questions:

1. **C**onquest—Am I always standing behind him and letting him know I support him in his work and endeavors in his field?
2. **H**ierarchy—Do I let him know I respect and appreciate his desire to protect and provide for me and the family? What have I said recently to communicate this?
3. **A**uthority—Have I gone on record that, because he has the primary responsibility for me (even to die for me), I recognize him as having the primary authority? Do I let him be the leader? How have I helped in that regard recently?
4. **I**nsight—Do I trust his ability to analyze things and offer solutions and not just depend on my "intuition"?
5. **R**elationship—Do I spend shoulder-to-shoulder time with him whenever I can? Do I let him know that I am his friend as well as his lover?
6. **S**exuality—Do I honor his need for sexual release even when I don't feel like it?

As a husband spells out love to his wife through C-O-U-P-L-E and a wife spells out respect to her husband through C-H-A-I-R-S, they can't help but meet each other's needs. The beauty of it is, if you meet a need in your spouse, it will come back to you as your spouse meets one of your needs. The key is in always being willing to cut your spouse some slack, as this woman discovered:

> I think I might have just realized something. . . . It is not that
> my husband is not showing me love or trying to understand me.
> It is that I am back to that place where, if he doesn't do it
> exactly the way I want it, it's no good. Okay, I am an idiot! He
> is showing me love, kindness, etc., in many ways and I have
> chosen to focus on one thing that I don't like! . . . So can you
> extend your 2x4 through the computer and hit me upside of the

head?! What I need is to rejoice in the ways my husband shows his love for me and express my appreciation for those. Would you please pray for me to really get this, internalize it, act on it and have it be my *first* response instead of having the negative, critical spirit come first?

I love this wife's honesty, not to mention her insight. She realizes she is a lot like Eve, who had paradise but wanted more (see Genesis 3). In a fallen world, you cannot always have "more." You can't grasp the Holy Grail of perfection, which is always beyond your reach. But you can embrace Love and Respect, which will always provide *more than enough* to energize your marriage. Act on the principles embodied in C-O-U-P-L-E and C-H-A-I-R-S, and your relationship as husband and wife is bound to be less negative and more positive. (If you have not read appendix C yet, do so now to learn how to share your needs with each other.)

FROM THE ENERGIZING CYCLE TO THE REWARDED CYCLE

In part 3, I will discuss how you can complete the Love and Respect process, which is designed to bring your marriage from bad to good, and from good to better. I will discuss how you can combine your faith with everything you have learned to bring you the reward of a happy marriage. I call this the Rewarded Cycle:

> HIS LOVE BLESSES REGARDLESS OF HER RESPECT;
> HER RESPECT BLESSES REGARDLESS OF HIS LOVE.

The Rewarded Cycle will show you the best way to develop the ability to give your spouse what he or she needs most as you bring your faith in Christ directly into your acts of Love and Respect. You will learn how a husband's unconditional love mirrors Christ's love for the church and how a wife's unconditional respect is like the church's reverence for Christ. I will share how the Rewarded Cycle develops your inner maturity and freedom of spirit, how it can make you good examples to those around you, and how you can win your spouses in a wise way.

PART THREE

THE REWARDED CYCLE

REGARDLESS OF

HIS LOVE

REGARDLESS OF

THE REWARDED CYCLE

HER RESPECT

Throughout this book I have emphasized that if the husband and wife are both people of basic goodwill, they can use Love and Respect principles to make a bad marriage into a good one and a good marriage into a great one. I have stressed the idea that you must trust your spouse; you must be the first to act on these principles, and not withhold what your spouse needs most in order to get your spouse to give you what you need most. We've also seen in preceding chapters that not only does God command men to love their wives and women to respect their husbands, but that we must do this *unconditionally*.

But what if your husband doesn't show you love when you show him respect? What if your wife doesn't show you respect as you show her love? If you get no results from practicing Love and Respect, why bother? The Rewarded Cycle gives you the answers to these questions. In a real sense, the Rewarded Cycle is the most important part of this book. Read on, and you will see why.

CHAPTER TWENTY-THREE

THE REAL REASON TO LOVE AND RESPECT

Perhaps the major problem that keeps so many couples somewhere between the Crazy Cycle and the Energizing Cycle is the fear that, even though they try to practice the Love and Respect Connection, it won't work. Here are some sample remarks I receive by e-mail or in person in conferences: "My fear is that I'm going to move forward in good faith but my spouse will mistreat me" . . . "My wife will continue showing disrespect, riding a bigger broom than ever" . . . "My husband will continue to be unloving. He'll re-enroll in the A-1 Jerks School and be first in his class."

Of course, there is always the exception—someone who is afraid to try respect because it just might work! A wife wrote:

Your suggestion to apologize and let him know how much I respect him is great. I intend to do that. But my heart is afraid that he may react positively, and I don't know if I am ready for more than what we have now: a mutual understanding for our roles as parents. It frightens me that I can do something so powerful and not be ready if he took a different kind of interest in me.

Another question I often hear is, "Why show love and respect when it isn't reciprocated?" One couple attended one of our conferences. She agreed to try respect, but according to her husband:

> . . . it faded away like a mist. She returned to her old self. She has not trusted me due to her relationship with her father. She has in the past been a vocal man-beater with her negative thoughts and comments about men, in general. I feel like an orphan in my own home. I feel like a husband with no wife. What I do experience of her presence is her critical, negative, hostile and judgmental attitude. . . . My emotions for my wife are being buried daily by her attitude towards me when she makes me feel less than a man. . . . I need to understand my wife and I need wisdom on how I can respond to her attacks.

Don't Give Up—Trust God to Work

Letters like the one above are heartbreaking, but my advice is always the same: *Don't give up because it doesn't seem to be working.* Keep showing your spouse unconditional love or unconditional respect. Look for even the slightest improvements. A husband doesn't bring flowers, but he does fix the leaky faucet. The wife still has a headache more than you like, but she has toned down the negativity. Remember the pink and blue lenses? We don't readily see what is happening in our favor, nor do we see the impact we might be making on our spouse.

"Do what is right without being frightened by any fear" (1 Peter 3:6).

One graphic example is a letter from a wife who explained that her husband called from his night job to tell her he got an unexpected bonus check. "Praise God!" she said, and that made him angry. Then he started to complain about how hard he had to work. She tried to remind him they really needed the extra money and,

"Why not be thankful?" As he continued to pour out his dissatisfaction with his lot in life, she (who was very much the lecturing type) decided not to give him another gentle lecture to stop feeling sorry for himself. Instead, she got respectfully quiet. As her silence continued, he said, "You better stop this quiet stuff. I mean it; it isn't like you and it's making me nervous. Something is wrong here. I don't like it. I never said for you to be quiet. I said to listen to me without always saying something. So stop being quiet!"

When she wrote to say that her respectful quietness "apparently wasn't working," I replied that actually it was working big time. At this season of their marriage, her husband's bad habits had to go, and he was already under conviction. The quietness probably caused him to hear himself, and he didn't like what he was hearing. So he lashed out. But her quietness *was* working in a powerful way. I urged her to be patient and let the Holy Spirit convict her husband.

Ultimately, we must depend on "the Helper," the Holy Spirit, to "convict . . . concerning sin" (John 16:7–8).

Months later she wrote back: "We are doing so well in our marriage. Our arguments have changed for the better." Her husband's spiritual life had significantly improved, and she gave credit to God but added, "I'd like to think it had a lot to do with my new attitude and silence, and respect in word and deed." This wife is a perfect example of how it's so easy to have doubts when things don't look as if they are going well. It takes time—in many cases, months—before there is a shift. Don't doubt the light from God's Word in your dark times.

Here's another example of a wife who felt nothing was happening but later was amazed. She called her ex-husband and apologized because she hadn't always respected his position in their home. (She is a Christian, and he is not.) There was silence, and then he responded, "Thank you." That ended the conversation, but several days later he called back at midnight in tears, wondering why she had made her apology. She explained she had to ask forgiveness for not being what she should have been as a wife. Again, the conversation ended abruptly. Not much seemed to be happening. Another week passed, and again he called at midnight. He had been thinking of everything he had done, and he was sorry. He went on about all of his mistakes—"some of the few kind words he has ever said to me."

In another situation, a wife moved out and bought another home. I coached the husband on how to behave toward her in more loving ways. This went on for some time, and he was seeing little progress. Then one day she said, "Are you wanting me to beg you to ask me to come back home?"

The above are just a few examples of what can happen. Don't give up because weeks or months pass with no response. Don't interpret delay as defeat. Don't assume that what you are doing is unfruitful. Most often, love or respect is working on your spouse more than you realize. Something is transpiring in the soul of that person. Have confidence that God will work.

WHEN IT SIMPLY DOESN'T WORK—WHAT THEN?

What is your worst fear in marriage? As a husband, is not your worst fear that you put on love but your wife shows you contempt? In response to your good-willed attempt to be close, open, understanding, peacemaking, loyal, and esteeming, she remains disrespectful.

As a wife, is not your worst fear that you put on respect but your husband is more unloving than ever? You have learned the "foreign language" of respect by appreciating his work efforts, his desire to protect and provide, to serve and lead, to give you his insights. You have also tried to give him shoulder-to-shoulder friendship and more sexual intimacy. Despite all this, he remains unloving. In good faith you moved first as the mature one, but your spouse did not change.

As Jesus spoke of the trials and tribulations believers might have to go through for Him, He mentioned that "a man's enemies will be the members of his household" (Matthew 10:36). For you, it may feel just this way. So should you simply say, "This Love and Respect thing doesn't work"? When you love or respect unconditionally, you are following God and His will for you. Ultimately, your spouse and your marriage have nothing to do with it. You are simply demonstrating your obedience and trust in the face of an unlovable wife or a disrespecting husband. *Unconditional love and unconditional respect will be rewarded.* I call this the Rewarded Cycle. Jesus said, "For if you love those who love you, what reward do you have?" (Matthew 5:46). Jesus could have had your troubled marriage in mind when He said that.

I believe Paul also had your marriage in mind when he penned Ephesians 6:7–8: "Serve wholeheartedly, as if you were serving the Lord, not men, because you know that the Lord will reward everyone for whatever good he does, whether he is slave or free" (NIV). In the immediate context, Paul refers to how slaves can serve their masters, but notice that he ends the passage by saying it applies to free persons as well. In other words, this idea is for all believers. If you trace his thinking back a few verses, you find him mentioning this same principle concerning children and their parents (see Ephesians 6:1–4) and also husbands and wives (see Ephesians 5:22–33). Paul is saying that whatever we do as to the Lord we will receive back from the Lord. In marriage, everything you do counts, even if your spouse ignores you! This is what the Rewarded Cycle is all about (see page 265 for a visual of it):

> *"Don't pay back unkind words with unkind words. Instead, pay them back with kind words"* (1 Peter 3:9 NIRV).

His love blesses regardless of her respect;
her respect blesses regardless of his love.

When I first began teaching this biblical truth as it pertains to marriage, I was unsure how people would receive it. Amazingly, many welcomed the Rewarded Cycle message with open arms. Those who feel hopeless suddenly catch the truth that what they do matters to God; *nothing is wasted.* This thought not only rejuvenates poor marriages, but it is helpful to good marriages. The key principle of the Rewarded Cycle is just as relevant for a good marriage as a poor one. Ultimately, all husbands and wives should be practicing Love and Respect principles first and foremost out of obedience toward Christ. If they do not, it is so easy to start being arrogantly proud about "our great marriage."

All couples must take heed. Those who think they stand could easily fall. So many marriages seem to be getting along just great and then, *wham!* The wheels come off. If we take our eyes off Christ (or never put our eyes on Christ in the first place), we are building on sand, and when the storms come we can be swept away (see Matthew 7:24–27).

Another benefit of the Rewarded Cycle for a good marriage is that you can understand why you are treating each other as you do and be more equipped to explain the Love and Respect Connection to other couples. And as other couples learn the Love and Respect Connection, the rewards increase exponentially. What are the rewards? We get some of them on earth, but we get an incredible reward in heaven.

HEAVEN'S REWARD—THE ETERNAL "AHHH!"

I heard a godly man with cerebral palsy speak. He had a delightful wit: "God is preparing me for heaven. . . . I am in His oven, so to speak. I am being baked for an eternal purpose. I am not finished yet. When I die and stand before Him, He is going to say, 'Well done.'" I laughed with delight as tears streamed down my cheeks.

Jesus is preparing us to hear, "Well done." He wants to say, "Well done, good and faithful servant! You have been faithful with a few things; I will put you in charge of many things. Come and share your master's happiness!" (Matthew 25:21 NIV).

Have you ever thought about what it will mean to "share your master's happiness"? It will be joy without measure. Think of your graduation day, wedding day, birthday, child's birthday, summer vacation, promotion, retirement, good times with friends, affirmation from your parents, leading all family members to Christ, good health. What if every hour of every day you experienced the glory and joy of all these events at once in their fullest intensity? Realize that when you "share your master's happiness," the intensity will be a trillion times greater.

How will you feel when you experience that endless first moment of joy? Remember when you wanted a bike for Christmas, but your parents wouldn't say if you would get one or not? You were in limbo, and then Christmas morning arrived. There under the tree was your bright, shiny bike, and you gasped, "Ahhh!"

Or think of the woman who is surprised with a diamond ring. She gasps, "Ahhh!" While speaking to a group of Wall Street investors in New York, I asked if anyone there had had an "Ahhh!" experience. One man said, "Yeah, when I got my first unexpected bonus check of $100,000." I swallowed hard then said, "Yes—that sort of gets at the idea!"

Do you realize that the greatest "Ahhh!" experience of your life is ahead? The Lord is closely watching and intends to reward you. "Each man's praise will come to him from God" (1 Corinthians 4:5). To keep in mind what's in store, memorize Ephesians 6:7–8: "Serve wholeheartedly, as if you were serving the Lord, not men, because you know that the Lord will reward everyone for whatever good he does" (NIV). Envision the scene as believers ascend into heaven and stand before Christ. To one husband He says, "Well done. You've put on love toward your disrespectful wife. You are about to receive back every act of love you did toward her." To a wife He says, "Well done. You've put on respect toward your unloving husband. I watched. You are about to be rewarded for every act of respect."

Next, Jesus directs you to enter the place called Paradise (see Luke 23:43). He has brought you "safely to His heavenly kingdom" (2 Timothy 4:18). As you enter with Jesus, you experience a holy rush. "You stand in the presence of His glory blameless with great joy" (Jude 24). At that moment, unexpectedly, you behold a gift of such great value you gasp a holy "Ahhh!" What you behold is beyond anything you could imagine. Suddenly, instantly, you are enveloped by love and glory. You are literally "in glory" never to leave (Colossians 3:4).[1]

To try to describe heaven is to describe the indescribable. Even Paul could only say that "momentary, light affliction is producing for us an eternal weight of glory far beyond all comparison" (2 Corinthians 4:17; see also Romans 8:18).

Let's go back to Matthew 25:21: "You were faithful with a few things." What would some of those "few things" be? Surely they include what Paul describes so clearly in Ephesians 5: "love [your] wife . . . respect [your] husband" (see v. 33). When you make a decision to love or respect your spouse, the dividends are without end. Jesus is offering you a bargain. Do a few things on earth in this life and get many things forever in heaven.

What Matters to God, Matters!

To the world it may make no sense for a wife to put on respect toward a husband who is harsh and unloving. It makes no sense for a husband to put on love toward a contemptuous, disrespectful woman. But it makes sense to God. These seemingly fruitless efforts matter to God because this is the kind of service He rewards. What is wisdom to God is foolishness to the world (see 1 Corinthians 3:19).

One way I like to picture this is that there is a *cha-ching!* effect in heaven when believers do things the world might call stupid. It's as though a billion angels are holding a gigantic handle. Each time you do something loving or respectful toward your spouse, the angels pull down on that handle. A secret treasure dumps into a colossal golden bowl and *cha-ching!* The lead angel exclaims, "He did it again! He put on love toward that disdainful woman!" . . . "She did it again! She put on respect toward that pathetic man! Okay, everyone, hit it again! *Cha-ching!*"

Admittedly, this imagery sounds a little fanciful, but it may not be that far off. The prayers of the saints are collected in "golden bowls" (Revelation 5:8). The Lord is keeping track somehow. As Paul says, "Whatever good thing each one does, this he will receive back from the Lord" (Ephesians 6:8). God's divine system is in place, and all is accounted for. The books will be opened and all will be judged according to their deeds (see Revelation 20:12).

Am I suggesting in any way that we are supposed to earn our salvation? Obviously not. Paul clearly says we are saved by grace through faith—"it is the gift of God; not as a result of works" (Ephesians 2:8–9). But look at Ephesians 2:10. We are to do the good works that God has already planned for us. Why? Not to appease the Lord or somehow pay "just a little bit" for our salvation, but simply to please Him. And when we please Him, He rewards us.

In 1 Corinthians 3:11–15, Paul clearly distinguishes salvation from rewards. Each believer should build with care on the only real foundation—Jesus Christ. "If any man builds on this foundation using gold, silver, costly stones, wood, hay or straw, his work will be shown for what it is, because the Day will bring it to light. It will be revealed with fire, and the fire will test the quality of each man's work. If what he has built survives, he will receive his reward. If it is burned up, he will suffer loss; he himself will be saved, but only as one escaping through the flames" (vv. 12–15 NIV).

Some of us may be tempted to say, "I'm not concerned about

Some say rewards are unimportant, but Jesus says, "I am coming soon! I bring my rewards with me. I will reward each person for what he has done" (Revelation 22:12 NIRV).

rewards—I just want to follow the Lord and reach heaven." But think for a moment. If Christ says He intends to reward you, then who are you to declare, "I don't care about that"? There is a certain false humility in saying, "Oh, rewards are so unimportant." Rewards are important because Jesus reveals them as important. I do not believe it is wise to take issue with the Son of God.

Yes, the rewards are waiting. *Nothing we do is wasted.* The Lord is watching with intense interest. A husband who loves his wife as Christ loved the church, and the wife who respects her husband "as to the Lord," will be rewarded throughout eternity (see Ephesians 5:22–33).

IT'S ABOUT YOU AND JESUS CHRIST

After more than a quarter of a century of counseling married couples and conducting Love and Respect Conferences, I have concluded that we don't have a "marriage crisis" in the Christian community; we have a crisis of faith. The point is that we all have to come to grips with one question: "Do I or do I not believe what Jesus Himself said?" The whole point is that you really can't do Love and Respect unless you do it unto Jesus Christ. And if you doubt the reality of Christ, if He is not truly Lord of your life, it won't work.

Many husbands and wives need to come to the point where they say, "Lord, I do believe; help my unbelief. I want to follow You, and I want to do this as unto You" (see Mark 9:24; Ephesians 6:7–8). One wife who made this discovery wrote:

I used to become very defensive and wounded by men. Now I have learned that my sufficiency is in Christ, my acceptance, my security, my significance comes through Christ. It's not about me, it's all about Him. I have nothing to prove to anyone. . . . I can relax and allow the Holy Spirit to work in me and through me.

Yes, there will be times when you will fail, but Proverbs 24:16 says, "A righteous man falls seven times, and rises again." Nobody can love perfectly and no one can respect perfectly. However, when we do this as unto Christ, we may fall but we can get up. The difference between successful couples and unsuccessful couples is that the successful ones keep getting up and keep dealing with the issues. Unsuccessful couples want it easy. They want it now. They want their needs to be met. They don't want conflict; they just want everything to be "happy." This approach is the epitome of immaturity.

The mature husband admits, "I blew it big time. I was wrong. I was unloving again. I've got issues I must deal with." The mature wife says, "You know, I just keep dishonoring you and not respecting you. I keep thinking it's all about love. I can't even remember that simple word *respect*."

I actually had one woman say, "What's that word again?" I said, "It's *respect*." She said, "Oh, yeah, that's it."

Fortunately, there are many more wives who learn and apply the word *respect*. One wife discovered her unsaved husband was having an affair, and her respect for him plummeted. Later he came to Christ, they reconciled, and he is now trying to grow into the role of spiritual leader in the home while she tries to be the best wife possible. They have a long way to go, but they are making progress. She writes:

It is easier for me to respect my husband out of obedience to God than necessarily because he is behaving respectfully. Thank you for helping me see how fragile a male ego can be. I never realized how much his own self-worth as a husband and a man hinges on a wife's respect. I have been keeping your words in mind if and when an argument would brew. Several times, by making a concerted effort to speak respectfully, rather than just going with my emotions, I have been able to ward off hurt feelings and harsh words between us.

Another wife who had suffered physical and verbal abuse from her husband (which I absolutely condemn as wicked and urge a wife to seek protection and help for) and had gone back to him after he repented, realized she had not completely forgiven him and certainly wasn't showing him respect. After coming across our materials, she began showing him respect, mostly by remaining quiet and dignified instead of arguing. Their relationship improved considerably, and she says:

My heart's desire is to win my husband to the Lord through my respectful behavior. I must admit I have to "mull over" some of your teaching, but it IS biblically based, and the Holy Spirit keeps revealing my rebellion, contempt, disobedience, etc. I keep asking the Lord for strength to implement your suggestions, and He is so faithful!

"Lord, When Did I Feed You?"

The Rewarded Cycle will deepen your love and reverence for Christ as you render love and respect to your spouse as unto Him. In the parable of the last judgment (see Matthew 25:31–46), the righteous ask, "Lord, when did we see You hungry, and feed You, or thirsty, and give You something to drink? And when did we see You a stranger, and invite You in, or naked, and clothe You? When did we see You sick, or in prison, and come to You?" (v. 37–39). And the king answers the righteous and says, "Truly I say to you, to the extent that you did it to one of these brothers of Mine, even the least of them, you did it to Me" (v. 40).

There is a basic principle we can take from this parable: whatever I do for my spouse, I do it to Christ as well. A husband's unconditional love for his wife reveals his love for Christ. The husband who loves God should love his wife also. If you are not loving your wife, then you must ask yourself, "Am I really loving Jesus Christ?"

A wife's unconditional respect for her husband reveals her reverence for Christ (see Ephesians 5:21–22; 6:6–7). The wife who respects God should respect her husband. If you are not respecting your husband, then you must ask yourself, "Am I really loving Jesus Christ?" For husband or wife, the conclusion is the same:

> *"'In the resurrection, when they rise again, which one's wife will she be? For all seven had married her.' Jesus said to them, 'Is this not the reason you are mistaken, that you do not understand the Scriptures, or the power of God? For when they rise from the dead, they neither marry, nor are given in marriage, but are like angels in heaven'"*
> *(Mark 12:23-25).*

IN THE ULTIMATE SENSE, YOUR MARRIAGE HAS NOTHING
TO DO WITH YOUR SPOUSE.
IT HAS EVERYTHING TO DO WITH YOUR RELATIONSHIP
TO JESUS CHRIST.

Yes, you will fail to perfectly love or respect, but that doesn't mean that you don't love Christ. In fact, your love for Christ is what gets you started again. You repent and confess, realizing you are not expecting your spouse to meet all your needs. But ultimately, whatever you do toward your spouse by way of love or respect is not done to motivate your spouse to get off the Crazy Cycle, nor is it to motivate your spouse to meet your needs. Ultimately, you practice love or respect because beyond your spouse you see Jesus Christ and you envision a moment when you will be standing before Him at the final judgment, realizing that your marriage was really a tool and a test to deepen and demonstrate your love and your reverence for your Lord.

Every time you do reach out with love or respect, heaven is watching. Those billion angels yank that big lever and, *Cha-ching! Cha-ching!*

I was talking to a friend of mine who is vice president of a large TV network. When he heard this teaching about the Rewarded Cycle, he said, "Whoa, it's not about my spouse, is it? It's about me and Jesus Christ. I have never heard this." My friend is a believer, but he never had clearly understood it's not about him and his spouse. It's about him and his Lord.

"Watch out that you don't lose what you have worked for. Make sure that you get your complete reward"
(2 John 1:8 NIRV).

But there is even more to the Rewarded Cycle. There is this whole area called "maturity"—having true inner freedom in Christ and the overflow that comes out of that as you are an example to your children and others around you, especially your spouse. We will look at these rewards in the next—and final—chapter.

CHAPTER TWENTY-FOUR

THE TRUTH CAN MAKE YOU FREE, INDEED

So far, so good on the Rewarded Cycle. You agree that the rewards of heaven will be overwhelming. That heavenly first moment, "Ahhh!" is beyond description. To realize that the "Ahhh!" will last forever is beyond the beyond. And you understand that your marriage is not primarily about you and your spouse but that it's about you and Jesus Christ.

Marriage is a test of how you unconditionally love and respect your spouse as you obey, honor, and please the Lord. *Primarily*, you don't practice love and respect to meet your needs in your marriage, as important as these are. Your first goal is to obey and please Christ. When you try to do this, often (but not always) your needs are met, and these are wonderful by-products and blessings. But your first goal is to obey and please the Lord.

HEAVEN WILL WAIT—WHAT ABOUT NOW?

There is still more to the Rewarded Cycle. There are rewards to help you cope right here, right now. Heaven will wait. God's timing is in control of that, but you can always use a little more help with understanding and living with your less-than-perfect spouse. I could fill a book with letters from couples who are trying the Love and Respect Connection but it isn't working out too smoothly. There are many couples who get the idea about stopping the Crazy Cycle, but they remain in a sort of limbo, not quite getting on the Energizing Cycle. And some couples seem barely able to keep the Crazy Cycle from cranking up to full speed again.

One couple heard our Love and Respect Connection tapes, and the husband wrote to admit that he knew he wasn't loving his wife as God wanted him to, and his wife had problems as well. He continued:

> You put your finger, or God's finger, right on it. I began to write down each time my wife said something that cut to the core of my being. I did not tell her that I was writing down these incidents, and I don't intend to use them against her. I was amazed at how I felt my honor being attacked on a daily basis. I don't want to judge my wife, but respect is certainly the issue . . . the male "withdraw and be quiet" response is very real. . . . Please be praying for me as I try to love my wife unconditionally, regardless of her words or actions.

Sometimes the Love and Respect Connection can seem to backfire as it did for this wife, whose husband monitored her "respect meter," so to speak, to see how well she was doing:

> Now whenever he senses anything that smacks of disrespect, even when it isn't, it reminds him of our past and he gets infuriated. I haven't seen such rage in awhile. . . . Actually, I regret letting him know about what I had learned from you because he uses it against me each time. . . . I can take on the criticism—I

feel I deserve it—but his rage is withering and makes me want to get away and hide.

I understand this woman's feelings. I grew up in the kind of environment she describes. My father would become enraged at my mother. To offset his strong feelings of personal guilt, he would take offense at things my mother innocently did and then explode. But she never saw herself as a victim. Not once in all my years growing up did I hear Mom bad-mouth Dad. When I griped about him, she would reply, "Your dad lost his dad when he was three months old, so he doesn't know how to be a daddy."

"When you do what is right and suffer for it . . . this finds favor with God" (1 Peter 2:20).

My mother could have moved in for the kill, defaming my father in order to bolster herself and win my heart. She chose not to do that. Years later I realized why. Mom's parents had suffered terribly. Several of her siblings had died, and her own father was wheelchair-bound all his life. It would have been easy for my mother to have the victim mind-set, but she realized that never got you anywhere. My mother made a choice to be positive. She knew if she could discover creative alternatives to the conflict, she would never believe for a moment she was helpless and hopeless, and she never was. Eventually, Mom was instrumental in bringing Dad to Christ.

"Sometimes the Issue Is Me!"

My heart breaks for husbands and wives who continue to struggle with a spouse's rage or withering criticism. While I can sympathize, I know that my sympathy isn't what they really need. What they need to know is that the Rewarded Cycle is the way to finding inner freedom and maturity of spirit. What I am about to say may sound hard and even judgmental, but hear me out. I am trying to help you, not simply hold your hand. The answer lies in the word *unconditional.* The key to being on the Rewarded Cycle is *unconditional love and respect* (see page 265).

First, you must get to the place where you can say, "My response to my spouse is my responsibility." In my own marriage, Sarah doesn't cause me to be the way I am; she reveals the way I am. When my reactions to her are unloving, it reveals that I've still got issues. There is still lack of love in my character and soul, and I have to own up to this. Maybe it is 70 percent her fault and only 30 percent my fault (and, then again, maybe it isn't), but the point is, what about my 30 percent?

"For from within, out of the heart . . . proceed . . . envy, slander, pride and foolishness" (Mark 7:21–23).

Don't play the percentages game with your spouse. It's an easy way to get yourself off the hook. And once off the hook, you can't mature spiritually. In fact, a typical result is that you feel like a victim. You get the victim mind-set. You want to be rescued. You want paradise on earth. You begin to resent your spouse and other people because they haven't healed your hurts or comforted you. Get rid of the victim mind-set! Realize that the only real healing and comfort you're going to get is by looking to the Lord and trusting Him with your situation, painful as it is. To do otherwise is to sin. This is hard to accept because you are the one being sinned against, at least most of the time, in your opinion. Nonetheless, you must grasp this principle:

NO MATTER HOW DEPRESSING OR IRRITATING MY SPOUSE MIGHT BE, MY RESPONSE IS MY RESPONSIBILITY.

Here is a letter from a husband who is making progress as he rides the Rewarded Cycle:

I also understand that I am often reading her reactions and actions incorrectly. I am not getting offended when she doesn't respond like I think she should. I am better at translating her feedback. We are arguing much less. We were miserable prior to the conference. As I love her more, my wife is acting more friendly to me. But she still has not acknowledged her part in the Crazy Cycle we always used to end up in. My prayer is that she will in time. She still seems to get stuck on how she is feeling. I'm trying to help her understand my heart. But this mindset that the man is mostly to blame for conflict is going to be difficult to overcome.

What's Inside Will Come Out

Think of a speck of sand. If the sand gets in the human eye, it causes irritation, then infection, and if not cared for, eventually loss of vision. But put that same speck of sand in an oyster. It causes irritation, then secretion, and eventually the oyster forms a pearl. Was the sand the primary cause of the results in the eye? Was the sand the primary cause of the results in the oyster? No. If it were, the results would be the same. The sand was an agent that revealed the inner properties of the eye and of the oyster. In a real sense, when life with your spouse causes irritation, you can let it develop into an infection or you can allow it to become a pearl.

Another example is the sun shining down on butter and clay. It melts the butter but hardens the clay. Heat from the sun reveals the inner properties of the butter as it reveals the inner properties of the clay.

Your spouse is an irritant (or worse) at times. That's a given. We don't have to dwell on that point. Your spouse puts pressure on you, has expectations of you. Your spouse puts heat on you. In these pressure situations, you always face a choice: to react in a godly way or in a sinful way. It is easy enough to just blame your spouse—after all, your spouse is to blame for whatever is happening to you, right? But if you go the blame route, you wind up only a victim and you miss out on God's rewards.

When the pressure is on and when the heat is turned up, you must remember to tell yourself, "As a mature person with inner freedom to make my own choices, I know that my response is truly my responsibility." Living this is not easy. One husband shared that there are many times when he feels like a doormat. Nonetheless, he says, "It is encouraging to know that Jesus is 'affixed' on my response to my wife and stands ready to reward me for a godly response. In other words, I am responsible for my response. Knowing this makes it much easier to love her regardless."

INNER FREEDOM DEVELOPS GREATER MATURITY

Obviously, what I have been talking about takes great spiritual maturity. You may say, "I'm just not that far along. I'm just not that strong." But Jesus is, and He can help. In John 8, Jesus is in a heated discussion with scribes and Pharisees trying to help them understand who He is and why they should follow Him. Some in the crowd appear to believe Him (see v. 30). Then Jesus says, "If you continue in My word, then you are truly disciples of Mine; and you will know the truth, and the truth will make you free" (vv. 31–32). Now there is a note of protest. The Jews don't get it. After all, they are Abraham's offspring and have never been anyone's slave. What does Jesus mean by becoming free? Jesus answers, "Truly, truly, I say to you, everyone who commits sin is the slave of sin. . . . if the Son makes you free, you will be free indeed" (John 8:34, 36).

What do Jesus's words about freedom have to do with you and your marriage? Everything. When Jesus said, "You shall be free indeed," He wasn't talking about political freedom of some kind. He was talking about inner, spiritual freedom—freedom from sin. Even though your spouse is being difficult, hateful, or full of contempt, Jesus can help you be dignified and loving. No matter how difficult your spouse may be, you cannot blame your negative reactions on your spouse. If you do, you are letting those negative reactions control your inner person. You are becoming a hopeless, helpless victim. When your spouse is unloving or disrespectful, if all you can do is react negatively, you are destined for unhappiness. But according to Jesus, you are free if you want to be. Your spouse can affect you, but your spouse does not control you. You can experience disappointment, but it is your choice to disrespect or be unloving. Memorize this principle and live by it:

"The deeds of the flesh are evident, which are: . . . outbursts of anger, disputes" *(Galatians 5:19–20).*

I CAN EXPERIENCE HURT, BUT IT IS MY CHOICE TO HATE.

One wife reports that since she has determined to take the "inner freedom" approach, her husband is still unloving at times. She writes:

> But if I am disrespectful to him, the Holy Spirit convicts ME to apologize! Yuck! But I feel so much better afterwards it's worth it. I know it's not my husband I am apologizing to, but Jesus. I hope and pray that my husband's eyes will be open to the Holy Spirit, but I leave this up to God since I know that only He can change his heart.

YOU CAN BE FREE IN ANY CIRCUMSTANCE

In 1 Peter 2:16–17, the apostle is talking to Christians who are under pressure. They can choose to react in godly or ungodly ways. Peter says,

"Live as free men. . . . Show proper respect to everyone: Love the brother-hood" (NIV). There are two truths here for a spouse trying to get on the Rewarded Cycle. First, the phrase "live as free men" (v. 16), refers to the same inner freedom Jesus describes in John 8. As Peter will show in chapter 3 of his letter, this inner freedom must be lived out in marriage as well as in the arena of citizenship. In any setting, you can experience inner freedom independent of your circumstances.[1]

Remember the husband (in chapter 5) who was arrested for domes-tic violence? While spending a couple of nights in jail, he had what he called an "epiphany." As he repented and confessed, he experienced the unexplainable presence of the power of God. Something took place inside of that husband. Though in jail, he said, "I am freer than I have ever been." Some call this a power encounter with the living God. We cannot grasp how it happens, but all we know is that something works in our hearts. As Paul wrote, "The peace of God, which surpasses all comprehension, will guard your hearts and your minds in Christ Jesus" (Philippians 4:7).

Second, we see the evidence that we are inwardly free when we can honor and love others. When Peter wrote this letter during the first century, he was trying to help believers who had all kinds of issues—with the government, with neighbors, and with each other. I'm sure they were saying to Peter, "Look, I cannot honor or love people who have offended me." Or can't you hear a wife saying to Peter, "I cannot honor my unloving husband"? Or perhaps a husband was telling him, "I cannot love my disrespectful wife." Peter is saying in effect that if you are inwardly free, you can do these things that seem impossible. If you do not do them, that is your issue. You are not free.

I also get many letters from spouses who are living in inner free-dom, or at least they are starting to. One wife shared that she learned that her husband of eleven years had been unfaithful to her numerous times. Her whole world fell apart, as did her relationship with God. How could this person whom she loved so much hurt her like this? He arranged for counseling, and for twenty months she poured out her heart—as well as her anger. The counseling transformed her husband into a loving, godly man, set free and walking in God's truth. But the wife continued to be angry and full of hate. She realized it was bondage, but she couldn't help it. Her respect for him was gone, and he could never earn it again.

By chance she was at a friend's house and saw some of our materials. When she read the word *respect,* she thought, *Oh, here we go again; it's all about the man . . . They don't know my husband or what he did, so this doesn't apply.* But she read on, and she thanks God she did. She said, "Suddenly my eyes were opened and a freedom came into my heart. I didn't have to respect him based on his behavior but on who he is as a man, made in the image of God. I had never heard of that before!"

Other wives have also conquered contempt by experiencing inner freedom. Here are two more letters:

> God is moving in my heart. I have had contempt in my heart for my husband. That was very hard to admit but very liberating. I have confessed this to God and have asked my husband to forgive me as well.

———

> It helps me so much to want to show respect to him when I realize that, in doing that, I am really showing respect and love to God most of all as well as trying to meet the deep needs of my husband. The verse, 1 Peter 2:16, that you shared really motivates me. Because I am free in Christ, I can show honor because He is meeting my security and love needs.

Sometimes you have to start at the very beginning with what doesn't seem to be much. Specific truths can help set you free. Yes, your spouse may be harsh, unloving, or disrespectful a lot of the time, but just remembering that your spouse is really a person of goodwill can put you on the road to the Rewarded Cycle. As one spouse wrote, "It was freeing to reflect on the fact that she was well-intentioned and good-hearted toward me."

INNER FREEDOM REWARDS YOU WITH A LEGACY

The Rewarded Cycle offers still more, because the mature husband or wife does not go unnoticed by his or her children. As you learn the truth and seek to act upon it with unconditional respect or unconditional love, realize that you're leaving a legacy.

How do your children feel about you? When you are gone, do you want your children to be excited because you left them an inheritance? Some children are so excited about their inheritance that they can hardly wait for their parents to die. What did their parents do to make them think like that? Parents want their children to love and respect them, but if they aren't showing love and respect to each other, what kind of legacy are they leaving behind?

A husband provides a good example for his children when he unconditionally loves their mother. He shows his children how a person who believes in Jesus Christ and who has inner freedom in Christ should act. What will the children of such a man say at his funeral? I believe they will say, "What a man my dad was. I didn't fully appreciate it when I was young, but now as an adult with a wife and children of my own, I realize he put on love to my mother even in the times when she had issues and she wasn't so pleasant to be around. I hope I can be half the man my dad was."

The same principles apply to a wife. What do you want your children to say at your funeral? If throughout their lives, they saw you put on respect to your husband, they will say, "Mom was really something. Dad wasn't always easy to live with, but she still respected him, because she knew it wasn't about Dad. She did it out of love and reverence for Christ. And even though I took advantage of her and was rebellious, she always forgave me and loved me. There is just nobody else like Mom."

The apostle John wrote of the great joy that comes when children walk in the truth (see 2 John 4). To walk in the truth means to order your life by the Word of God. If we want our children to walk in the truth, we must live that same truth before them.[2]

Each day you are on the edge of something; you face some kind of crossroads. Today could be the day something happens that will make all the difference, and when it does you will want to be ready for it— you will want to be mature with inner freedom. As your children see you living out Christ's words, "The truth shall make you free," you will set them on the path of following Jesus as well. What greater joy can a parent have than that?

But what if you've already blown it? Perhaps your kids are teenagers by now and you're just discovering the Love and Respect Connection and beginning to figure out what the Rewarded Cycle is all about. You're thinking

> *"Set an example . . .*
> *in speech, in life,*
> *in love, in faith*
> *and in purity"*
> *(1 Timothy 4:12 NIV).*

about mistakes you've made, the times you haven't been a good example and those numerous scenes where you didn't show love or respect to your spouse. Don't despair. God has a unique way of eliminating past mistakes. Where there has been sin, His grace abounds. He erases your mistakes and puts more grace in their place. One wife writes:

> My husband and I were having a discussion, and he said that he felt as if I did not respect him . . . he was right . . . and it was obvious because we have two daughters, six and a half and three,

and they do not show much respect for him either, which is a sign to me that I was not giving it to him. So, I bought your book. I've been showing respect in various ways. In the time that I have put some of the ideas into practice, his relationship with the girls has grown much more loving and so has our relationship. He knows that I am trying to make things the best that they can be. He has gone out of his way to do extra things for me and give me some extra time by myself on days when I work by taking the girls shopping. I am so excited to see 1 Peter 3:1–2 work in our marriage.

Another wife tells of observing her own parents being married unhappily for thirty-eight years. Her mother got some of our materials and started applying some of the ideas. She had always known what God wanted but had never understood how to do it. As the daughter observed her mother making major changes in her attitude and her marriage, it deeply affected her. The daughter, who had been married almost fifteen years herself, explains:

> [I] have not been very successful in getting along with my husband. We both have strong personalities. I have seen such a change, not in my parents' relationship but in my mom's attitude toward my dad that I have been calling for advice a lot lately. . . . I have always known that doing the will of God is what will ultimately bring me joy. I am just thankful for what it has already done for my mom and the peace that it has brought into her life.

Another woman with a son (twenty-one) and a daughter (eleven) wants to pass on the Love and Respect message because, as she writes,

"I have taught them to be disrespectful of their father, but now I can remedy this by showing respect regardless of what happens. . . . I have asked for forgiveness from God, my husband and my children in regard to this sin."

The Reward of Winning Your Spouse God's Way

We have already studied 1 Peter 3:1–2 and know its importance in understanding the Love and Respect Connection. Peter writes, "In the same way, you wives, be submissive to your own husbands so that even if any of them are disobedient to the word, they may be won without a word by the behavior of their wives, as they observe your chaste and respectful behavior." Here Peter clearly says that a husband who is unloving, rebellious, even far from God, can be won by his wife's respectful behavior.

The Rewarded Cycle principle of unconditionally respecting your husband out of obedience to the Lord can win him. This is power. And this same power is available to husbands. Your unconditional love for your wife with no strings attached, simply wanting to obey God and serve Him, can win her.

A good example is the prophet Hosea, who married Gomer. Gomer proved to be an adulterous woman, and Hosea was separated from her for a time. Then God said, "Go, show your love to your wife again, though she is loved by another and is an adulteress" (Hosea 3:1 NIV). Talk about unconditional love! Hosea even had to buy Gomer back (the custom of the time) to restore her to her wifely status (see Hosea 3:2).[3]

A modern-day Hosea wrote to say that we had "connected many dots" for him. He had lost hope for any change in his difficult marriage, and he cried out to God, not knowing what to do, how to do it, or how to love his wife.

"All I heard from the church was 'love, love, love,'" he said. "I tried, tried, tried and couldn't." But when he attended one of our conferences, he understood why he felt so discouraged and rejected:

> I hadn't put the words on it, but I wanted her to respect me and be my friend—neither of which I was experiencing. I knew I had failed to love her (maybe even more than she did not respect me). . . . Thanks be to God for knowledge that leads to understanding and allows me to act lovingly in service to Jesus Christ. I realize tests and trials are coming. My wife has many hurts from not being loved for so long, but we now have a way to move forward.

Letters from other spouses who are trying to win their mate God's way keep pouring in. One came from a successful thirty-four-year-old woman who felt trapped between the world's views on respect for men and God's plan. But as she read our materials, she couldn't put them down. She said, "It was like finally there was freedom in knowing the truth in such a straight-forward manner. It's so simple to know."

Another woman wrote to say that she had already been trying to make some changes her husband had suggested, but when she heard our CD:

> . . . I began to do other things. I changed my attitude. I changed my tone of voice and my facial expressions. I even changed my prayers from "bless me and change him" to "change me and bless him." Due to my new understanding, I had a passion for my husband that was not there before, so I began to see him differently. I have begun to see fruits from these changes already.

The Rewarded Cycle always reveals what you are inside. What does it mean to be the mature one? The concept is more easily grasped than lived. The following testimony is proof that you can live and act with maturity:

> Most of us are fully aware of the power of words, but the power to destroy by a disrespectful attitude is just as damaging. . . . The Lord has really given me self-control and conviction in this area. I think when we know that we are full and complete in Christ, and our identities are not given to us by our husbands, it is so much easier to Love and Respect. . . . My situation is not any easier at home, my husband has been "on the run" from the Lord for many years now, but I do not feel so hopeless and, therefore, do not have a need to have the final word, be right, win an argument, worry about a decision, etc. And by honoring my husband . . . I am choosing life, Christ's life, and then I am blessed. Even if my husband never changes, I know the Lord wants me to honor Him. I know some women get a cruise out of this (ha ha), but really, I feel better about myself as a Christian being able to overlook an offense.

This wife is one of many I could quote who has taken that vital step toward maturity that you may need to take. As you do so, remember that you will be tested because your marriage is a test of your devotion to Christ. Some people fear God's tests—they think He might be mean or somehow deceptive. You must understand something crucial about God's tests. He does not test you to show you how dumb, insincere, and sinful you are. He tests you to show you that you *can* do this, and when you do, your inner freedom will increase (see James 1:2–12). Don't be afraid of God's testing. As soon as you let Him know that you want to take this step, He will allow you to enter into the discipline of this new way of thinking.

So, in your mind's eye, step into the future. Try to envision where and when the first test might come. What might your spouse do or say that will test you? When it happens, the Lord will speak gently and softly. He will help and strengthen you. But now is the moment to make the decision to change. Do it now—and never look back!

PINK AND BLUE CAN MAKE GOD'S PURPLE

One of the favorite analogies in our Love and Respect Conferences is comparing women and men to pink and blue. There is an immediate ripple of recognition and agreement in the audience when I talk about how she sees through pink sunglasses and hears with pink hearing aids while his world is shaded in blue. He sees life differently through blue sunglasses and hears what she is saying differently through blue hearing aids.

Although it is impossible to sum up the Love and Respect Connection with one illustration, the obvious difference between pink and blue is a good start. Because husband and wife see and hear differently, they can't easily decode the signals they send each other. The result is the Crazy Cycle: without love (her deepest need), she reacts without respect (his deepest need); without respect (his deepest need), he reacts without love (her deepest need).

We spent part 1 talking about how to recognize and slow down the Crazy Cycle. We learned, however, there is no way to get rid of the Crazy Cycle completely. Because pink and blue are human, the Crazy Cycle is always there, ready to spin. The key is knowing how to spot trouble before it starts, how to keep the Crazy Cycle in its cage.

In part 2, we looked at the best way to keep the Crazy Cycle contained by having wives show husbands respect and then having husbands show wives their love. We call this the Energizing Cycle: his love motivates her respect; her respect motivates his love.

We learned all kinds of practical, as well as biblical, ways to do this: six for him and six for her. All the tools in C-O-U-P-L-E and C-H-A-I-R-S are extremely useful, but improving marriages takes more than helps and how-tos. One husband wrote to tell me he had attended a Love and Respect Conference and found it a breath of fresh air. He and his wife had been going to marriage conferences during the twenty-six years of their marriage, and he felt they always did one of two things: taught lots of techniques or preached the "men are bad" message. He had become convinced that focusing on human effort and training to improve marriages missed the heart of God's call to walk in the Spirit.

As he listened to our presentation of the Love and Respect Connection, he appreciated the Energizing Cycle, but he was more impressed by the Rewarded Cycle (his love blesses regardless of her respect; her respect blesses regardless of his love). He realized that he had been "loving" his wife out of endurance and obligation. His letter continues:

> Endurance is a good thing and it has probably preserved our
> marriage to this point, but my joy tank has been empty for
> about twenty-five of my twenty-six years of marriage. Through
> your message, the Lord breathed new life into me and has given
> me a new joy and freedom to love.

This husband's letter gets to the very heart of our Love and Respect message. We are not simply about helping you save or improve your marriage. Those can be very important by-products, but the real purpose behind showing love and respect to one another is to glorify God and to obey what He teaches in His Word.

Only recently have I seen the key passage of this book in a new light. Ephesians 5:31–33 says, " 'For this reason a man will leave his father and mother and be united to his wife, and the two will become one flesh.' " This is a profound mystery—but I am talking about Christ and the church. However, each one of you also must love his wife as he loves himself, and the wife must respect her husband" (NIV).

Paul is, indeed, correct when he says marriage is a profound mystery. How can two become one? In math, two is never one. Think about it: can you see a man and a woman coming together into one being? In your mind's eye, what do you envision? Some sort of unisex figure? Or we might ask ourselves, "Is each to be what the other is? How can a wife be one with her husband if he is to be one with her?" We say, "Well, the husband would have to become more feminine, more pink." But turn the question around. "How can a husband be one with his wife if she is to be one with him?" Now we tell ourselves, "It seems the wife has to become more masculine, more blue." But a male is not to be a female nor a female a male! So how are two to become one?

Paul answers the question in verse 33. The best and most practical way for two to become one is through the Love and Respect Connection. Oneness is undermined, not through daily problems, but when he has an unloving attitude and she has a disrespectful attitude. Said in another way, if two people agreed on every decision but she still felt unloved and he still felt disrespected, neither would feel one with the other. But as a husband puts on love, especially during conflict, his wife will feel one with him. When a wife puts on respect during those moments, the husband will feel one with his wife. A disagreement may not be solved, but oneness will be experienced. When a wife feels her need for love is met, she bonds with her husband. When a husband feels his need for respect is being met, he bonds with his wife. This can happen simultaneously. Two do, indeed, become one!

There is much information in this book. Many people have said that they have never heard this particular slant on marriage, but all this information is nothing without trust, love, and reverence for the Lord. The road to a lasting Love and Respect marriage is a lifelong one, and there is no way you can travel it in your own strength. The task is overwhelming, and you need help from your heavenly Father, who knows your heart. If you want to do your marriage as unto Christ, you must ask Christ for help. Remember, Jesus said, "Apart from me you can do nothing" (John 15:5).

HAVE YOU REALLY TRIED PRAYER?

I often tell couples that they should try prayer. That sounds like a cliché, I know, but I repeat, try prayer. Talk to God. It is amazing to me how many people say they think about praying but never really pray. Scripture says, "You do not have because you do not ask" (James 4:2).

I'm not talking about reciting your wish list to God. James 4:2 does not refer to asking God for health and wealth. It is talking about asking for power to cope with life's real problems. If anything is heard in heaven, it is the unselfish prayer, based on the heart of God. Too many people pray, "God, here is what is on my heart. Please fulfill my desires for me." What we should be praying is, "God, here is what is on *Your* heart. Please fulfill Your desires *in* me."

What is on God's heart is clearly spelled out in Scripture: that husband and wife be one. I am told that when blue blends with pink, it becomes purple and that purple is God's color—the color of royalty. The way for pink and blue to blend is spelled out in Ephesians 5:33: "[Every husband] also must love his wife as he loves himself, and the wife must respect her husband" (NIV). Here is the key to blending together to reflect the very image of God.

Quoting Ephesians 5:33 is easy enough, but living it in the daily here and now takes commitment. Hear the words of husbands and wives who are committed to living out the Love and Respect Connection in any and all circumstances:

> I have regained my walk with God in a way that has convinced me that this trial has produced a good result . . . I am committed to the restoration of my marriage, whatever it takes.

> Although I know our marriage has never been all that happy and I have biblical grounds for divorce. . . . I have decided to stay . . . my husband says he is committed to our marriage now and is willing to do what it takes.

> We are both too committed to Christ to divorce. We have several strikes against us. My husband is a doctor and I am an RN, so we have a medical marriage—which equals a high divorce rate. We are the parents of a handicapped child—which equals a high divorce rate. We experienced a child's death—which equals a high divorce rate. We are totally committed to Jesus and the marriage; however, we just don't like each other very much. The term one marriage counselor used was the "gruesome twosome." Now we are the grandparents of two special needs children, which is even more stressful. All that to say, we have been through many marriage programs [and] all these things together were not as helpful as your simple message from Ephesians 5:33. For the first time in our lives, I can talk to him . . . we are trying to love and like each other for the rest of the years we have together. We're back on track to Love and Respect one another again.

Two years in this marriage have been the most painful of my life.
. . . I have been begging God to let me out of this, but I am committed to my vow and I KNOW leaving isn't HIS will.

I have learned to be keenly aware of what I am communicating
(including facial expressions and tone of voice) and my husband
has responded by allowing me to tell him when I am feeling
unloved. We have avoided the Crazy Cycle completely since I committed to being obedient to God in this.

All of the above letters—and we could quote many, many more—
thrill us, but especially gratifying was a letter we received from a lady
who had gone through the pain of an unfaithful husband. She went
through obsession, depression, and "insanity" before, during, and after
the divorce. Her view of men dropped well below zero. She decided to
try to reconcile with her ex-husband for the sake of her two boys, but
she had little hope for a fulfilling marriage. Then she found a class
taught by her aunt, offering our Love and Respect series. She had heard
plenty from the church about being submissive, but not much about
being respectful. The class changed her life forever. She learned to bury
her baggage and understood for the first time the real meaning of submission and respecting men. She decided to quit men-bashing and
realized men were part of God's perfect design instead of God's mistakes. As she concluded her letter to us, she said:

Marriage is a tool and a test to allow God's will to be revealed in
our lives . . . we should do all this as unto God, not as unto the
person, but *for God* because He commanded us. . . . All of you

have definitely earned a reward in heaven as a result of the changes that your efforts made in me. "CHA-CHING! CHA-CHING!"

Perhaps there is no better note to conclude on than that. Every move that any of us makes to teach, share, or cause Love and Respect results in the sound that comes ringing across the heavenlies as those billion angels pull down on that big lever. *Cha-ching! Cha-ching! Cha-ching!*

A Prayer of Commitment

Dear Father,

I need You. I cannot love or respect perfectly, but I know You hear me when I ask You for help. Forgive me where I have been unloving or disrespectful. I open my heart to You, Father. I will not be fearful or angry at You or my spouse. I see myself and my spouse in a whole new light, and I forgive my spouse. I will appreciate my spouse as different, not wrong. Lord, fill my heart with love and reverence for You. Ultimately, this is about You and me. It isn't about my spouse. Thank you for this enlightenment. My greatest reward comes from doing this unto You. Prepare me this day for those moments of conflict. I especially ask You to put love or respect in my heart when I feel unloved or disrespected. There is no credit for loving or respecting when it is easy. At this moment, I believe You hear me. I anticipate Your response. I have on my heart what is on Your heart. I thank You in advance for helping me take the next step. I believe You will reward me, and I believe this touches Your heart as I do this unto You. It's between You and me. I am a true believer.

In the name of Jesus Christ,
Amen.

A Lexicon of Love and Respect: Reminders of What to Say, Do, or Think to Practice Love and Respect in Your Marriage

Always ask yourself:

- Is what I am about to say or do going to feel unloving to her?
- Is what I am about to say or do going to feel disrespectful to him?

Things to remember:

- Even though feeling disrespected, pull back from being unloving toward her.
- Even though feeling unloved, pull back from being disrespectful toward him.

- When she is being critical or angry, she is crying out for your love; her intent is not to be disrespectful.
- When he is being harsh, or stonewalling you, he is crying out for respect; his intent is not to be unloving.

- If you defend your lack of love, she will feel unloved.
- If you defend your lack of respect, he will feel disrespected.

- When you feel disrespected, you tend to react in unloving ways and don't see it.

- When you feel unloved, you tend to react disrespectfully and don't see it.

- When you feel disrespected, it is not natural for you to be loving in return; you must love her in an act of obedience to Christ.
- When you feel unloved, it is not natural for you to be respectful in return; you must respect him in an act of obedience to Christ.

- Ultimately you show your love for Christ when you unconditionally love your wife. If you are not loving your wife unconditionally, you are not loving Christ.
- Ultimately you show your reverence for Christ when you unconditionally respect your husband. If you are not respecting your husband unconditionally, you are not reverencing Christ.

- If you have failed to love her, do something loving.
- If you have failed to respect him, do something respectful.

- The best way to motivate her is by meeting her need for love.
- The best way to motivate him is by meeting his need for respect.

To communicate feelings or start discussion:

For wives: Never say, "You are unloving." Instead, say, "That felt unloving. Did I come across as disrespectful?" If he says yes, say, "I'm sorry for being disrespectful. Will you forgive me? How can I come across more respectfully?"

For husbands: Never say, "You are disrespectful." Instead, say, "That felt disrespectful. Did I come across as unloving?" If she says yes, say, "I'm sorry for being unloving. How can I come across more lovingly?"

Taboos:

- Never tell a wife she must earn your love in order for you to love her inner spirit created in God's image.
- Never tell a husband he must earn your respect in order for you to respect his inner spirit created in God's image.

- Never say, "I won't love that woman until she starts respecting me."
- Never say, "I won't respect that man until he starts loving me."

- Never say, "Nobody can love that woman!"
- Never say, "Nobody can respect that man!"

- Never blame your lack of love on her lack of respect. Your lack of love is disobedience to Ephesians 5:33a.
- Never blame your lack of respect on his lack of love. Your lack of respect is disobedience to Ephesians 5:33b.

Things to say to lighten up the relationship:

"We're like two hamsters on the Crazy Cycle."

"Are you trying to take a spin on the Crazy Cycle?"

"Are we trying for a new record on the Crazy Cycle?"

"I think your pink/blue sunglasses are fogging over."

"Put on my pink/blue hearing aids and listen."

"May I borrow your pink/blue hearing aids? I have no idea what you are trying to say."

"You're seeing this in pink; I see it in blue. Let's agree to disagree."

"You're seeing this in blue; I see it in pink. Let's agree to disagree."

"We've been flipping the light switch for twenty minutes. Let's try something else."

"Pardon me, but you're standing on my air hose!"

APPENDIX B

PERSONAL LOVE AND RESPECT INVENTORY FOR HUSBANDS AND WIVES

"Yes" answers mean you need to pray for change and improvement.
"No" answers mean you are doing great. Thank God and keep it up!
"Perhaps" or "Maybe" answers mean you are aware of a need for change. Keep trying!

Regarding myself:

- As a wife, did I react disrespectfully because I felt unloved?
- As a husband, did I react unlovingly because I felt disrespected?

- As a wife, am I afraid to say, "That felt unloving. Did I come across disrespectfully?"
- As a husband, am I afraid to say, "That felt disrespectful. Did I come across unlovingly?"

- Do I refuse to say, "I'm sorry," when my husband says, "That felt disrespectful"?
- Do I refuse to say, "I'm sorry," when my wife says, "That felt unloving"?

- As a wife, am I too proud to make the first move and start being more respectful?

- As a husband, am I too proud to make the first move and start being more loving?

Regarding my spouse:
- As a wife, do I neglect to energize my husband by failing to meet his need to be respected?
- As a husband, do I neglect to energize my wife by failing to meet her need to be loved?

- Do I say, "No way am I going to respect him until he starts loving me"?
- Do I say, "No way am I going to love her until she starts respecting me"?

- When I feel unloved, am I quick to claim my husband is unloving?
- When I feel disrespected, am I quick to claim my wife is disrespectful?

Regarding God:
- As a wife, do you give little thought to God calling you to show unconditional respect, especially when your husband is unloving?
- As a husband, do you give little thought to God calling you to show unconditional love, especially when your wife is disrespectful?

- As a wife, do you justify your lack of respect and thus do not confess this sin to God?
- As a husband, do you justify your lack of love and thus do not confess this sin to God?
- As a wife, have you put off making a decision to show God you reverence Him by showing respect to your husband?
- As a husband, have you put off making a decision to show God you love Him by showing love to your wife?

APPENDIX C

HOW TO ASK YOUR MATE TO MEET YOUR NEEDS

You cannot hope to get what you need—whether it be love or respect—by withholding what your spouse needs most. But while you are trying to meet your spouse's needs, what happens during those moments when your needs are not being met? Must the Energizing Cycle sputter as the Crazy Cycle starts to turn? Must you remain mute, hoping your mate senses your deflating spirit and realizes exactly what is wrong? One of the basic skills I have been trying to teach husbands and wives in this book is how to communicate their needs to each other. Here are some "need communicators" husbands and wives can use to let each other know how they are feeling.

Wives can humbly and softly say:

Closeness: "When you want to work in your shop all evening and not be with me, that feels unloving. You have a right to your hobbies, but I need some face-to-face time with you too."

Openness: "When you said you didn't want to spend time talking about my concerns, that felt unloving to me. I know we don't always have time to talk at length, but sometimes I need to feel reassured that everything is okay."

Understanding: "When you gave me a quick solution to what I was trying to tell you, that felt unloving. I know you were trying to be helpful, but I really need to feel your care and you can do that by just listening and understanding."

Peacemaking: "When you tell me to, 'Drop it, let's forget it, it's over,' that feels unloving. I know some things need forgetting, but first I need to know that you aren't angry anymore and that we really are at peace."

Loyalty: "When you look at other women, that feels unloving to me. I know temptations are real, but I need to know you have eyes only for me."

Esteem: "When you make negative comments about my mothering or homemaking, that feels unloving. I know I'm not perfect and that I fail, but I need to hear from you when I do a good job, and I need your encouragement even when I don't."

Husbands can humbly and softly say:

Conquest: "When you make negative remarks about my work goals, that feels disrespectful. I struggle with balancing work and family, and I am not against our family or you."

Hierarchy: "When you suggest that I am irresponsible, that feels disrespectful. I admit I blow it at times, but overall I am a good provider and protector, and what you're saying hurts."

Authority: "When you make decisions regarding the children that exclude me, that feels disrespectful and I even feel insignificant. Please include me even in the day-to-day stuff whenever you can."

Insight: "When you roll your eyes and say, 'That's really ridiculous,' that feels disrespectful. I know you have intuition in many areas, but I have insight that can often help."

Relationship: "When you refused to go to the basketball game with me, that felt disrespectful. I know you cannot always go to events with me because of the kids, but I need you to be with me as my friend, and lately that's lacking."

Sexuality: "When you said you were just too tired to have sex, that felt disrespectful to me. I understand that you're tired, but I hope you understand my need as well. It's not that I'm just oversexed; I really need to hold you close."

Appendix D

What about Exceptions to the Love and Respect Pattern?

At times I receive mail or personal inquiries at our conferences to the effect: "We don't fit your description of husband and wife. She is the one who stonewalls, and he is the one who 'lets it all hang out.'" My answer is that cultural and personal applications can vary. My parents were a good example. My father would come at my mother ranting and raving in anger—confronting her because he wanted to communicate. She simply shut down and withdrew. Then he would withdraw also, and there would be icy silence for many hours and sometimes days.

Both my parents wanted to connect with each other, but they could not out of ignorance or fear. Mom longed to connect with Dad (as every woman wants to connect with her husband), but she would pull back because she feared his anger. And Dad wanted to connect with Mom, but his feelings of being disrespected (she was the key breadwinner for many years) kept him in a state of frustration and anger. At the deepest core, however, my mother still was seeking love and my father was seeking respect.

We get other inquiries regarding "exceptions." For example, a woman wrote to tell me that in certain aspects of personality her husband was more "pink" than "blue" and she was more "blue" than "pink." She was reared in a home dominated by her father's values: education, intelligence, strength, pride, and lack of emotions. She wrote: "Subsequently, as I became a woman, I thought that to be loved (the kind of love that would touch the core of my being), I had to seek recognition for all the things that came naturally to 'blue' instead of to 'pink.'"

On the other hand, her husband was raised in a very warm, nurturing environment, full of unconditional love. "So naturally," she continued, "[he] grew up with a HIGH regard for those very 'pink' tendencies that made him feel so complete and unconditionally loved."

In short, this wife focused on "respect" in order to get love. Her husband focused on "love" in order to get respect. Until I helped them unpack their puzzle, she thought respect was her deepest value and he thought love was his deepest value. In truth, he was doing "the pink thing" to get respect, and she was doing "the blue thing" to be loved.

If you have further examples or questions regarding "exceptions" to my general thesis on the Love and Respect Connection, please feel free to contact me at www.loveandrespect.com, "ask emerson."

Appendix E

What If Your Husband Is a Workaholic?

I have counseled many wives whose husbands are workaholics of one degree or another. First, I caution that I cannot guarantee that what I have to say will automatically get a husband to quit working so many hours and be at home a lot more. I do, however, offer three observations that usually help a wife deal with the situation in a more positive way.

First, some husbands work because it is the place they feel respected. If a wife is negative, complaining, and disrespectful, what man wants to come home? I know of a man who whistled and hummed on Monday mornings as he went joyfully to work. On Friday he did not whistle and hum as he came home for the weekend. When asked why, he said, "I have to be home over the weekend with my wife." Now, it is quite possible that his wife did not cause him to work the long hours at first. But as the pattern went on, her loud and bitter complaints increased, and her negativity persuaded him to stay at work as long as possible. A man does not hear the deeper cry of his wife's heart when she makes a personal attack on him and his work. He does not hear, "Rescue me." Instead he hears, "I despise you." So he asks for (or chooses) overtime at work.

Second, if a change is to happen, whining or contempt will not draw him home. You need not praise him for all the work he is doing away from home. (Don't feel that you must respect what may be a negative obsession.) Instead, look for non-work areas in which to express respect. This book is designed to help you find these areas and learn about how to express them. Remember, you cannot devalue what he is doing at work in order to get him to value the family more. Do not say or imply, "I am not going to respect you until you start helping me and the children." That is equal to having him say or imply, "I am not going to show you and the family any love until you start honoring me for what I do at work." *Disrespect never motivates love, and lack of love never motivates respect.*

Third, to influence him directly, respectfully say, "Your son (daughter, children) needs you at home more. You have a unique influence on him. In certain areas, nobody matters to him as much as you do. It may not appear that way to you, but your positive presence has the power to mold him. I know you are swamped and have little time, but I also know that you want to give him that part of you that no one else can give to him. Thanks."

After delivering your "we need you at home more" message, don't repeat it for anywhere from ten to twenty days. Then mention it again, quietly and positively with the general tone of "just a positive reminder because of your importance." Always choose your words carefully. Never even remotely imply that you are really saying, "If you don't make a positive change, you idiot, you will destroy me and the children."

Have confidence in God's Word. Quietness shouts to a husband. A gentle spirit will bring out the gentleman in him. Respectful encouragement to your husband about his unique value to the family will have influence over time. Unemotional and positive appeals will have their effect on any good-willed man.

Having said all of the above, I know that this is not easy advice for many wives to heed. Women tend to want to respond to family concerns *now*. Men, however, will begin to make improvements over a season of time. Stay with a positive and short message, and eventually he will turn his ship around. Just remember, ships are not rowboats. Allow for time and the Holy Spirit to work. As hard as this is to hear, you will need to see this being a twelve-month project at the very least. Give your husband time to bring some things at work to completion and to introduce "no" into his vocabulary on the job. Give him time to taste what it's like to be an influence in his own home with his own children (not to mention you).

One way to look at it is that in family matters, you are the hare and he is the turtle. You can tear down the track and leave him in the dust, but that will not make you win the race. Your respect will bring him out of his shell and motivate his movements. His movements will be much slower than you prefer, but it will do you little good to run circles around him, tapping on his shell with your stout stick of judgment. Be patient and make the following your motto: "If I can't say anything respectful, I won't say anything at all."

For more information and resources on the Love and Respect Connection, go to www.loveandrespect.com

E-mail your personal story to Dr. Emerson Eggerichs: story@loveandrespect.com

---

NOTES

Chapter One: The Simple Secret to a Better Marriage

1. I believe it is important to make a distinction between theology and theory. My biblical theology of Ephesians 5:33 is simple: a husband is commanded to love his wife unconditionally, and a wife is to respect her husband unconditionally. This is what the text says—period. The Love and Respect Connection (my theory) is inferred from verse 33. So far, every couple I work with seems to experience the Crazy Cycle to one degree or the other. Ephesians 5:33 reveals that a wife needs love and a husband needs respect, and when those needs are unmet each spouse reacts at some level. My theory says that the wife has a tendency to react in ways that feel disrespectful to the husband (thus, the command to her to respect). And the husband has a tendency to react in ways that feel unloving to the wife (thus, the command to him to love).

Chapter Two: To Communicate, Decipher the Code

1. John Gottman, *Why Marriages Succeed or Fail* (New York: Simon & Schuster, 1994), 61.

2. In Ephesians 5:33, Paul uses the Greek word for love (*agape*) in the present active imperative, and the word for respect (*phobetai*) in this usage becomes a practical imperative. Both usages in this text are meant as a command. This is why the NIV uses the word "must" for both these phrases. (A. T. Robertson, ed., *A Grammar of the Greek New Testament in the Light of Historical Research*, 4th ed. [New York: Hodder, 1923], 994.)

Chapter Three: Why She Won't Respect; Why He Won't Love

1. The NIV translates the Greek word *hina* as "must" to leave no doubt that this is a command from God's heart.

2. When I refer to the feminist movement, I am referencing the more radical elements. Many positive benefits for women have come out of feminism. However, what profoundly disturbs me is that a substantial segment of the feminist movement has promoted a negative, contemptuous attitude toward men simply because they are men. As a follower of Christ, I see both men and women created in God's image. I am to love and respect God's creation. Though men and women are sinful and in need of Christ, the Lord Himself yearns for every soul to experience His love and glory (i.e., highest respect!). To have a demeaning attitude toward males simply because they are males is to look down on sons, brothers, uncles, grandfathers, fathers, husbands, and male friends in a way that God Himself does not.

3. Professional survey data quoted in Shaunti Feldhahn, *For Women Only: What You Need to Know about the Inner Lives of Men* (Portland, Ore.: Multnomah, 2004). Survey performed for Shaunti Feldhahn by Decision Analysts, Inc. and tabulated by Analytic Focus. Shaunti Feldhahn, a best-selling author, has a master's in public policy from Harvard University, is a financial analyst at the Federal Reserve Bank of New York, and is a weekly columnist on women's issues for the *Atlanta Journal-Constitution*. Based in Dallas, Texas, Decision Analysts, Inc., is one of the most in-demand survey firms in the nation. Analytic Focus, a separate firm headed by Chuck Cowen, former Chief of Survey Design at the U.S. Census Bureau, is based in Alabama. For more information, visit the website at analyticfocus.com.

4. I appreciate the significant contribution women are making to the military, but my observation is that the military is a particularly natural place for the male, especially in combat. In fact, a broad policy in the military, no matter what the branch of service, is not to use women in combat situations. For policy statements, see U.S. Marines—http://www.Marines.com/officer_programs/FAQ.asp?format=/ and Center for Military Readiness—http://www.cmrlink.org/WomenInCombat .asp?docID=154. My point is that, by the very nature of who they are, men are better equipped to serve, fight, and die if need be; and this same drive transfers to the home and the family, where the man fills the role of protector.

Chapter Four: What Men Fear Most Can Keep the Crazy Cycle Spinning

1. Professional survey data quoted in Shaunti Feldhahn, *For Women Only: What You Need to Know about the Inner Lives of Men* (Portland, Ore.: Multnomah, 2004). Survey performed for Shaunti Feldhahn by Decision Analysts, Inc., and tabulated by Analytic Focus.

2. Gottman, *Why Marriages Succeed or Fail*, 152.

3. Ibid.

Chapter Five: She Fears Being a Doormat; He's Tired of "Just Not Getting It"

1. Gottman, *Why Marriages Succeed or Fail*, 175.

Chapter Six: She Worries about Being a Hypocrite; He Complains, "I Get No Respect!"

1. Gottman, *Why Marriages Succeed or Fail*, 159.

Chapter Ten: Openness—She Wants You to Open Up to Her

1. For an in-depth discussion of the difference between the compartmentalization of men and the integration of women, see Stephen B. Clark, *Man and Woman in Christ* (Ann Arbor: Servant Books, 1980). In his thorough study of the differences between men and women, Clark references two specialists in the trait-patterns of male

and female: Dietrich von Hildebrand, *Man and Woman* (Chicago: Henry Regnery, 1965), and Edith Stein, *The Writings of Edith Stein* (London: Peter Owen, 1956). Clark writes: "Both von Hildebrand and Stein say that men and women differ in the way their minds, emotions, and bodies function together. A woman's emotions, intellect, and body form a more integrated unity than those of a man. She confronts decisions, activities, and relationships as an entire person—a blend of emotions, intellect, and body. On the other hand, a man's emotions, intellect, and body are more differentiated. He more easily compartmentalizes elements of his personality, treating them as aspects of his identity which he can at times temporarily ignore."

Chapter Twelve: Peacemaking—She Wants You to Say, "I'm Sorry"

1. In Isaiah 54:6, the plight of Judah in exile is likened to the sorrow of the wife who is forsaken, grieved in spirit, and rejected by her husband.

2. See William Barclay, *The Daily Study Bible, The Letters to the Corinthians* (Edinburgh: The St. Andrew Press, 1965), 67.

3. In Matthew 19:1–6, Jesus is answering the Pharisees' query, "Is it lawful for a man to divorce his wife for any reason at all?" (see v. 3). Instead of taking either of the rabbinical positions—one liberal, one more conservative—Jesus focused on Genesis 2:23–24 and the concept of "one flesh." Marriage is to be "the deepest physical and spiritual unity." See Charles E. Ryrie, *The Ryrie Study Bible* (Chicago: Moody, 1976), 1478.

Chapter Thirteen: Loyalty—She Needs to Know You're Committed

1. Now Columbia International University.

2. Robertson McQuilkin, *A Promise Kept—The Story of an Unforgettable Love* (Wheaton, Ill.: Tyndale, 1998), 21–23.

3. Ibid.

Chapter Fifteen: C-H-A-I-R-S: How to Spell Respect to Your Husband

1. In 1 Corinthians 7:25–38, Paul gives the Corinthians "wisdom" that he admits is not a direct command from the Lord Jesus in the Gospels. Because he felt that time for winning people to Christ was short, he preferred that Christians not be married, so they could concentrate on doing the Lord's work. Paul isn't putting down marriage. He is simply stating a fact about what happens when good-willed men and women marry: they will be concerned about how to please one another. Paul realizes that married people can still serve the Lord.

2. A loving wife is called upon to overlook certain failures and mistakes by her husband "because love covers a multitude of sins" (1 Peter 4:8). And a husband overlooks words or actions by his wife that may seem disrespectful because "a prudent man overlooks an insult" (Proverbs 12:16 NIV).

Chapter Sixteen: Conquest—Appreciate His Desire to Work and Achieve

1. Charles F. Pfeiffer, ed., *The Wycliffe Bible Commentary* (Chicago: Moody, 1987), 5.

2. Feminists do, in fact, severely differ with several of Paul's observations in 1 Corinthians 11:3–16. As Paul discusses a problem in the church at Corinth, he advises women to appear in worship services with their heads covered, something that some of them apparently were not doing as part of their "traditions" (11:2). He states: "For a man ought not to have his head covered, since he is the image and glory of God; but the woman is the glory of man" (1 Corinthians 11:7). From the feminist point of view, this verse seems to be feeding the male ego at the expense of a woman's dignity. From the Love and Respect point of view, however, men need to feel honored and respected in the same way women need to feel loved. Consider this statement: "Women were created to be loved by men in the same way Christ loved the church; therefore, men are created to bring love to women." Few women would object to this, but it is a little harder to accept what Paul is saying in 1 Corinthians 11:7. In giving advice on a protocol problem in the church at Corinth, Paul has uncovered a profound truth. A man needs to feel honored for who he is— the image and glory of God—because God made him that way. This is not chauvinist egotism. It is a fundamental need built into the male by the Creator. Yes, there are chauvinists among men just as there are prima donnas among women, but these exceptions should not be the rule. I believe our culture, which is heavily influenced by feminism, has missed the beauty of God's design.

3. In his book *The Essential Difference: The Truth about the Male and Female Brain,* Simon Baron-Cohen reported his findings after twenty years of research on gender differences in which he concluded that the female brain is predominantly hard-wired for showing empathy while the male brain is hard-wired for understanding and building systems. Baron-Cohen developed his theories by observing infants in the crib and noting the kind of stimuli they responded to. Girl babies responded better to faces above them while boy babies responded to mobiles. For a review of Baron-Cohen's book, see Carolyn See, "His and Hers," *Washington Post,* 5 October 2003.

4. In their discussion of the sociology of the family, Talcott Parson and Robert F. Bales hold that the basic model of the family consists of two adult partners (husband and wife) living together with their children. Roles tend to revolve around internal tasks for the wife and external tasks for the husband. The authors describe these as the expressive versus instrumental orientations—see Talcott Parson and Robert F. Bales, *Family, Socialization and Interaction Process* (Glencoe, Ill.: Free Press, 1955). Though various voices differ with this model, it still doesn't go away! I hold to this as reflecting the basic nature and interests of men and women. Generally, women will be focused on relationships in the family, expressing the wonders of love. Though a career for the woman is important in our present cul-

ture, we still find career being an *option* for women if they want children. A career is a freedom of choice for them, whereas a man feels *compelled* to work outside the home in the field.

Chapter Seventeen: Hierarchy—Appreciate His Desire to Protect and Provide

1. See Donald G. Bloesch, *Is the Bible Sexist?* (Westchester, Ill.: Crossway, 1982), 36–37). Bloesch points out that the Bible "nowhere sanctions the abuse and exploitation of women. Instead, it emphasizes the need for their care and protection. Some feminists call this 'condescension,' but deference to woman as woman belongs to the very nature of masculinity, just as a certain dependency on the male is the very essence of femininity."

2. From *Family News from Dr. James Dobson*, February 1995. This account in Dr. Dobson's newsletter recounted the story as the late Dr. E. V. Hill told it himself on a *Focus on the Family* radio broadcast, "E. V. Hill on the Death of His Wife."

3. See Deborah Tannen, *You Just Don't Understand—Women and Men in Conversation* (New York: Ballantine, 1991), 24–25. As she did research on her book, Tannen observed her husband as "simply engaging the world in a way that many men do; as an individual in a hierarchical social order in which he was either one-up or one-down. In this world . . . people try to . . . protect themselves from others' attempts to put them down."

Chapter Eighteen: Authority—Appreciate His Desire to Serve and to Lead

1. See Wayne Grudem, *Systematic Theology: An Introduction to Biblical Doctrine* (Grand Rapids: Zondervan, 1994), 465–66.

2. Beware of certain cultural voices. Some say submission never strengthened any institution except slavery. Others say submission only applies to the first century, which, by the way, they say about every New Testament teaching with which they differ. It would do all of us good to heed the scripture: "For there are many rebellious men, empty talkers and deceivers . . . who must be silenced because they are upsetting whole families, teaching things they should not teach for the sake of sordid gain" (Titus 1:10–11).

Chapter Nineteen: Insight—Appreciate His Desire to Analyze and Counsel

1. Based on a story in Jo Berry, *Beloved Unbeliever* (Grand Rapids: Zondervan, 1981).

Chapter Twenty: Relationship—Appreciate His Desire for Shoulder-to-Shoulder Friendship

1. See Deborah Tannen, *Gender and Discourse* (New York: Oxford University Press, 1994), 96.

Chapter Twenty-one: Sexuality—Appreciate His Desire for Sexual Intimacy

1. See Charles C. Ryrie, *The Ryrie Study Bible* (Chicago: Moody, 1976), 944. The "wise teacher" who wrote Proverbs 5:19 is probably King Solomon, who is said to have spoken three thousand proverbs and more than one thousand songs (see 1 Kings 4:32). He is generally credited with writing many parts of the book of Proverbs, including chapters 1–9. Unfortunately, Solomon wound up with seven hundred wives and three hundred concubines, most of whom were idol-worshiping women from outside of Israel who turned his heart away from God (see 1 Kings 11:1–8). Solomon could not follow his own advice about sex, but that does not preclude the wisdom of what God inspired him to write.

Chapter Twenty-three: The Real Reason to Love and Respect

1. To say that we will be overwhelmed by our entrance into heaven is the epitome of understatement. Whatever you think ecstasy means, multiply that by a billion times infinity. For just a few passages on what it will be like to experience Paradise and be in heaven with God forever, see Romans 8:17, 30; 1 Corinthians 13:12; 2 Corinthians 12:4; Philippians 3:21; 1 Thessalonians 4:17; Hebrews 7:25; Hebrews 10:14; 1 John 3:2; Revelation 2:7; Revelation 21:4.

Chapter Twenty-four: The Truth Can Make You Free, Indeed

1. In this section, 1 Peter 2:13–3:7, Peter has a clear outline, which he sums up in 3:8. The outline is discovered by noticing the repetition of the phrase, place yourselves under authority (1 Peter 2:13; 2:18; 3:1). Notice another repetition when he addresses wives and husbands. He uses the phrase "in the same way" (1 Peter 3:1, 7). We might say the four main points of the outline are: citizens, slaves, wives, and husbands. Each of these groups is to submit. In Peter's mind, the greatest evidence of submission is Love and Respect! "Live like free people. . . . Show proper respect to everyone. Love the community of believers. Have respect for God. Honor the king" (1 Peter 2:16–17 NIRV). In other words, a wife who is inwardly free submits by respecting her husband, which Peter clearly states (3:2). By implication, a husband who is inwardly free submits by loving his wife—that is, he lives with her in an understanding way and honors her as an equal.

2. See Ryrie, *The Ryrie Study Bible*.

3. Ibid., 1338.

LOVE & RESPECT

Workbook

BEFORE YOU START YOUR STUDY OF LOVE AND RESPECT . . .

Welcome to the *Love & Respect Workbook* experience. You are about to discover and apply the single greatest secret to a successful marriage. Today, you and your mate can start fresh with the ground-breaking guidance that Dr. Emerson Eggerichs provides in this workbook and the book it accompanies—*Love & Respect*. These two books are designed to be companions, so you'll benefit most if you have a copy of the book as well as this workbook.

Based on three decades of counseling experience, as well as scientific and biblical research, the book offers you the information and tools you will need to understand what is wrong in your relationship and begin the process of correcting it. The workbook gives you and your mate a private place to complete a wide variety of exercises that are crucial to the process of making Dr. Eggerichs' breakthrough techniques a permanent part of your marriage.

Before you start your actual study, here are some helpful hints on how you can benefit most from your experience:

Come ready to let God help you work on your marriage. As you experience *Love & Respect* you will be amazed at how these two simple but powerful concepts can affect your marriage. This is no quick and easy fix, but if you are willing to spend a reasonable amount of time and effort, and make the tiniest of adjustments, this study will change you and your marriage for the better.

Study at your own pace and preference. Some of the questions are quite simple—others take more thought and effort. But as you interact with *Love & Respect* concepts, you will begin to see what Emerson is talking about. In Emerson's words, you will "get it" and once you "have it," you will never be the same.

Get acquainted with how this workbook is constructed. It covers all the *Love & Respect* book in fourteen sessions. Some sessions cover one chapter of the book, and others cover as many as three chapters. As you go through each chapter, you will note that every subhead denotes a block or section of study, and generally there is at least one question for every section. The goal is to get you involved with what Emerson is saying, to see if you agree or disagree as you apply his concepts to your marriage. When some questions deal with difficult concepts, there is extra input and explanation in the form of Emerson's Additional Commentary (see *Workbook* Appendix VI).

This workbook was designed to be used by both individuals *and* couples, so you'll notice ICONS throughout that will help you understand which questions apply to you.

First, take note that the questions *without* icons apply to *all readers.* In each chapter, be sure to answer all these questions first. Then, take note of the three types of icons used in the workbook. There are certain questions designed especially for men, while others address women only. And some of the questions should be answered as a couple. Here is a quick review:

> **Unmarked questions should be answered first in each chapter by both the man and the woman.**

Men answer these questions.

 Women answer these questions.

 Couples answer these questions together. Answer these questions last in each chapter.

You can study this book solo. The questions are written primarily for individuals and then for couples. Therefore, if your spouse is not yet interested in *Love & Respect*, you can gain much from working alone. But as you begin putting *Love & Respect* principles into action, your spouse may decide to join you!

For maximum benefit, study with your spouse. Virtually every question has a section for spouses studying together. Remember, these questions are marked with an icon of a couple. Both of you should answer these questions together *after* you answer each question individually. As you compare and discuss your answers, you will gain new understanding of each other and how each of you sees your marriage.

Take your time. There is no hurry and no requirement to cover every last question completely. Break each session into workable parts. Concentrate on the questions that really speak to your needs as husband and wife.

Treat each other with Love and Respect. Because some of the questions probe sensitive areas, it is possible that tension will develop—even irritation and anger. Your rule should be: when dealing with sensitive issues, be sensitive to each other! If a question becomes a bit too sticky, and one of you doesn't feel up to dealing with it at the moment, table that question for possible discussion later.

Handle each other with care. As you proceed, you will soon see that a question may reflect the strength of one spouse and the vulnerability of the other. Where you are strong, or not so sensitive, your spouse is weaker and more sensitive. Where you can quickly see the need to change your attitude or something you are doing, your spouse may struggle, seeming to stubbornly hang on to habits you know have to go! By-words for your study of *love and respect* should be: patient, non-judgmental and forgiving. Always remember that God made us male and female—not wrong, just different. If both of you approach each question with compassion and empathy for each other, there will not be a critical or judgmental spirit on the part of the stronger one, and the vulnerable one will feel greater freedom to address issues and get feelings on the table.

As you study, expect God to work. To be sure, *Love & Respect* was written to put you in closer touch with your spouse. But the ultimate goal is to put you in closer touch with your Lord. Every session in this workbook includes scripture studies to guide you in times of meditation and prayer. Without prayer, your study will yield minimal returns. Pray without ceasing, and you will see God work at His pace, in His way, as He strengthens you " . . . with power through His Spirit in the inner man" (Ephesians 3:16). Love and respect each other as God loves and respects you. He will be forever pleased, and you will be forever rewarded.

Are you ready? Then let's begin!

Part One:
The Crazy Cycle

Sessions 1 to 4 cover the Introduction and Chapters One to Seven of
Love and Respect

A personal word from Emerson . . .

Welcome! You are beginning a journey to love and respect, a "new"
way to approach marriage that is as old as the New Testament itself.
Nestled in the fifth chapter of Paul's letter to the Ephesians, hidden in
plain sight, is the "secret" to controlling what I call the Crazy Cycle—
and beginning to enjoy a marriage built on love for her and respect for
him. Everyone who has ever been married knows what it is like to be
on the Crazy Cycle: without love from him, she reacts without respect;
without respect from her, he reacts without love. And so husband and
wife go round and round saying and doing the same wrong and hurtful things, with seemingly no way to stop it.

As you study the first four sessions in this workbook, you will learn
how the Crazy Cycle starts and why it often continues indefinitely.
Most importantly, you will come to understand how to slow the Crazy
Cycle and eventually bring it to a halt. I know this can happen because
God empowered my wife, Sarah, and me to defeat the Crazy Cycle.
He can and will empower you as well.

SESSION ONE

In preparation for this session, read the Introduction to *Love & Respect* ("Love Alone Is Not Enough") and Chapter One, "The Simple Secret to a Better Marriage." The following questions are for use in individual study or study by a husband and wife together. Remember to answer all unmarked questions first, then answer questions marked by the male or female icon (whichever applies to you). Finally, answer the questions with the couple icon, if you're studying with your mate. (Suggestions for anyone planning to use this study with a small group are in *Workbook* Appendix I, page 201.)

Questions for Chapter One

1 On page 1 of *Love & Respect,* Emerson "absolutely disagrees" with the Beatles' conclusion that "all you need is love." Emerson goes on to say that five out of ten marriages are ending in divorce because love alone is not enough. Love is vital for the wife, but what we have missed is the husband's need for respect. *Love & Respect* is all about how the wife can fulfill her need to be loved by giving her husband what he needs—respect.

Do you agree or disagree with the paragraph above? Can a wife get the love she needs simply by showing her husband respect? What if he doesn't deserve respect? Do you think Emerson is talking about conditional respect, or unconditional respect? Put down some of your thoughts here:

Compare what you wrote. Be aware that this very first question in the workbook could possibly be sensitive, so be cautious as you declare your "firm opinion." If you disagree with each other on the answers to the questions above, hold them until later in this session, when they may come up again.

2 On pages 2–4 of the book are different testimonial statements by wives who have attended a Love & Respect conference, or read Emerson's books:

"I never ever realized how important, how life-giving, respect was to my husband."

"Just a few days ago, I decided to tell my husband that I respect him. It felt so awkward to say the words, but I went for it and the reaction was unbelievable! . . . I watched his demeanor change right before my eyes."

"I wrote my husband two letters about why I respected him. I am amazed at how it has softened him in his response to me."

"I GOT IT! God granted me the power of this revelation of respecting my husband . . . [it] has changed everything . . . my approach, my response, my relationship to God and my husband."

From your point of view as a spouse, what do these statements say to you?

 As a husband I think:

As a wife I think:

 Compare your answers and talk about what you have covered so far. Some couples may find it easier to talk than others—do not force it; be sensitive to each other's feelings. Your study is just getting started, and you should have many good sharing times as you get farther into this workbook.

---

3 In an introduction to Part One (page 6), Emerson writes:
"I wrote this book out of desperation that was turned into inspiration. As a pastor, I counseled married couples and could not solve their problems. The major problem heard from wives was, 'He doesn't love me.' Wives are made to love, want to love and expect love. Many husbands fail to deliver. But as I kept studying Scripture and counseling couples, I finally saw the other half of the equation. Husbands weren't saying it much, but they were thinking, *She doesn't respect me.* Husbands are made to be respected, want respect, and expect respect. Many wives fail to deliver. The result is that five out of ten marriages land in divorce court (and that includes evangelical Christians).

"As I wrestled with the problem, I finally saw a connection: without love from him, she reacts without respect; without respect from her, he reacts without love. Around and around it goes. I call it the Crazy Cycle—marital craziness that has thousands of couples in its grip."

You will be learning and talking about the Crazy Cycle a lot more as this study progresses, but for now, understand that Crazy Cycles come in all shapes and sizes, as Emerson's daily mail attests. One man caught in a severe Crazy Cycle wrote:

"We were in the middle of one of our fights . . . . My wife was saying things that made me fume. She had no respect for me at all. I knew she loved me but her belligerence was too much. Fed up, I turned and went into my computer room. I left her screaming in the kitchen."

Granted, the above letter describes a marriage with the Crazy Cycle out of control. But there are other ways to be on the Crazy Cycle or to start one. Here are three more examples, based on mail Emerson has received:

A husband and wife are looking at jewelry together while shopping. The husband points excitedly and says, "Look, honey, I think those earrings are what you're looking for!" Her condescending response: "No, they aren't! Those are yellow gold and I don't like yellow gold; I want white gold!"

A wife greets her husband as he comes in from work. She wants to share what happened that day while she visited a friend. He cuts her short with: "Don't bother me. Traffic was a nightmare. I just want to kick back and watch the news until dinner."

A husband and wife have had a disagreement (the same one they usually have). She wants to talk about it; he clams up. As she badgers him to share his feelings, he picks up a newspaper and is soon engrossed in the sports page.

Choose one or more of the situations reported above. What is going on? Why could the husband feel disrespected or the wife feel unloved?

Compare notes on the examples above of how the Crazy Cycle can start up (or just keep going). If you don't seem to have a lot to discuss at this point, move on. You are just getting introduced to what the Crazy Cycle is and how it affects marriages.

4 What is your response to the term, Crazy Cycle? Does it seem to apply to your marriage—at least some of the time?

___ YES   ___ NO   ___ MAYBE

I think:

Check any of the following that apply.

I see the Crazy Cycle starting up when:

___ a. My spouse appears unreasonable

___ b. I appear unreasonable

___ c. My spouse doesn't make sense

___ d. I don't make sense

___ e. My spouse is harsh and/or critical

___ f. I am harsh and/or critical

___ g. My spouse is inconsiderate

___ h. I am inconsiderate

___ i. We argue about sex, money, in-laws, or _____

___ j. My spouse won't talk

___ k. I won't talk

___ l. My spouse talks too much

___ m. I talk too much

___ n. Other (describe your experience or viewpoint):

 Share your answers. Take note of what each of you has checked, but do not get into a lengthy discussion at this time. The main idea is that you both recognize how either of you could start the Crazy Cycle.

---

5 In 1 Corinthians 7:28 the apostle Paul writes: "Those who marry will face many troubles in this life, and I want to spare you this" (NIV). Did you ever stop to think that all married couples will have trouble? In other words, all married couples take a spin on the Crazy Cycle from time to time. Should couples conclude they have a bad marriage simply because they sometimes have troubles and things get a bit crazy? (Additional commentary is available in *Workbook* Appendix VI.)

Share ideas on what each of you thinks about Emerson's claim that there will always be "trouble" of some kind to deal with in marriage. It may be small, it may be huge, but trouble is something that does come up from time to time.

6 In Chapter One, Emerson recounts his early life and first years of marriage as he and Sarah rode the Crazy Cycle. Reread the story of "The Jean Jacket 'Disagreement'" (pages 9–10) and analyze what Emerson learned. What was Sarah feeling? What was Emerson feeling?

 Compare what you wrote down. Can either of you relate to this story? Have you had similar things happen?

7 During an argument after attending a Bible study (book pages 10–11), Emerson responds to Sarah's criticisms by saying: "Sarah, you can be right but wrong at the top of your voice." Does this statement ring a bell for you? Is your spouse ever right but wrong at the top of his/her voice? Are you ever right but wrong at the top of your voice? How does this keep the Crazy Cycle spinning?

As you discuss this question with each other, the wisest approach is not to accuse your spouse, but to confess the times when you may have been "right but wrong at the top of your voice."

8 Read the story of "And Then I Forgot Her Birthday" (book page 12). Has something like this happened in your marriage? Did you feel unloved or disrespected? Did your spouse? Think back and describe what happened as you remember it.

Recalling a forgotten birthday may not make much difference to him, but it will to her. If a husband is the one at fault, he would do well to apologize. For more on how important birthdays and anniversaries are to wives, see Session Eight, page 115.

9 On pages 13–14 Emerson describes a pattern in his marriage of "Loving Times and Spats of Ugliness." He and Sarah love each other, but they still irritate each other in certain ways—even to this day. Can you relate to their experience? In what way?

This is another question where you should go easy on each other. Try to identify what happens when the positive times turn negative. Are certain words said? Are certain things done or not done? Always remember the key questions: Does she feel loved? Does he feel respected?

---

10 In Song of Solomon 2:15, the lovers resolve to "Catch the foxes . . . the little foxes that are ruining the vineyards." In other words, they don't want anything to spoil their relationship. What are some "little foxes" that threaten to spoil your marriage and keep the Crazy Cycle rolling along?

Though we will have "trouble" in marriage (1 Corinthians 7:28), that doesn't mean we should assume trouble is always inevitable. Some trouble can be caused because we have not dealt with the "little foxes" that we know are there. What could you do to reduce some of the crazy negativity that causes unnecessary trouble? Write down some different steps you can take to drive out the "little foxes."

Share ideas on how to go "fox hunting." Each spouse will do well to think of things he or she needs to do, not what the other spouse needs to do.

---

11 In "The 'Secret' Hidden in Ephesians 5:33" (book pages 14–15), Emerson explains how God helped him see the secret to defeating the Crazy Cycle. This secret is in Ephesians 5:33 (NIV):

However, each one of you also must love his wife as he loves himself, and the wife must respect her husband.

In "How God Revealed the Love & Respect Connection" (book pages 15–17), Emerson explains how his study of Ephesians 5:33 began to show him a definite link between love and respect. He realized that a husband is to obey the command to love even if his wife does not obey the command to respect, and a wife is to obey the command to respect even if the husband does not obey the command to love. As Emerson saw it, Ephesians 5:33 didn't leave much wiggle room. A husband can't say, "I will love my wife after she respects me." Nor can a wife say, "I will respect my husband after he loves me" (see page 16). A husband's love for his wife must be unconditional, and a wife's respect for her husband must also be unconditional.

What do you think? Is there any "wiggle room" in Ephesians 5:33? Many wives believe (some with good reason) that their husbands don't deserve respect. What is Paul saying to wives who may feel like this deep down? (Additional commentary available in *Workbook* Appendix VI.)

Keep in mind each other's comfort zone. (For example, some spouses like discussing the meaning of the Greek more than others.) The key point Emerson is making is Ephesians 5:33 clearly teaches that husbands must unconditionally love their wives and wives must unconditionally respect their husbands. This can be new and striking information for a wife, so the husband should be sensitive to her need to process this idea over time.

---

12 For more on the concept of unconditional respect, read "Why Love & Respect Are Primary Needs" (book pages 17–19). See especially pages 18–19, which give additional comment on Ephesians 5:33 and then show how 1 Peter 3:1–2 also teaches unconditional respect for husbands. What kind of a husband is Peter talking about? How can a wife feel respect for a man who does not believe, or who is not treating her lovingly? Is she supposed to feel respect, or is Peter asking her to do something else? Write your thoughts below. (For additional interpretation of 1 Peter 3:1 and its application to husbands, see *Workbook* Appendix II.)

 As you share answers, you may want to just touch on this question. To go into it in depth (see *Workbook* Appendix II) may be something you want to do at another time. The key point is that 1 Peter 3:1 is a cross-reference support to Ephesians 5:33. Both passages teach unconditional respect for the husband by the wife.

13 On page 16 of *Love & Respect*, Emerson relates that he still did not totally understand the Love & Respect Connection until God guided him to see that it is a connection that can be strained or even broken. Without love she reacts without respect, and without respect, he reacts without love—the Crazy Cycle.

Read pages 15–16 again to be sure you follow Emerson's reasoning. Does it make sense? Why or why not? How do his ideas apply to your marriage? Husband, do you think you understand how to love your wife? Wife, are you certain you understand how to respect your husband? What are some examples of how you believe you are doing this?

 I love my wife by:

 I respect my husband when I:

You can take one of two approaches on this question:

- Keep your answer to yourself at this point and use it as your personal checkpoint on how you are treating your spouse.

- Share your answer with your spouse and get his or her feedback. Try to give each other positive suggestions and encouragement whenever possible.

---

14 On page 20, Emerson describes and illustrates the "life-changing decision" he and Sarah have both made. He has decided to believe that no matter what Sarah says or does, she does not have evil intentions. She might have a nasty or peevish moment but deep in her heart she intends to do good. She may come across in a way that seems disrespectful to Emerson, but that is not her real purpose. And Sarah has decided to believe that, no matter what Emerson says or does, he does not intend, deep in his heart, ill will toward her. He may come across in an angry way, and give her a cold stare that seems unloving, but his real purpose is not to be uncaring. (See his accounts on pages 20–22 of the book concerning peppered eggs and wet towels to see how this plays out in their marriage.)

Take a few minutes to end your study of Session One by thinking and praying about a woman's deep need for love and a man's deep need for respect. Consider how the decision Emerson describes on page 20 of the book applies to you. If you are studying alone, you may be in one of several situations: You may be trying to find answers for your marriage, but your spouse isn't interested in studying anything with you at this point. You would like to decide that no matter what your spouse says or does, deep down your spouse loves (or respects) you, but you aren't quite sure this is always true. In fact, at this point you may be thinking you need more time and more study of how love and respect work in a marriage. Emerson has many more insights to share, beginning with Session Two, which covers why men and women are so different, and which often causes communication problems.

Talk about what this chapter has been saying to both of you. Share any "light bulb moments," questions, or concerns you may have. Perhaps you are ready to make the same decision about each other's good intentions that Emerson and Sarah have made (see book page 20). Perhaps one of you isn't quite ready. Wives, in particular, if your husband seems unwilling or uncomfortable about taking this step so early in your study together, do not be critical or disrespectful. Do not rush something like this. Be willing to pray and think about it. Both of you may need more time, or more information about the Crazy Cycle and why people can't seem to slow it down. As Emerson says, there is much more he wants to tell you. In Session Two he will talk about how husbands and wives can learn to communicate, despite their differences as men and women.

A JOURNAL OF MY JOURNEY TO LOVE & RESPECT

Every session will conclude with Emerson's meditations on foundational Scripture passages cited in *Love & Respect*. The space provided below for you to interact with his observations will allow you to create a personal journal of your journey to love and respect. By the time you finish this workbook, you'll have a permanent record of your growth and development as an individual or as a couple.

SCRIPTURE MEDITATIONS

1. "Enjoy life with the woman whom you love" (Ecclesiastes 9:9). When on the Crazy Cycle, many a husband wants to throw up his hands in defeat. Does Ecclesiastes 9:9 suggest that a husband could influence the emotional temperature of his marriage more than he might think? As a husband, what might you do for or with your wife in the next several hours that is wholesome and enjoyable—something to ignite a smile in both of you?

2. The Crazy Cycle is, indeed, "the evil of folly and the foolishness of madness" (Ecclesiastes 7:25). When the Bible speaks of "madness," it does not refer to someone who is mentally deranged. This person has a sound mind, but he or she is acting or reacting in ways that God deems foolish, unfruitful, even "crazy." Think about it: how crazy is it for a husband to react in unloving ways when feeling disrespected? How crazy is it for a wife to react in disrespectful ways when feeling unloved? You might say, "But it's natural to react sometimes in an unloving or disrespectful way." Natural, yes, but effective, no. What do unloving or disrespectful reactions do to the spirit of a spouse?

3. In Ephesians 5:33, Paul writes: "Each one of you also must love his wife as he loves himself, and the wife must respect her husband" (NIV). Because Ephesians 5 contains what is considered the greatest treatise in the Bible on marriage, it is safe to say that Ephesians 5:33 is, in effect, God's "last word" to us on this subject. But God's last word on marriage won't help you if it isn't heard. Do you believe that if, as a couple, you apply love and respect to your marriage you will experience marriage in the way God intended? Do you believe love and respect will guide the two of you in responding correctly to troubles that are bound to come to your marriage? Do you believe that at the end of your life, after living out love and respect, you will be able to pray: "Thank You, Lord, for showing me Your simple plan for marriage"? (Put down your honest thoughts here. If you have any doubts write them out, then give them to God in prayer.)

My current thoughts about our marriage:

SESSION TWO

In preparation for this session, read Chapter Two in *Love & Respect*, "To Communicate, Decipher the Code." The following questions are for use in individual study, or study by a husband and wife together. Remember to answer all unmarked questions first, then answer questions marked by the male or female icon (whichever applies to you). Finally, answer the questions with the couple icon, if you're studying with your mate. (Suggestions for using this workbook with a group are in *Workbook* Appendix I, page 201.)

Questions for Chapter Two

1 On page 25, Emerson opens Chapter Two by asserting that husbands and wives communicate in "code" and must learn how to decipher the messages they send each other. What do you think?

How often does your spouse seem to communicate in a "code" that is hard to decipher or understand?
CONSTANTLY ___ OFTEN ___ NOW AND THEN ___ SELDOM ___

Discuss this question gently and sensitively, particularly if your answers fall in the "constantly" or "often" range. If you do have a communication problem, this session is designed to get you talking about it and learning how to work on it. Guard against getting into an argument about "who communicates the worst."

2 Read the story of the "Tenth Anniversary Card" that turned out to be a birthday card (book pages 25–27.) When the wife responded in anger, what coded message was she sending to her husband? What coded message was he sending to his wife when he responded defensively by saying, "I made an honest mistake; give me a break"? How did they start the evening anticipating a wonderful tenth anniversary and wind up on the Crazy Cycle?

Compare notes with your spouse (and with Emerson's additional commentary on Question 7 found in *Workbook* Appendix VI). Talk about how the couple wound up on the Crazy Cycle on a night when they should have been celebrating.

3 Read the story that starts under the heading, "All You Want Me for Is Sex!" (book pages 27–29). What message was the wife sending in code as she reeled off a barrage of problems, appointments, and

assignments the minute her husband returned from his trip? What message was the husband sending in code when he said sarcastically, "Great to see you after a week"?

———————

4 Later, when this same husband and wife go to bed after their exhausting day, what coded messages do they send each other? What mistakes do they make in doing so? Why can't either spouse decipher the other's code? How did they get on the Crazy Cycle?

Compare your answers to Questions 3 and 4. If you aren't sure you have identified the encoded messages correctly, hold them for discussion in Question 7, where Emerson will review this story and make comments on what the encoded messages meant.

———————

5 Under "Craziness—Just Keep Flipping the Light Switch" (book page 29), Emerson compares the Crazy Cycle to mindlessly flipping a light switch over and over when the light won't come on. Instead of figuring out the problem, you just keep flipping that switch. Emerson's point is simple: "Craziness happens when we keep doing the same things over and over with the same ill effect." What things do you or your spouse do over and over that help start you both on the Crazy Cycle?

 Go easy with each other when discussing this question. Confess your faults, not your spouse's. Try to have some fun with this, and don't call each other "crazy." The truth is, any couple can get on the Crazy Cycle together, and you must work together to slow it down and stop it.

6 In "Why Do Couples Communicate in Code?" (book page 30), Emerson paraphrases a well-known explanation of why and how we send messages in code and don't communicate: "What I say is not what you hear, and what you think you heard is not what I meant at all." Read the story about Emerson and Sarah almost getting into a serious argument about who was listening to what on the radio. How did Emerson finally break the codes they were sending and stop the problem from escalating?

You can learn a lot about communicating as you discuss your answers to this question. The way Emerson stopped the Crazy Cycle from spinning was to realize he was not being clear (and not very loving either). Once he broke the pattern of miscommunication, he and Sarah were able to understand each other and prevent sparks from becoming a fire.

7 Read the section titled, "When the Issue Isn't the Issue" (book pages 31–32). What was the real issue when the husband gave the wife the wrong kind of greeting card?

What was the real issue as the businessman's wife turned him down when he wanted sex?

Compare your answers. Did you agree that the real issue in these stories, as it usually is in all marital arguments or fights, is love and respect? She doesn't feel loved or she desperately needs a kiss or a hug—something to assure her she is loved. And he doesn't feel respected. He needs to feel he is appreciated and that he is someone his wife looks up to, not down upon. For interpretation of the encoded messages the spouses were sending each other in each story, see additional commentary on Question 7 in *Workbook* Appendix VI.

Are you beginning to see the importance of "decoding" each other when one or both of you sounds irritated, angry, or sarcastic? No spouse can decode his or her mate perfectly, but it is vital to understand that the need to decode is always there, and the more you both work on doing it, the better your communication will be.

---

8 In "We're as Different as Pink and Blue" (book pages 32–35), how is male-female communication described? According to Emerson, women see the world through _____ sunglasses and hear with _____ hearing aids. Men see the world through _____ sunglasses and hear with _____ hearing aids. Why is it important to understand these differences? How could understanding their pink and blue perspectives have helped the couple whose tenth anniversary was spoiled by the wrong kind of greeting card or the couple who reconnected so badly after his week on the road?

Compare your answers, as well as your respective under-standings of the pink and blue analogy. This question is really a continuation of Question 7. Obviously, the pink and blue perspectives of the wife and husband have everything to do with the kinds of codes they send and the decoding that needs to be done. Try working together to re-create each story to make it come out with a happy ending, or at least with the Crazy Cycle slowing down and even stopping. In either story, what might the husband have said or done that would have felt more loving to the wife? What might the wife have said or done that would have felt more respect-ful to the husband?

---

9 Emerson constantly receives letters from spouses who finally "get it" concerning the deep need in wives for love and the deep need in husbands for respect. Following is one such letter, from a wife, who came to see clearly the difference between "pink" and "blue":

I read your book this week and I have been convicted. I have always felt that if I just loved my husband enough, he would come around and be the kind of man my father was. Then God proceeded to show me the many ways I have been disrespectful towards my husband—and my father!

I now see that most of the arguments have been started by me, in my mis-understanding of the way my husband thinks. I have been arrogant and self-righteous in my misguided attempts at communication in hopes of bringing us together. What a fool I've been! It sounds so dumb when I write it down!

I wrote him a letter today in apology and my desire to change. He called to say, "It's okay, it was nothing!" What a man!

I never saw my disrespect as disobedience to Christ before. That really hurt. I know now what a grievous sin it is and I pray for grace and help to change. Thank you for this liberating truth.

Grace and peace to you and may I see and hear in blue!

What has this wife understood? What does she mean when she says: ". . . may I hear and see in blue!"?

Here's another letter, from a husband who also finally "got it." He and his wife had started going to a counselor before they attended a Love & Respect Conference, and they continued to go afterward as they tried to apply love and respect principles. He writes:

Recently, I had forgotten to do something for my wife. She expressed hurt and anger toward me at the next [counseling] session. Our counselor concluded that I have not been "hearing" her because I react in a "defensive" way to her comments, and this has hurt her and caused her to shut down. He has challenged me to learn her "language" [pink] so that I will "hear" her. Subsequently, she will melt and then respond with respect. . . .

I accept my divine command to unconditionally love my wife through any technique that works. I still do fall into the Crazy Cycle, but I try my best to stay off of it. I do intend to sign up for "pink language lessons."

What has this husband understood? What does he mean when he says he wants to "sign up for 'pink language' lessons"?

You may wish to discuss one or both of these letters at length. In each case the spouse writing the letter has gotten the point: "pink" and "blue" must try to see and hear in the other color. When pink or blue sees it only one way, the Crazy Cycle will keep on spinning. If both spouses are agreed, now would be a good time to pledge to each other respectively:

As a wife, I want to see and hear in blue a lot more.

As a husband, I want to see and hear in pink a lot more.

10 What does Emerson mean near the bottom of book page 34 when he sums up the wrong anniversary card debacle by saying: ". . . and so two essentially good-willed people wound up spinning on the Crazy Cycle with no clue about how to slow it down or stop it"? How does he define *good-willed* on the top of page 35? Put his definition in your own words beginning with: "My spouse . . ."

Compare your definitions of *good-willed*. This term will be popping up again and again in this study. The key point to remember is that no matter how nasty, irritating, or unreasonable your good-willed spouse is, he or she does not mean to hurt you in the ultimate, long-range sense. Oh, there may be some intent to hurt on a short-range basis, but this is not what your spouse really wants. What every spouse wants is love for her and respect for him. (For more on the concept of "good will" and questions like: "How can a sinful person have good will?" go to http://loveandrespect.com/pearl/.)

---

11 In "Scientific Research Confirms the Centrality of Love & Respect" (book pages 35–37), read the conclusions of marriage research expert John Gottman, who studied two thousand couples who had been married twenty to forty years to the same partner. What single factor stood out as a reason they stayed together for the long term?

_____ a. having enough money

_____ b. attending church regularly

_____ c. a loving, respectful tone to their conversations

_____ d. spending enough time together

Gottman adds that contempt is "perhaps the most corrosive force in marriage." Do you think he is right?

 Compare your answers. Talk about how contempt can hurt and how a loving, respectful tone can heal.

---

12 Read the analogy described under "You're Stepping on My Air Hose!" (book pages 37–38). Emerson pictures the wife with an air hose leading to a big tank labeled "Love." What happens when the husband does something to "step on her air hose"?

Which of the following statements are examples of how a husband can step on his wife's air hose?

    ____ a. "I'll do the dishes, honey. You had a rough day with the kids."

    ____ b. "Can't you get that kid to be quiet? I'm trying to get a few minutes rest."

    ____ c. "I know we planned to spend some time tonight talking, but the guys want to come over to play cards."

    ____ d. "Sorry I couldn't call sooner. The meeting ran late, but I should be home about 6:30."

 Compare your answers. These choices should be "no brainers" for both of you, but use this question to get into your own discussion of how a husband can step on his wife's air hose. (Try not to step on each other's air hose as you talk together.)

---

13 On book pages 37–38, Emerson continues his illustration by picturing the husband with an air hose leading to a big tank labeled "Respect." What happens if his wife happens to "step on his air hose"?

Which of the following statements are examples of how a wife can step on her husband's air hose?

___ a "The bills keep piling up. Why can't you bring in more money?"

___ b. "Honey, I know things are tight, and I'm so thankful that you get out there every day, working hard to make a way for us."

___ c. "Jane's husband doesn't lie around watching so much TV."

___ d. "I'm so grateful you like being home and being available when I need help."

You should find the right choices fairly easy to identify, but use the question to get into a discussion of what happens in your home. How can you step on each other's air hose, perhaps in all innocence?

---

14 In "Men Hear Criticism as Contempt; Women Feel Silence as Hostility" (book pages 38–40), Emerson gives valuable insight on just how pink and blue sunglasses and hearing aids can affect a marriage. List at least three statements or phrases that stand out for you, from your pink or blue point of view.

1.

2.

3.

Compare notes on what you find. Note that Emerson observes that spouses may have good will (they intend no evil toward each other), but because they don't decipher each other's code, she sees only his failure to love and he sees only her failure to respect. They lash out and the Crazy Cycle continues to spin! Talk about how to decipher each other's codes, how to slow and stop the Crazy Cycle. (For more ideas, see *Love & Respect* Appendix A, pages 305–7.)

---

15 The following is a letter from a wife who describes her life with her husband on the Crazy Cycle. As you read it, make notes on the following: Who is stepping on whose air hose and why? What starts this Crazy Cycle? What keeps it going?

We have been married for a long time . . . . We have difficult and challenging jobs and he feels that if I want to discuss something with him, somehow I think I know more than he does. I have never been a shrinking violet and the thing my husband hates about me is what my boss loves about me. I can be very aggressive and I get things done. Should I keep my mouth shut? It's getting worse because we don't seem to be able to come to any kind of agreement, which is distressing at the very least. I am losing hope because we don't ever seem to get anywhere. I try to talk and he stonewalls me; he tries to talk and I stonewall him. It goes nowhere.

My notes:

Talk about what you have noted in the letter above. How does the wife's "Type A Personality" step on her husband's air hose? What is his basic way of fighting back that steps on her air hose? What does their "he stonewalls me, I stonewall him" routine tell you about this couple?

---

16 On book page 40 Emerson gives the secret to at least start decoding your spouse's messages: "Whenever a wife is complaining, criticizing, or crying, she is sending her encoded message: 'I want your love!' And whenever a husband is speaking harshly or sometimes not speaking at all, he is sending his encoded message: 'I want your respect.'"

 How well do you decode your wife's complaints? Though not all of her complaints are cries for love (she can just be having a "bad hair day"), it helps to think first that her complaint might be rooted in her cry for love. Describe a time when you heard her cry for love underneath her complaint and responded lovingly. (If you can't think of any, just write your thoughts about how willing you are to listen better and decode her complaints.)

To complete this exercise, fill in the following: "The next time my wife complains or criticizes I will show her love by . . ."

How well do you decode your husband's actions or words when he needs respect? Silence or harshness are not always cries for respect, but they can be. Sometimes pride, or the inability to verbalize his need for respect can keep the need covered. Never forget that his "Respect Tank" is there and that you could be stepping on his air hose. Can you think of any times recently when you heard his cry for respect underneath his silence or harshness? (If you can't, just write your honest thoughts about how willing you are to decode his behavior and try to show respect.)

To complete this exercise, fill in the following: "The next time my husband appears unloving or harsh, I will show him respect by . . ."

 Go slowly as you compare what you have written. This could be sensitive, but the benefits are well worth it. One area to explore is how the messages one spouse is sending another could be misread. For example, when a wife complains or criticizes, it's possible that she is frustrated about something unknown to the husband. She is not necessarily feeling a husband's lack of love. Of course, it still doesn't hurt if a husband reaches out with a touch or a hug to say, "It's okay, I'm still here for you." On the other hand, a husband's lack of love can also be hard to read. Sometimes the "big, dumb buck" is not looking for respect; he's just being selfish, unaware, or ignorant of how to treat his wife. A good approach for both husbands and wives is in *Love & Respect* Appendix A, under "To communicate feelings . . ." (book page 306). Spouses should never say, "You're being unloving," or "You're being disrespectful." As calmly as possible, she can say, "That felt unloving," or he can say, "That felt disrespectful." Then go on from there as explained on page 306.

17 As you complete your personal study of Session Two, take some time to think and pray about the messages you may be sending your spouse in code (and vice versa). And as you pray, ask yourself some basic questions: when I see the spirit of my spouse deflating, do I understand that the issue is never the real issue, which is a lack of love and respect? Do I grasp the importance of "pink" and "blue"—how different my mate and I are? Am I fully aware of my "air hose" and how it can be stepped on? Am I fully aware of how I might be stepping on my spouse's "air hose"?

If necessary, review book pages 31–35 and pages 37–40. These ideas are simply put, but they are profound. How well you embrace and practice them will have everything to do with how well you play your part in stopping, or at least slowing, the Crazy Cycle.

Talk about what this chapter has been saying to both of you. Share any "light bulb moments," questions, or differing perceptions. Write down how well each of you responds to the following principles or concepts in this chapter (use a scale of 1–10, with 10 meaning "totally get it," as one way to measure your responses):

____ The issue at hand may not be the real issue.

____ Pink and Blue are very different.

___ Each of us has an air hose that can be stepped on by the other.

___ Her complaints can mean, "Please come across more lovingly!"

___ His withdrawal can mean, "Please come across more respectfully!"

Although Emerson's word pictures (pink and blue, air hose) are playful, they contain vital and practical truths. The better you understand and actually practice them, the better you will communicate with each other. Be aware that it may sound simple, but it is not. In Session Three, based on Chapters Three and Four of the book, Emerson will explain why.

A JOURNAL OF MY JOURNEY TO LOVE AND RESPECT

As part of your journal, every session includes a study of foundational scripture passages quoted in the margins or text of the book. As you interact with Emerson's meditations below, make notes as part of your journal. There is additional space at the end to record your current thoughts about your marriage and the progress you hope to make with this study.

SCRIPTURE MEDITATIONS

1. When counseling couples I often quote to them James 4:1: "What causes fights and quarrels among you?" (NIV). I point out that the apostle James wants each of us to evaluate why he or she is having conflicts—particularly if we are married. James continues: "You want something, but don't get it" (James 4:2 NIV). What happens when a spouse does not get love or respect? As a wife, if you feel unloved, what do you do to try to get your husband's love? Do any of these words or actions sometimes lead to quarrels? As a husband, if you feel disrespected, what do you do to get your wife's respect? Do unloving words or actions (or just stonewalling her) help? Evaluate what you have been doing to this point while on the Crazy Cycle. How effective is fighting and quarreling to get what you want?

2. Runaway divorce statistics reveal that ". . . insanity is in their hearts . . ." (Ecclesiastes 9:3). As a wife, when you do disrespectful things in

a misguided attempt to motivate your husband's love, has it ever occurred to you that this is a little bit crazy? How often each week do you go a bit "insane" in an effort to get your husband to love you more? As a husband, when you do unloving things to make your wife respect you more, does it ever occur to you, "I am acting a little nuts here"? How many times this past week did you say to yourself (consciously or unconsciously), "I am not going to show love to that woman until she starts respecting me more"? If you both continue with this sort of "insanity," how likely is it that you could be pushing your marriage over the edge? How long will it be before you become a divorce statistic?

3. What can happen when a husband tries to obey a command from God's heart? In Ephesians 5:33, Paul is not making a mere suggestion when he writes, ". . . each one of you also must love his wife as he loves himself" (NIV). A husband who took this verse seriously wrote to tell me, "The information God gave you is working all over in my life. I have seen the glow in [my wife's] eyes when I apply it and the defeat [and] the despair . . . when I fail to practice the principles you are trying to teach me through your material and God's word." Husband, what is Ephesians 5:33a for you? A command? Or a "suggestion"? Wife, read Ephesians 5:33b, which tells you to respect your husband. For you, is this a clear command, or a suggestion you can follow if he "earns" your respect?

My current thoughts about our marriage:

SESSION THREE

In preparation for this session, read Chapter Three, "Why She Won't Respect; Why He Won't Love" and Chapter Four, "What Men Fear Most Will Keep the Crazy Cycle Spinning." The following questions are for individual study, or study by husband and wife together. Remember to answer all unmarked questions first, then answer questions marked by the male or female icon (whichever applies to you). Finally, answer the questions with the couple icon, if you're studying with your mate. (Suggestions for anyone planning to use this study with a small group can be found in *Workbook* Appendix I, page 201.)

Questions for Chapter Three

So far you have been introduced to the Love and Respect Connection and the Crazy Cycle. You have learned about "pink" and "blue" and differences between men and women. You know how to be more careful about stepping on your spouse's air hose. You understand the dynamics of how the Crazy Cycle can affect a marriage: When she feels unloved, she can react in ways that feel disrespectful to him. When he feels disrespected, he can react in ways that feel unloving to her. And around and around they go. Nobody wants to be on the Crazy Cycle, even for a short time. Some couples, unfortunately, have been on it for years. Getting off and staying off is not as easy as you might think. In the two chapters of *Love & Respect* covered in this session, you will dig a little deeper into why wives find it hard to respect and why husbands in turn won't love.

1 No one has ever expressed the Crazy Cycle dilemma better than the husband whose letter appears on pages 41–42 of *Love & Respect*. Read his letter carefully. What do you hear him saying from deep within his soul? What is his wife saying about him and their marriage? What do you think it does to this man to hear, "You're not the man I thought you were"?

Compare notes on how you think a husband might feel when told, "You're not the man I thought you were." Then, to add a "fair and balanced" tone to your discussion, also consider this question: "What do you think it does to a woman when her husband angrily delivers his own message, which blames her for their problems?"

2 Read "Unconditional Respect—An Oxymoron?" (book pages 42–44). In his many years of counseling, Emerson has often heard women say they have never heard the two words "unconditional respect" put together in the context of a relationship (page 43). To these women unconditional respect sounds like an oxymoron (a term created by putting together two words that appear to be incongruous or contradictory). Why do you think so many women feel this way?

Choose from the following ideas, or write your own:

    ___ a. They think respect is something a husband has to earn.

    ___ b. They think husbands are so unloving, they don't deserve respect.

    ___ c. They think that giving a husband unconditional respect is giving him license to do anything he wants.

    ___ d. I think:

Discuss the answers you chose above. You may also want to tackle questions like the following: why does telling a husband he has to earn his wife's respect put him in a lose-lose situation? What is the difference between showing respect and feeling respect? Is it okay for a wife to show respect, even though she doesn't feel respect? What do facial expressions and tone of voice have to do with how a wife shows her husband unconditional respect?

3 In "It All Goes Back to Pink and Blue" (book page 45), a wife is quoted: "We think so differently, I don't even relate to what he considers respect (or the lack of it)." How could this wife adjust her pink sunglasses and pink hearing aids so she might begin to understand her husband's need for respect? Would it help if she remembered her husband's need for respect is just as great as her need for love? At the same time, how could this woman's husband adjust his blue sunglasses and hearing aids? How crucial is it that he respond patiently to his wife's struggle with the new idea of "unconditional respect" for him, especially if he has done things that deeply hurt her? Write your thoughts here and on the next page:

 Talk about your respective perceptions of "respect." What positive things could happen if each of you made a slight adjustment?

4 Continuing on book page 45, Emerson admits that for years as a pastor he went along with the cultural emphasis on unconditional love by the husband for the wife as the key to a good marriage. When he switched his message and started giving equal weight to unconditional respect for husbands, he got a mixed reception. One women's group actually fired him after he taught two sessions! They wanted someone to speak on "How to Love Your Husband." What they failed to see was that the way for a wife to fully love her husband is to respect him in ways that are meaningful to him. What do you think this might entail? How can a woman respect her husband in meaningful ways? When a wife attempts to show this kind of respect, what can a husband do in response to show his appreciation? Put your thoughts in writing:

Share what you have written. If either or both of you are struggling a bit with the concept of a man's deep need for respect, be sensitive to each other. It also might help to use some of the suggestions under "Things to say to lighten up the relationship," *Love & Respect* Appendix A, page 307.

5 In "Respect Is a Man's Deepest Value" (book pages 49–52), Emerson reports on a national survey in which 400 men were asked which they could endure better: (a) to be left alone and unloved in the world, or (b) to feel inadequate and disrespected by everyone. Seventy-four percent said they would prefer being left alone and unloved over feeling inadequate and disrespected (see page 49).

Would you have been among the 74 percent who believed the more negative experience would be feeling inadequate and disrespected? Why or why not?

 Do the results of this survey question surprise you? Why or why not?

 Compare your answers and also talk about Emerson's analogy (bottom of book page 49) in which he compares love and respect to food and water. Do you agree with his statement, "For men, love is like food, and respect is like water"? If love is like food (important) and respect is like water (even more important), what does this suggest for your marriage?

6 Emerson is often asked if there is any passage in Scripture where men are instructed to respect their wives as well as love them. Under "Husbands Are to Value Wives as Equals" (book pages 52–54), he cites 1 Peter 3:7, where Peter tells the husband to show his wife honor as ". . . a fellow heir of the grace of life." How does Emerson interpret this phrase (see last paragraph, page 52)? How does Galatians 3:28 teach the same idea?

Discuss the concept that although husband and wife are very different, as male and female they are equal in the eyes of God (see Galatians 3:28). How might a husband appear to forget this equality and unintentionally come across to his wife in a condescending manner? What does his wife feel during such moments? What practical things can a husband do to show he values his wife as his equal?

7 On book page 53 Emerson develops the concept that women are to be first in importance, while men are to be first among equals. As you think about how comfortable you are with these "firsts," consider these questions:

 Do you think your wife longs to be first in importance because she is a prima donna or because she wants to respond, give, and serve?

Do most husbands want to be seen as first among equals because they believe it is their "right" to dominate, or because they believe it is their responsibility to lead, protect, and even die for their family?

 Compare your answers. In the second paragraph, book page 54, Emerson states: "When he honors her as first in importance and she respects him as first among equals, their marriage works." Do you think he is right? Are you willing to make this a major goal in your marriage? Is your spouse?

8 Under "Husbands: Do Not Say, 'I Told You So!'" (book page 54), Emerson cautions husbands that the concept of unconditional respect can be a "huge piece of information" for a wife to process. Why should a husband *never* say, "I told you so!" or try to use unconditional respect as a weapon?

Talk about what each of you is thinking and feeling. Obviously, a wise husband will not "rub it in" if his wife is struggling to process what Scripture teaches. Also read together on book page 55 the two letters from husbands after they attended a Love and Respect Conference. What insights did each man receive, and how did this information affect his attitude toward his wife?

Questions for Chapter Four

9 As he starts Chapter Four on page 57 of the book, Emerson discusses a powerful factor that can keep the Crazy Cycle spinning: the male fear of criticism, and especially contempt. Men may look powerful and impervious to their wives' words, but underneath they are very vulnerable. The male species is often labeled as the one that likes to get into fights, and as Emerson pointed out in Chapter Three, it is the male who primarily responds to the call to war, to protect home and family. Nonetheless, males do not handle conflict with their wives well at all when they feel disrespected (see survey questions results, page 58). Emerson writes: "Men know deep down that their wives love them, but they are not at all sure that their wives respect them." Are men being overly sensitive or perhaps a bit arrogant by being so concerned about being respected? Write down what you honestly think:

Share what you wrote with each other. Also read together Emerson's idea that among men there is an "honor code"— from boyhood men learn there are certain things men just don't say to one another. A woman will talk to a husband in the home in a way that a man would never talk to him. "He can't believe she can be so belligerent, so disrespectful" (bottom of book page 59). Does your experience as a husband bear this out? As a wife, do you think you ever talk to your husband in a "belligerent" manner?

10 Read "Are You a Criticizer or a Stonewaller?" (book pages 60–61), then answer these questions: Who is the criticizer and who is the stonewaller in your marriage? Why do men (as a rule) stonewall their wives?

This can be a delicate question for a husband and wife to discuss, so go easy on each other. Be sure you both define *stonewalling* the same way. Simply put, stonewalling is refusing to talk, period.

11 On book pages 61–62, "How Women Deal with Conflict Between Themselves" describes a typical female approach to conflict with another female, like a best girlfriend. Why do a wife's complaints and criticisms, expressed during conflicts with her husband, seldom result in shared sorrow, hugs, and even laughter as often happens with a best girlfriend? Choose from one of the ideas below, then add your own thoughts:

____ a. Husbands are too proud to admit they are wrong.

____ b. Husbands don't see their wives' deeper goal of reconciliation.

____ c. Husbands clam up because ongoing criticism feels like contempt.

___ d. Wives are more critical and judgmental of their husbands than of their girlfriends.

___ e. I think:

Share your answers. How do your perceptions differ? Do you see examples of "pink" (her viewpoint) and "blue" (his viewpoint)? Why is it obviously not a good idea for a wife to deal with her husband in the same way she deals with a best girlfriend?

12 In "A Wife's Self-Image May Depend on Her Husband's Approval" (book pages 62–63), read the letter from the wife who realizes that negative confrontation (being way too demanding and critical of her husband) doesn't work. As you analyze her confession of mistakes, what would you suggest that might work much better?

Compare your findings on the wife's letter. Discussing this question can be a real opportunity to work together positively to understand how Love and Respect principles apply to your marriage. Can both of you fill in the Crazy Cycle maxim below, without going to the diagram on page 5 of *Love & Respect?*

Without _____ she reacts without _____.

and

Without _____ he reacts without _____.

---

13 Read "A Wife's Scolding Can Start the Crazy Cycle" (book pages 63–66). Why do wives often make the innocent mistake of scolding (or mothering) their husbands?

Talk about any "scolding" that might be going on in your marriage. Husband, be gentle in describing what you might think is scolding. Wife, try not to be defensive if he labels what you think are "constructive comments" as scolding. How can the male need for unconditional respect cause him to interpret certain comments by his wife as "scolding"? (For ideas on what the wife can do, see Question 14 below.)

14 To avoid sounding like she is scolding, which of the following questions is the best one for a wife to ask herself as she interacts with her husband?

_____ a. Is what I am about to say/do going to let him know that we are equals and he cannot treat me as "lesser than"?

_____ b. Is what I am about to say/do going to come across as loving or unloving?

_____ c. Is what I am about to say/do going to come across as respectful or disrespectful?

 Talk about which response on the previous page is the best question for a wife to ask. Then identify the best question for a husband to ask himself before interacting with his wife. (See *Love & Respect* Appendix A, page 305, under "Always Ask Yourself." Also go over the "Taboos" on page 307.)

15 On book page 66 is an account of how one woman asked her husband: "Do you want me to tell you I love you or respect you?" What was his answer?

At this point in the study, are you comfortable with asking your husband this same question?
YES___ NO___ NOT SURE_____

What would be your answer? Love_____ Respect_____

If you feel comfortable doing so, share your answers and feelings. If a husband answers "Respect," he should try to help his wife understand without shaming her. Put a "U" next to any statements below that would help a wife Understand and a "D" next to any statements that would put her on the defensive.

_____ The reason I am so unloving is because you are so disrespectful.

_____ I'm sure you love me, but I don't always have assurance you respect me.

_____ I know you don't intend to be disrespectful, but sometimes you come across as disrespectful. At those moments I know I should love you anyway, but I don't know how and it's safer to stonewall.

_____ If you would just meet my need for respect, this marriage would be great.

_____ I couldn't care less about your love; just give me respect.

_____ I know you often feel I don't deserve respect, and you're right. But I need you to respect who I am deep down, even though on the surface I'm somebody neither one of us likes at times.

---

16 In "So That's It . . . I Need Respect!" (book pages 67–69), analyze the letter on page 68 from a wife whose husband strayed into an affair. Without excusing the husband's wrongdoing, what were some reasons he strayed? What do these reasons suggest about ways to respect a husband?

Discuss the contents of the letter. As a wife you may be tempted to dismiss its many valuable tips because an adulteress is described as using her wiles to seduce the husband. This would be a mistake. What is wrong with seeing your husband as handsome, witty, and intelligent? Obviously all this can be overdone, but there are suggestions here for how a wife can respect her husband and give his ego a respectful, but not phony, boost. At the same time, there is a warning here for both spouses. A wife may not be tempted in the same way her husband can be tempted, but she is vulnerable nonetheless. The wise husband pays attention to his wife's vulnerabilities and never ignores or belittles them. Many a wife has been drawn into an affair because she felt lonely and unloved. The best way to protect your marriage from an affair is love and respect—love for her, respect for him.

---

17 Read the section, "All This Should Be Obvious, Right?" (book pages 69–71). How true does the following statement at the very bottom of page 69 sound to you: "We easily see what is done to us before we see what we are doing to our mate"?

VERY TRUE ____   SOMEWHAT TRUE____   NOT TRUE AT ALL ____

Does this saying remind you of any scripture passages (see Matthew 7:12; Luke 6:31)? Why do husbands and wives often find it hardest to practice the Golden Rule with each other?

Talk about what it means for a Love and Respect couple to practice the "Love and Respect Golden Rule": the wife should respect her husband as she wants to be loved; the husband should love his wife as he wants to be respected. Why is practicing this particular rule difficult? How can you help each other do it more consistently? (For some good review, see Chapter Two in *Love & Respect*.)

18 On book page 71 Emerson states that he believes married couples are at a crossroads. Then he asks some penetrating questions. These questions appear below, restated to apply directly to you and your spouse:

Will you appreciate your husband's need for respect, or will you denounce his feelings? Will you discover that the best way to love a husband is by respecting him in ways that are meaningful to him? Or will you focus on what you might feel is the key to a happy marriage—your womanly feelings—and dismiss his needs as antiquated chauvinism or male arrogance?

Will you appreciate your wife's need for love or just continue to ignore her feelings? Will you discover the best way to love your wife is to look beyond her criticisms and complaints to see why she isn't feeling loved? Or will you just cower before her apparent contempt and retreat to the shelter of your "stone wall?"

Spend some time in prayer as you answer these questions. It may be that you and your spouse are at the crossroads Emerson mentions. Will you take the fork labeled "Love and Respect?" Read the letter from the wife who, together with her husband, took that fork (book page 72). At this point in your study, are you gaining confidence that the simple message of *Love & Respect* really can work? Why or why not?

 The many questions above can be heavy for both of you to deal with, but they can pay off handsomely in slowing and stopping the Crazy Cycle. Be honest, but sensitive to each other and share from the heart.

19 On book page 72, Emerson closes the chapter by admitting that at times he may sound like he is hammering wives for their lack of unconditional respect for their husbands. He continues: "But I'm not trying to hammer wives—I'm trying to help them, because I know how pivotal the wife's respect can be in slowing down the Crazy Cycle. Yes, many men are unloving clods to one degree or another, but they can change. In fact, many of them want to change, and the best way to get them to change is treating them with unconditional respect."

Respond to the above paragraph from your point of view as a wife or a husband. Do you think Emerson is trying to help wives, not hammer them?

YES ___ NO ___

NOT COMPLETELY SURE, NEED TO KNOW MORE ___

I think . . .

Give this question some careful thought and discussion. Husband, if your wife is still feeling a little "hammered" even after reading Emerson's assurances that he is really trying to help, listen to what she is saying and do not simply say things like, "You're foolish to worry," or, worse, "You may feel hammered, but it's what you needed to hear." Tell her that you want to be a more loving husband, and her respect can do nothing but help you achieve that goal.

20 As you complete this session, it may be a good time to review Question 18 and the answers you gave. Are you truly ready to take the fork in the road labeled "Love and Respect"? Write down your honest feelings at this point:

You may feel the need to go over the heavy questions in Question 18 and talk about them a little more. Go slowly with this. Be sensitive to each other and honor any doubts or questions either of you may have. You may want to go back over Question 19 as well. Wives need understanding as they process what unconditional respect means to them and how they should act toward their husbands. Even though Emerson assures wives he is trying to help, not hammer, them, they may still feel a bit sensitive. Pray together about your study so far and your marriage. The Crazy Cycle is not easily slowed or stopped. It can be hard work, so let God help.

A JOURNAL OF MY JOURNEY
TO LOVE AND RESPECT

Continue creating your own journal by interacting with the following scriptures cited in *Love & Respect*. You may wish to make notes as you interact with Emerson's meditations. There is additional space to write your current thoughts about your marriage and your study so far.

SCRIPTURE MEDITATIONS

1. In 1 Peter 3:1–2 Peter instructs wives to be submissive (give respect) to their husbands, even if they do not believe or obey God's Word and are undeserving of respect. If a wife does this, Peter writes, her husband may be won over as he observes her "respectful behavior." What does Peter mean by "respectful behavior" on the part of a wife before her husband? I believe that part of what Peter had in mind includes a wife's tone of voice and facial expression. When he isn't the man she wants him to be (loving and considerate), can she still show him unconditional respect with the way she talks and the look on her face? She is not asked to endorse his unloving actions; she is asked to show him unconditional respect, just as he is supposed to show her unconditional love. Difficult? Very. But it can work wonders. As Peter implies, it is less about what a wife says (verbal language) and far more about how she comes across (nonverbal language). A good-willed husband, no matter how badly he might be fouling things up at the moment, will find it hard to continue resisting unconditional respect.

2. Why is it that Scripture instructs men to "fight for your . . . wives" (Nehemiah 4:14), but women are never instructed to fight for their husbands? On the pages of any piece of well-known literature, does the prince see himself as the rescuer of the princess, or does the princess want the prince to depend on her for protection? If an intruder enters a home, what will the wife think if Harry screams, "Sally! Protect me! Go get that mean man out of here so I can stop huddling in the corner!"? What does a husband feel when his wife never respectfully acknowledges and praises his desire to protect her? Question for her: "Does my husband have a need to be respected (looked up to) in a way that I have been overlooking?"

3. In a marriage especially, "Reckless words pierce like a sword . . ." (Proverbs 12:18 NIV). How deep is the wound if a husband snarls in anger, "Nobody could ever love you!"? How deeply does it cut when a wife retorts: "Nobody could ever respect you!"? Neither spouse "means it" but the effect is like a sword thrust, nonetheless. The Love

and Respect couple works hard at never using "reckless" words, and instead heeds the rest of Proverbs 12:18: ". . . the tongue of the wise brings healing" (NIV).

4. A good passage for any married couple is Proverbs 14:8: "The wisdom of the prudent is to give thought to their ways . . ." (NIV). As you reflect on your study of *Love & Respect* so far, have you given much thought to your "ways"? As a husband, when you feel disrespected, is your way of reacting loving or unloving? As a wife, when you feel unloved, is your way of reacting respectful or disrespectful? It is so very easy to rationalize that your way of reacting is solely the fault of your mate and to tell yourself, "If my spouse changed, all would be well." Take the rest of Proverbs 14:8 as the Lord's warning: ". . . but the folly of fools is deception" (NIV). In other words, fools deceive themselves.

My current thoughts about our marriage:

SESSION FOUR

This session is the last in Part One: The Crazy Cycle. Session Four covers Chapters Five, Six, and Seven of the *Love & Respect* book and deals with some of the most frequently voiced issues raised by the thousands of couples Emerson has helped slow or stop the Crazy Cycle. In preparation for this session, read Chapters Five through Seven of *Love & Respect*. As you read, you may identify with many of the questions and concerns others have voiced. You may prefer to concentrate on only one or two of the chapters, or you may find all three helpful. Choose what fits your situation. It is possible that none of these chapters will seem to fit your experience exactly. We suggest you go over them anyway, using the questions in Session Four as a review of key issues and principles that affect this marriage. Remember to answer all unmarked questions first, then answer questions marked by the male or female icon (whichever applies to you). Finally, answer the questions with the couple icon, if you're studying with your mate. (Suggestions for anyone planning to use this study with a small group can be found in *Workbook* Appendix I, page 201.)

Questions for Chapter Five

1 In the opening paragraph of Chapter Five (book page 73), Emerson relates that during many years of counseling couples, he has observed that old Crazy Cycle habits are hard to break. She may want to change, but "the rat needs to earn my respect" attitude dies hard. He would like to be different, but he fears looking like an unloving fool—again. As you begin this session, where are you on this continuum?

 Do you have any fears of being a "doormat" if you really try to respect your husband unconditionally? Write your honest thoughts here:

 Do you have any fears of looking like a fool if you try to unconditionally love your wife and fail—or she doesn't respond with respect? Write your honest thoughts here:

 One (or both) of you may feel a little uncomfortable discussing your answer(s) to the questions above. Admitting your fears and then talking about them can be beneficial, but only if both of you are willing to share your hearts.

2 The concerns described in Question 1 raise another major question that spouses have. Read "Who Should Make the First Move?" (book pages 74–75) carefully. What is Emerson's answer to spouses who wonder: "Should I make the first move?"

Why does Emerson claim that the spouse who makes the first move can rarely lose?

 This is another question that you may feel reluctant to discuss. Even so, being willing to discuss this is, in a sense, being willing to make the first move! If one of you is willing to take the risk, the rewards will be well worth it.

3 In "Not a Doormat but a Woman with Power" (book pages 75–77), Emerson attempts to assure wives he is not a chauvinist in disguise, trying to lure them into a life of subservience. Read this material carefully, then go down the "list of a wife's fears" below and check off anything that you believe is a concern in your marriage.

 Which of the following fears concerns you to some degree at this time?

____ If I respect him, he won't really be more loving.

____ If I respect him, I will wind up a doormat, and doing whatever he wants.

____ If I respect him, I'll have to bury my brains, never think for myself or speak my mind.

____ If I respect him, he will ignore how I hurt and where I'm vulnerable.

____ If I respect him, he'll become arrogant and self-centered.

____ If I respect him, I'll have to do something I don't really feel, and that's impossible.

____ My fear, in my own words, is:

 Do you see anything in the above list that may be of concern to your wife? Check those concerns and be ready to talk about them.

This question provides plenty of opportunity for sensitive sharing. Wife, if you don't have any of these fears, you should tell your husband, which will be a big encouragement to him. Husband, if your wife does have fears about showing you unconditional respect, you can do several things: First, be thankful that she is courageous and humble enough to tell you. Second, remember she is a good-willed woman who wants your love. Third, do not dismiss her fears as "silly" or just say, "Oh, you don't have to worry about that." Fourth, seek to understand her and empathize as much as possible.

4 According to "Not a Doormat but a Woman with Power" (book pages 75–77), one of the ways a wife feels empowered is when she corrects or "mothers" her husband (page 76). According to Emerson's counsel, why doesn't this work? Finish his observation on page 77: when a wife continues to mother, correct, or goad a husband into changing, she wins the battle but loses ____ _____.

 This question is similar to Questions 13 and 14 in Session 3, which dealt with the wife's scolding. If you choose to discuss this one, be careful of stepping on each other's air hose. If the two of you can share without arguing, it will be helpful for him to explain when he feels he is being "corrected and mothered," and for her to learn how she can come across a bit differently as she constantly sees things that need putting right. Remember, if you can avoid battling each other, and see each other as an ally, not an enemy, you will win the war of the Crazy Cycle.

5 In "What If You're Afraid to Take the Risk?" (book pages 77–80), there are several letters from wives who were hesitant to try showing their husbands respect—but who trusted God anyway. Read these letters carefully. Write out phrases that may give you help, hope, or assurance for your marriage.

 Husbands, while this question is designed primarily for wives, you can benefit from answering it as well and then comparing notes with your wife. Can you identify with why the husbands described in these letters were so energized? As you share with your wife, what can you say to her to alleviate any fears or questions she may still have? Whatever you do, refrain from shaming your wife as she awakens to your need for respect.

---

6 In "Husbands, Remember Only One Idea—Love" (book pages 80–82), Emerson admits that there have been plenty of times when he has felt like the husband who wrote in to say: "I have spent the last twenty years literally consumed with trying to figure out what is going on in our marriage." What has helped Emerson during those times? What are the two questions a husband must focus on when his wife gets critical or negative? (See book page 81.)

Even though Question 6 is directed primarily toward the husband, the wife can benefit by answering it as well and then comparing her answers to her husband's. As a wife, do you agree that when you get critical or angry you are actually saying, in one way or another, "I need your love, please love me!"? As a husband, are you remembering to ask yourself: "Will what I do or say next come across as loving or unloving?" Ask your wife how she thinks you are doing in that department.

---

7 Read the story of how "This Husband Decoded in Jail" (book pages 82–85). As he spent the entire weekend in jail, this man had an "epiphany experience" that helped him to finally understand his wife's angry messages. What stands out in this story from your point of view as a spouse?

Compare your answers, which may be quite different. Concerning this man's story, Emerson says: "Husbands and wives please note: physical violence against a wife is reprehensible and evil. Sharing this man's letter should not be construed as sanctioning such evil in any way. The story shows what can happen when God works in a husband's life and he learns how to decode his wife."

---

8 Two more letters from husbands who learned to decode their wives are on book pages 85–86. As you read these letters, make notes on some important ways a spouse can decode. What phrases or ideas stand out? Which ones should you use more often?

Compare your answers. How are all of these ideas about decoding summed up in Emerson's observation, "The Crazy Cycle can be slowed—and stopped—if only we would have eyes to see and ears to hear"? Not only is it important for you to "get it" (understand what you need to do), it is also very important to listen and respond when your mate "gets it" as well. (See Emerson's additional comments on Question 8 in *Workbook* Appendix VI.)

Questions for Chapter Six

9 Chapter Six opens with a letter from a woman who was trying to respect her alcoholic husband, but she did not "want to be a hypocrite." How does Emerson answer this concern (book pages 87–88)? Why does continuing with criticism and anger only mean that a wife shoots herself in both feet?

This could be a delicate question, especially if the wife has any feelings about being a hypocrite as she tries to show the husband unconditional respect. Go slowly and gently and remember that practicing Love and Respect isn't about feelings; it's about doing what the Scriptures teach.

—————

10 On book page 89 Emerson tells of having asked a wife: "Are you afraid that your respectful manner will lessen your chances of motivating your husband to change?" Read her response, then write your own. According to Emerson, "Obeying God's Word does not make a wife a powerless hypocrite." Do you agree? Explain.

 Husband, while this question is directed to your wife, write your answer as well, then discuss it with her. As your wife shows you respect, especially when you are not as loving as you could be, do you see her as "power-less" or "power-full"? Why?

—————

11 Read the letter from a wife at the bottom of book page 90, plus the paragraph at the top of page 91. What did she get out of being respectful? What has she made sure to do in response to all his loving acts? How do you think the husband feels when he comes home to a clean house, a hot meal, and a wife who looks good and acts like she is happy to see him?

 You and your mate may see this question as rather simple, not to mention that it flies in the face of a culture where a stay-at-home-spouse is unrealistic in many households. Nonetheless, there are principles here any couple can apply. Today's woman expects her emotional needs to be met, even if she has a career, because her traditional need for love has not changed. Conversely, a husband has a traditional need for respect, but when he expresses it, some want to tar and feather him. If the way your spouse wants to be treated seems unrealistic or outdated, look beyond all the cultural baggage and see the deeper need to be loved or respected. Talk about why the Love and Respect Connection is so simple, yet sometimes so difficult. Why can it be so powerful when used by two good-willed people?

———

12 Read "Refuse to Play Rodney Dangerfield—Don't Stonewall!" (book pages 91–92). Instead of muttering, "I just don't get no respect," husbands are to move toward their wives even when they are receiving "verbal deathblows." How does Proverbs 12:16 help a husband when his wife is being abusively disrespectful?

Handle this question (and each other) with care. As a husband, you have the opportunity to apologize for the times you "stonewalled" your wife when you received what felt like "verbal deathblows" from her when she felt angry (and unloved). Tell her that from now on you want to follow Proverbs 12:16 and "conceal the dishonor." In other words, no stonewalling—no getting angry in return. You just want to keep coming with unconditional love. As a wife, you have the opportunity to apologize for your anger and promise to give your husband unconditional respect. Both of you realize you can't be perfect at practicing Love and Respect, but you also know that just being willing to try means real progress. Pray together for guidance as you seek to slow and stop the Crazy Cycle.

———

13 In "I Used to Say, 'I'll Show Her!'" (book pages 92–94), Emerson confesses how he reacted badly to Sarah when feeling disrespected. Then he discovered a way to motivate her to be more respectful, which in turn motivated him to be more loving! Read this section carefully and find the combination of short sentences Emerson used to develop what amounts to the "Love and Respect 'I' Message." Also turn to *Love & Respect* Appendix A, page 306, "To communicate feelings or start discussion," where an example is given for the wife as well as the husband. To start memorizing the "Love and Respect 'I' Message," fill in the blanks below:

As a husband, you can say: "That felt _____.
Did I just come across as _____?"

As a wife, you can say: "That felt _____. Did I just come across as _____?"

Note on book page 306 what you are to say if your spouse answers yes to your question. Is the "Love and Respect 'I' Message" something you can use in your marriage? Write your thoughts:

 Compare your answers and also discuss what Emerson and Sarah have done when angry, which is stated in Ephesians 4:26 (see "It Works—Even on Our Bad Days," book page 94). Read this verse together. Could this verse change the way you deal with anger?

———————

14 In "If I Can Do It, So Can You" (book pages 95–97), there are two letters from struggling husbands (bottom of page 95, top of page 96). Finish this bit of advice Emerson gives both of them:

"Gentlemen, it is true you are not designed by God to enjoy contempt, but He does call you to _____ _____ _____."

 As you talk together, note the comments by marriage researcher John Gottman who concluded it is more effective for a husband to embrace his wife's anger (bottom of book page 96). (For more discussion ideas, see Emerson's additional comments in *Workbook* Appendix VI.)

---

15 At the bottom of book page 96, top of 97, Emerson suggests what a husband can say if his wife vents her feelings with venomous remarks: "Honey, I love you. I don't want this. When you talk this way, I know you're feeling unloved. Let's work on this. I want to come across more lovingly, and I hope you would like to come across more respectfully."

 Because a husband does not love naturally, God commands him to do so (see Ephesians 5:25–33). It may never feel "natural" to say something like what is quoted above, when your wife is venting her anger at you, but as a man of honor, are you willing to try it?

YES ___   NO ___   NOT SURE ___

 If your husband used Emerson's suggestions when you were venting your anger at him, how might this make you feel? Would it help? Why or why not?

Compare your answers. Is Emerson's suggestion for turning aside a wife's anger something that could work in your marriage right now? Talk about how it would feel in the middle of an argument or angry exchange for the husband to talk about wanting to be more loving and hoping the wife could be more respectful. (For more ideas on defusing anger, see "Things to Remember," *Love & Respect* Appendix A, pages 305–6.)

16 Read the story of "The Husband Who Never Stopped Loving" (book pages 97–99). Note two or three things that stand out for you in the wife's letter about how her husband wouldn't give up on her, even when it seemed hopeless.

Compare notes, then talk and pray about your own marriage. Emerson adds this note on the value of prayer: "As you go through this study of *Love & Respect*, you may have moments of feeling overwhelmed. All husbands and wives who are believers in Christ have His promise: 'Come to Me, all who are weary and heavy-laden, and I will give you rest' (Matthew 11:28). And Peter adds: '[cast] all your anxiety on Him, because He cares for you' (1 Peter 5:7). If you are feeling weary and heavy-laden, will you pray to the Father? Will you cast your anxieties on Him? Do this because He cares for you. Jesus, the Perfect One, depended on the Father while on earth. All God's children are free to do the same. Depend on God for all your needs. He is eager to help you!"

17 Read carefully the second paragraph on book page 99 (beginning, "No matter how desperate or hopeless a marriage may seem . . ."). What do you think? Can love and respect, plus basic goodwill in both spouses, conquer anything?

I TOTALLY AGREE ____   I PARTIALLY AGREE ____   I DOUBT IT ____

My comments:

You may know people who face tremendous problems in their marriage such as adultery, abuse, or addictions. You may face tremendous problems yourself. Does Love and Respect work when the going gets really tough? (Those who may need specific help to deal with adultery, spousal abuse, and drug addictions, go to the following Web site: http://www.loveandrespect.com/pearl.)

Questions for Chapter Seven

18 As he has counseled wives over the years, Emerson often hears comments like these: "Forgive him? Yes, I know what Jesus said about seventy times seven, and I've forgiven him at least that many times! But when is he going to ask me for forgiveness? When is he ever going to care about how much he hurts me?" Is there some truth in comments like these? Shouldn't a husband ask for forgiveness in order to be forgiven? Can granting forgiveness, even when it isn't wanted, really help the situation at all? Read the opening book pages of Chapter Seven (101–3). Then put down your response to Emerson's teaching:

Talk about what it means to forgive. Do you agree with Emerson's assertion that when you forgive someone for being unloving, you give up your right to hold a grudge? Note the letter from the wife on page 103. What insights does she provide that might make forgiveness possible, even if it doesn't seem practical? Husbands, don't skip this material because it seems to be directed to wives. You may need to do some forgiving yourself, or perhaps it is time you asked for forgiveness. Forgiving someone, or being forgiven, can be a humbling experience. Each of you should try to be sensitive to the other's needs at this time.

19 At the bottom of book page 105, Emerson writes, "Nothing is easier than judging, nothing is harder than forgiving, and nothing can reap more blessings." Read the letters from the wife whose husband strayed into adultery (pages 104–5). How did she find it in her heart to forgive him? What was her driving motivation?

Compare notes on what you see in this woman's letters. She faced having to decide to forgive her husband at the hardest level: for his immorality. It may be of help to spend time together reading and discussing Emerson's views on forgiveness at two levels (see *Workbook* Appendix III, page 207). He gives sound biblical advice to the spouse who has been wounded deep in the heart by a mate's adultery. For the woman who wrote the letters, her strongest motivation was, obviously, her faith and trust in God. She had no trust for her husband, and little or no inclination to forgive. But when she did, he responded. Emerson adds: "Situations like this do not always have such a happy ending, but God calls us to obey Him and His word, one step at a time, and to accept what happens as His will."

---

20 Read book page 106, "If You Fail to Love Her, Rebound," then respond to the following:

 How good a rebounder are you? (In other words, how well do you bounce back when you are unloving and get clobbered with contempt?)

 How good a rebounder is your husband when you criticize him with good reason? (For that matter, how good a rebounder are you when he reacts to your disrespect?)

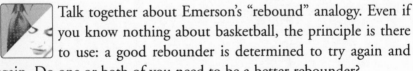 Talk together about Emerson's "rebound" analogy. Even if you know nothing about basketball, the principle is there to use: a good rebounder is determined to try again and again. Do one or both of you need to be a better rebounder?

21 Read Emerson's humorous account of how he has had to rebound after blowing it with Sarah (bottom of book page 106 to top of 109). What truths in his transparent admissions stand out for you?

As a husband, note especially the two choices you have if your wife comes at you "with disrespect flashing in her eyes and venom shooting from her tongue": defend your pride or surrender with unconditional love. As a wife, how would you respond if your husband said, "I'm sorry. I know I've been unloving"?

22 In "Marriage—A Two-Become-One Proposition" (book pages 109–12), Emerson claims that when couples practice love and respect, "Bad marriages become good, boring marriages become exciting, and good marriages become better." Note these words from a husband who from all appearances had a good marriage (and even conducted marriage seminars with his wife): "On a scale of 1–10 we were living with a 5–6 marriage most of the time." When he and his wife started making Love and Respect a priority, that number went way up. How would you rate your marriage right now on a scale of 1–10, with 10 being "great"? Our marriage is a _____.

 Be aware that this question could be difficult to discuss. Be sensitive to each other and willing to hear the other person's reasons for the number he/she chose. Concentrate on agreeing about how you can work together to make that number higher.

23 In "From the Crazy Cycle to the Energizing Cycle" (book pages 112–13), Emerson reminds spouses that you can slow or stop the Crazy Cycle, but you can never get off completely. He and Sarah know they have to work continually at controlling the Crazy Cycle, and some of the best ways they have learned to do this are stated in capsule form in *Love & Respect* Appendix A, especially in "Always Ask Yourself" and "Things to Remember" (pages 305–6). Take time to go over these suggestions now, and write down several ideas that stand out as things you want to practice as you move into Part II—The Energizing Cycle.

As you complete your study of Part I: The Crazy Cycle, share and pray together concerning these questions:

1. How much progress have we made in slowing and stopping the Crazy Cycle?

2. What can we do, as a couple, to keep the Crazy Cycle under control?

A JOURNAL OF MY JOURNEY TO LOVE AND RESPECT

This section of your workbook is your private area to write whatever you are thinking or feeling at this time. The Scripture Meditations can help you start thinking and praying and putting down what is on your heart. There is also room to record any other current thoughts about your marriage.

Scripture Meditations

1. In your marriage, be the first to "seek peace and pursue it" (1 Peter 3:11). Can you say you are the one in your marriage who consistently seeks peace and pursues it? Do you ever seek peace at any price, ignoring or compromising the clear teaching of Scripture? Or, do you stubbornly and selfishly demand your own way in small matters because you foolishly make these "little things" symbols of how you are unloved or disrespected? Consider this wife's letter: "I turned the temperature down last year . . . [then] my husband bought a plastic box that fits over the dial complete with lock and key. . . . I was appalled when he put a locked box over the temperature dial. . . . I found a way to change the dial without using the key [and] I turned the heat down to 68. This has always been an area where we don't agree. He told me last month that he felt I was being disrespectful." How would you answer this wife? At this rate, why will she and her husband not experience peace? How could they change in an attempt to seek peace?

2. It is always wise for a husband to be "humble in spirit" (1 Peter 3:8). What does it mean for a husband to be humble in spirit? Will a wife walk all over a husband who approaches her in this way?

3. Over the years, as I have blown it and been unloving to Sarah, I have found solace in Proverbs 24:16: "Though a righteous man falls seven times, he rises again"(NIV). The husband who tries to live an honorable life with his wife, but fails, knows two things: (1) He is "righteous" only through the blood of Christ; (2) he can no more always show his wife perfect love than she can show him perfect respect. What does Proverbs 24:16 tell the husband or wife to do in the moment of failure? The last time you came across as unloving or disrespectful what did you do?

4. To stop the Crazy Cycle, and keep it in its cage, seek to obey God's Word "which also performs its work in you who believe" (1 Thessalonians 2:13). We have God's promise that His Word will do His work deep in our souls! Your marriage isn't first about performance; it's about God doing a work in and through you: ". . . for it is

God who is at work in you, both to will and to work for His good pleasure" (Philippians 2:13). As you live with your spouse, stop at least once each day and pray, "Dear God, perform Your work in me. Do Your work through me. Please, Lord, I need You!"

My current thoughts about our marriage:

PART TWO:
THE ENERGIZING
CYCLE

Sessions 5 to 12 cover
Chapters Eight to Twenty-Two of *Love & Respect*

A PERSONAL WORD FROM EMERSON:

I hope you have made progress to this point in slowing or stopping the effects of the Crazy Cycle on your marriage. Your next step is to learn how to keep the Crazy Cycle from spinning, or how to stop it if it seems to be starting up again. You can do this by getting on the Energizing Cycle in which his love motivates her respect and her respect motivates his love.

To help you get on the Energizing Cycle and stay there, I developed two acronyms covering six important principles for each spouse. The acronym C-O-U-P-L-E contains advice for husbands in six brief chapters on Closeness, Openness, Understanding, Peacemaking, Loyalty, and Esteem. The acronym C-H-A-I-R-S contains advice for wives in six brief chapters on Conquest, Hierarchy, Authority, Insight, Relationship, and Sexuality.

Keep in mind that if you are studying together with your spouse, discussing some of these questions may be tough going. Husbands and wives need to be sensitive to each other and take it slowly, easily, and gently. There is no rule that says you must exhaustively discuss every question. Some questions may prove sticky, even irritating to one or both of you. The first rule in being a Love and Respect couple is to do just that—show love and respect to each other! This will mean not always saying everything that may be on your mind. Be honest, but not brutally honest. (Speak the truth in love—Ephesians 4:15.) Remember, having a difference of opinion or a different understanding of something does not mean you have major problems as a couple. What you must guard against, however, is allowing disagreements to turn into disapproval of the other person. Always, the goal is Love and Respect, whether you agree or disagree. The husband should focus on loving his wife, the wife on respecting her husband. If you do this, the Energizing Cycle will hum along nicely and the Crazy Cycle will not have a chance to spin.

SESSION FIVE

In preparation for this session, read the first two chapters in Part Two of *Love & Respect*, which covers the Energizing Cycle. Begin with Chapter Eight, "C-O-U-P-L-E: How to Spell Love to Your Wife," and Chapter Nine, "Closeness—She Wants You to Be Close." The following questions are for individual study or study by a couple. Remember to answer all unmarked questions first, then answer questions marked by the male or female icon (whichever applies to you). Finally, answer the questions with the couple icon, if you're studying with your mate. (Suggestions for leading a small group can be found in *Workbook* Appendix I, page 201.)

This session opens your study of C-O-U-P-L-E, six important principles that will help a husband learn important aspects of loving his wife. In Love and Respect, just under the title of Chapter 8, is a brief note to wives saying the next several chapters are for "husbands only, but wives are invited to read along." Wives are also invited to study along in Sessions 5-8 of this workbook, so please do! As your husband discusses the six parts of C-O-U-P-L-E with you, he will learn more about how to love you (and you will learn how to help him do it better!).

A SPECIAL WORD FOR HUSBANDS FROM EMERSON:

Welcome to the Energizing Cycle and your study of the acronym C-O-U-P-L-E: Closeness, Openness, Understanding, Peacemaking, Loyalty, Esteem. These are the six principles you can practice to make your wife feel loved. More than that, you can use C-O-U-P-L-E as a diagnostic tool to tell when you and your wife are slipping off the Energizing Cycle and back on the Crazy Cycle. According to the Crazy Cycle, a wife acts disrespectfully when she isn't feeling loved. Her disrespect is not justified, but when it does happen you can say to yourself, "Since my wife is reacting in ways that feel disrespectful to me, there is a good chance I have done something to make her feel unloved. I have two choices: react to her unlovingly, or try to decode. Which one of the principles in C-O-U-P-L-E might I be neglecting in her view?" This way you soften your reaction, as you remember that your wife is basically a good-willed woman who is not intending to show you contempt.

Next, depending on the situation (what has been going on between the two of you), you can probably make a good guess at what's wrong. For example, you've been working long hours, and she is feeling the need for closeness. Talk to her and ask if this is what is wrong. If she says it is, you can say you are sorry for your behavior, make adjustments, and get the Energizing Cycle going again.

But what do you do if, for whatever reason, you can't decode (figure out what is bothering her)? If that happens, you can communicate your feelings to your wife by gently (not defensively or aggressively) saying, "I'm feeling disrespected right now. Have I been coming across as unloving? How can I come across more lovingly?" (In other words, tell me where I am messing things up.)

I believe that as you go through C-O-U-P-L-E for husbands and C-H-A-I-R-S for wives, you will get to know each other better than you ever have before as you are challenged, stretched, and, I hope, blessed. But remember, if any of the questions in the following sessions makes either of you uncomfortable, agree together to table that item for right now. Later, you may be ready to come back and discuss the topic with real profit as you go to new levels of Love and Respect. But for now, let's get going with the Energizing Cycle—and have a great trip!

Questions for Chapter Eight

1 To get started with Session Five, the six words represented by C-O-U-P-L-E are listed below. Next to each word is a brief definition. Under each word, write what it suggests to you. Does your definition match the one given?

Closeness: She wants you to be close.

 My definition:

Openness: She wants you to open up to her.

 My definition:

Understanding: Don't try to "fix" her; just listen.

 My definition:

Peacemaking: She wants you to say, "I'm sorry."

 My definition:

Loyalty: She needs to know you're committed.

 My definition:

Esteem: She wants you to honor and cherish her.

 My definition:

Which of these six principles sounds most interesting? Which is most necessary to a happy marriage? Why?

Husbands and wives should compare their respective definitions and discuss them. How did they differ from the definitions given? How does your definition differ from your spouse's? How do your answers to the other two questions differ? When your study of C-O-U-P-L-E is complete, see if your opinions have changed and note why they might have changed.

---

2 On book page 118, Emerson defines the acrostic word C-O-U-P-L-E as "two people connected together." What does it mean to you to be "connected" to your spouse?

This question could prove sensitive, especially if the husband sees his wife's efforts to connect with him as an effort to control him. Go over book page 118 again. Wife, do you agree that when you come across as negative and offensive you are really crying out for C-O-U-P-L-E, the things your husband can do to connect with you? Husband, can you see yourself starting to decode your wife's messages, which may sound negative, but are really her cries for your love?

---

3 Farther down on page 118 Emerson writes, "Wives want connectivity. . . . Women confront to connect." Why is this good? How can it turn out "not so good"?

Discuss your answers and learn a little more about one another.

4 In "This Husband Wouldn't Believe Me Until . . ." (book pages 118–20) is a story about a husband who saw his wife's effort to connect by confronting as an effort to control him. He finally "got it" and realized this was not true, but only after attending a Love and Respect Conference. Why do many men fear being controlled? How could understanding this fear help prevent the Crazy Cycle from spinning? Who needs to understand it more—the husband or the wife?

Generally speaking, men want to be responsibly in control. See especially Session Ten, under C-H-A-I-R-S, which talks about the wife respecting the husband's desire to protect, provide, serve, and lead. All of these involve being responsibly in control to one degree or another. When a husband feels his role in any of these areas is threatened, he may start to think his wife is trying to control him. ("She's trying to mother me.") On the other hand, if a wife feels her husband is being too dictatorial or demanding, she will feel unloved. ("He treats me like a doormat!") Talk together about the issue of control. Wife, let your husband know you are not trying to "wear the pants"; you only wish to connect with him. Husband, ask your wife for honest feedback about how "controlling" you are in your marriage. A good-willed husband wants to be a loving and responsible servant-leader. Talk about how the husband's control can be good as long as a wife feels secure, but bad if she starts to feel unloved. Perhaps the key phrase is "responsible servant-leader." What does that look and feel like to each of you?

———————

5 Read carefully the "Learn to Trust Your Instruments" section on pages 120–21. How can practicing C-O-U-P-L-E prevent "marital vertigo?" Husbands, are you willing to "trust your instrument panel"?

NO PROBLEM ___   NOT TOTALLY SURE ___   DOUBTFUL ___

Husband, discuss your answer with your wife and share any doubts you may have about how well you can practice the principles in C-O-U-P-L-E (that is, "trust your instrument panel"). For example, are you willing to ask her if she confronts you to connect or control? (In other words, does she want to connect to create mutual understanding or is she confronting to control you and get her way?) Many wives are also mothers (or want to be), and it is in their nature to be helpful. Not only that, but wives are called to be "helpers" (Genesis 2:18). Can a wife seek to help her husband and come across as controlling without meaning to? Should the husband be willing to trust her goodwill, even though her helping can make him feel like she is being "bossy" at times?

6 In "In the Ocean of Conflict, Men Sink Unless . . ." (book pages 121–22), Emerson shares the story of one husband who had the guts not to stonewall his angry wife. How would you describe what he did as he "trusted his instrument panel"?

Compare your answers, which could be very revealing by showing how each of you think. Also see *Love & Respect* Appendix C (page 311), which lists "need communicator" statements both of you can use when appropriate.

7 At the bottom of book page 122, as he summarizes Chapter Eight, Emerson writes, "To turn to your wife in the middle of a conflict and say, 'I am sorry, will you forgive me?' takes guts. I know because I have been there. It isn't pleasant, but it works powerfully. Over time it becomes easier, but it is never natural. Even so, this response gives you the power to drain negativity out of your wife in conflict after conflict." Why does it take guts to say "I'm sorry"? What often stands in a husband's way?

This can be a good question to discuss, but only if both of you are "up for it." Be sensitive to each other's needs and, if feasible, talk together about why it's hard for him to say, "I'm sorry." Is it pride? Or is it fear that later she will use his apology against him in a disrespectful way?

Questions for Chapter Nine

8 Chapter Nine opens with a biblical definition of *closeness* (book page 125). Write that definition below and be sure to add what it means "to cleave." Obviously "cleaving" involves sex, but what other kinds of closeness are involved?

 Talk together about what closeness means to each of you. How important is it for the husband to let his wife know he wants to be close with a look, a touch, or a smile?

9 Read carefully "The First Few Seconds Set the Tone" (book pages 126–27). Why are those moments when a couple comes together after being apart all day so important to the wife?

Share your answers, then talk about how you are doing during the first few moments when you arrive home. How easy is it to be perfunctory, preoccupied, and self-absorbed with your own needs? Is Emerson saying couples have to spend a lot of time reconnecting? What is more important—quantity or quality? Take a good look at what the two of you have been doing to reconnect after a busy day. What is your typical routine? Is Emerson right when he says, "The first few moments of reconnecting will set the tone for the rest of the evening"? If you agree with him, you may want to talk about changing your usual routine and spending at least a few minutes talking about what each of you did that day—achievements, frustrations, humorous incidents . . .

10 How important is face-to-face connection? (Read "What My Four-Year-Old Taught Me . . ." book pages 127–28.) Question for husbands: How are you doing at face-to-face with your wife? Question for wives: How can you respectfully ask your husband for more face-to-face connecting? (See *Love & Respect* Appendix C, under "Wives can humbly and softly say," page 311.)

Not every husband will appreciate being confronted about his face-to-face time with his wife, particularly if he hasn't been doing it that much. Wives should be sensitive to this. In addition, Emerson adds an important point: "If a wife wants to encourage her husband to be close face-to-face, she must always consider what her face looks like. I'm not talking about looking like some cover girl; I mean the facial expression, which can be sweet and welcoming or sour and rejecting. From his extensive research with thousands of married couples, John Gottman concluded that 'Wives who make sour facial expressions when their husbands talk are likely to be separated within four years.'[i] When a husband does move toward a wife face-to-face, she should think about showing respectful interest. At the same time the husband should place importance on looking like he wants to be close and loving, not like he is in a board meeting. For both spouses the emphasis is always on being humble and gentle as you seek to meet each other's needs."

11 Read the sections entitled, "Involvement or Independence?" and "Only Chickens Get Henpecked" (book pages 128–30). Then mark the line below according to what you need—more involvement with your spouse or more independence from your spouse.

Involvement

Independence

 According to Emerson, "In the typical marriage relationship, she leans more toward the 'Involvement' side while he leans more toward the 'Independence' side." Talk together about the amount of tension you see in your marriage, between her need for involvement and his need for independence. Remember, this kind of tension is normal, so think positively about how you can solve his need for 'space' and her need to be 'close.' If this subject isn't too sensitive, discuss what Emerson says on book page 129 about a wife not wanting her husband to become like a "girl friend," but how even small moves toward closeness by the husband can energize the wife. Wife, do you agree? Husband, are you willing to give up a little independence in order to be a little closer to your wife? What might happen if you did? For more tips and helps for talking together about something like this, see *Love & Respect* Appendix A, page 305–307, especially "Always ask yourself," "Things to remember," and "Things to say to lighten up the relationship."

Husband, take time to ask your wife what she would like. (Maybe she will just want you to surprise her.)

A JOURNAL OF MY JOURNEY TO LOVE AND RESPECT

Always take at least a few minutes to write down your feelings, questions, insights gained, and other comments when you finish a study session. Months, or even years, from now, you will appreciate reviewing this record of your growth as a person and a spouse.

SCRIPTURE MEDITATIONS

1. "When I found him whom my soul loves; I held on to him and would not let him go" (Song of Solomon 3:4). A woman in love longs for closeness. Husband, does your wife's need for face-to-face closeness seem like "clinging" to you? At the same time, is it okay for her to request face-to-face talking and physical closeness without wanting sexual intimacy? Serious tension can develop if a husband constantly reads his wife's desire for closeness as an invitation to have sex. What can a couple do if this is the case? One solution that I have seen work in many marriages is getting on a schedule to take the guesswork out of when you will be sexually intimate. This kind of schedule leads in turn to regular, scheduled times for face-to-face interaction without the husband pushing the sexual issue, because he knows the schedule. Does this sound rigid and nonspontaneous? Nonetheless, it can work miracles in a marriage.

2. A wife always hopes, "Now my husband will hold me close" (Genesis 29:34 CEV). Husband, have you ever heard your wife say, "I need a hug"? God seems to have made women for closeness and hugs. When women friends greet each other, do they hug or shake hands? For a group photo, do several women stand shoulder to shoulder as men would do, or do they squeeze close together, almost cheek to cheek for the camera? When your wife wants you to hold her close in a nonsexual way, does she have

12 According to Emerson, there is a battle to the death going between the Crazy Cycle and the Energizing Cycle (p 130–31). What suggestions does he make in this section to help bands win that battle and have a great marriage? Check off ph that sound helpful to you, or write down your own ideas.

___ Always seek to motivate and not demoralize.

___ Always be trying to adjust your "sunglasses" and "he aids."

___ Always try to do the positive, loving thing.

___ I think:

 While this question is directed primarily at helping bands love their wives, the suggestions listed above car ily be used by wives who want to respect their husb; Do you both agree with Emerson's assertion that "this is a war—a tle to the death between the Crazy Cycle and the Energizing Cy Why or why not?

13 Chapter Nine closes with tips and techniques for being (book pages 131–33). Go down the list and find thing; you are doing well. Then find one thing that you have not done while. Write it here, then plan how you can do it in the next tw four hours.

some problem with you, or is she simply a woman expressing her womanly desires? Is she wrong for having these desires, or just different from you? If you have not been that aware of this female need for hugs and closeness that don't always lead to sex, what little change will you make that can make a huge difference in your wife's feeling loved?

3. As Paul seeks to advise the Corinthians concerning a dispute that had arisen in their church, he says, "In the Lord, however, woman is not independent of man, nor is man independent of woman" (1 Corinthians 11:11 NIV). In other words, the basic New Testament principle is that women and men are equal before God. Eugene Peterson puts it well when he paraphrases this verse in *The Message:* "Neither man nor woman can go it alone or claim priority." there is great truth here for today's Love and Respect couple: there is always the temptation to become too independent of one another, particularly on the man's part. Because a man leaves father and mother (Genesis 2:24), his tendency is toward independence. The typical man, who does not have the same emotional need to connect as his wife does, should continually ask himself some important questions: Am I choosing activities that keep me too far away from her? Am I engaging in activities that keep me too independent and justifying them as "my right" or "something I need"? Do I sometimes change my plans but do not bother to inform her? Do I take on still more responsibilities (for example, in the church, on the job, in the community) even though my wife is overwhelmed at home with our children? Do I withhold information from her that she should know? Do I make decisions without including her, even though these decisions impact her significantly? Go over these questions, and anything else where your wife may be complaining about your being too independent (not involved enough at home). If the answer to any of these questions is yes, perhaps it is time to talk and pray with her about changes you could make.

My current thoughts about our marriage:

SESSION SIX

In preparation for this session, read Chapter Ten, "Openness—She Wants You to Open Up to Her," and Chapter Eleven, "Understanding—Don't Try to 'Fix' Her; Just Listen." The following questions are for study by an individual or by a husband and wife together. Remember to answer all unmarked questions first, then answer questions marked by the male or female icon (whichever applies to you). Finally, answer the questions with the couple icon, if you're studying with your mate. (Suggestions for anyone planning to use this study with a small group can be found in *Workbook* Appendix I, page 201.)

Questions for Chapter Ten

1 As he begins Chapter Ten (book page 135) Emerson shares from his counseling experience, describing how couples act when they come in to see him. Men tend to be closed, playing it close to the vest. The wife is much more open, wanting to talk and connect with her husband. Does this describe you and your spouse—the husband more quiet and closed, the wife more open and talkative?

FITS US PERFECTLY ____   SOMEWHAT TRUE OF US ____
NOT TRUE OF US AT ALL ____

 Compare your answers. If you both believe this is true of the two of you, at least to some degree, talk about it as much as feels comfortable. The typically "closed" husband may not want to go into it to any extent, at least at this time in your study. (Note that it is also possible for a wife to be closed, which could be perfectly normal for her. And, there are husbands who are quite expressive. If this reverse situation is true of your marriage, discuss how it affects your communication. For more on "exceptions" to the Love and Respect norm, see *Love & Respect* Appendix D, page 313.)

—————

2 Read the material "Smash One of Her Lights . . ." (book pages 136–37) very carefully. It is one of the most important analogies in this entire workbook. Emerson illustrates the difference between the typically expressive-responsive wife and the typically compartmentalized husband by picturing two electrical circuits, both with 3000 lights. On the first circuit, if you smash just one light, the whole thing shuts down. On the second circuit, if you smash two thousand lights, the other thousand will stay lit. According to Emerson's explanation, why is the expressive-responsive wife like the first circuit? Why is the compartmentalized husband like the second?

Compare notes on what you wrote down concerning the electric circuits analogy. It will probably be useful to read pages 136–37 together to grasp how important it is that the husband understands how one minor tiff can affect his wife all day and still be bothering her when they reconnect at day's end. The husband has probably forgotten all about whatever happened earlier because he has compartmentalized it—shoved it aside where it can't bother him. His wife, however, is an integrated personality who does not compartmentalize things. Everything is connected and one small remark that hurts her stays with her until the hurt is repaired. Talk together about what this can mean to each of you in different situations, for example, if you are invited out for the evening . . . if you planned to work together on something related to the house . . . if he hoped to make love that evening.

---

3 In "Wives See Husbands As Mysterious Islands" (book pages 137–39), Emerson describes a typical phenomenon: the husband is open, communicative, and charming during courtship, but after getting married he closes up. Why does this happen? How does it make the marriage vulnerable to the Crazy Cycle?

This could be a sensitive question, particularly if the husband thinks he is being accused of doing one thing during courtship and then the reverse after marriage. Compare what you wrote and talk about what is comfortable for both of you. His "closing down" after marriage could well be his not fully understanding how to love his wife properly. He is good-willed, but unaware (and possibly quite willing to learn). On the other hand, it is quite possible that after they got married, his wife started criticizing and being disrespectful, and then he closed up. Do not dwell on deciding if it was "the chicken or the egg." Talk together about adjustments you both can make right now to keep the Crazy Cycle from starting to spin. And always be aware of the possibility that, basically, you may already be married to a loving husband or a respectful wife. There are things you can improve upon, but 80 percent or more of your marriage already consists of love and respect. If this is the case, be thankful and build on that foundation.

---

4 Do you keep your wife up-to-date? Read "Sarah Prefers . . ." (book pages 139–40) and see if you have ever struggled (or perhaps you are struggling now) as Emerson did. Following are questions a husband could ask himself if he is tempted to think his wife is snooping or prying. How he answers each question can tell him a great deal concerning why he may not be keeping his wife informed. (**Wives should answer these questions as well.**)

Is my wife a good-willed woman?	YES ___	No ___
Is she trying to control me?	YES ___	No___
Is she trying to connect and be close?	YES___	No___
Is she trying to make me feel guilty?	YES___	No___

Share with each other how you answered the questions above from your individual perspectives. If the husband perceives the wife as coming across as "prying or controlling," this is her chance to reassure him of her good intentions. And if the husband realizes he has been reading his wife wrong (decoding her incorrectly), this is his chance to apologize for misinterpreting her heart, to say that he is sorry and from now on he will try to do a better job of decoding (and keeping her up-to-date).

---

5 In "Beware of Becoming Embittered" (book pages 140–42), Emerson describes a disturbing problem that can be caused when a husband is closed toward his wife. As he withdraws and refuses to talk about much of anything, the husband can appear to be irritated, even bitter. His wife thinks he is secretly (or not so secretly) angry with her. What can a husband do to guard against coming across as bitter or harsh? See Colossians 3:19, and especially the letters from wives on page 142, for some simple but powerful ideas. Write down some things that may be useful in your marriage.

This question may be a sensitive one for discussion. If a husband is embittered because he secretly feels his wife is disrespectful, he may want to justify his attitude instead of seeing his wife's need for love. And if the wife is hurt by his harshness or irritation she will want to judge him as unloving and minimize her own disrespectful actions. Good-willed spouses who don't want to hang on to being angry or hurt over past problems can work their way into a discussion by comparing what they found in the letters from wives on book page 142. Also, if both of you are comfortable with the idea, look at Colossians 3:19 together. Paul's words are God's command to the husband to love his wife and not be embittered toward her. Why is bitterness never effective, always destructive? If a husband tries to use bitterness to "teach his wife a lesson," what kind of "lesson" will she learn? (Also note: As a husband, you may be saying this question is not for you, because you're not bitter. Nonetheless, husbands must always guard against sounding or looking bitter with a harsh tone or dark countenance. If a wife is perceiving her husband as "bitter and angry," which of the following are the most useful: a loving look, a friendly gesture, a gentler tone? All of these?)

6 To close Chapter Ten, Emerson asks husbands a practical question: "How Will You Then Live with This Sensitive Creature?" (book pages 143–44). As a husband, what practical ideas do you find on these pages that you can or should use? As a wife, what do you see on these pages that you would like to respectfully point out to your husband?

 Compare what you found on pages 143–44. Husband, did you ask yourself, "How often do I come off as harsh when I'm just telling her what I think?" Wife, did you think about, "How sensitive am I to my husband's words and moods? Am I letting him know tactfully and respectfully when he steps on my air hose because he sounds harsh?"

7 On book page 144, just before the chapter on openness ends, is some excellent advice for husbands concerning sex. According to Emerson, which of the following statements is true?

_____ To get sex I must try to appear to be more open.

_____ If I am genuinely open to my wife, she is more likely to be open with me sexually.

Talk together about the right answer, which is rather obvious, but not necessarily easy to practice for the typical husband. While the husband must be sensitive to his wife's need for

openness, she needs to be sensitive to his need for sex. This will be covered more thoroughly in Session 12.

———————

8 Look over the list of tips on book page 144. Husband, which ones
are you already using? Which ones are you going to try? Wife,
which of these tips would you like to have your husband try?

 Share together about these ideas and how they might help
your relationship. For starters, a husband should try at least
one idea that he and his wife agree would be helpful.

Questions for Chapter Eleven

9 Chapter Eleven opens with a discussion of 1 Peter 3:7, which says
a husband should live with his wife in an understanding way because she is the "weaker partner" (NIV) or "weaker vessel" (NKJV).
Feminists tend to bristle at this, claiming it says men are stronger, and
therefore superior to women. What has been your understanding of
"weaker partner"? Write your thoughts here, then compare them to
Emerson's explanation of what the verse means on book pages 145–46.

Discuss what you each wrote about 1 Peter 3:7. What do you think Emerson means when he says the wife is the weaker vessel (or partner) "because of her vulnerability to her husband within the marriage relationship"?

---

10 In "Always Handle Porcelain with Care" (book pages 146–47), wives are seen as porcelain bowls and husbands as copper bowls. Is this a good analogy? Why or why not? What does this comparison have to do with the husband needing to "understand" his wife?

Compare notes on your reaction to the porcelain/copper analogy. Talk about times when a wife wants to be "handled with care." What are some specific ways a husband can do this?

11 The bottom half of page 147 talks about something you may have noticed: The principles in C-O-U-P-L-E connect and even overlap. How can practicing closeness and openness help a husband with understanding his wife? Write your ideas here.

 Compare what you wrote. As you work on the rest of this session, take note when anything you wrote above matches up with some of the key truths in the rest of Chapter Eleven.

12 Read book pages 148–51. What does Sarah usually want from Emerson—a "solution" or a listening ear? How is the man's typical desire to "fix" whatever seems to be wrong an example of "blue" thinking? How is the woman's typical desire to "just want to talk" an example of "pink" thinking?

Compare yourselves with Sarah and Emerson. Does the wife usually want to "just talk"? Does the husband prefer to exchange information, come to conclusions, or "fix a problem"? If the two of you fit this profile, how does it sometimes lead to problems? What can each of you do about it?

***

13 "'Just Talking' Is a Key . . ." (book pages 151–52) presents some valuable help for men who are trying to show their wives understanding. Husbands, read this section carefully, then list key phrases and sentences you want to remember and ideas you want to try. Wives, what do you see in this section that describes you? How important is "just talking" to you?

***

Compare notes on what you have each written above. If "just talking" is even moderately important to the wife, she can elaborate on why this is true. Wise husbands will "just listen" and try to understand.

***

14 Do you agree that "Understanding Takes Scheduled Time"? (See book pages 152–54.) How does this idea strike you? Be totally honest.

    ____ a. I agree completely and already do this, or plan to do this regularly.

    ____ b. I'm not sure it would work . . . What would we talk about?

    ____ c. I'd like to try it, but doubt we have the time.

    ____ d. I think understanding is something you feel, not something you schedule.

    ____ e. I think:

 Compare answers, then discuss how useful it would be to schedule time to talk. (See Emerson's additional comments on answers *b*, *c*, and *d* in *Workbook* Appendix VI.)

15 Look over the list of tips at the bottom of book page 154. Husbands, pick at least one thing you will try this coming week. Wives, choose at least one thing you would like your husband to try this coming week. Write your choices here.

Compare your choices and agree on what the husband is going to try. (The wife should not be judgmental if her husband doesn't perform flawlessly. Be encouraging as he tries things that are probably new to him.)

A Journal of My Journey to Love and Respect

Take time to add your thoughts to the points below as you continue to create a record of your journey toward Love and Respect.

Scripture Meditations

1. Proverbs 31:12 says, "She does him good and not evil all the days of her life." Do you believe this about your wife? Does this motivate you to be more open with her?

2. The wise husband is "quick to listen, slow to speak" (James 1:19 NIV). As you deal with your wife, do you find it easier to give solutions or give empathy (put yourself in her shoes and think about how she feels)? If you are more solution-oriented, recall a recent conversation with your wife where it would have been better to listen than to speak. Would it help to pray daily asking God to help you be more empathy-oriented?

3. In 1 Peter 3:7, the apostle tells husbands to ". . . live with your wives in an understanding way . . . show her honor as a fellow heir of the grace of life." God has made your wife with needs and vulnerabilities that are different from yours. Can you name some of them? Do you find yourself being impatient with some of her needs or vulnerabilities? How can you begin treating her with more understanding and respect in one or two of these areas?

My current thoughts about our marriage:

Session Seven

In preparation for this session, read Chapter Twelve, "Peacemaking—She Wants You to Say, 'I'm Sorry.'" The following questions are for study by an individual or by a husband and wife studying together. Remember to answer all unmarked questions first, then answer questions marked by the male or female icon (whichever applies to you). Finally, answer the questions with the couple icon, if you're studying with your mate. (Suggestions for anyone planning to use this study with a small group can be found in *Workbook* Appendix I, page 201.)

1 On book page 156, Emerson introduces what he calls "the fourth side to connectivity"—peacemaking—and adds that it might be even more important than the three principles you have studied so far in C-O-U-P-L-E: closeness, openness, and understanding. As you began reading this chapter, what was your response to seeing peacemaking as a major principle for a husband to employ in "spelling love to his wife"? Choose from the statements below, or write your own response.

___ a. "Peacemaking" suggests there has been a fight; frankly, I always try to avoid conflict. I just want us to get on with our lives.

___ b. The best way to resolve a fight is to speak your mind and then drop it and move on.

___ c. I don't want to sound arrogant, but if my spouse would defer to my good judgments we wouldn't have these arguments and peace would reign.

___ d. Feeling at peace, because things are up-to-date with nothing between us, has a lot to do with my feeling okay about our relationship.

___ e. I think:

Husband, which of the comments above captures your feelings? Wife, which statement captures yours? As this session of study will show, it is vital for a wife to feel at peace, with nothing between her and her husband.

2 Continuing on book page 156, Emerson mentions a "paradox" he found as he studied the Scriptures: "God intended for some conflict to exist in a marriage." He goes on to say that secular research confirms that the best marriage relationships have conflict and that it almost seems that a marriage needs to have some conflict to keep the passion in it. What do you think? Do you agree that conflict puts just enough spice in marriage? Choose from these responses, or write your own:

___ a. Sometimes conflict helps; sometimes it doesn't.

___ b. Conflict is never good; it squelches passion for me.

___ c. A little conflict is good, because it's fun to make up afterward.

___ d. I think:

Discuss your answers, then compare your conclusions to what Emerson says about the risk involved when "the sparks fly" (book pages 156–57).

3 In "Husband and Wife Can 'Work It Out,'" book pages 157–58, Emerson makes some comments that may be new to you concerning how spouses can deal with conflict in their marriage. Read these pages carefully, then jot down phrases or sentences that strike you as a different approach to working out conflict. (If you are studying with your spouse, you can discuss what you find at this point, or wait until Question 4.)

4 What in particular does Emerson say on book pages 157–58 about how couples should view a conflict over sex? To put it in practical terms: "Tonight, after a particularly stressful day for both of you, who decides if you will be sexually intimate? First Corinthians 7:3–5 says both spouses have authority over the other's body, so who decides?" When Emerson speaks at Love and Respect Conferences, his answer to this question is: "Yes!" This usually gets a laugh, but the real answer is found in 1 Corinthians 7:5, plus what Emerson says on page 158. How would you sum up his description on page 158 of "one of the great principles of the New Testament"?

Discuss the ideas you both put down, then compare your conclusions with Emerson's further thoughts on this crucial question. (See Emerson's additional comments in *Workbook* Appendix VI.)

<hr />

5 In "My Wife Is Always Getting Historical," book pages 158–60, Emerson gives husbands another important tip for making peace. Husband, as you read this section, think about how "historical" your wife has been or can be. Does she bewilder you with her seemingly endless memory? Wives, how do you see yourself regarding your tendency to "get historical" with your husband?

   ___ a. Extremely historical (memory like an elephant)

   ___ b. Somewhat historical (might bring something up now and then)

   ___ c. Not historical at all (never bring up anything from the past)

   ___ d. I think:

 Compare your perceptions. What does the husband think of his wife's historical propensities? Does she agree that she can be historical? Discuss your answers. If tension begins to rise, try to keep things light: "May I borrow your pink/blue hearing aids? I need help understanding what you're trying to say." (For more "lighten things up" ideas see *Love & Respect* Appendix A, page 307.)

6 According to book page 160, why is it usually not helpful for the husband to say, "Let's drop it—just forget it"? At the bottom of page 160, what does Emerson recommend a husband say if he wants to make peace with his wife? Write out these three short sentences below and commit them to memory.

 Take plenty of time to discuss this one. Be sure to read the letter from the frustrated wife on book page 160. Work together on the real issue: love for her, respect for him.

---

7 The section captioned "Why It's Hard for a Man to Say, 'I'm Sorry'" (book pages 161–62) offers important insights on how men think. Emerson speaks from experience when he observes: "When a woman says, 'I'm sorry,' to her it's an increase of love. But when a man says, 'I'm sorry,' he fears he will lose respect." Do you agree or disagree with his observation? What does your experience tell you?

_____ a. I agree on all counts.

_____ b. I partially agree.

_____ c. I disagree on all counts.

_____ d. I think (write your reasons for your answer above):

---

8 Read the story about the couple who had a childish fight, but then he said the words that made her "fall in love with him all over again." Why is saying, "I'm sorry" so powerful? What dynamics are at work?

Discuss your answers and share what you think of Emerson's belief that when a husband humbly expresses sorrow for what he did, his wife melts. He doesn't think many men "grasp" this. Is he right?

9 Which points made in "A Short Course on Peacemaking," book pages 162–64, are most helpful, in your opinion? Some of the more obvious ideas are listed below. Choose from these, or find others you like as much or better:

_____ a. A husband should have absolute confidence in the power of his loving demeanor (see Proverbs 15:1).

_____ b. When a husband says he is sorry, he must be sure he means it, or be ready for another spin on the Crazy Cycle.

_____ c. The husband will make peace with his wife when he doesn't blame her but, instead, confesses his part of the blame (see James 5:16).

_____ d. When a husband says, "I'm sorry," it's a big turn on for a woman, but an even bigger turn-on is when he adds, "I think I understand your feelings and why you react as you do. Will you forgive me?"

_____ e. If a husband utters sincere words of apology, forgiveness, and love, his wife will trust his words and trust him. It can heal the whole thing.

_____ f. Other points I like:

The wife should be sure to fill out her answers to the above question along with her husband. Discussing your ideas can give you both more insights into how each of you thinks.

---

10 Chapter Twelve closes with a list of tips: "She'll Feel at Peace with You When . . ." (book page 164). Do you see anything else here that would help the peacemaking process in your marriage?

 As you compare notes on this question, you might want to review your answers to Question 9. Then, agree on one thing the husband can do differently during the coming week. When he attempts to practice what you both have agreed upon, if at all possible, stop and talk about how it worked, how it felt. Always be positive and encouraging to one another. If he makes real progress on his "one thing to do differently" go over the tips and ideas again and choose another action or attitude he can use to improve your peacemaking process.

A Journal of My Journey to Love and Respect

Build another "chapter" of your journal to Love and Respect by interacting with the following points.

SCRIPTURE MEDITATIONS

1. After giving advice to wives and husbands in 1 Peter 3:1–7, Peter writes this summary: ". . . all of you be harmonious, sympathetic, brotherly, kindhearted, and humble in spirit" (v. 8). As a spouse, which of these do you do best? Which does your spouse do best? Do you both bring strengths to the marriage that can make for peace?

2. "If possible, so far as it depends on you, be at peace with all men" (Romans 12:18). Peace is possible if you believe the other person wants to be at peace with you and will respond if you take the initiative. As a husband, do you have faith that if you were to apologize for being unloving, your wife would respond? As a wife, do you have faith that if you were to apologize for being disrespectful, your husband would respond? If your answer is yes, then as far as it depends on you, you can be at peace with your spouse.

3. "Be humble in the presence of God's mighty power, and he will honor you when the time comes" (1 Peter 5:6 CEV). We fear that if we seek to make peace by humbling ourselves and confessing our lack of love and respect, our spouse will not reciprocate. Ultimately, however, this is not about our humility before our spouse, but being humble in the presence of God. According to this verse, when we are humble in the presence of God what eventually happens? How can we have the courage to humble ourselves in this way (see v. 7)?

My current thoughts about our marriage:

SESSION EIGHT

In preparation for this session, read Chapter Thirteen, "Loyalty—She Needs to Know You're Committed," and Chapter Fourteen, "Esteem—She Wants You to Honor and Cherish Her." The following questions are for an individual or a husband and wife studying together. Remember to answer all unmarked questions first, then answer questions marked by the male or female icon (whichever applies to you). Finally, answer the questions with the couple icon, if you're studying with your mate. (Suggestions for anyone planning to use this workbook with a small group can be found in *Workbook* Appendix I, page 201.)

Questions for Chapter Thirteen

1 Read the opening of Chapter Thirteen on book page 165. What are your first impressions of the idea that a wife needs reassurance of her husband's love?

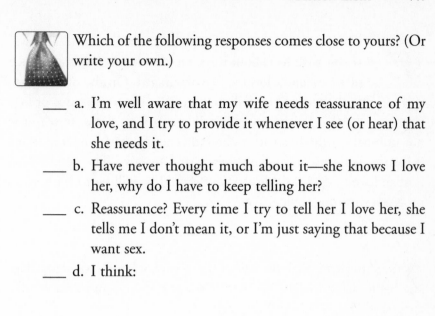

Which of the following responses comes close to yours? (Or write your own.)

___ a. I'm well aware that my wife needs reassurance of my love, and I try to provide it whenever I see (or hear) that she needs it.

___ b. Have never thought much about it—she knows I love her, why do I have to keep telling her?

___ c. Reassurance? Every time I try to tell her I love her, she tells me I don't mean it, or I'm just saying that because I want sex.

___ d. I think:

What is your reaction to page 165? Is reassurance of your husband's love something you like to hear fairly often? Check the answer that comes close to your ideas (or write your own).

___ a. Reassurance is important to me, and I think most women feel the same.

___ b. I've had my husband use that "Don't worry, I'm not going to trade you in for a new model" line, and I didn't think it was that funny.

___ c. My husband is always telling me he loves me, and I never get tired of hearing it.

___ d. I think:

Compare notes on your answers checked or written above. If you both feel about the same concerning the importance of a husband's loyalty, be encouraged. On the other hand, it is possible the two of you will not agree on the importance of loyalty, or even what loyalty looks like in a marriage. For example, it is not unusual for the husband to be rather unaware of how important it is to reassure his wife of his loyalty and his love. The good-willed husband who falls into this category should be willing to learn as he proceeds with this session.

2 Read the letter from the wife at the top of book page 166. How does her husband reassure her? Are there any key words or principles you appreciate or find useful? Write them here:

 Compare notes on what you see in the wife's letter that might be helpful in your own marriage. Spend some time on how the wife tells her husband she feels "emotionally disconnected" from him at certain times and what he does about it. Is "I'm feeling disconnected" something one or both of you might be able to say to communicate a need, or would it just trigger arguments?

3 Read the sections "She's a One-Man Woman . . ." and "It's a 'Swimsuit Issue' World," book pages 166–68. Is a wife being overly sensitive if she wonders about her husband's commitment, particularly with the barrage of beautiful females that bombard his eyes daily—in person and in the media? Choose from the following answers, or write your own opinion.

    ___ a. A wife can't help but wonder sometimes.

    ___ b. Either spouse might struggle with commitment.

    ___ c. It would be nice for a wife to be reassured now and then, especially as her body reflects the aging process.

    ___ d. What's a man to do? His wife should know he might look, but she has nothing to worry about.

    ___ e. I think:

This can be a sensitive issue, so beware of stepping on your mate's air hose. Try comparing the answers you checked or wrote. Wife, if you do feel at least a little insecure, let your husband know without condemning him. Husband, how can you reassure your wife of your commitment? Does Job have some good advice when he says: "I made a covenant with my eyes not to look lustfully at a girl" (Job 31:1 NIV)?

4 How does Song of Solomon 8:6 catch a wife's deep feelings about needing to always be sure of her husband's loyalty? Also read Emerson's thoughts on the wedding ring (book page 168). Why is a wedding ring so important? Write your ideas here:

Be sure not to skip this one. Share honestly with each other about your perspective on wearing a wedding ring. Is Emerson right when he says: "No husband should leave home without one"? Why or why not?

5 The prophet Malachi warned Israel against the prevalent practice of easy divorce that was going on in Israel as husbands dealt treacherously with their wives (see Malachi 2:14–15). Read "Are You Being As Loyal As You Could Be?" (book pages 168–69). Emerson is not saying that today's good-willed husband is trying to be treacherous toward his wife—but what is he saying? How can heeding Malachi 2:14–15 help keep you and your spouse off the Crazy Cycle?

Discuss your answers to this question with sensitivity to each other. Try to dwell on the positive idea that "his love motivates her respect." A big part of a husband's love for his wife is being loyal in every way he can think of. In Malachi 2:16, the prophet tells husbands, ". . . take heed to your spirit, that you do not deal treacherously [with your wives]." Is this passage only for husbands in Malachi's time, or is this also a warning for today's husband to be on guard against things that can undermine faithfulness to God and his wife? What are some of those "things" that can tempt a husband to be unfaithful?

———————

6 On book pages 169–70 read the story of Robertson McQuilken, who left his position as a seminary president to care for his wife who was slowly dying of Alzheimer's disease. What does McQuilken's "sacrifice" tell you about the meaning of being loyal as a husband? Write down some of the thoughts he expressed when he faced his decision.

You and your mate may want to read Robertson McQuilken's story together, then share your thoughts. See especially the quote, "Almost all women stand by their men; very few men stand by their women." How can a good-willed husband turn this statement from a possible guilt trip into a motivator to be more loyal to his wife?

7 Which of the tips included in "She Is Assured of Your Loyalty When . . ." (book pages 171–72) could be a real help in sparking the Energizing Cycle for your marriage? Pick out one and write a brief reason why this particular idea could help you and your spouse.

 Compare your choices, then agree on which tip the husband should practice during the coming week. If you each have a strong preference, perhaps he can practice both ideas. Be sure to talk about and encourage what he decides to live out on a daily basis.

Questions for Chapter Fourteen

8 Wives often ask where Scripture talks about the husband respecting his wife. On book pages 173–75 Emerson spells out what it means for a husband to respect (honor and cherish) his wife. (See especially 1 Peter 3:7.) Which of the following ideas, taken from this section, are most useful to you as a spouse?

_____ a. God has made women so that they want to be esteemed, honored, and respected.

_____ b. The honor a wife seeks is a different kind of honor from what her husband seeks as a man.

_____ c. To your wife, respect, honor, and esteem are not qualities in and of themselves; they are components of the love she wants from you.

_____ d. Other:

A wife studying with her husband should be sure to give her opinion on this one to see how closely it matches her husband's choices. Talk together about Emerson's claim, "Your wife wants to know that you have her on your mind and heart first and foremost. This is what I mean by 'esteem'; when it's there, your wife will feel treasured as if she's the most loved woman on earth" (book page 175). Do you both agree he is right?

---

9 In "Our Kids Often Made Sarah Feel . . ." (book pages 175–76) Emerson shares a practical way he esteemed his wife, Sarah, at a critical time in their marriage. What did he do, and why was it effective?

 If you have children growing up in your home, this story can be very applicable to your marriage at this time. Parenting is difficult at best. What does the final paragraph in the section tell you about why moms usually need more support and encouragement than dads as they do parenting tasks?

10 Back in Session 1, question 8 dealt with the time Emerson forgot Sarah's birthday—completely! This was good for several more turns on the Crazy Cycle for both of them. For further insight on how much store women put in birthdays and anniversaries, read "Use Symbols to Show Your Wife Esteem" (book pages 176–79). Following are some quotes from this section. Write down your response to each of Emerson's observations, whether you agree or disagree and why.

a. "You will never be able to show her the amount of emotional openness and esteem that she really wants—no man could—but symbolic things can do a great deal to bridge the gap."

AGREE ____   DISAGREE ____   **Explain:**

b. "Women are the ones who have babies, and that's one reason that birthdays are a big deal to them. . . . In a woman's mind, who could possibly forget a birthday? She never would."

AGREE ____   DISAGREE ____   **Explain:**

c. ". . . a marriage date is etched in the woman's soul. Since childhood, your wife dreamed of the wedding day. . . ."

AGREE ____   DISAGREE ____   **Explain:**

This section offers some great discussion possibilities. As a wife, do you feel about birthdays and anniversaries the way Emerson describes? As a husband, do you begin to grasp how important this can be to a woman? Discuss the example of giving the wife a Mercedes or a little rock with a sentimental message inscribed on it (see book page 178). Is Emerson overstating his case when he claims most women would treasure the rock more? What is his point? And be sure to read the letter from the wife whose husband "went all out" for Valentine's Day. Should more husbands try things like this? Why or why not?

---

11 Read the story included in "Does Your Wife Ever Want . . ." (book pages 179–81). Is Emerson right when he says, "Every husband has been expected to read his wife's mind"? What do you think of Emerson's suggested solution to the husband's problem when his wife doesn't want to go to the restaurant he picked? Is coming up with some alternative restaurants too much to ask of the typical husband?

The two of you can have fun with this story, as long as it doesn't crimp somebody's air hose. (You may want to borrow each other's pink or blue sunglasses and hearing aids!) For other ways to lighten up the discussion see book page 307. Also talk about how a husband can disagree with his wife and keep her esteem intact (see the last paragraph in the section, page 181, where Emerson offers three responses a husband can make). What is the key to disagreeing agreeably?

12 Read "Thank Her for All She Does" and "Your Wife Will Feel Esteemed When . . ." (book pages 181–82). Which of these ideas and tips for ways to make a wife feel esteemed seem most practical to you? Write down your choices and when you plan to try them.

Be sure the wife gets to contribute her opinion on what the husband might like to try. Later, after the husband tries at least one of these tips, talk about the difference it made and how this practice can be continued.

A JOURNAL OF MY JOURNEY TO LOVE AND RESPECT

When you have opportunity, review the journal entries you have made since beginning your journey to Love and Respect. Are you encouraged by your progress?

SCRIPTURE MEDITATIONS

1. Because Christians live in a secular culture, they are susceptible to the argument that it is unrealistic for two people to remain faithful to each other "'til death us do part." More than one Christian husband or wife has rationalized, "A person's needs change. In fact we just aren't the same people we were when we got married. I need to move on. I know God wants me to be happy." Is there any passage in the Bible that can "divorce-proof" your marriage? We know God "hates divorce" and He advises all husbands, "So guard yourself in your spirit, and do not break faith with the wife of your youth" Malachi 2:15 NIV). But on the positive side, what can a husband do? Proverbs 5:18–19 offers wisdom: ". . . may you rejoice in the wife of your youth. A loving doe, a graceful deer—may her breasts satisfy you always, may you ever be captivated by her love" (NIV). Not only does this passage assume that a marriage is to be long and lasting, but it tells us how to make it so. The loyal husband not only refuses to gaze on other women, but he fixes his eyes on his wife, refusing to see the negative, and rejoicing in her positive features and the loving person she is.

2. A woman never tires of hearing her husband call her "my darling, my beautiful one" (Song of Solomon 2:10). In your opinion, why is this true? Have you, husband, said this to your wife lately?

3. "Does a young woman forget all about her jewelry? Does a bride forget her wedding jewels?" (Jeremiah 2:32 NIRV). What is the prophet saying about the nature of the female? Is there any such language about men in the Bible? Why did God design women to remember in detail and forever those things related to being the object of her husband's loyal love? Her wedding jewels (today, her wedding ring) symbolize her husband's loyal love, reserved only for her. Do you as a husband appreciate how God designed your wife? If you have daughters, are you mindful that He made them the same way? Is it any wonder, then, that if your loyalty wobbles—or appears to wobble—that she will be filled with fear? Is it time to take her out to dinner (or just take her by the hand) and tell her how much you love her, how glad you are God gave her to you?

4. In 1 Peter 3:7 the apostle instructs the husband to live with his wife in an understanding way and to "show her honor as a fellow heir of the grace of life, so that your prayers will not be hindered." Peter continues in the passage (see 1 Peter 3:8–12) with general instructions to all believers on how to live the Christian life and sums up his teaching with a quote from Psalm 34:15–16: "For the eyes of the Lord are upon the righteous, and his ears attend to their prayer, but the face of the Lord is against those who do evil." The entire passage (vs. 7–12) shows that God watches a good-willed husband who treats his wife with understanding, and that husband's prayers are not hindered. One husband wrote Emerson to say, "You spoke of our prayers being hindered due to our relationships with our wives. Well, it hit me like a ton of bricks. I knew something was hindering my prayers, but this opened a new door to me." Questions for every husband: "Am I honoring my wife, esteeming her for all she is and does? Or are my prayers being hindered in any way because of how I treat her?"

My current thoughts about our marriage:

SESSION NINE

In preparation for this session, read Chapter Fifteen, "C-H-A-I-R-S: How to Spell Respect to Your Husband," and Chapter Sixteen, "Conquest—Appreciate His Desire to Work and Achieve." The following questions are for individual study or study by a couple. Remember to answer all unmarked questions first, then answer questions marked by the male or female icon (whichever applies to you). Finally, answer the questions with the couple icon, if you're studying with your mate. (Suggestions for leading a small group in studying this workbook can be found in *Workbook* Appendix I, page 201.)

This session opens your study of C-H-A-I-R-S, six principles to help a wife learn important aspects of respecting her husband. Note that just under the title of Chapter Fifteen in *Love & Respect* is a notice to husbands saying the next several chapters are "for wives only but husbands are invited to read along." Husbands are also invited to study along as well, so please do. As the wife discusses the six parts of C-H-A-I-R-S with the husband, she will learn more about how to respect him (and he will learn how to help and encourage her to do it better!).

A Special Word for Wives from Emerson:

What I told the husbands about how to use C-O-U-P-L-E (book page 118) also applies to wives regarding their acronym, C-H-A-I-R-S. The Crazy Cycle says that when a husband is acting unlovingly, there is a good chance he is feeling disrespected. And, as C-H-A-I-

R-S explains, there can be six good reasons for this. For example, if he feels you aren't really appreciating his desire to protect and provide for you (hierarchy), he can react in an unloving fashion. As C-O-U-P-L-E serves the husband as a diagnostic tool to figure out what is happening in the marriage, C-H-A-I-R-S plays the same role for the wife. She can say to herself, "Since my husband is acting in ways that feel unloving to me, perhaps it is because he feels disrespected. I can react in one of two ways: be even more disrespectful because he is so unloving, or I can decode by checking C-H-A-I-R-S to see where I might be saying or doing something wrong."

With this approach, you can temper your hurt feelings and resist the temptation to go after him with angry tears or criticism. You can try to decode his words or actions as you trust he is a good-willed man who wishes you no evil (even if it seems that way at the moment). Vital to your decoding process is to remember that C-H-A-I-R-S spells out six desires that are deep in a man's soul, given to him by God. For example, he has a desire to protect and provide, to serve and to lead, and others. Unconditional respect by the wife means she respects these God-given desires, even if her husband doesn't always fulfill them as well as he (or she) would like. (For more on understanding and respecting your husband's God-given desires, visit the Web site: http://loveandrespect.com/pearl/)

In a real sense, C-H-A-I-R-S is your "decoder" as you try to pinpoint what it is you may have done that felt disrespectful to your husband. For example, you recall a recent conversation in the car, when he started to offer his opinion on what should be done to get the kids to do their homework. You remember cutting him off in mid-sentence, saying you had already talked to their teachers and had it all worked out. Obviously, you stepped on his air hose big time in the area of Insight—his desire to analyze and counsel. What can you do? Apologize and ask for forgiveness for being disrespectful. (It also won't hurt if you start asking his opinion about things you have been handling alone because "it's just easier that way.") Chances are he may shrug it off and say "No problem," but deep down he will like being shown respect, if only through an apology. And the Energizing Cycle will start humming again.

As I mentioned to the husbands, there may be times when you can't decode what's wrong. Your best bet is to communicate your feelings with the "need communicator" statements at the bottom of page 306 in *Love & Respect*. Let him know that what he's been doing feels unloving and you wonder if you have done something disrespectful. He may or may not spell something out, but you can go ahead and say, "I'm sorry if I have been disrespectful. Please tell me how I can come across more respectfully." At this point, he may give you some idea of what is bothering him. Remember, many men have a hard time expressing that they feel disrespected and can struggle with describing their feelings. The better you know and understand C-H-A-I-R-S, the more successful you will be in decoding the situation.

Questions for Chapter Fifteen

1 To get started, the six words represented by the acronym C-H-A-I-R-S are listed below. Next to each word is a brief definition. Under each word write what it suggests to you. Does your definition match the one given?

Conquest: His desire to work and achieve.

My definition:

Hierarchy: His desire to protect and provide.

My definition:

Authority: His desire to serve and to lead.
My definition:

Insight: His desire to analyze and counsel.
My definition:

Relationship: His desire for shoulder-to-shoulder friendship.
My definition:

Sexuality: His desire for sexual intimacy.
My definition:

Which of these words piqued your curiosity as a husband or as a wife? Which seems most important to a happy marriage? Why? When the study of C-H-A-I-R-S is complete, come back to this question and see if your opinions have changed and talk about why they may have changed.

---

2 On the opening pages of Chapter Fifteen, Emerson reviews something he said earlier: for many wives the words "unconditional respect" seem like a foreign term, even an oxymoron. According to Emerson's research and experience with thousands of couples, a wife may buy into the idea of giving her husband unconditional respect, but have trouble with how to go about it. Take a moment to put down your honest thoughts about "unconditional respect" from your pink or blue perspective:

 I think "unconditional respect" is:

 I think "unconditional respect" is:

Be sensitive to each other as you share your answers. You may want to pass on discussing this now. If you want to try, it might be of help to go over the testimonial letters from wives on book pages 184 and 185. What worked for these women as they tried to start giving their husbands unconditional respect?

---

3 "How to Use the 'Respect Test' with Your Husband" (book pages 185–87) includes Emerson's description of one of the most effective tools he has developed to help wives tell their husbands, "I respect you!" Read this section carefully, then record your honest response. Could the Respect Test work in your marriage? Are you willing to try it?

Because you are studying together, obviously it will be impossible for a wife to "surprise" her husband by telling him, "I just want you to know I respect you." Suggestion for wives: write him a "respect note" sometime in the next few days. It doesn't matter if he knows the note is coming. What it says, surprise or not, is what will count. Suggestion for husbands: it is important that you receive and read this note without sarcasm or even teasing such as, "You just wrote this because Emerson told you to." All a husband need remember is how he would feel if he tried to do something loving that is suggested in *Love & Respect*, and his wife responded with, "You're just doing that because you read it in the book." Obviously the whole idea behind saying or writing a message of respect is that the wife wants to do it, even if she isn't sure what will happen.

4 Read the rest of the chapter, from "Be Ready with Reasons That You Respect Him" to the end (book pages 187–92). Emerson stresses that when a wife tells her husband, "I respect you," she must be ready with good reasons why, because he will want to know! A key problem for many wives, especially those just getting acquainted with the concept of respect, is that they can't think of what to say. Look over Emerson's suggestions and make some notes on what could work.

You may agree to leave this question strictly for the wife. If the Respect Test or writing a Respect Note has any favorable results at all (and it usually does) husband and wife will have lots to discuss afterward. As Emerson says on book page 189, the typical good-willed husband wants a happy marriage, and ". . . wives who try the Respect Test can be amazed at what will happen. Men are starving for respect." For examples of what can happen when wives start practicing respect, see the letters on pages 189–91.

Questions for Chapter Sixteen

5 Read the opening of Chapter Sixteen on book pages 193–94, especially the part about what not to say to a man who has lost his job. Why would it probably be nonproductive, even harmful, for a wife to say, "It's okay, honey; we have each other"? What does a man's job have to do with his sense of self-respect? Because his job is so important to him, does that mean his wife is unimportant? Write your thoughts:

Talk together about how important work is to a man. Keep in mind that in this day and age work may be quite important to a woman as well. Later in Chapter Sixteen, Emerson observes that many wives work, but the typical woman likes to have the option of being able to leave the workplace if she so chooses (see book page 199).

6 In "From the Start, Adam Enjoyed His Work" (book pages 194–96), Emerson shares insights from Genesis about the first man and his career path. What does this section tell you about men and their work? Emerson claims that working—being involved in adventure and conquest out in the field of life—is not an option for a man but rather, "it is a deep-seated trait." Write down some of your thoughts about why you agree or disagree with this idea.

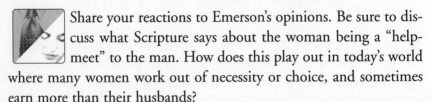

Share your reactions to Emerson's opinions. Be sure to discuss what Scripture says about the woman being a "helpmeet" to the man. How does this play out in today's world where many women work out of necessity or choice, and sometimes earn more than their husbands?

7 Read "A Man's First Question: 'What Do You Do?'" (book pages 196–98). What was the real threat to Emerson's two friends who faced dying of cancer?

The wife should be sure to answer this question and then talk with her husband about his work and its importance. According to the bottom of book page 197, what happens to a husband's air hose if she even implies unknowingly that his work is not all that important?

8 In "Do Women Want to Have It All?" (book pages 198–200), Emerson makes it clear that while women may desire to work out of the home, and may be extremely capable in their jobs, there are questions to ask about how this affects the family, especially the children. Do you agree or disagree with the following statements? Write brief reasons for your answers.

A woman should be able to work if she wants to.

AGREE _____   DISAGREE _____

If at all possible, the man should be the main breadwinner.

AGREE ____   DISAGREE ____

A woman should be able to stop working if she wishes (to take care of a new baby, for example).

AGREE ____   DISAGREE ____

Although there can be exceptions, generally speaking women make the best care-givers for children.

AGREE ____   DISAGREE ____

For the typical wife, her first desire is not for a career but for a home and family.

AGREE ____   DISAGREE ____

Comparing your answers to the above statements can provide much valuable sharing. If both of you are working, try to come to some mutual conclusions as to why you both work, how long this will continue, and where the children fit in.

9 Read the last two sections of Chapter Sixteen: "Have You Ever Said, 'Thanks for Working'?" and "He Wants a Woman Who Believes in Him" (book pages 200–03). Then take the True or False test that pertains to you:

Mark each statement T for True, or F for False.

____ I have told my husband numerous times, "Thanks for working."

____ I sometimes think my husband works too long and too much.

____ My husband is much more than a "meal ticket" to me.

Mark each statement T or F.

____ It would be (is) nice to be told, "Thanks for working."

___ I know I work too many hours, but feel I have no choice.

___ I sometimes feel I'm just a "meal ticket."

Compare your answers and discuss them. Be sensitive to each other, particularly concerning "working too many hours." Note Emerson's comment on page 202 of *Love & Respect*: "If he is a good-willed man who is neglecting his family by working too much, he will realize it, and you can talk it through and work it out." (For more on a man working too much see *Love & Respect* Appendix E, page 315.)

10 Go over the tips on book page 203 ("Your Husband Will Feel You Appreciate His Desire to Work and Achieve When . . ."). Choose two or three you think could benefit your marriage. When do you see these being tried?

Compare notes on what each of you chose. If the husband's feelings about how his work is perceived did not come out in Question 5, they may be clearer as the two of you talk about it here.

A JOURNAL OF MY JOURNEY
TO LOVE AND RESPECT

You should be very comfortable at this point with recording your thoughts and impressions of your journey toward Love and Respect. Continue to follow through at the conclusion of each session until the end of the workbook.

SCRIPTURE MEDITATIONS

1. As you begin your study of C-H-A-I-R-S, remember that each letter in the acronym is designed to help the wife who may well be sailing in uncharted waters called "unconditional respect." Emerson has talked to many wives who want to respect their husbands unconditionally, but they are not sure how to go about it. To these wives I say, "How perfectly you do this is not the issue; how willing you are is what counts." A good verse to keep in mind is Proverbs 14:1: "The wise woman builds her house, but with her own hands the foolish one tears hers down" (NIV). One woman who had realized her mistakes wrote: "I am 'a nasty, big mouth wench' who emotionally abused her husband by her lack of respect and bad behavior. I know a foolish woman tears down her own house, now I want to build my house back up." Chances are you are not in this woman's shoes, but perhaps God is calling you to make some things right. What, specifically, can you start practicing as a way to respect your husband unconditionally?

2. The husband who finds a good spouse who supports, appreciates, and respects him "obtains favor from the LORD" (Proverbs 18:22). Have you ever heard your husband say, in one way or another, that he was a favored man because of you? If not, there are two possible reasons: he is overlooking the gift you are to him and needs to be more mature in his evaluation of you; or perhaps your disrespect has made it hard for him to feel and express his appreciation. Have you ever considered that you have been given by the Lord to your husband to

meet his need to be respected? Has it occurred to you that this is part of God's call on your life? Is this call getting easier to answer? Why or why not?

My current thoughts about our marriage:

SESSION TEN

In preparation for this session, read Chapter Seventeen, "Hierarchy—Appreciate His Desire to Protect and Provide," and Chapter Eighteen, "Authority—Appreciate His Desire to Serve and to Lead." The following questions are for study by an individual or study by a couple. Spouses studying together should note that Chapters Seventeen and Eighteen cover material that is complex and sensitive. Leave plenty of time for reading and discussing all of the additional commentary as well as *Workbook* Appendix IV, which deals with mutual submission. Remember to answer all unmarked questions first, then answer questions marked by the male or female icon (whichever applies to you). Finally, answer the questions with the couple icon, if you're studying with your mate. (Suggestions for leading a small group in studying this workbook can be found in *Workbook* Appendix I, page 201.)

Questions for Chapter Seventeen

1 According to the dictionary, *hierarchy* means "a body of persons organized or classified according to rank, capacity, or authority." When you read the phrase, "hierarchy in marriage," what immediately comes to mind? Check the answer that comes closest to your honest first response, or write your own.

    ____ a. Politically incorrect.

    ____ b. Men think they are superior.

___ c. God's plan is good, but men abuse it.

___ d. I think:

 Compare your answers. Did either of you check or write a definition that interprets "hierarchy in marriage" negatively? Discuss what Emerson says on page 205 of *Love &* *Respect*. Does he think the Bible supports chauvinism and the "superiority of the male"? Write down the gist of what you believe Emerson is saying:

2 According to the section "What Is the Real Meaning of 'Biblical Hierarchy'?" (book pages 206–8), what kind of hierarchy has God planned for marriage? (See also Ephesians 5:22–24.) What does God call the husband to do? What does He call the wife to do?

Talk about a husband's responsibility to love, protect, and provide for his wife. Take a second look together at the letter from a wife on book page 207. How did she first interpret her husband's firm, even a bit gruff, efforts to lead and protect her? What changed her mind about his leadership?

---

3 According to Emerson (book pages 207–8) an evil-willed man might abuse his position as head of the family but a good-willed man would not take advantage of his wife or children because "that is not his nature. He will not use his position as 'chair' of the family against those he is to love and protect."

 Do you think Emerson is right? How do you see your husband in his role as "head" of the family? Which statement comes closest to describing him?. Or if you prefer, write your own:

_____ a. I am comfortable with my husband as "head." He does a good job.

_____ b. I agree he should be the "head," but I wish I could have more input.

_____ c. I am not completely comfortable with my husband as "head." He thinks he is being biblical, but he puts the children and me down at times.

_____ d. I think:

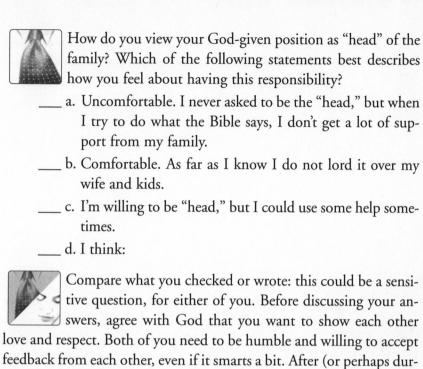

How do you view your God-given position as "head" of the family? Which of the following statements best describes how you feel about having this responsibility?

_____ a. Uncomfortable. I never asked to be the "head," but when I try to do what the Bible says, I don't get a lot of support from my family.

_____ b. Comfortable. As far as I know I do not lord it over my wife and kids.

_____ c. I'm willing to be "head," but I could use some help sometimes.

_____ d. I think:

Compare what you checked or wrote: this could be a sensitive question, for either of you. Before discussing your answers, agree with God that you want to show each other love and respect. Both of you need to be humble and willing to accept feedback from each other, even if it smarts a bit. After (or perhaps during) your discussion, read together Emerson's additional commentary in *Workbook* Appendix VI to get additional input.

Following are some questions for a good-willed husband to help him evaluate how he feels when his wife chooses quietness rather than being verbally contentious. As a husband, which of the following comes closest to what you might think? (As a wife, which of the following would you say your husband would choose?)

_____ a. Her quietness is an endorsement of my position and no further discussion is needed. I get what I want.

_____ b. I'm afraid her quietness is short term and insincere; she will verbally attack me if she doesn't get her way.

_____ c. Her quietness gets my attention and calms me down. I often feel convicted about where I have been unreasonable and want to make amends.

_____ d. I think her quietness is one of two things: weakness and fear, or rebellion and anger. Either way, when she won't talk to me I get irritated.

_____ e. Her quietness? That would be nice. I have not encountered what Emerson describes.

_____ f. I think:

This can be sensitive. Remember that both of you have goodwill and want to treat each other with love and respect. The good-willed wife may want to assure her husband that she never uses quietness as a ploy or a weapon. The good-willed husband may want to reassure his wife that as she seeks to obey God, he will seek to respond in good faith as well. (For more examples of how a wife's quiet respectfulness can influence her husband, go to http://www.loveandrespect.com/pearl/)

4 Read "Paul Versus Today's Culture" (book pages 208–9). In an "ideal marriage relationship," how does a husband act? What are some reasons a wife might be hesitant to place herself under her husband as "the head"? Which of the following comments might apply to you and your spouse?

_____ a. He can be the head, but will he really care about my needs?

_____ b. I want him to be the head, but not too much.

_____ c. What if headship becomes dictatorship?

____ d. I make more than he does, so why does he get to be the head?

____ e. My comment:

Compare the answers you checked or wrote down. Is "the husband as head" an accepted concept in your marriage, or are there concerns and questions? At the bottom of book page 208 and top of 209, Emerson describes a problem many wives have (and that includes Christian spouses). They want to be treated like a princess but "deep down they resist treating their husbands like the king." Do you think he is right or wrong? Or, would you say this is true of some marriages but not yours?

5 In "How to Deflate a Husband with Seven Words" (book page 209), find the remark a wife made that deflated and disrespected her husband. Fill in the blanks:

"You need _____ _____ _____ _____ _____.**"**

Why would this remark hurt a husband so badly? List some reasons here:

Compare your answers and discuss what happened in the incident described on book pages 209–10. Was the husband too sensitive? Did the wife have any clue about what showing him respect might mean? In earlier sessions you covered the question that any Love and Respect spouse can ask to guard against being unloving or disrespectful. For husband or wife, the question begins: "Is what I am about to say or do . . . ." How does this question end for the husband? For the wife? (If you need help, see "Always ask yourself" in *Love & Respect* Appendix A, page 305.)

6 Read the touching story in "Showing Respect by Candlelight," book pages 210–11. What stands out in this account of how and why Dr. E. V. Hill and his wife, Jane, ate by candlelight? Write down your strongest impressions.

Compare your answers. Wife, if something like this would happen to you and your husband, would your natural response be similar to what Jane Hill did? Husband, if you found yourself in the same situation as Dr. Hill, how would you have responded to the "candlelight dinner for two"? Talk together about how important finances are to a marriage. Is Emerson correct in saying: "Mark it down. Men are more vulnerable to criticism when it is related to headship issues"?

7 Read "The Card He'll Keep Forever" (book pages 211–13). Why does being told by his wife that she respects his leadership work so powerfully on the typical husband? Write your own ideas. How do they compare with what the husband says in his letter on page 212?

Compare your answers. This could possibly be an awkward question for one or both of you, so be sensitive to each other's feelings. (The use of a Respect Test or Respect Note was covered in Session 9, but it is well worth repeating here, in this session on hierarchy.) Wife, are you willing to write such a card or note to express appreciation for his leadership and protection? Husband, what would you think if she did? Would you save such a card or note to read and reread it?

8 Go over the tips in "Your Husband Will Feel You Appreciate His Desire to Protect and Provide When . . ." (book pages 213–14). Choose one or more that you believe would benefit your marriage. Write down your choices, putting them in your own words as much as possible, and adding ideas of your own that would apply.

Husbands should write down their choices too. Compare the ideas each of you chose and then agree on at least one thing the wife can do or practice during the coming week. At the end of the week, talk together about how it went for each of you. Is it worth continuing? What other ideas could you try?

Questions for Chapter Eighteen

9 Read "Who's the Boss at Your House?" (book pages 216–17). Then indicate whether you agree or disagree with the following statements and write a brief reason for your answer.

a. Men and women are totally equal, and husbands don't have any more responsibility and authority than their wives do.

AGREE ____   DISAGREE ____   **Explain:**

b. The good-willed husband who acts responsibly and lovingly as leader of his home always works out compromises that are mutually pleasing.

AGREE ____   DISAGREE ____   **Explain:**

c. If a wife is a better decision maker and has better judgment than her husband, she should demand equal say regarding what they buy, where they go, what they do.

AGREE ____   DISAGREE ____   **Explain:**

d. The good-willed wife who is more competent than her husband needs to demonstrate her abilities by her respectful speech and deferential attitude, with the confidence that in time her husband will prize her giftedness.

AGREE ____   DISAGREE ____   **Explain:**

Compare your answers to these statements. This could be a sensitive area, particularly if the wife is inclined toward the feminist view, which claims that men and women should have equal authority and responsibility. A good goal is not to cater to what society and culture are saying about husbands and wives but work to understand what Scripture says. Many wives are like the young woman in the opening of Chapter Eighteen (book page 215) who said: "I want him to be the head. I want him to be the leader. I just want to make sure that he makes decisions in keeping with what I want."

10 Read "Does Scripture Teach Mutual Submission?" (book pages 217–19), where Emerson discusses the concept of "mutual submission" which says husbands and wives should submit to one another with neither one being owed any special deference. What impressions or opinions do you have about "mutual submission?" Choose from the statements on the next page, or write your own assessment.

____ a. Mutual submission sounds unworkable. Ultimately, someone has to be responsibly in charge.

____ b. These mutual submission people may have something. I need to get more info.

____ c. I prefer the Love and Respect approach.

____ d. I think:

As you compare your answers, be aware that for some couples this could be a sensitive question. Biblical feminists have argued in recent years for a certain kind of "mutual submission," which they base on Ephesians 5:21: "Submit to one another out of reverence for Christ" (NIV). Those proposing this particular mutual submission approach interpret Ephesians 5:21 to mean that the wife owes no special submission to her husband. However, Ephesians 5:22 clearly says: "Wives, submit to your husbands as to the Lord" (NIV). The Love and Respect approach to marriage is based on Ephesians 5:22, which does not give a husband a mandate to treat his wife poorly. On the contrary, he is to defer to his wife's need for love in all situations. This is his goal, even though he is certain to fall short at times. Review page 218 of *Love & Respect*, especially the discussion of how to deal with honest stalemates. For more on mutual submission and a detailed explanation of the apparent contradiction in Ephesians 5:21–22, see *Workbook* Appendix IV, page 213.

11 Read "Husbands Are Responsible to 'Make the Call'" (book pages 219–21). How does a Love and Respect couple reach a decision when there is an honest stalemate, a difference of opinion where husband and wife both have good points and reasons why they believe their way is best? List some steps they can take to keep Love and Respect working in their relationship. According to book page 220, if the husband has to "make the call" and his wife does not agree with it, how does she cope with the temptation to feel unloved at the moment? How does she show him respect?

Compare your answers and talk about how you deal with stalemates in your own marriage. Wife, do you agree with Emerson's advice on book page 220 to remain respectful and quiet? Husband, do you accept your responsibility to "make the call" when necessary if a decision is needed and you can't agree with each other? For additional help with your discussion, see *Workbook* Appendix IV, as well as Emerson's additional commentary in *Workbook* Appendix VI.

12 The following paragraphs are excerpted from the section in "Authority Must Come with Responsibility" (book pages 221–23). Mark your reaction to each paragraph and put down a brief reason why.

a. ". . . because God has made your husband responsible (review Ephesians 5:25–33), he needs the authority to carry out that responsibility. No smoothly running organization can have two heads. To set up a marriage with two equals at the head is to set it up for failure. . . . God knew someone had to be in charge, and that is why Scripture teaches that, in order for things to work, the wife is called to defer to her husband."

AGREE ____   DISAGREE ____   **Explain:**

b. "If you want to work with your husband to reach mutually satisfying decisions most of the time, follow this principle: GO ON RECORD WITH YOUR HUSBAND THAT YOU SEE HIM AS HAVING 51 PERCENT OF THE RESPONSIBILITY AND, THEREFORE, 51 PERCENT OF THE AUTHORITY. Once you go on record about his authority, he will not feel you are trying to be the boss. As you submit (which simply means recognizing his biblically given authority), you will not be a doormat. In fact, you will get your way far more often than you would if you 'stood up for your rights,' which usually means being disrespectful."

AGREE ____   DISAGREE ____   **Explain:**

c. ". . . among good-willed couples, if there are one hundred decisions over a three-month period related to the family, the wife will have a strong opinion on ninety-nine of them, and her opinion will usually be respected and have strong influence."

AGREE ____   DISAGREE ____   **Explain:**

For spouses studying together: compare your answers and discuss as many as possible. If you have definite disagreement on a certain paragraph, you may want to focus on that. For additional discussion ideas, see the additional commentary in *Workbook* Appendix VI. (For more on how a wife's submission can strengthen a marriage, see *Workbook* Appendix IV.)

13 Look over the tips in "He Will Feel You Appreciate His Authority and Leadership When . . ." (book pages 224–25) and choose one or more that sound useful for your marriage. Here and on the next page write down what you have chosen, and start thinking of how this idea might be carried out.

Compare your choices. Discuss why you think these particular ideas are important. Be sure the husband gives his input on what he would like his wife to try.

A Journal of My Journey to Love and Respect

Write your responses to any Scripture Meditations that seem to speak especially to your regarding your marriage. Also, put down something, no matter how brief, about your current feelings, fears, or questions.

Scripture Meditations

1. "Those who talk a lot are likely to sin. But those who control their tongues are wise" (Proverbs 10:19 NIRV). Some wives feel nothing can be resolved apart from talking. Proverbs 10:19, however, says that sometimes too much talk ends up in sin. This is especially true because of the thoughts that precede the talk, as one wife discovered. She wrote to me to say she had begun to realize the many ways she had been disrespectful to her husband during twenty-six years of marriage. The result was she didn't have the marriage she would have liked and she began asking God to alert her when she was going to say something disrespectful. At first she couldn't recognize the disrespect until after it was out of her mouth, but then she began recognizing the disrespectful words as they were going through her mind and realized they could be stopped. It also helped to hear her pastor preach on the need to control the tongue, that what comes out of our mouths is what we put in our hearts. Her letter concludes: "If we feed on God's

Word, that is what comes out of our mouths; likewise I recognized that if we feed on being irritated with our husbands, thinking about how they fail us, hurt, or offend us, that is what comes out of our mouths . . . . Luke 6:45 says, 'What's stored up in the heart overflows in the mouth.' (That may be paraphrased.) Sounds like love and respect to me!"

2. A wife's willingness to show her husband respect and defer to his authority should not undermine her God-given abilities, as the Proverbs 31 woman clearly demonstrates: "She considers a field and buys it; from her earnings she plants a vineyard" (Proverbs 31:16). As a husband, have you considered designating authority to your wife in certain areas, which will empower her to use her God-given talents? I have done so in my marriage, with wonderful results. My wife, Sarah, is an efficient administrator when it comes to finances. I have entrusted her with the day-to-day bills and financial decisions because I trust her heart and competencies. I am grateful to God, because this has freed me to focus my abilities elsewhere. Why has this worked? One reason is that Sarah has never been afraid to communicate to me that she sees me as the one having 51 percent authority. Another reason is that I have never feared designating the day-to-day authority to her for the finances. She looks to me for approval and sanctioning when new and more major questions arise, and I ask for her counsel as we come to a final decision. In our case this has worked beautifully. I feel respected as the one who is ultimately responsible, but I give her the authority as the one who is immediately involved.

My current thoughts about our marriage:

SESSION ELEVEN

In preparation for this session, read Chapter Nineteen, "Insight—Appreciate His Desire to Analyze and Counsel." The following questions are for individual study or study by a couple. Remember to answer all unmarked questions first, then answer questions marked by the male or female icon (whichever applies to you). Finally, answer the questions with the couple icon, if you're studying with your mate. (Suggestions for leading a small group in studying this workbook can be found in *Workbook* Appendix I, page 201.)

Questions for Chapter Nineteen

1 On the opening pages of Chapter Nineteen, read the story of the wife who decides to visit her husband where he works. What does she see? What does she learn? What has she been missing?

 Compare the notes you made with what your mate discovered. Did you see the same things? Where did you differ? Discuss the story to see if it has any relevance to your marriage. If it does, be sensitive to each other and express your ideas with the "Is what I'm about to say or do . . . " question in mind. (See *Love & Respect* Appendix A, page 305.) Analyze together the letter from the wife at the bottom of book pages 228–29. Has either one of you thought much about the importance of a man's insight? How would you rate your typical daily exchanges? Are they conversations or monologues?

2 In"I No Longer Believe Totally in Womanly Intuition," book page 229, Emerson admits he no longer gives complete credence to two beliefs he once held: (1) that the vast majority of men are opinionated, one-sided, and inattentive; and (2) that women possess an exclusive and unique power of intuition that is always right. Why did he change his mind? Check the answer that fits or write your own thoughts:

    _____ a. He realized he was getting a very one-sided view from the wives he counseled.

    _____ b. He read some helpful books that straightened him out.

    _____ c. He realized that constantly pounding on men to "listen to the intuition of your wives. . . . God will teach you through your wives" was tipping the scales too much.

    _____ d. My thoughts:

The problem of "lack of spiritual leadership by the husband" may or may not apply to your marriage. As a husband, if you are taking spiritual leadership, rejoice with your wife in that fact. As a wife, if you wish your husband would take more spiritual leadership, first ask him if he would mind discussing this. If he is open, proceed to explain what you wish the two of you could work out in matters such as family devotions, praying together, and church life. (For additional discussion material on the husband's spiritual leadership, see Emerson's commentary in *Workbook* Appendix VI.)

(For more on how a wife can help her husband, see Question 5 below. And for more on the husband's spiritual leadership go to http://www.loveandrespect.com/pearl/)

---

5 At the bottom of book page 232, Emerson lists some questions for the wife to ask herself about any area of leadership where she feels her husband's leadership is lacking or questionable. Which of these questions, if any, apply to your marriage? Write them here:

Also, read the rest of page 233 and most of page 234, down to the next subhead. Do any of the following statements by Emerson from these pages apply to your marriage at all?

    ____ a. ". . . ask yourself if you may possibly have an attitude of self-righteousness—at least to some degree. . . . You may well believe, as many women do, that you are a better person than he is and that he needs to change."

My thoughts on this:

___ b. "What I see happening in some marriages is that the wife believes—or appears to believe—that she does not sin. In many other marriages the only sin that a wife will readily admit to is her negative reaction to her husband's failure to be loving or for losing patience with the children."

My thoughts on this:

___ c. ". . . it's easy for a wife to discount or disparage a husband's suggestion that she has some problem that needs correcting. Even if he is gentle and diplomatic in suggesting that she needs to make a correction . . . he is quickly silenced. She is offended, wounded, and angered by his assessment. He is accused of being without understanding and compassion. He has no right to speak. And he will often wind up being shown contempt."

My thoughts on this:

Be sensitive to each other as you share your thoughts on these statements, which are quite confrontational to the wife. None of them may apply in your marriage, and if so, celebrate this fact together. If something does apply to some degree, discuss it calmly, always invoking the "Is what I am about to say . . ." rule (see *Love & Respect* Appendix A, book page 305). You may not be able to agree on every point, but try to follow Emerson's advice: "I believe husband and wife together need to examine any situation where something is amiss and try to come to a solution or, if needed, seek godly counsel."

6 In "Are You Trying to Be Your Husband's Holy Spirit?" (book page 234–237), Emerson warns that in many marriages, wives see their husbands as unrighteous. He writes, "Because she is the one who constantly seems to have to be on top of things, such as correcting the children (and him), she slips into an attitude of self-righteousness without realizing it. It is often subconscious, but a subtle judgmental spirit comes over a woman. Many women have admitted to me, 'I've got to stop being my husband's Holy Spirit.' . . . I never hear men saying, 'I've got to stop being my wife's Holy Spirit.'" How can a wife avoid slipping into a judgmental attitude (even though she may have good reason)? See especially pages 235–36 for practical ideas and list them here.

This can be another sensitive question, so walk softly to avoid stepping on each other's air hose. On book page 235, Emerson cites the account of Mary and Martha (Luke 10:38–42), which contains wisdom that is equally good for husbands and wives. Humbly focusing on Christ is a good way to avoid being or sounding judgmental. To paraphrase Jesus, "Don't look for the speck in your spouse's eye, be aware of the possible log in your own!" (see Matthew 7:1–5). Talk together about what this section may be saying to one or both of you. Note the wife's letter, bottom of page 236, top of 237, for more good advice.

7 Check the tips under "Your Husband Will Feel You Appreciate His Insight and Counsel When . . ." (book page 237). Choose one or more that look applicable for you and write them here for reference later. (Note how many of these tips parallel tips under Understanding, in Chapter Eleven. A husband is a natural-born "fixer," so in some cases you may have to accept his insight, when all you think you need is his listening ear.)

 Compare notes on what you chose. As a wife, it might be especially appropriate in this instance to ask for your husband's insight. Which ideas did he choose? What does he want you to do first?

A Journal of My Journey to Love and Respect

Write any thoughts prompted by the following Scripture Meditations by Emerson, or just record your perception of how the study has gone to this point.

Scripture Meditations

1. Proverbs 3:7 tells us, "Do not be wise in your own eyes. . . ." This warning is often applied to men, who can be very firm about their view of things. But doesn't this verse apply to women as well? For instance, a group of wives may gather for coffee, even Bible study, and wind up talking about their marriages and how their husbands "just don't get it." The implication: the wife always "gets it" regarding what God had in mind with creation of male and female. Yes, the wife certainly has her very pink point of view, but does she really "get it" regarding the very blue point of view of her husband? "Do not be wise in your own eyes" cuts both ways. Husband and wife both need to adjust their sunglasses and hearing aids and become wise together as they seek God's counsel.

2. I have counseled many wives who admit that, deep down, they consider themselves better than their husbands—at least "better" in the sense of how to love the family and run the household. It is not hard to see why a wife may feel this way, but she should be aware that this is a dangerous state of mind. Listen to Paul's words in I Timothy 2:14: "Adam was not the one deceived; it was the woman who was deceived and became a sinner" (NIV). Paul isn't letting Adam off the hook. He followed as his wife lead him like a lamb to the slaughter and wound up being held responsible for the Fall (see Romans 5:12–19). The point is, husbands and wives are both sinners; both face their own private temptations. In 1 Timothy 2:14 Paul reminds today's wife that Eve was the one who was deceived (and by implication, so can she be deceived). When a woman, for

whatever good reasons, begins to think she is intrinsically better than her husband, she slips into being self-righteous and judgmental (all in a "loving way," of course). To those who might say or even think, "I am holier than you," God replies that this kind of attitude is "smoke in My nostrils, a fire that burns all the day" (see Isaiah 65:5). First Timothy 2:14 is not there to shame the wife but to remind her she can be deceived. She must ask herself, "Am I a better person because God made me one way and my spouse another? Can either of us be saved apart from Jesus and His grace?" These questions are equally good for the husband. They enable husband and wife to come together in mutual confession and joyful connection.

3. As a wife, are you looking for ways to make it easier for your husband to lead and give insight? Peter has a lovely thought in 1 Peter 3. He says your real beauty "should be that of your inner self, the unfading beauty of a gentle and quiet spirit, which is of great worth in God's sight" (1 Peter 3:4 NIV). As you get dressed for the day, it is important to look well-groomed, fresh, and attractive on the outside, but the more important thing is what is inside. A good daily prayer might be: "Lord, as I dress this morning, please clothe me in a gentle and quiet spirit."

My current thoughts about our marriage:

SESSION TWELVE

In preparation for this session, read Chapter Twenty, "Relationship—Appreciate His Desire for Shoulder-to-Shoulder Friendship" Chapter Twenty-one, "Sexuality—Appreciate His Desire for Sexual Intimacy," and Chapter Twenty-two, "The Energizing Cycle Will Work If You Do." The following questions are for an individual or a husband and wife studying together. Remember to answer all unmarked questions first, then answer questions marked by the male or female icon (whichever applies to you). Finally, answer the questions with the couple icon, if you're studying with your mate. (Suggestions for anyone planning to use this workbook with a small group can be found in *Workbook* Appendix I, page 201.)

Questions for Chapter Twenty

1 Read book pages 239–40 in *Love & Respect*. Is your marriage anything like the marriage described in the opening of Chapter Twenty? In your marriage, does he just want her to "be with him" with little or no talking? Check the answer that comes closest to describing you and your spouse.

OFTEN THE CASE ____   SELDOM HAPPENS ____
NEVER HAPPENS ____

My comments:

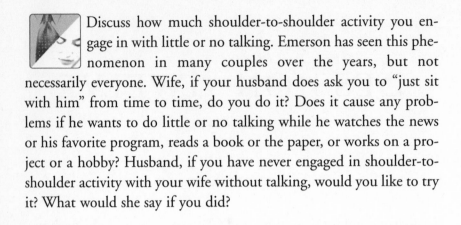

Discuss how much shoulder-to-shoulder activity you engage in with little or no talking. Emerson has seen this phenomenon in many couples over the years, but not necessarily everyone. Wife, if your husband does ask you to "just sit with him" from time to time, do you do it? Does it cause any problems if he wants to do little or no talking while he watches the news or his favorite program, reads a book or the paper, or works on a project or a hobby? Husband, if you have never engaged in shoulder-to-shoulder activity with your wife without talking, would you like to try it? What would she say if you did?

This session can take the two of you in three possible directions: (1) the wife will learn a new way to meet a basic need in her husband for shoulder-to-shoulder activity; (2) you both will better understand why he needs this kind of activity and why it energizes him; or (3) you both will agree he doesn't need shoulder-to-shoulder much, if at all.

2 Read "How Can 'Doing Nothing' Build a Relationship?" (book pages 240–42). What are some reasons a wife might have trouble with just sitting with her husband watching TV or watching him work on a project in his workshop? How does this need in many husbands illustrate major differences between "pink" (wives) and "blue" (husbands)?

Compare your answers, then discuss them. The typical wife could have real problems with just sitting "doing nothing" when she has so many chores and other activities. But would it be worth the time if it leads to feeling closer as a couple—and, possibly later, face-to-face talking?

---

3 In "For a While There, Sarah Wasn't Friendly" (book pages 242–43), Emerson recounts a time when Sarah was not too friendly, not only toward him, but the rest of the family in general. Her cleanliness standards were being violated, and she was always on everyone to pick up, wash up, and shape up. What happened to change Sarah's mind?

Talk about this story together. Here, indeed, was a case of "pink" and "blue" needing to like each other in spite of weaknesses and faults. Go back to the top of book page 242. Talk about how husbands and wives need to be lovers, yes, but also shoulder-to-shoulder friends. In Song of Solomon 5:10–16, the wife describes her husband in the most amorous of terms, but she also adds, "This is my beloved and this is my friend" (vs. 16).

---

4 Read the section under "Wives, Be Patient with 'Just Sit by Me'" (book pages 243–45). Which of the following sentences or paragraphs excerpted from this section give you insights into the male need to just be "shoulder-to-shoulder" with little or no talking?

___ a. "When the husband calls the wife in to 'just sit by him,' he is working on their relationship in a significant way. . . . This is the way a husband communicates."

___ b. "Males prefer shoulder-to-shoulder communication instead of face-to-face communication, and this can occur in the simplest of ways."

___ c. "In most marriages, then, there is a real difference in basic needs. As we saw in Chapter Nine, she wants to talk, to be close. But in this chapter we see that the natural bent of the male is to be shoulder-to-shoulder with a lot less talking. Obviously, there must be some give and take at this point as there should be in so many other areas of marriage."

Regarding "shoulder-to-shoulder with little talking" I think:

Compare any notes you have made concerning choices *a*, *b*, or *c* above. As mentioned earlier, not all husbands have this need, but many do. If shoulder-to-shoulder is something he wants to do, how can his need be balanced with her need to be close and just talk?

5 Read the experiences of three different wives in "Spend Time Together, Stay Together" (book pages 246–47). What can be learned from the wife in Peoria? From the letters by wives who are benefiting from being shoulder-to-shoulder? Write down any key words or phrases you find.

Compare notes on what you found in these accounts. And be sure to discuss the last two paragraphs in this section. Does Emerson's "twelve-week experiment" sound worth trying? Is it too much to ask a wife to do something that feels unnatural? Are the possible benefits worth it?

6 Go over the tips in "Your Husband Will Feel You Value His Shoulder-to-Shoulder Friendship When . . ." (book pages 247–48). Which of these might benefit your marriage? Write them here, with any added notes on how they can best be implemented.

Compare your choices and decide on what should be tried first. After a week or so, compare notes on how it is going. Make adjustments, if any are needed.

Questions for Chapter Twenty-One

7 Read the opening story of the doctor and his wife, plus the section called "They Kicked the Devil out of Bed" (book pages 249–51). How did the doctor's wife turn their impasse into a win-win?

Which of the following statements from this section speak most directly to you and your marriage?

_____ a. "If there ever were an issue that isn't really the issue, it is sex."

_____ b. "Sex for him and affection for you is a two-way street."

_____ c. "Sex is symbolic of his deeper need—respect."

Complete this sentence: In our marriage, sex is . . .

 There is a lot to compare and talk about in Question 7 that could lead to tension. Much depends on how satisfying your sex life as a couple is at the moment. Ideally, husband and wife meet each other's major needs: his for sex, hers for intimacy through affection mixed with plenty of talking. Then both are content.

But often there is an imbalance that leads to friction and fighting or a dull and boring relationship. Be sensitive to each other as you talk through this three-part question. If he doesn't think he gets enough sex, or she doesn't think she gets enough affection and closeness with talking, do not condemn one another. Share what you can, always seeking to show each other love and respect. (For more ideas and suggestions, see *Workbook* Appendix V, "Sex: Love and Respect Come First—Then, 'Just Do It!'"(page 218).

---

8 Read "Two Keys to Understanding Your Husband" (book pages 251–53). Emerson describes two aspects of why a husband has sexual desire for his wife. What are they? Put each one in a sentence or two at the most.

On book page 252 is a story about a mother who gives her daughter some advice concerning sex. Do you agree or disagree (explain your choice) with her when she says, "Why would you deprive him of something that takes such a short amount of time and makes him soooooo happy"?

AGREE _____   DISAGREE _____

Compare your answers to the two aspects of a man's sexual desire for his wife. Put in its simplest terms: he sees her and he wants her. If she wants him, she can make him sooooo happy. But it isn't always that simple, as most couples can attest. Talk about how the husband needs to woo his wife with closeness, openness, and sincerely talking with her to connect with her. When the wife feels close, she may want to become close physically, but it is an interplay that both spouses must work out in terms that are unique to their relationship. As always, this kind of interplay should be governed by love and respect.

---

9 In "The Golden Rule Works with Sex Too" (book page 253), Emerson describes the tension in every marital sexual relationship. She wants to feel close emotionally in order to connect sexually. He wants to feel close sexually in order to connect emotionally. Neither is wrong, just different. In the second paragraph in this section is a rule (see line in italics) that applies to every principle covered in the Energizing Cycle, and especially sexuality. This rule, which never changes, is (copy it here and commit it to memory):

 Talk together about the rule that never changes. Are you at a point where you are getting better at sharing your needs with each other openly, without stepping on each other's air hose? This could be a good time to review together *Love & Respect* Appendix C: "How to Ask Your Mate to Meet Your Needs" (see page 311–312). See especially what she can say about closeness and openness, and what he can say about sexuality. Obviously, these "scripted statements" are only suggestions. Each spouse can and should work out her or his own way of communicating needs to the other.

———————

10 "A Dose of Respect Beats a Dose of Viagra Any Day" (book pages 254–55) includes two letters, one from a wife whose husband committed adultery, and one from a husband who also strayed. In both cases, why was the husband vulnerable to infidelity? What does this say about the link between sex and respect?

Share your answers, which may or may not be similar. In both cases the husbands were being deprived of sex, but the thing that really drew each man into an adulterous relationship and held him there was that his adulterous partner made him feel admired and respected. As one of the straying husbands wrote, "Somebody thought I was okay." What does this say about the constant need to let each other know, "You are okay, lovable, respectable, wanted, and needed"? Are these positives being communicated in your marriage?

11 Read "If He Loves Me, How Can He Be Tempted by Other Women?" (book pages 255–58). Which of the following statements, taken from the paragraphs near the bottom of page 257 and top of 258, are most helpful to you as a spouse? Add your comments below.

_____ a. "A man is responsive to what he sees. He needs his wife's understanding of his struggles. If he wanted to be untrue to her, he would never allude to the problem at all."

_____ b. "A wife longs to receive her husband's closeness, openness, and understanding. You can achieve this in two ways: (1) do your best to give him the sexual release he needs, even if on some occasions you aren't in the mood, or (2) let him know you are trying to comprehend that he is tempted sexually in ways you don't understand."

_____ c. "If your husband is typical, he has a need you don't have. When you shame him, punish him, or deprive him, he feels dishonored for who he is. . . . But he needs you. . . . As you recognize his need and seek to meet it, you will find him, reaching out to meet yours."

My comments on the quote I chose:

Compare your choice of quotes, realizing this can be a very sensitive subject. You may want to discuss one or more of the quotes above, or you may want to come back to this at another time. One solution for this problem that has worked for some couples is for the husband to meet with other men and share with them. In this way they can encourage each other to resist sexual temptation, as well as keep each other accountable.

12 Choose from the tips under "He Will Feel You Appreciate His Desire for Sexual Intimacy When . . ." (book page 258) and choose one that you believe can benefit your marriage. Write it down, with an estimated date for when it could be tried.

Compare notes and talk about how the two of you can make this happen. The husband should not put the entire burden on his wife. This is definitely a time for love on his part, respect on hers.

Questions for Chapter Twenty-Two

13 You have covered C-O-U-P-L-E and C-H-A-I-R-S, which give the husband and wife six ways each to love and respect each other. On book page 259 is the definition of the Energizing Cycle: His love _____ her _____. Her respect _____ his _____.

If you haven't memorized this yet, do it now, and never forget it. The Energizing Cycle is the answer to keeping the Crazy Cycle from turning on.

Now go to page 260. In "How Does a Husband Spell Love to His Wife?" is a brief review of C-O-U-P-L-E, six tools the husband can use to maintain his side of the Energizing Cycle for his marriage. If you are a husband, make some notes below on which of these six tools you have understood in a new way or even learned about for the first time. Which ones are easiest for you to use? Which ones are harder? Which ones have made a definite difference in your relationship? If you are a wife, make notes below on the six tools in C-O-U-P-L-E. Which ones has your husband been using? Which ones would you like to see him use more? Why?

Compare what you wrote. What does the husband think he has been doing well? Where does he see he could be doing better? What does the wife think he has been doing well? If the wife has suggestions on what the husband could be doing better or more often, she should be encouraging, not negative and complaining. The point is, even small steps of progress on the Energizing Cycle are symbolic of a big step of progress for your marriage.

14 "How Does a Wife Spell Respect for Her Husband?" (book pages 260–61) is a brief review of C-H-A-I-R-S, six tools a wife can use to maintain her side of the Energizing Cycle for her marriage. If you are a wife, make some notes below on which of these six tools you have understood in a new way, or even learned about for the first time. Which ones are easiest for you to use? Which ones are harder? Has using any of these tools made a real difference in your relationship to your husband? In what way? If you are a husband, make notes below on the six tools in C-H-A-I-R-S. Which ones has your wife been using? Which ones would you like to see her use more? Why?

Compare your answers. What does the wife think she has been doing well? What does she think she could be doing better? What does the husband think she has been doing well? If the husband has some suggestions on what his wife could do better, he should be encouraging, not complaining (or even teasing).

15 Is it easy or hard to "cut your spouse some slack" as he or she tries to practice the principles in C-O-U-P-L-E or C-H-A-I-R-S? Read the wife's letter that begins on book page 261. What has she learned that all spouses should try to practice?

Compare your answers to see if you both included what the wife said about what her "first response" should be. To put it briefly: always try to find positives about your spouse, not negatives. This is not easy. The negative comes naturally. The positive is often much harder, because, look, your spouse has stepped on your air hose again!

On page 262 Emerson writes, "You can't grasp the Holy Grail of perfection, which is always beyond your reach. But you can embrace Love and Respect, which will always provide more than enough to energize your marriage." Is he right? Do you believe enough to act on the principles embodied in C-O-U-P-L-E and C-H-A-I-R-S? If you do, your marriage will not only be less negative and more positive, it will be the kind of marriage that honors Christ in every way. (To look ahead to the Rewarded Cycle, Part III, see "From the Energizing Cycle to the Rewarded Cycle" (pages 262–63.)

A Journal of My Journey
to Love and Respect

Emerson's Scripture Meditations, below, are one possible source of journal entries you may want to make. Or just write your thoughts on where you are in your marriage. What do you see happening? What do you need to do or stop doing?

Scripture Meditations

1. A woman should consider how to be a companion to her husband. After all, God did say, "I will make a helper who is just right for him" (Genesis 2:18 NIRV). Have you, as a wife, considered that a most helpful activity for you that is just right for your husband is a shoulder-to-shoulder activity? Many husbands are energized by a wife's mere presence. As your husband's helper, have you been overlooking a very fruitful way to help your husband and energize your marriage?

2. In marriage, timing is everything. There is, indeed, "A time to be silent, and a time to speak" (Ecclesiastes 3:7). Have you seriously considered that there are times when talking is not a good thing? For example, if a husband has been unloving or disobedient to Christ in some other way, the shoulder-to-shoulder wife can find new meaning in "won without a word" (1 Peter 3:1). Although "without a word" may make little sense to you as a woman, God's Word is worth trusting. In the past, how persuaded have you been that the only way to convict your husband was by voicing your complaint to him? During this "season" of your marriage, is it a time to be silent? Could it be that when you are respectfully silent a husband can better listen to God and his own conscience?

3. "Your two breasts are like two fawns . . . that browse among the lilies" (Song of Solomon 4:5 NIV). This passage is describing the attraction a wife's breasts have for her visually oriented husband. When you courted, were you aware of his visual orientation? Now that you

are married, do you still acknowledge that orientation, or do you act as though it should not be there? What about your emotional orientation? Should he act as though it should not be there? If a husband denies his wife's emotional orientation, what could happen? If a wife denies her husband sexually, what could happen? For rather explicit details on how not to deny each other's needs, read Song of Solomon 4:1–15, which is Solomon's song of praise to his wife's charms. Also note verse 16, where the wife gives her husband a passionate invitation to be sexually intimate.

4. "With her flattering lips she seduced him" (Proverbs 7:21 NKJV). It is possible that a husband might be seduced by a sexy, sensual woman, but he is far more likely to be seduced by an admiring woman. We could assume the woman spoken of in Proverbs 7:21 flattered her victim with false respect and phony admiration. Actually, what she said to him could have been true enough, but her motives were false and manipulative. Why was he so easily manipulated? A good guess is that he could have been living with a wife who never said anything respectful to him, much less admiring.[i] When the adulteress laid her trap (see Proverbs 7:6–20), he fell for it completely, just as a wife who gets no emotional intimacy can be seduced by a man who is "kind and understanding." How can you affair-proof your marriage? With love, respect, and trust in God.

My current thoughts about our marriage:

PART THREE:
THE REWARDED
CYCLE

Sessions 13 and 14 cover Chapters Twenty-three and Twenty-four, and the Conclusion of *Love & Respect*

A PERSONAL WORD FROM EMERSON:

In Part One you learned how to slow and stop the Crazy Cycle. In Part Two you learned how to build a better marriage with the Energizing Cycle. In Part Three the message is different and has multiple applications: the Rewarded Cycle is for couples who are trying the Love and Respect Connection but it isn't working well. They have slowed the Crazy Cycle but aren't quite on the Energizing Cycle. The Rewarded Cycle is also for spouses hanging on by a thread in a marriage where his unconditional love for her, or her unconditional respect for him, is getting little or no results. And finally, the Rewarded Cycle is for all couples who want to know the real reason for love and respect.

Ultimately, all husbands and wives should be practicing Love and Respect principles first and foremost out of obedience to Christ. If they do not, it is so easy to start being arrogantly proud about "our great marriage." So many marriages seem to be getting along just great, and then *wham!*—the wheels come off. If we take our eyes off Christ (or never put our eyes on Christ in the first place), we are building on sand, and when the storms come, we can be swept away (see Matthew 7:24–27).

What follows contains comfort, encouragement, and plenty of straight talk for any spouse who wants to learn the deepest meaning of respecting or loving unconditionally. The Rewarded Cycle explains that you love and respect, not because you want to save your marriage, or even strengthen your marriage (worthwhile as those goals are). You love and respect because you want to love and reverence Christ. In the ultimate sense, your marriage has nothing to do with your spouse. It has everything to do with your relationship to your Savior and Lord, and how much you want to serve and glorify Him.

SESSION THIRTEEN

In preparation for this session, read Chapter Twenty-three, "The Real Reason to Love and Respect." The following questions are for an individual or a husband and wife studying together. The suggestions for spouses studying together are of two kinds: (1) for couples who have managed to slow the Crazy Cycle, but are struggling to get on the Energizing Cycle; (2) for couples who are on the Energizing Cycle, but who can still profit from what the Rewarded Cycle has to tell them about how central Jesus Christ should be in a marriage. Remember to answer all unmarked questions first, then answer questions marked by the male or female icon (whichever applies to you). Finally, answer the questions with the couple icon, if you're studying with your mate. (Suggestions for anyone planning to use this *workbook* with a small group can be found in *Workbook* Appendix I, page 201.)

1 Read "Don't Give Up—Trust God to Work" (book pages 268–70). If you are a spouse who is struggling, which of the following quotes from this section speak to you the loudest right now?

    ___ a. "Don't give up just because it doesn't seem to be working."

    ___ b. "Don't doubt the light from God's Word in your dark times."

    ___ c. "Most often, Love or Respect is working on your spouse more than you realize."

    ___ d. "Have confidence that God will work."

Write your thoughts here and on the next page regarding what you checked above. How can one or more of these ideas help you right now?

If you have slowed the Crazy Cycle but can't seem to get the Energizing Cycle started in your marriage, look at the quotes above. If you haven't already checked one or more of them, do so now. Then, if both of you are willing, talk about where you are now and how you must trust God and His Word to work in your lives. (If yours is a marriage that is on the Energizing Cycle, rejoice together and give God the glory for what He has done, and what He will continue to do as you trust in Him.)

2 In "When It Simply Doesn't Work—What Then?" (book pages 270–71), Emerson explains what the Rewarded Cycle is all about. Following are some key quotes to consider if you have been ready to say, "This Love and Respect thing just doesn't work." Choose one of Emerson's statements and write some reasons why it encourages or enlightens you regarding your situation.

_____ a. "When you love or respect unconditionally, you are following God and His will for you. Ultimately, your spouse and your marriage have nothing to do with it."

___ b. "Unconditional love and unconditional respect will be rewarded. I call this the Rewarded Cycle."

___ c. "I believe Paul also had your marriage in mind when he penned Ephesians 6:7–8: 'Serve wholeheartedly, as if you were serving the Lord, not men, because you know that the Lord will reward everyone for whatever good he does . . . (NIV)."

___ d. "In marriage, everything you do counts, even if your spouse ignores you!

This is what the Rewarded Cycle is all about:

HIS LOVE BLESSES REGARDLESS OF HER RESPECT;

HER RESPECT BLESSES REGARDLESS OF HIS LOVE."

Write your thoughts here regarding the statement you chose. Does the Rewarded Cycle sound too hard? Or is it strangely encouraging, even inspiring?

As a couple you may have had trouble putting the Energizing Cycle in gear. Go over the four statements above that describe how the Rewarded Cycle works. Does the Rewarded Cycle sound helpful or too hard? If you can talk with your spouse about these things, share your deepest thoughts and feelings. (Couples on the Energizing Cycle: read together the third paragraph

on book page 272, beginning with "All couples must take heed . . . ."
Then talk about how you can keep your marriage on a foundation of
rock, never letting it shift to sand.)

---

3 Read "Heaven's Reward—The Eternal 'Ahhh!'" (book pages
272–74). Have you ever thought of heaven in the terms that
Emerson describes in this section? Suppose you could put all the
happy, joyful experiences you have ever had into one big package that
you could enjoy all the time. When you share your Master's happiness,
the intensity of being with Christ forever will be "a trillion times
greater" than that! Emerson concludes this section by saying, "When
you make a decision to love or respect your spouse, the dividends are
without end. Jesus is offering you a bargain. Do a few things on earth
in this life and get many things forever in heaven." As you think about
hanging in there with a marriage that just doesn't seem to be working,
what is your reaction to Emerson's words? Do you agree that the endless, boundless, indescribable pleasures of heaven will be worth the
"momentary affliction" you are feeling now? Write your thoughts here.
Be very honest—tell God how it really is. (You can read Emerson's additional comments in *Workbook* Appendix VI.)

 If you are able to talk to each other about your marriage,
this is a good question to chew on together. Is heaven
worth the rough trip you are having here on earth right

now? Can you begin to catch a vision of God using your "momentary light affliction" to bring you eternal joy? The first thing the two of you have to do is commit to your marriage because you are doing this as unto Christ, and you look forward to the matchless rewards He has waiting. If you can do that, it will open the way for things to happen here on earth as you struggle between the Crazy Cycle and the Energizing Cycle.

(Couples on the Energizing Cycle: never cease to remind yourselves that you are loving and respecting each other "as unto Christ." When you someday meet Christ face-to-face, He will ask you: "Did you do what you did in your marriage for Me?" How sad if a person must reply, "Lord, I had a good marriage, but I must confess I never thought about You." I know of one wife who had a very good marriage, but she had been overlooking where Christ really fit in. Then she heard the Love and Respect challenge and wrote to say: "The image of myself looking through my husband and seeing Christ was exactly what I needed to hear. Knowing that when I hold my tongue [and] have self-control over my responses, it is not only out of respect for my husband but in obedience to God. What a breakthrough!")

———

4 Read "What Matters to God, Matters!" (book pages 274–76). Does the "cha-ching!" effect offer any hope and encouragement? Note that Emerson is not talking about earning your salvation; but he is talking about earning rewards (see 1 Corinthians 3:11–15). Which of the following quotes from this section give you hope and encouragement? Pick one and write down why it appeals to you.

    ___ a. To the world it makes no sense to respect a harsh, unloving husband or to love a contemptuous, disrespectful wife. "But it makes sense to God. These seemingly fruitless efforts matter to God because this is the kind of service He rewards. What is wisdom to God is foolishness to the world" (see 1 Corinthians 3:19; also 1 Peter 2:19; 4:13).

    ___ b. ". . . look at Ephesians 2:10. We are to do the good works that God has already planned for us. Why? Not to appease the Lord or somehow pay 'just a little bit' for our salvation, but simply to please Him. And when we please Him, He rewards us."

    ___ c. "Yes, the rewards are waiting. Nothing we do is wasted. The Lord is watching with intense interest. A husband who loves his wife as Christ loved the church, and the wife who respects her husband 'as unto the Lord,' will be rewarded throughout eternity (see Ephesians 5:22–33)."

About rewards, I think:

It may be hard, if not impossible, for the two of you to think about "rewards in heaven" right now. You are having enough struggles on earth. Nonetheless, Scripture does promise rewards for those who earnestly seek to do God's will, however imperfectly. If you have chosen one of the paragraphs above, talk about what it means to you and how its truths can energize you right now. Emerson heard a wife who had been ready to divorce her husband tell a large group of women that the Rewarded Cycle had gotten her eyes off her husband and on the Lord. God revealed to her heart that her first step was to respect her husband unconditionally, "as to the Lord." Until that realization she was feeling defeated and without energy. (Couples on the Energizing Cycle: be sure to look at what Emerson has to say about "not needing rewards, just wanting to reach heaven" [book pages 275–76]. Rewards are important because Jesus reveals them as important. Thank God together for your marriage and any rewards He may have waiting for you.)

———————

5 Read what Emerson says in "It's About You and Jesus Christ" (book pages 276–78). Then answer the three questions below:

a. What is the vital prerequisite if love and respect are to work in your marriage?

b. What is the difference between the successful couple and the unsuccessful one?

c. What is the epitome of immaturity?

The previous three questions are important ones for the struggling couple to answer.

Concerning *a*: if Christ is not the Lord of your life, Love and Respect will not work in God's eyes. Only love and respect done in faith pleases God. If one of you "isn't quite sure" where he or she stands with Christ, this spouse can pray what Emerson suggests: "Lord, I do believe; help my unbelief. I want to follow You, and I want to do this as unto You." (See Mark 9:24.)

Concerning *b*: the difference between the successful couple and the unsuccessful couple is found in Proverbs 24:16. Only Christ can make us righteous, but only we can get up after we fall. Couples who have gotten on the Energizing Cycle have kept dealing with the issues. They never give up!

Concerning *c*: the epitome of immaturity is wanting everything to come easy, with no struggle. Read the letters starting at the bottom of book page 277 to see how two wives took the high road to maturity. (Couples on the Energizing Cycle: read Proverbs 24:16, then talk about why you are successful and what you must continue to do to be successful.)

———

6 Read in "Lord, When Did I Feed You?" (book pages 278–80). What is the basic principle we can take from Christ's parable of the last judgment? Write your answer here:

Do you agree with what Emerson spells out beginning at the bottom of page 279?

". . . ultimately, whatever you do toward your spouse by way of love or respect is not done to motivate your spouse to get off the Crazy Cycle, nor is it to motivate your spouse to meet your needs. Ultimately, you practice love or respect because beyond your spouse you see Jesus Christ and you envision a moment when you will be standing before Him at the final judgment, realizing that your marriage was really a tool and a test to deepen and demonstrate your love and reverence for your Lord."

Write your thoughts here. Tell God what you really feel right now:

For the struggling couple, the questions above could produce a critical moment. If both of you can agree with what Emerson is saying, you can take a giant step forward in your marriage. If one of you is reluctant or just not sure, the other spouse should be patient and wait for God to work according to His timing. (Couples on the Energizing Cycle: talk about why you show each other love and respect. Is it because you want a happy marriage? Because you are trying to get your spouse to meet your needs? Because you want to serve Christ and reverence Him? All of the above—at least to some degree?)

A JOURNAL OF MY JOURNEY TO LOVE AND RESPECT

Emerson's Scripture Meditations may serve as a basis for new entries in your journal or you may prefer to record insights and thoughts that have come to you during this session.

SCRIPTURE MEDITATIONS

1. Scripture acknowledges that we can be afraid, and at least one passage teaches that although we have fears we can deal with them. As Peter told his flock, "Do what is right without being frightened by any fear" (1 Peter 3:6). As a husband, are you afraid of loving your wife, especially if she is disrespectful? Why? As a wife, are you afraid of respecting your husband, especially if he is unloving? Why?

2. "Don't pay back unkind words with unkind words. Instead, pay them back with kind words" (1 Peter 3:9 NIRV). Next time your wife says something disrespectful to you, say something loving; next time your husband says something unloving, say something respectful. Watch what happens. Yes, I've often heard the complaint: "My spouse is different! You don't know my spouse. What you think will happen with my spouse won't happen!" Perhaps not, but why deprive yourself of God's reward by imitating your spouse's negativity? Care enough about God's heart, and what He has in store for you, to do things His way. In all likelihood, the tone of the conflict will turn more positive.

3. "Watch out that you don't lose what you have worked for. Make sure that you get your complete reward" (2 John 1:8 NIRV). The apostle John is teaching something here that has staggering implications. You can go twenty years in your marriage loving and respecting, building up your personal "reward account." Then something could happen in your twenty-first year of marriage and you wind up having contempt, even hatred, for your spouse. John is saying, "Beware, God is gracious; your salvation is assured, but you could fall into sin that would negate some of the rewards God

has planned for you." John is not naïve; he knows believers are being tempted by sin of all kinds, all the time. He is warning his flock because he knew people wouldn't slip into sin when times were good. No, it was far more likely they could lose some of their rewards because they would lose heart in the face of unexpected challenges. John's words are also for you, today, in your marriage. Are you determined to finish faithfully no matter what?

My current thoughts about our marriage:

SESSION FOURTEEN

In preparation for this session, read Chapter Twenty-four, "The Truth Can Make You Free, Indeed" and the Conclusion, "Pink and Blue Can Make God's Purple." The following questions are for an individual or a husband and wife studying together. As in Session 13, the suggestions for spouses studying together are of two kinds: (1) for couples who have slowed the Crazy Cycle, but can't quite get on the Energizing Cycle to their satisfaction; (2) for couples who are on the Energizing Cycle but who can still benefit from what the Rewarded Cycle has to say about how central Jesus Christ should be in a marriage. Remember to answer all unmarked questions first, then answer questions marked by the male or female icon (whichever applies to you). Finally, answer the questions with the couple icon, if you're studying with your mate. (Suggestions for anyone planning to use this study with a small group can be found in *Workbook* Appendix I, page 201.)

Questions for Chapter Twenty-Four

1 Read "Heaven Will Wait—What About Now?" (book pages 281–83). On page 283 Emerson shares his boyhood experiences, when he watched how his mother handled his father's fits of rage. What did she do as she lived with a less-than-perfect spouse? How many things can you learn from her? Write some of them here:

If the two of you are struggling but can still talk together, rejoice in that fact as you begin this session. Compare notes on what you found in the example Emerson's mother set for him as she coped with his father's anger. How easy is it to fall into a "victim mindset"? How hard is it to "choose to be positive"? Do either one of you see yourself having a victim mindset? Are you willing to confess it and move on by making the choice to be positive? (Couples on the Energizing Cycle: you will find much in this session about how to stay there and keep the Crazy Cycle in its cage. Talk together about what it might mean for the two of you to look for "creative alternatives" when you do have a conflict from time to time.)

2 In "'Sometimes the Issue Is Me!'" (book pages 283–85), Emerson states the Rewarded Cycle Principle (which he admits is useful for anyone on the Energizing Cycle as well). That principle is: no matter how depressing or irritating my spouse might be, my response is my responsibility. What if you are doing everything you can to love or respect your spouse and you still get back cruelty, harshness, contempt, unreasonableness, or indifference? Read the letter from a husband beginning at the bottom of page 284. Then write your thoughts about the Rewarded Cycle Principle. Are you willing to take responsibility for your response, no matter what?

 If at all possible, discuss this question together. Talk about Emerson's admission on book page 284 that "in my own marriage, Sarah doesn't cause me to be the way I am; she reveals the way I am. When my reactions to her are unloving, it reveals that I've still got issues. There is still lack of love in my character and soul, and I have to own up to this." Even though Emerson and Sarah are on the Energizing Cycle, there are always moments when they need wisdom from the Rewarded Cycle. As Emerson puts it: "When we are on the Energizing Cycle, we are also on the Rewarded Cycle, given that we are conscious of loving and respecting each other because we do it as unto Christ. The point is, everyone trying to live out the Love and Respect Connection is on a continuum, trying to become a more loving, respectful spouse. No one is perfect; everyone struggles at some point." Do Emerson's words encourage you in your own situation? (Couples on the Energizing Cycle: realize that, like Emerson, you still have "issues" like everyone else. When you talk together about whatever happens in your marriage, each of you should always say, "My response is my responsibility.")

---

3 Read "What's Inside Will Come Out" and "Inner Freedom Develops Greater Maturity" (book pages 285–87). The grain of sand illustration on page 285 teaches that when your spouse puts heat or pressure on you, you always face a choice (fill in the blanks): "to react in a _____ way or in a _____ way." The "secret" to reacting in a godly way is found in John 8:30–36. In an exchange with Jewish leaders, Jesus reveals the way to true spiritual freedom. What do His words have to do with your marriage? See page 287 for answers and then put some of these truths in your own words here:

If you are struggling as a couple, the key to ending (or start-ing to end) your struggles is in the lengthy paragraph at the top of page 287. Read this paragraph together, down through the principle it entails: I can experience hurt, but it is my choice to hate. What is all this saying to each of you? To both of you? (Couples on the Energizing Cycle: you can find much in this section to talk about and digest. Share especially how John 8:36 can keep you on the Energizing Cycle: "So if the Son makes you free, you will be free indeed.")

4 Under "You Can Be Free in Any Circumstance," Emerson continues to describe how you can have inner freedom no matter what situa-tion you are facing. Read 1 Peter 2:16–17. Also, be sure to study Endnote 1 for Chapter Twenty-four, book page 324. Where are you right now with putting Peter's instructions into practice in your marriage?

____ a. "Not sure I can do it. You don't know what my spouse is like!"

____ b. "I'm willing to try, but I feel so weak and unsure of what to do."

___ c. "Through God's grace I will do this; I am trying to do it already!"

___ d. I think:

If you and your mate are on the Rewarded Cycle, or trying to be, your answers probably ranged between *b* and *c* above, or perhaps you had your own way of putting it. Look together at the letters on page 289. How did these wives conquer their contempt and lack of respect for their husbands? Also discuss the top paragraph, page 290, in which a husband writes, "It was freeing to reflect on the fact that she was well-intentioned and good-hearted toward me." As Emerson points out, if you believe at all that your spouse is "good-willed" despite those times of being unloving or disrespectful, it can put you on the road to the Rewarded Cycle, and you can build on that. (Couples on the Energizing Cycle: talk about how Peter's instructions in 1 Peter 2:16–17 can apply to your marriage. Are you living as "free men" while you work on your Love and Respect Connection? Look together at Endnote 1, Chapter Twenty-four, page 324. Do you agree that ". . . the greatest evidence of submission is Love and Respect"?)

5 Read "Inner Freedom Rewards You with a Legacy" (book pages 290–93). Which of these quotes from this section speak to you the most?

___ a. "Parents want their children to love and respect them, but if they aren't showing love and respect to each other, what kind of legacy are they leaving behind?"

___ b. "Each day you are on the edge of something; you face some kind of crossroads. Today could be the day something happens that will make all the difference. . . . As your children see you living out Christ's words, 'The truth shall make you free,' you will set them on the path of following Jesus as well."

___ c. "You're thinking about mistakes you've made, the times you haven't been a good example, and those numerous scenes where you didn't show love or respect to your spouse. Don't despair. God has a unique way of eliminating past mistakes. Where there has been sin, His grace abounds. He erases your mistakes and puts grace in their place."

My thoughts about leaving a legacy:

If you can discuss this kind of question together, be sure to do so. How does thinking about the legacy you are leaving (how your children see you and how they will respond to Christ) relate to where you are in your marriage? For what happens when love and respect are tried, see the letters on book pages 291–93. (Couples on the Energizing Cycle: you will want to think about the legacy you are leaving. Have you even thought of how your Love and Respect Connection looks to your children? What specifically can you do, or continue to do, when your kids are watching that which will prepare them for having their own families some day?)

—————

6 "The Reward of Winning Your Spouse God's Way" (book pages 293–96) includes several letters from husbands and wives who are moving forward on the Rewarded Cycle by living out Love and Respect. Which of the following excerpts contain kernels of truth you can use right now?

_____ a. "I wanted her to respect me and be my friend—neither of which I was experiencing . . . . Thanks be to God for knowledge that leads to understanding and allows me to act lovingly in service to Jesus Christ."

_____ b. "I changed my attitude. I changed my tone of voice and my facial expressions. I even changed my prayers from 'bless me and change him' to 'change me and bless him.'"

_____ c. "My situation is not any easier at home, my husband has been 'on the run' from the Lord for many years now, but I do not feel so hopeless and, therefore, do not need to have the final word . . . , worry about a decision, etc. And by honoring my husband . . . I am choosing life, Christ's life, and then I am blessed. Even if my husband never changes, I know the Lord wants me to honor Him."

Most meaningful to me of the quotes on the previous page is _____ because:

As you have seen while studying Sessions 13 and 14, the Rewarded Cycle is for couples in many different states of mind. They know love and respect is the way, but walking in that way is a struggle. If the two of you have been able to discuss any of the questions in these sessions, thank God for a major step of progress. If one or more of the quotes above speak to you, talk about why and what it might mean to your marriage. (Couples on the Energizing Cycle: you may complete this final session in the Rewarded Cycle and have one of two basic reactions: (1) "All of this is nice, but we really didn't need it" or (2) "Now we see what love and respect is really about. It's not about us; first and foremost, it is about our relationship to Jesus Christ. When that is strong, our marriage is strong." Carefully read the paragraphs on the bottom of page 295 and the top of page 296. Do you agree that once a couple attempts the vital step toward marital maturity that the tests will come? How can you be ready?)

Questions for Conclusion

7 Read book pages 297–98. Why did one husband find the Love and Respect Conference to be a "breath of fresh air"? What is the real purpose behind showing each other love and respect? Put your thoughts in writing here.

Do you agree with the husband who wrote in to say that at a Love and Respect Conference he was impressed the most by the Rewarded Cycle? If you have not attended one of these conferences, perhaps it is time to do so. For information on how to attend a Love and Respect Conference, or how to purchase a video of a conference, please go to http://www.loveandrespect.com. (Couples on the Energizing Cycle: set aside time to go over C-O-U-P-L-E and C-H-A-I-R-S and how you can live out these principles by keeping your eyes on your ultimate goal—glorifying God and obeying His Word. During a Love and Respect Conference, Emerson asks each husband and wife in attendance to "see" with the eyes of faith that just beyond the shoulder of his/her spouse stands Jesus Christ. Jesus is saying, "This isn't about your spouse, who may not deserve love or respect. This is about your living with love and respect as you show reverence for Me." With this image in mind, husbands and wives can go through C-O-U-P-L-E and C-H-A-I-R-S and receive divine help for living out any of these principles. A husband may not want to say, "I'm sorry," but he makes peace with his wife anyway, because just over her shoulder he sees his divine Master, and he does what he needs to do as unto Christ. A wife may rebel against acknowledging her husband's authority, but she does so anyway, because just over his shoulder she sees the Lord, and she does what she needs to do as unto Him. Living out C-O-U-P-L-E and C-H-A-I-R-S "as unto Christ" does not prohibit disagreeing with each other and confronting issues; the couple living on the Energizing Cycle "as unto Christ" can deal with any problem. They look at each other, and just over each spouse's shoulder is Jesus Christ. This is not just "incentive to be good"; it is power to live with love and respect.)

8 On book page 299 Emerson relates how "two can become one" as stated in Ephesians 5:31–33: ". . . as a husband puts on love, especially during conflict, his wife will feel one with him. When a wife puts on respect during those moments, the husband will feel one with his wife. A disagreement may not be solved, but oneness will be experienced. When a wife feels her need for love is met, she bonds with her husband. When a husband feels his need for respect is being met, he bonds with his wife. This can happen simultaneously. Two do, indeed, become one!" Do you think what Emerson says is possible for you and your spouse? What stands in the way?

Before writing your thoughts, consider these additional ideas by Emerson:

"In order to be 'one' as God intended, the Bible teaches we need to depend on Christ. Do you find encouragement in these words spoken by Christ: 'Apart from Me you can do nothing' (John 15:5)? As a man do you feel it is 'unmanly' to depend on Christ? Can you show love to your disrespectful wife in your own natural strength? As a wife, you can love naturally (it is the way God created you), but you don't respect naturally when you feel unloved. As a man, or as a woman, do you admit you need Christ's help to show your spouse love or respect? What a comfort to know God has sent 'the Helper,' His Holy Spirit, to help the one who looks to Him! Does knowing God is there to help you uplift your heart?" Write your thoughts:

Like so many questions in these sessions covering the Rewarded Cycle, this may be difficult for you and your mate to discuss. But if you can talk about it at all, rejoice in your progress! Talk about your conflicts and disagreements. Why do these differences of opinion leave you feeling your needs are not being met—hers for love, his for respect? What would happen if you had a disagreement, agreed to disagree, and assured each other of your mutual love and respect? Be sure to look at the last paragraph of this section starting on the bottom line of book page 299. The best kind of help is available for the asking. (Couples on the Energizing Cycle: you can benefit from evaluating how well you "agree to disagree." During times of conflict or disagreement, does she still feel loved? Does he still feel respected? How can you both be sure of this? [For ideas, review *Love & Respect* Appendix A, "A Lexicon of Love and Respect . . . ," especially pages 305–6. Also see *Love & Respect* Appendix C, "How to Ask Your Mate to Meet Your Needs."])

9 In "Have You Really Tried Prayer?" (book pages 300–3), Emerson uses another analogy to describe being one in Christ. When pink (the wife) blends with blue (the husband) the result is purple (God's color of royalty). The challenge is in the blending. The answer to "how to blend" is in the verse that began this book: Ephesians 5:33. Write that verse here, followed by your statement of commitment to pray—really pray—for the power to allow God to fulfill His desires in you.

If one or both of you is still struggling, blending your pink and blue to make God's purple may sound too difficult. But do not put the idea totally out of reach, because it may be only a prayer away. Read the letters on book pages 301–2. Then consider the Prayer of Commitment on page 302. If you can pray this prayer, do it now. (Couples on the Energizing Cycle: you will also want to go over the Prayer of Commitment. It may be of benefit to write out this prayer, inserting your own thoughts and decisions as you go.)

A JOURNAL OF MY JOURNEY
TO LOVE AND RESPECT

Since this is the final session in your study of Love and Respect, you may want to look back to where you were when you started and record your thoughts about the progress you have made.

SCRIPTURE MEDITATIONS

1. "For from within, out of the heart . . . proceed . . . envy, slander, pride and foolishness" (Mark 7:21–22). What is Jesus saying to each

one of us? That our response is always our responsibility! Our Lord does not let us rationalize our sins. When we do wrong, it is a choice of the heart, who we are deep within. There is no copping out, no blaming others. The husband who barks, "I was unloving because I get no respect" only confirms Christ's words. The wife who shrills, "I can't respect him; I get no love!" speaks from a heart that needs Christ's touch. Pray daily for His touch, and always begin, "Lord, help me. My response is my responsibility."

2. Paul told Timothy, "Set an example . . . in speech, in life, in love, in faith and in purity" (1 Timothy 4:12 NIV). We all know the over-whelming power of example, especially in the home in front of the children. When we come across as unloving, angry, disrespectful, or harsh, it drowns out all our advice, teaching, instruction, or admonition. When one of our personal needs goes unmet and we lash out with hate or contempt, the kids only learn that our faith in Christ appears meaningless. If you have already blown it, ask God for His abundant grace and forgiveness. If you are blowing it right now, with children still in the home who are watching you, ask God for help— the power to love, the strength to respect. He will grant what you need, as you trust in Him.

3. It is right and good for a husband to love his wife and for a wife to respect her husband. But a husband will suffer when loving a disre-spectful wife, and a wife will suffer when respecting an unloving hus-band. What incentive is there, then, to suffer like this? Peter tell us: ". . . when you do what is right and suffer for it . . . this finds favor with God" (1 Peter 2:20). Yes, as you endure the suffering your spouse may be causing you, it wins God's favor. This is something of which the carnal world knows nothing. The unbeliever sneers, "You are stupid for suffering this way. Be done with this!" But the believer knows that the day is coming when those who suffer this way will be seen as wise, not stupid, because the favor of God rests on them. Be encouraged. You have God's Word on it!

Now may the God and Father of our Lord Jesus Christ,
by the power of the Holy Spirit, bless you with wisdom
and strength to grace your marriage with love and respect.
And may He eternally reward you because you chose
to trust and obey Him. Amen.

My final thoughts as I conclude my study of *Love and Respect*:

APPENDIX I

Suggestions for Group Leaders

USING THE *LOVE & RESPECT WORKBOOK* IN A GROUP SETTING

Before using this workbook with your small group . . .

1. Read the introductory pages, read the introductory pages, "Before You Start Your Study of *Love & Respect*" (page 6). Become familiar with the workbook's primary purpose: to take an individual spouse or a couple through each chapter of *Love & Respect* as they interact with the thinking of its author. Dr. Emerson Eggerichs, in addition to seminary degrees, has an M.A. in Communication and a Ph.D. in Child and Family Ecology. Beyond that, he spent more than twenty-five years in the pastorate, where he counseled many couples struggling in their marriages. In 1998, as a result of meditating on Ephesians 5:33, he experienced a significant breakthrough in his understanding of this marital struggle. At that time, he recognized why this struggle happened between good-willed people. Emerson felt that God illumined his heart, so to speak, to see the remedy to these marital tensions. The *Love & Respect* message is this remedy. In 1999 Emerson left a thriving congregation of 2,000 to found Love and Respect Ministries. Since then, he and his wife, Sarah, have conducted Love and Respect Conferences in churches and other settings throughout the nation.

2. Complete several sessions of the workbook to become thoroughly acquainted with its design and function. You should always be a session or two ahead of the group to provide adequate time to internalize the material and decide which questions to emphasize with your group. If possible, have your spouse study along with you and use the discussion ideas for couples throughout the workbook. (Look for the icon that indicates questions for spouses studying together.)

Additional helpful information for the group leader is contained in Appendices II–VI (see pages 205–223). All of these additional resources are a gold mine of information for a group leader. Read and study them, then use what works for your group.

3. Check your leadership style. Facilitating a group study of a book like *Love & Respect* is a great responsibility. The spouses in your group represent marriages in different circumstances and stages—some strong, others weak. As you lead your group, seek to be:

Relaxed and casual, but organized and able to keep things moving. Let people share, give opinions, and even disagree a bit, but don't be afraid to sum things up and move to the next question or topic.

Caring and sensitive, always trying to be aware of what others might be thinking or feeling at the moment. Some couples in your group will probably see a lot of humor in certain questions and be quite able to enjoy what is going on. Others could be hurting and unhappy, not finding the proceedings to be as much fun. You may spot couples or perhaps individuals you need to contact outside the group, to guide them in their study, pray with them, or possibly refer them to someone who can give help that you cannot.

Acceptant and nonthreatening. For example, if someone comes up with an opinion that is totally counter to what Emerson sometimes refers to as "typical" or "generally speaking," do not be defensive or argumentative. Let everyone who wishes to give opinions, then sum up by saying, "According to Emerson's extensive experience and research, this is what he finds to be the norm or what is typical of men and women, husbands and wives. He knows there are exceptions to any 'general rule,' but he has also found that regardless of how people think or act, they all need love and respect."

Experienced and empathetic. Ideally, you and your spouse have studied the workbook together, and you have learned how to slow and stop the Crazy Cycle. You know what it takes to keep the Energizing Cycle humming. And you know and readily admit that at times you need wisdom and humility that you can get only from the Rewarded Cycle. Your enthusiasm and transparency about sharing your own problems and what you and your spouse have learned will do much to get the rest of the group to relax and open up to what *Love & Respect* has to offer. (You don't have to have a perfect marriage to qualify to lead a small group through the workbook. Ideally, however, if you and your spouse are leading the group together, it would be beneficial for you to have worked completely through the workbook and be in agreement about living in the Rewarded Cycle in your own marriage.)

Willing to use tough love in regard to everyone doing the homework. As a rule, any couple willing to join a study of *Love & Respect* should be highly motivated to put in the necessary time to improve their marriage. If you are holding meetings once a week, suggest that couples will need to invest a minimum of two hours weekly to the workbook. As they get into their study, they may soon be spending much more than that. Remind everyone: "Your study of *Love & Respect* should be top priority because your marriage is top priority. Your *Love & Respect Workbook* assignments are 'homework' done for the sake of your marriage and your home. This study has to do with improving (even saving) your marriage. It deserves your best effort because your marriage deserves your best effort."

Dependent on God's leading. Prayer must be a major part of your preparation for every meeting. And while leading a meeting, be praying silently: "Lord, help us all right now; give me the right words to say, or prompt another member of our group to share something that can help someone else."

If you get a question you can't answer, admit it and say you will try to find an answer by next meeting. Throughout the week, pray for each of your group members, and for each marriage represented. Contact your group members during the week to see how they are doing. If a couple is on the Crazy Cycle, offer to pray with them over the phone. Never be pushy, but always be available and interested.

4. Plan your meetings and what you want to cover. As you have probably already seen, there is a lot of material in this workbook. The fourteen sessions are organized around the flow of material in *Love & Respect*, as you move from the Crazy Cycle to the Energizing Cycle and finally the Rewarded Cycle. Some sessions cover one chapter of *Love & Respect*; others cover two chapters, and a few cover three. Obviously many sessions contain far more material than you can cover in one meeting. You will want to pick and choose questions that you believe will meet the needs of your group.

Also important is how much time you have for each meeting. You should plan on one hour minimum, but ninety minutes or two hours would be better, particularly as people get involved in discussing their problems and sharing insights they have gleaned from reading *Love & Respect*. As you divide the material to develop meeting plans, keep these points in mind:

a. Go through a session and decide how much of it you will use for a meeting.

b. Choose questions that cover the key truths of a given chapter in *Love & Respect*. All of the material is interesting but keep in mind your goal for the meeting—the essential points you want to make.

c. Go over all the questions you think you might use and analyze each one for how suitable it is for "public group consumption." Some of the questions asked in this workbook are sensitive; the answers people write will be, in some cases, things they want to keep private. Some questions are probably best avoided altogether; others could be used if you do some checking with your group members and also give some introductory explanations. Always stress that no one has to talk or share what is written in his or her workbook.

d. For more help planning meetings, see http://loveandrespect.com/LEADER/ and view "Meeting Plans for Your Small Group," which gives ideas for planning fourteen meetings that cover the fourteen sessions in the workbook. They can easily be expanded to cover more meetings, according to the interests of your group.

APPENDIX II

1 PETER 3:2: ADDRESSED TO GOD OR TO WIVES?

I am sometimes asked about my emphasis on 1 Peter 3:2 and why I take the position that the Greek word *phobos* should be translated "respectful behavior" toward husbands, which is the way the New American Standard Bible translates it.

Those who challenge my preference for the NASB translation refer to the New International Version of 1 Peter 3:2, which translates *phobos* as "reverence of your lives." This translation implies that wives are not commanded to show respectful behavior toward their husbands; instead their respect, or reverence, is to be given to God. My reply is that a wife who reverences God will come across in respectful ways to her husband. First Peter 3:2 is part of a larger passage—1 Peter 2:12–3:7—within which context it is clear why the NASB translates 1 Peter 3:2 as it does.

Peter's theme throughout 1 Peter 2:12–3:7 is that Christians are first to have vertical respect (or reverence) toward God, and then live out their reverence for Him with horizontal respect toward others. As Peter puts it, because of our vertical relationship to God we are to show "excellent behavior," specifically submissive behavior that comes across to others as honorable and respectful. For example:

In 2:12, why are we to show excellent behavior among the Gentiles (unbelievers)? Because it will glorify God.

In 2:13, why are we to submit to human institutions and authority? For the Lord's sake.

In 2:15, why are we to do what is right before other people? It is God's will.

In 2:16, since we are free, why should we be sure never to use that freedom as a cover for evil? Because we are God's bondslaves.

In 2:17, when we are commanded to honor all, love the brotherhood, and honor the king, we realize this means unconditional love and honor. Those we are commanded to honor and love may not deserve such treatment.

In 2:18, why are servants to submit by showing respect toward those who are harsh and unreasonable, not just toward those who are gentle and good? Because this finds God's favor.

In 2:19, why should a believer do what is right toward people? Because this is how to follow Christ's example.

Regarding wives, what is Peter's application of his concept of living with excellence? Go to 1 Peter 3:1, which begins, "In the same way, you wives be submissive to your own husbands . . . ." In the same way as what? In the same way Christians are to be submissive to (have respect for) those already mentioned in the total passage: kings, governors, other believers, masters (review 1 Peter 2:13–18). In 3:1–2 why are wives to act in this same submissive way in order to win their disobedient husbands? Because their actions and attitudes are precious to God.

So, coming back to the original question, does 1 Peter 3:2 say a wife wins her disobedient husband through her respectful behavior (NASB translation) or through her reverence for God (NIV translation)? As I like to say with questions like this: Yes! These choices are the front and back of the same coin. When a believing wife reverences God, her behavior spills over onto her husband as respect. On the other side of the coin, when she shows respectful behavior toward her husband, it comes out of her reverence for God, her "excellent behavior," which is what Peter has been talking about throughout the last half of 1 Peter chapter two!

The overall tone and message of 1 Peter 2:12–3:7 teaches us to show excellent behavior and a reverence for God, which displays itself through submissiveness that comes across as unconditional respect.

APPENDIX III

FORGIVENESS HAS TWO LEVELS

When counseling a couple on the Crazy Cycle, I find it helps many spouses to understand that forgiveness involves two levels:

1. Forgiving a person for having a personal preference at odds with your own personal preference.

2. Forgiving a person for a moral transgression.

First, how should you forgive someone for "wronging" you by preferring something you do not? Consider some examples:

- A husband prefers to leave the sink or a room (or the entire house!) less than neat, but his wife prefers everything neat and clean.

- A wife prefers to drive the car on a full tank or nearly so, but the husband prefers to live on the edge and drive it another twenty miles with the red "Fuel Low" indicator blinking merrily.

- A husband prefers to save "discretionary money" but his wife prefers to spend it.

All of the above examples are personal preferences, not moral transgressions. But the "rub" comes when one spouse starts resenting the other spouse for having different personal preferences. Then the personal preference can become a supposed moral transgression. The "logic" runs thusly: "If I mattered to you, you would do it my way. I can see, however, that you don't care. Obviously, I don't matter!" Easily carried a bit further, this kind of logic continues: "Because you don't care and think I don't matter, you are wrong, unloving, disrespectful—even ungodly!"

Actually, the only thing "ungodly" that is going on is that you have made a moral mountain out of a personal preference molehill. God knew that Christians, especially spouses, would experience tension over personal preferences, and He inspired writers such as the apostle Paul to lay down helpful principles about how to handle this kind of thing (see, for example, Romans 14). If you ignore God's principles and become bitter and unforgiving over personal preference problems, it reveals a character flaw in you, not your spouse. Because your husband has his own standard of cleanliness (that is, being comfortable with less-than-perfect neatness) does not mean he is ungodly. Because your wife is not as frugal as you are and loves to find a good sale that may blow the budget for that month, she is not a loose woman. To get upset to the point of becoming angry and unforgiving is to be judgmental and self-righteous.

When I am counseling a couple, right about here is where the wife may get a bit exasperated. Her husband is driving her nuts with his sloppiness. Can't he do anything to help just a little? My reply is that having differences on personal preferences leaves plenty of room for disagreement, debate, and even some anger (as long as the anger doesn't last past sundown (see Ephesians 4:26–27). If a couple has truly bought into *Love & Respect* principles and techniques, they can work out any disagreement. Messy husbands can reform (at least to a point) because they want to love their wives better. Spendthrift wives can reform (at least to a point) because they want to respect their husbands more.

But what cannot happen is for one spouse or the other to stay angry and unforgiving over differences in personal preferences. You may become upset by your spouse's choice to act in a certain way (the personal preference), but to stay argumentative and bitter about it is overkill. To repeat: *a personal preference is not a moral transgression.* To take offense at something that is not a true offense flies in the face of all that the Love and Respect Connection stands for in your marriage.

But what about the other level of forgiveness? What about forgiving things that are true offenses because they are moral transgressions?

And within the boundaries of marriage, how does one tell the difference between a personal preference and something serious enough to fall in the category of "moral transgression"? I believe this kind of sin is committed consciously and willfully. In the New Testament there is no final summary of such trespasses, but in Galatians 5:19–21 Paul mentions such sins as immorality, idolatry, and drunkenness and ends a rather long list with ". . . and things like these . . . ." Obviously, Paul is intending to be illustrative, not exhaustive. He is talking about following after the flesh (the sinful nature, see Galatians 5:16–17) in such a way that it grieves God's heart and deeply wounds your spouse.

If you are the spouse who is wounded, how do you respond to "things like these"? First of all, you must confront such sins in the right spirit. For example, suppose you learn of your mate's act of adultery. You may be stunned, devastated, and extremely angry, but you should not confront your spouse with lasting bitterness and contempt. God forgives a momentary angry response, but a continually bitter person cannot be God's instrument to restore a straying spouse. The confrontation needs to be done with a respectful and forgiving spirit, even if your heart is breaking. A forgiving spirit says, "I refuse to become a bitter and contemptuous soul, though you have wounded me with a near fatal blow."

"But," you may object, "if I display a respectful and forgiving spirit, my spouse will not repent!" The error here is to think that a contemptuous and continually angry spirit is the means God intends to use to motivate a spouse to repent. This is not God's means to achieve His holy end. Your truthful and humble confrontation of sin by stating the clear facts can lead to another's repentance when your belligerence never will.

"Okay," you might respond, "what if my sinful spouse remains unrepentant after being confronted and accuses me of being judgmental and unforgiving?" Unrepentant spouses often make this claim. The typical line is, "You are so intolerant and self-righteous. Don't judge, lest you be judged!" The offender uses this kind of line to shame the godly spouse into the conclusion, "to prove I am forgiving and not judgmental, I will no longer confront my spouse's wrongdoing." The spouse who has been wronged must not fall for this kind of manipulation. Confrontation must still occur, but in a forgiving manner.

Some spouses may question me right here because they know what Jesus says in Luke 17:3: "If your brother sins, rebuke him; and if he repents, forgive him." What if your spouse refuses to repent? Is Jesus saying that you don't have to forgive as long as your spouse remains unrepentant? That's a fair question. My answer is that the kind of forgiveness Jesus mentions in Luke 17:3 (the ending of the confrontation or rebuke) is different from the spirit of forgiveness, which Jesus also teaches in many places (see for example, Matthew 18:21–35). A spouse who has been wronged can forgive the offending spouse (with a spirit of forgiveness from the heart), but still confront the offender until he or she repents. Having a forgiving spirit does not mean that you announce, "Because I have a forgiving spirit, I will no longer confront your adultery and alcoholism. Go ahead and continue in your sin." Jesus would not want you to be so foolish or uncaring. He intends that you care enough to confront, but in a loving and respectful way.

For example, a husband can have a forgiving spirit toward his wife for her alcoholism, but for her sake there must be confrontation and consequences. Having a forgiving spirit does not mean letting the transgressor off the hook. The wife may adamantly insist she has changed (alcoholics often do), but somehow she turns up drunk again. The husband must say, "Honey, I love you and I forgive you, but I cannot trust you."

It is important to differentiate between forgiving and trusting. To be real, repentance must lead to some kind of change in behavior or attitude. Paul taught his listeners to "repent and turn to God, performing deeds appropriate to repentance" (Acts 26:20). Some evidence should exist that the sinner has sincerely turned the corner on his or her sin. When this "fruit" is plainly there, the offended party should be encouraged and thank God. Yes, the fear that "it could happen again" may always be there, but it should not be allowed to control the situation. If an offending spouse repents and has a real change in behavior, full forgiveness should be extended. You should not be in your spouse's face confronting a grievous sin that is no longer there. You stop dwelling on the past and look to the future.

Sadly, a spouse may commit grievous sins, but after supposedly "forgiving" those sins the offended party ends up committing worse sins. I have watched this kind of thing happen all too often over the years. The sinful spouse comes clean in repentant humility, but the offended spouse chooses to be relentless with questioning and accusing. For example, a husband commits adultery and then repents, asking God's forgiveness and his wife's. His fellowship with God is restored, but his wife is bitter and judgmental. Even though the husband turns his heart back to Christ and tries in every way he can to restore the marriage, his wife continues to defame him to anyone who will listen, including their children.

What is more common than the repentant spouse who remains unforgiven is the spouse who refuses to repent, or the spouse who claims repentance but the "appropriate deeds" don't follow. Returning to the example of the alcoholic wife, her husband can have a forgiving spirit, but that does not include allowing her to go to a bar or to stay home alone for any period of time. The facts are clear: at present, her addiction does not make her trustworthy regarding alcohol. The husband should say, "I love you, but you must go to the rehab center at the hospital. You are too weak to fight your addiction alone."

There is no contradiction between extending forgiveness and enacting consequences for the offender. Because you forgive someone doesn't mean that everything goes on just as it did before, that nothing has to change. For example, a wife may forgive her husband's adultery with his secretary, but that does not mean the husband can continue to work with the secretary. The forgiving wife need not "prove" her forgiveness by allowing her husband to do whatever he chooses in relationship to the secretary. But the husband does need to prove that he is truly repentant and intends to be loyal to his wife by "bear[ing] fruit in keeping with repentance" (see Matthew 3:1–10).

I know of one man who committed adultery with a female associate at work, and he decided his only course of action was to resign. He did this not only to remove further temptation, but also to demonstrate to his wife that his repentance was real. He knew her forgiveness was real, but he also knew he had to reestablish trust. The onus was on him, not his wife. This marriage has been restored now for over fifteen years.

When the husband quit his job he took a huge hit financially, but God honored his decision. Today, he owns his own company and loves what he is doing. He and his wife love each other more than ever and are actively involved together in ministries at their local church.

But what about the wife who confronts her husband's sin and he refuses to repent? In 1 Peter 3:1–2 the wife is called upon to win her disobedient husband "without a word." Peter understood that after awhile a wife's words of rebuke repulse a disobedient husband. Her fire and brimstone preaching just turns him off. From a human perspective, "without a word" makes no sense, especially to a wife who is continually being wronged. However, God's revelation is to be obeyed. When it is clear that her husband will not listen, she must cease her confrontation. She must walk in a quiet, gentle, respectful, and forgiving spirit, trusting that God will defend her and convict her husband.

Does Scripture teach that a wife should go quietly on and on while her unrepentant husband continues, for example, to commit adultery? If the transgressing party refuses to repent and cut off the adulterous relationship, divorce may be inevitable (see Matthew 5:32; 19:9). The innocent spouse may have a forgiving spirit, but ongoing hardness of heart, unfaithfulness, and betrayal by the guilty spouse can kill whatever is left of the marriage.

What about physical abuse? The abused spouse can have a forgiving spirit, but immediate physical separation may be necessary. An abused wife need not "prove her forgiveness" by subjecting herself and her children to more violence. That would not only be absurd, it could be fatal. My counsel is that an abused wife should bodily remove herself and her children from a violent husband. There are people in every community ready and able to help abused wives.

I do not know your situation. Every marriage, every family, is different. But I do have a strong conviction. In any Bible-believing church there should be at least one person who can counsel you with godly wisdom. Paul says as much when he writes, "Is it possible that there is nobody among you wise enough to judge a dispute between believers?" (1 Corinthians 6:5 NIV). God is saying that there is such a person and that you must seek that person out and ask for help. For the sake of your children, for your own sake and for God's honor, find that person! God will direct your steps. I have seen it happen.

Do not assume that the only person who can help you is the pastor. It may well be that your pastor or an elder could be this person, but there may be others. Every church I have ever visited has a handful of happily married compassionate people who are humble servants ready to respond to a person in deep crisis. The ground rule is simple: when you turn to this person or couple for assistance, your attitude must not be, "I want to tell you the evils my spouse has committed against me to destroy me." Instead, your attitude is to be, "My spouse has stumbled and sinned. I need God's wisdom to restore our marriage. I want to face my own sin, which has contributed to this problem, but I also want to confront my spouse's sin in the right spirit. Will you help me?"

One last word: Jesus instructs us to do this. Humanly, there may be no reason to believe a sinful, straying spouse will respond to confrontation. I have seen, however, that when God's word is obeyed, it brings God's convicting power. When you step out in faith and in the spirit of forgiveness, love, and respect, God shows up. One person who had been confronted by his spouse and me said, "You have restored my confidence in the church." This carnal Christian knew what was happening and was thankful that people cared enough to get involved.

In another situation the person who was confronted told me, "After the confrontation, I lived in fear that God would take my life." I never advise telling someone, "You better shape up or God will get you." Nonetheless, loving but firm confrontation can bring people under deep conviction! The confronted person may act indifferent or rebellious, but things can be happening in his or her soul. I cannot count the number of small groups who confronted a wayward member of their Bible study for wrong behavior and that person returned to the fold. This works more often than most want to believe. And the reason it works is because God tells us to do it, and He backs up His commands.

Appendix IV

DOES EPHESIANS 5:21 SAY WIVES DON'T HAVE TO SUBMIT TO HUSBANDS?

Contrary to what some teachers and leaders in the church espouse, Ephesians 5:21— "Submit to one another out of reverence for Christ" (NIV)—does not "cancel out" Ephesians 5:22, where wives are instructed to "submit to your husbands as to the Lord" (NIV). In Chapter Seventeen of *Love & Respect*, I pointed out that the Greek word translated "submit" is *hupotasso*. Literally, this is a compound word meaning to rank under or place under. In Ephesians 5:23–24, Paul explains why a wife is to "rank under" or "place herself under" her husband: "For the husband is the head of the wife as Christ is the head of the church. . . . Now as the church submits to Christ, so also wives should submit to their husbands in everything" (NIV). Paul is simply saying that as Christ has authority over the church, so the husband has authority over his wife. But most importantly, the husband's authority is to be motivated by love and is based on his responsibility to be a Christ-figure. As Christ loved the church and gave Himself up for her, the husband is to be willing to die for his wife if necessary (see Ephesians 5:25–29).

Because God has given the husband primary responsibility, He has also given him primary authority. Nowhere in Ephesians 5 is the wife called to be the head of her husband. Nor is the wife called upon to be the Christ-figure dying for her husband. This kind of "mutuality" does not exist in the text. In summary, any teaching on "mutual submission" should never negate the fact that Scripture clearly and ultimately calls the wife to defer to her husband's God-given authority and responsibility. If a wife protests, saying, "We are equal; we are to submit equally to one another," she will hurt and frustrate her husband. Few things are as demeaning and disrespectful to a husband as denying or ignoring his primary responsibility before God. Those who seek to be politically correct might scoff, "Who cares how a man feels? He needs to get over it!" A wise wife, however, not only cares about how her good-willed husband feels, she understands this is how God created him, and she seeks to help him with his awesome task of leading and protecting her. Thus, she places herself under his authority and enjoys his protection.

Having said all this, we must note that while the husband has the greater general authority, his wife is not without specific authority in at least two areas. First, Scripture teaches that the husband is to submit to his wife's sexual authority. In 1 Corinthians 7:4, Paul writes, "The wife does not have authority over her own body, but the husband does; and likewise also the husband does not have authority over his own body, but the wife does." Half the time, so to speak, in the sexual realm (and this is a colossal realm!) the wife has authority over her husband's body. At those times the husband must submit to his wife's God-given authority, right, or need. For example, for a change she may need him sexually, and he should submit to her request to be sexually intimate. Or, she may be exhausted from a horrific day caring for sick kids and prefers to abstain from sex, at least that night. The loving husband must submit to his wife's request.

But doesn't 1 Corinthians 7:4 also say the husband has authority over his wife in the sexual realm? Clearly, it does, so how can this be worked out if both spouses have equal authority over the other's body? I believe Scripture is calling both spouses to mutually submit to the other's authority and need! Because both have equal authority, both must mutually submit. Is this a mystical idea that is impossible to apply? A simple explanation is to strike a balance (find a happy medium). An important point to grasp about mutual sexual submission is that it does not always have to be simultaneous. Work out a way you can "give preference to one another in honor" (Romans 12:10). The couple practicing Love and Respect can agree on a sexual pattern that is mutually acceptable to both of them. Paul leaves each couple to work out 1 Corinthians 7:4 in their own way, doing so with the confidence that God will guide both spouses in this area of mutual submission.

Does this mean there won't be times of tension or disagreement when an agreed upon pattern doesn't work out? No—but a good thing to keep in mind is that in Ephesians 5:21 Paul instructs husbands and wives to submit to each other "*out of reverence for Christ*" (NIV, italics mine). You aren't playing some kind of game of marital *quid pro quo*. You are using your marriage as a practical laboratory for living out your reverence for Christ. In the midst of the tension there is always a Third Party who can be trusted to give you help. Because you try to reverence Christ, He is there to get you through the tough times.

For example, I once counseled a husband who felt he was being deprived sexually. His wife seemed repulsed by the idea of having sex on a regular basis, and this had become a huge problem for them. I advised him to trust and reverence the Lord in the midst of his frustration and to seek to consistently love his wife as a person, even if she didn't always respond sexually. It is amazing what prayer and love can do! Their sexual intimacy is now better than ever. The husband, a medical doctor, truly sees God's hand in what has happened. You can too, if you reverence Him when you are feeling disrespected or unloved.

A second way a husband submits is indirectly stated in Ephesians 5:33, the passage on which *Love & Respect* is based: ". . . each one of you also must love his wife as he loves himself, and the wife must respect her husband" (NIV). I have learned in my marriage to Sarah that loving her isn't always convenient or easy, especially when I feel disrespected. So, in order to love Sarah at such times, I must choose to submit to Sarah's need to be loved. In that way, I show my submission to God's command and my reverence for Christ. And in the same way, respecting me isn't always easy for Sarah, especially when she feels unloved! In order to respect me at such times, she must choose to submit to my need to be respected. When she shows me respect, she shows her submission to God's command and her reverence for Christ.

Because Paul commands us to be subject to one another in Ephesians 5:21, and then in the immediate context he teaches husbands to love and wives to respect, I believe love and respect are part of mutual submission. I also believe that, outside the bedroom, mutual submission can and should happen simultaneously. In all other situations in marriage, we can simultaneously submit to each other's need to feel loved or respected. For example, during a serious disagreement Sarah and I can mutually submit by giving each other love or respect even though we remain at loggerheads about the decision over, let's say, buying a security system for our home versus increasing our health insurance. She wants the system; I want the insurance. When I truly seek to meet Sarah's need to feel loved, even while we are arguing in favor of our own position, the "conflict" does not escalate to hostility. In this case, even though I defer 90 percent of the time to what my wife wants for our home, I feel I have to go with the health insurance, where our coverage is dangerously low at some points. But in making my decision I am still called to submit to Sarah's need to feel loved; I don't have to be hateful as I make my choice. By the same token, Sarah does not close off her spirit. She respects my decision and me, even though she is disappointed. (It turns out that a few months later we were able to buy the security system anyway, so we were both happy.)

Admittedly, I have used a situation where everything came out nicely in the end. You may be saying, "That's fine for you, Emerson, but with my husband and me, I would want the security system and he would want a new set of golf clubs. According to your thinking, he gets his clubs and we get no security system, even though crime is going up in our town every month. I have to live with his bad decision, and that is just not right." My answer is that I have counseled many wives who have had to live with bad decisions by their husbands. In fact, Sarah has had to live with a number of mine. I am not saying that submitting to a bad decision is easy, but in the long run it will pay off. I have seen many wives override their husbands again and again with a disrespectful attitude. Finally the continual disrespect gets to these husbands. They say to their wives, "Fine, you take over; have it your way"—and they retreat into being uninvolved and passive. Later, their wives come to me and say they can't understand why their husbands aren't more involved with them on much of anything. There is no connection, no intimacy—he is just "out of it."

My point is that some bad decisions need to go the husband's way. If the wife submits and is quiet (not cold, complaining, or bitter), she has a better platform for making her case next time. What I have seen with thousands of couples is that a good-willed husband seldom ignores his wife's reasoned, respectful appeals on a continual basis. When a wife respectfully and calmly presents her position to her husband, he will seldom take issue with her motherly and womanly desires.

I believe the real issue is not with male dominance and bad decision-making, resulting in harm to wives. Yes, that can happen, but it does not happen that often among good-willed couples. The real issue is with female dominance and passive, angry husbands. What I am trying to get across to wives, and husbands, is that hierarchy and authority are not teachings designed to keep the wife in subjection, treated like a doormat. Instead, if the wife submits respectfully, it motivates the husband to stay engaged in the awesome task of leading his home on all fronts, including being the spiritual leader, which is the deepest longing of the wife. The problem isn't with a husband denying the rights of his wife. The problem that I have seen in many marriages is with the husband backing away from being responsible when his wife refuses to submit. When a wife does respectfully submit, a husband is much more likely to step up to the plate and be the leader she hopes and prays for. He may strike out now and then, but he is in the game. In fact they are in the game together, living out love and respect.

APPENDIX V

___

SEX: LOVE AND RESPECT FIRST—THEN, "JUST DO IT!"

Our Lord created sex to be holy and enjoyed. The Bible makes this clear in the Song of Solomon, which paints a picture of married love with sexual and romantic metaphors in the brightest of colors! God has never shied away from encouraging "eros" in marriage.

Although God designed sex for husbands and wives to draw closer, I have noted over many years of counseling experience that many couples clam up when the subject of sex comes up. And when I address sexuality at a marriage conference, a hush literally falls over the crowd. (It always makes me think of Christmas Eve: "Not a creature was stirring, not even a mouse!") The topic of sex makes many, if not most, people self-conscious. It is a very personal issue, which just freezes a lot of us, male or female.

Let's cut to the bedroom, where a typical "discussion" is taking place regarding sex. In one way or another, the husband is saying, "I know you want affection, but right now, I need to make love with you . . . BAD." To which the wife responds, in so many words, "(Sigh) All right, you can have your sex, but it's no fun for me, and I better get something out of it, or I'm likely to have chronic headaches."

Of course, many such discussions never get that far. She may just say "NO!" and that's the end of sex and the beginning of three days of stonewalling. Wanting (or not wanting, as the case may be) sex often leads to behavior and words that are unloving, disrespectful, manipulative, or self-serving.

It need not be.

There is a way to move forward, not necessarily to sexual nirvana, but to something that might be called "heaven on earth," at least compared to what many couples have now. How do you do it? The Love and Respect message calls on both of you to believe in the other's good will. Yes, I know you know my definition of "good will"–not really wanting to harm your mate in the long run. But sex is a short-run issue (at least for many husbands). Stick with me and I will show you how good will can help solve sexual stalemates. Here is my advice— first for husbands, then for wives:

As the husband, if you feel deprived sexually, you must not allow yourself to feel powerless and angry because you feel rejected. Instead, trust that while it doesn't seem like it, your wife does have good will toward you. Do not automatically conclude that she is disinterested in sex because she is mean-spirited and intends to punish you. Yes, she is angrily denying you at times, but this isn't necessarily the deepest desire of her heart. Realize the problem is more about her lack of sexual desire, which might be caused in part because she is hurt by how angry you have gotten when she refuses you. She may need help to reopen her heart to address her sexuality and her relationship to you, her husband. This may be the time to seek counsel from a godly, wise counselor who is competent to give you both advice about sex.

Whether or not you think a counselor is needed, this is a significant moment to let go of your negative beliefs about your wife. Her lack of sexual desire may have little to do with you. Seek her forgiveness for getting angry in the past as a way of "motivating" her to meet your sexual needs. Let her know you want to approach the problem differently, with the goal of creating mutual understanding.

As a wife, if you do have less sexual desire, one thing you should do is become aware of the message you are sending your husband: "Have eyes for me only, but don't touch me sexually—at least not very often. You can come close emotionally, but that's all. And as you stay away sexually, make sure, Buster, you stay faithful to me." What does this kind of message do to a husband? At best it hurts so deeply it can be devastating. At worst, it can drive him into another woman's waiting and willing arms.

At this point, I will make a significant qualification about what I have been saying concerning the sexual needs of men and women. So far I have pictured the husband as the one who needs sex and the wife as the one who often is not interested. I am well aware that many wives need sex more than their husbands. I have had many women tell me just that. The problem I have been addressing (he wants it; she doesn't) is what I see far more often than not. I am speaking about this subject in general terms. Twenty years of counseling experience convinces me it is safe to say, for every marriage where "the wife wants it and he doesn't," there are many more marriages where the reverse is true.

Having said this, I am insistent that couples look to (and believe) 1 Corinthians 7:3, where Paul clearly teaches that husband and wife must seek to meet each other's sexual needs. How does that happen? First, both spouses must ask, "Is it okay that God has created my mate to have a need I don't have, or at least not in the same way?" The wife must learn to ask, "Is it okay that my husband has a greater need for sex than I do?" The husband must learn to ask, "Is it okay that my wife has a greater need for affection and emotional connecting than she does for sex?"

If you both can say yes to those questions, that's a big first step toward sexual maturity. The mature husband realizes his wife has a need for affection in and of itself and he chooses to meet her need, even though he doesn't understand it completely. And the mature wife realizes that her husband did not ask to be created with an anatomy that needs sexual release on a regular basis. She chooses to meet that need, even though she does not understand it completely. Both of them realize that although God made husband and wife with needs that are equal in importance, He did not make them with needs that are the same in kind.

So far so good. Now, I have something more—something extremely important—to say to husbands. Yes, I realize you feel deprived, but a reminder is in order. If you neglect (or don't give much thought to) being close to your wife, open with your wife, understanding of your wife, at peace with your wife, loyal to your wife, or esteeming of your wife (C-O-U-P-L-E), you are shooting yourself in the foot. If you refuse her all these things I just listed to "teach her a lesson"—that she cannot deprive you sexually—you have shot yourself in the other foot. You have sent her the wrong message, and she will not hear your heart. She won't hear you trying to say, "Please respect my need for sex." All she will hear is, "I don't love you; I just want to use you." Bottom line: if you want to move forward to help your wife understand your sexual needs, you cannot deprive her of her emotional needs. By way of analogy, she cannot put her ear to your chest and listen to the deepest beat of your heart if you are figuratively screaming at the top of your lungs and banging her on the head. Some approaches just don't work.

Husbands, remember: God has designed your wife to nurture and empathize. When you share your sexual need in a reasonable, loving (and yes, respectful) way, most wives want to help. But you have to approach her humbly and honestly. You cannot mask your sexual need behind hostility and threats and expect her to decode your sexual pain. The typical good-willed wife knows her husband has this sexual need, and she isn't consciously trying to put her husband in a sex-starved state.

Then why, the husband is surely asking, do I get so little sex? In all probability, your wife isn't responding because you have not been consistently gentle and meek in this matter of sex. (For men who think "meek" is for sissies, remember Moses was called "meek" and he was no sissy [see Numbers 12:3 KJV].) In other words, you are not predictably tender with her as you share your need. Oh, you may be sweet and patient for a while, but then you explode with frustration and anger. This is the real problem: your inconsistent approach to her emotionally, which leads to the explosions. It is not her "evil will" to make you suffer. Your inconsistency sets you back each time. Patiently and consistently practice C-O-U-P-L-E and see what happens with your good-willed wife. (In fact, ask her if what I am saying is not true for her.)

Most wives want to connect emotionally and sexually with their husbands, but God did not design them to drool every time they have a thought about sex. The husband needs to see how God has designed his wife. Women are sexual beings, but there are moments during the month when they feel less sexual than others. Nonetheless, I believe the typical couple can enjoy a healthy and satisfying sexual relationship throughout most of the month, because God has created male and female to mutually satisfy each other (see 1 Corinthians 7:3).

Look at it this way: as a husband you can try to be close, open, and understanding but you won't satisfy your wife emotionally 100 percent of the time. Wives who think their husbands must satisfy their every emotional need all of the time must let go of unrealistic expectations. (For example, what man is able to discuss relationships, the needs of children, emotional feelings . . . in the same way a woman can?) The wife must let go of her dreams of what went on in Paradise before the Fall. Nonetheless, I do believe any husband can respond to his wife's emotional needs up to 80 percent of the time.

The 80 percent rule also holds for wives. A wife isn't going to "perform" sexually at the 100 percent level of a typical man's imagination. No wife is going to be available as he imagines Eve must have been available in the days before fig leaves. Nonetheless, I believe any wife can respond to her husband's needs up to 80 percent of the time. When a wife feels genuinely and consistently loved by her husband, she will respond sexually. And when a husband fails to be loving (and all husbands do from time to time), he must always remember to say, "Honey, I am truly sorry. Will you forgive me for being unloving?" When the typical wife hears that from her husband, it makes her melt, and puts her in a far better state of mind to be approached about sex.

Please know that I realize it isn't always as simple as I describe. As I talk about C-O-U-P-L-E principles I am not trying to give husbands six "new and improved sex toys" to lure their wives into bed. I am trying to give husbands pure and simple wisdom that will lead to a mutually satisfying sex life and a mutually satisfying emotional connection. Recent research in sex and marriage is bringing out some interesting information. Regarding the sex act, the traditional view has been: desire for sex leads to sexual arousal, which leads to orgasm (desire, arousal, orgasm). This sequence is still true for many. Today, however, some of the best research finds something different is true for the person with lesser sexual desire. Instead of waiting for sexual desire to surface, one chooses to enter into the act of sex and then the desire comes. This new view, which works for many, says: make a decision to have sex, which leads to arousal, which then leads to desire (sex, arousal, desire). The general idea is that desire for sex increases after one chooses to be sexual with one's spouse.

Stealing a line from the Nike commercial, sex specialists are calling on couples to "Just Do It!" Encouragingly, after "just doing it" those with lesser sexual desire are finding a wonderful change in their marriage and in improving personal sexual desires.[i]

The "Just Do It!" approach to sex reminds me of what Paul says in 1 Corinthians 7:3: "The husband must fulfill his duty to his wife, and likewise also the wife to her husband." I know the word "duty" makes it sound like sex is some kind of required obligation devoid of joy, but not so. The truth is, as we seek to do our "duty" out of love for each other and reverence for God, good things happen. It may seem like a meaningless duty to meet the emotional needs of a wife, but, oh, the pleasure this brings her! When a husband meets her needs, the typical wife in turn responds to her husband and both are happy. It may seem like a meaningless duty to meet the sexual needs of a husband, but, oh, the pleasure this brings him! When a wife meets his need, the typical husband responds to his wife and both are happy.

Again, I know it isn't always just as simple as finding some new research and a new approach, but as I say in Love & Respect, when it comes to conflict about sex, "the issue isn't the issue." The real issue is love for her, respect for him. Seek that together and sex will be a fantastic part of your total life as husband and wife.

---

[i] R. Basson, "Using a Different Model for Female Sexual Response to Address Women's Problematic Low Sexual Desire," *Journal of Sex and Marital Therapy*, 2001, 27:295–403.

APPENDIX VI

—————

EMERSON'S ADDITIONAL COMMENTARY

Session 1, Question 5

Some couples think they are the only ones having trouble in their marriage and they begin to feel defeated. In the face of this trouble one of the spouses may declare: 'I married the wrong person!' Be assured that marital troubles happen to everyone, everywhere. It is what is called a 'global experience,' so no husband or wife should feel alone or abnormal when trouble, big or small, hits the marriage. Actually, knowing that millions of married couples are in the same boat can become a source of encouragement. This kind of 'negative encouragement' can actually lighten the heart.

For example, a captain may tell his crew a bad storm is coming, and while this is not positive news, it prepares his sailors to remain inwardly calm and roll with the waves. The sailors can say to themselves, "Millions of other sailors have made it through bad storms and we can too." The same truth holds for marriage. The husband and wife can say, "Millions of couples have had marital troubles and made it, and we can make it too."

For excellent advice on how to deal with trouble in your marriage, look at Paul's general instruction in Ephesians 4:26: "Be angry, and yet do not sin." Paul is recognizing anger as a normal and (in some cases) correct emotion to have. But he also puts in a note of caution. Too much anger, or the wrong kind, can be sinful. In other words, "righteous anger" can become unrighteous, especially in a marriage. Just because my wife, Sarah, gets angry with me does not mean she is sinning and that I have a bad marriage. I cannot assume that I made a mistake in marrying this woman and start thinking that another woman would appreciate me and be more understanding and romantic. It could well be her anger is justified, and I need to be repentant and teachable because God is using her to correct me. If her anger is based on a misunderstanding, I need to be patient and try to clarify the issue. Do I want to go through all this trouble? No. But is this just the kind of trouble God told me would come? Yes. Should I conclude that I married the wrong person because she is angry with me? No. Should I realize this is part and parcel of normal marriage and be encouraged? Yes! I do not rejoice in the trouble we may be having, but I continually rejoice in the hope that God will make a way where there seems to be no way.

Session 1, Question 11

How Paul uses the Greek language in Ephesians 5:33 is extremely revealing and very important. Simply stated, when he uses the Greek words for love (*agape*) and respect (*phobetai*) he puts both expressions in the imperative mood. The imperative mood always means a command is being given. Clearly, God is giving a command to both the husband and the wife. That is why the New International Version, one of the best of the newer translations, leaves no doubt. The husband "must love his wife . . . and the wife must respect her husband" (Ephesians 5:33 NIV).

Sadly, however, some have interpreted Ephesians 5:33 to mean that the wife's respect for her husband can be conditional. She need only show respect for him after she feels loved. If, in her eyes, he has not been loving enough she may feel justified in ignoring God's command to her in Ephesians 5:33b. I have had many wives tell me, "If he loves me first, I'll respect him. If he does not love me in the way I want, it is foolish to show him respect."

What is so disturbing is that these wives are not trying to be mean or willful, just honest and sincere. But they might as well take a pair of scissors and cut Ephesians 5:33b out of their Bibles. What would we think of a husband who declares, "Lord, I don't have to obey Your commands to love my wife until she is lovable and triggers feelings of love in me"? The bottom line is very clear: just as a husband is commanded to love his wife even if she is not as lovable as he would like, so a wife is commanded to respect her husband, even if he is not as loving as she wants him to be.

Session 2, Question 7

In "The Tenth Anniversary Card" story, the encoded message sent by the wife in her angry response to getting a birthday card on her anniversary was, in so many words, "If you really loved me, you wouldn't foul up like this!" When the husband responded defensively (and unlovingly), his encoded message was: "Hey, don't get so angry with me. My heart was in the right place. Your disrespect is devastating me!" (Note: the typical husband does not always think consciously about being disrespected. He probably isn't aware of his need to feel respected, or if he is consciously aware, he feels uncomfortable voicing his need to his wife. Whatever his state of mind, the point is that deep down he feels disrespect.)

In the "All You Want Me for Is Sex" story, there are several encoded messages. When the husband walks in after a week on the road, hoping for a big kiss, his wife lets fly with everything that is on her mind. She is buried in details, crises, things to be done. She needs his reassurance that he loves and understands her, and to hear "How can I help?" Instead, he feels disrespect and sends his own encoded message with a bit of sarcasm for flavor: "Great to see you after a week!" Later that night in bed, when he attempts to be sexually intimate, his wife sends a short but simple encoded message: "Don't. I'm too tired." She could have used the timeless phrase, "I have a headache," but the real message was the same: "I don't feel loved, and you aren't getting any warm, intimate responses from me!"

More encoded messages follow: he rolls away, saying nothing, but the message is there: "Disrespected again! See if I give you any loving words at all." From her female perspective, she fires another code—

"You're so insensitive!"—which is once again her way of saying, "I want you to love me, not sexually at the moment, but just hold me and care about the week of misery I've just gone through!"

From there the conversation heats up and real feelings surface. From his male perspective, the husband lets his wife know he didn't appreciate not getting any kind of "Welcome home" greeting as he walked in the door. Instead he heard a litany of what sounded like complaints from a woman who seems to take for granted what he is going through for his family out there in the dog-eat-dog world. Feeling disrespected, he finally says, "Am I just a meal ticket to you?" In other words, "Don't you respect me at all?"

Feeling totally unloved, his wife unloads her frustration with another encoded message. He never asked her how she had been doing with the kids, the house, the school—*everything*. When he finally seems interested in her at all, it's for one thing. The husband is not cowed and sends his own encoded message in a short speech that lets her know he had been gone for a week (in other words, no sex for a week). He wasn't too pleased with no kiss (there were kisses once, earlier in their marriage) and being asked why he had gotten home "so early." He emphatically ends the conversation with: "Thanks. That makes my day." Another bit of sarcastic code that simply means: "I am sick of all this disrespect! What's the use?"

Session 4, Question 8

Although many husbands don't seem to "get it" about how to love their wives correctly, a wife must ask herself three questions: "Is his heart in the right place? Am I judging him too severely? Could the real problem be my lack of genuine respect for him?" One wife wrote to tell me:

"My husband left me and refused to take my calls or pleas. He tried to love me for twenty-one years and finally my facial expressions, tones, and negative disrespectful behavior became too much for him to bear. He broke and told me I was mean and he was not going to let me treat him like that again. I was devastated and hounded him for months. . . . I didn't know the damage I had already done the first month we were married [when I] removed my wedding ring and spat in his face, and many, many episodes after that for twenty more years."

This woman's letter is heartbreaking. The guy tried to love her for twenty-one years. He did "get it," but her disrespect sent the message, "You don't get it, stupid," and it defeated him. This story graphically illustrates a key truth, which is framed best in this question: even if my spouse isn't "getting it" as perfectly as I would like, will it help to criticize or to encourage him or her?

Session 4, Question 14

When a wife comes across as disrespectful to her husband, she thinks it's like a "wet noodle" across her husband's face, just annoying enough to get his attention and hear her real message: "I'm hurting. Please reassure me that you understand, value, and love me." But if a man used the same kind of disrespect toward another man, it would be like a brick in the face! He can think of few men, if any, who talk to him in this way. Difficult as it may be at times, the man of honor must decode his wife's words (which could be hitting as hard as any brick) and hear her real message, asking for his love.

Session 6, Question 14

Concerning answer *b*: don't worry, there will be plenty to talk about, and as I say on page 153 of *Love & Respect*, husbands can just mostly listen.

Concerning answer *c*: don't let the "urgent" things that fill your day squeeze out the truly important. Understanding a wife means talking to a wife; you can find the time if you really want to. Sarah and I did.

Concerning answer *d*: of course understanding takes feelings, especially feelings of empathy. But to know what and how to feel, spouses need to talk. You and your spouse may want to schedule regular time to talk. For some couples, twenty minutes every evening is satisfactory. For others, an evening dinner or Saturday morning breakfast once a week works best. Work out your own schedule. The point is that talking is the means, understanding is the end.

Session 7, Question 4

The more I studied Scripture, the more I saw 1 Corinthians 7:3–5 as a great illustration of how marriages can have trouble—actually trouble ordained by God, because He has wired male and female so differently. We might say that because God made you male and female, He created you to have conflict and intends that the two of you use the conflict to deepen your mutual understanding of one another. Is this fun to go through? No, it isn't, but you can trust that it is His will. Because you have conflict you are not outside of God's will, nor did you marry the wrong person. (See again 1 Corinthians 7:28!)

In 1 Corinthians 7:3–5, God lays down a basic truth for spouses: neither spouse has total authority over his or her body in the sexual area, because the other spouse has authority as well. Since Scripture gives both spouses "equal power" in making a sexual decision, they can and must work together to find a solution. So, how would a couple work out a possible conflict about having sex tonight as mentioned in the question above?

To those spouses studying this question together, I urge you to read page 158 of *Love & Respect* carefully, perhaps more than once. These paragraphs contain the "solution" to marital conflict.

Session 10, Question 3

Obviously, for biblical hierarchy to be lived out in a love and respect fashion, it is necessary for a husband to operate from an attitude of good will—never wishing his wife and children any harm. But a good-willed man can be stubborn, proud, and prone to poor judgment from time to time. Being good-willed does not guarantee perfect, or even competent, behavior on every occasion. Being the "head" is a difficult task, and a husband needs all the help he can get. Ideally, a wife is his willing helpmeet and he is willing to listen to her suggestions. If he resists her suggestions, another approach for the wife to take is Peter's advice to enter quietness (see 1 Peter 3:1–4). This does not mean giving him the cold shoulder or pouting. It does mean withholding comments and criticisms, even though the wife is sure that what she has to say has much merit.

Withholding her comments can be extremely difficult for the typical wife who believes talking is the way to solve problems. One "extremely verbal" spouse had a husband who let her handle the money, then later he would criticize her for "doing it all wrong." She tried to get him to talk about it (so she could argue her side vehemently), but he could never "find the right time." Finally, with great difficulty, she tried just "being quiet," and it worked! Slowly he changed, and the wife eventually wrote to me: "We are doing very, very well. My husband is transforming before my eyes. My being silent . . . [has] become a habit and I'll eat my words, or choose my timing, or . . . just let it go . . . [and] now my husband has become a leader. A man that's [sic] easy to admire and respect . . . and love."

"Just being quiet" seems counterintuitive to many wives. They wonder how anything can be decided if there is no talking. God's answer through 1 Peter 3:1 is: ". . . without a word. . . ." To a woman, this is absurd. Therefore, she must take God's word for it by faith and use respectful silence for a season of time to try to break a husband's bad habits and disobedience of God's call to love his wife. Many wives have told me how well it works to use respectful silence on a good-willed husband. Remember, "good-willed" means that a husband means no harm in the ultimate sense, even though in the "immediate now" he can be acting pretty badly. What a verbal and aggressive wife must remember is that her husband may be acting badly due to his fear of her verbal skills and disrespect. Silence on her part gives him a chance to deal with her on more even terms. That is when he will let down his defenses and quite possibly change, as the husband described above changed.

Session 10, Question 11

So, how does mutual-submission-even-though-the-husband-has-final-responsibility-and-authority work out in the daily stuff of life? If there is an honest stalemate between husband and wife that threatens to cause a real rift, the wife is called upon to submit to her husband. For example, a *Love & Respect* couple has a serious disagreement over homeschooling versus sending a child to a public school or a private

Christian school with high tuition. A decision must be made by September. Suppose they discuss this thoroughly as he tries in every way to show her love and she tries to show respect. Finally, all alternatives are exhausted, and they still strongly disagree. Because of some serious financial problems at present, and because he has checked the public school out and it gets a decent academic rating, the husband decides that this year at least the child goes to public school. His wife is not happy, but she is called to defer to her husband. She is not called to agree with him, and in the long run her position may prove to be the better one, necessitating a change of course. Nonetheless, because the husband has been given the greater responsibility, he must have the greater authority. So for now, the child will attend the public school even though the wife believes it will be at the expense of the child's spiritual welfare.

Secular culture says that such a decision is unfair to the wife, and in a sense that is true. However—and this is an extremely important point—would it be more unfair to the husband to hold him primarily responsible for the marriage and the family and not give him final authority? For a wife to say, "You can't do that, we're equal!" means she grabs veto power. Few things feel so unfair and dishonoring to a husband as that.

Egalitarians take the position that a husband and wife should make a decision based on who has the greatest expertise. But that begs the question, what do you do when both spouses claim to have greater insight? Coming back to our home school or public school debate, that was precisely the case. Neither one would give an inch. A couple may seldom come to an impasse like this, but they should have a theological and organizational understanding in place in the event there is the need for a tiebreaker decision. This idea may sound ridiculous to those who dream of a perfect egalitarian world, but it makes perfect sense to the couple who wants to make the institution of marriage work long-term. In a Christian marriage a woman does not have the biblical right to say, "I'm going to do what I prefer in spite of my husband's opinion. I feel I'm right. This is the twenty-first century!

Besides, I make more money than he does." That is not what Scripture plainly teaches. The woman is not the head; for better or worse, the man has that responsibility.

Does making the man the head always result in perfect decisions? Obviously not. We live in a fallen world, and husbands are quite fallible. Nonetheless the biblical model for decision-making in the marriage is better than the two alternatives: (1) the wife is in charge; (2) both are in charge. Egalitarianism sounds like it might be more fair, but there is no answer for the honest stalemate, and it often fosters exhausting negotiation or such strict boundaries concerning "who has authority over what" that spiritual oneness is undermined and eroded.

Session 10, Question 12

All of the quotes from pages 221–222 in *Love & Respect* center around what I call Leadership 101—the most basic of all leadership principles: if you give somebody primary responsibility they must have primary authority to carry out that responsibility. One way of looking at Leadership 101 is described in choice *b*. If the husband has 51 percent of the responsibility, he must have 51 percent of the authority. But ranking herself under her husband's responsibility and authority is a choice each wife must make for herself. According to Ephesians 5:22, she does this out of love and reverence for Christ: "Place yourselves under your husband's authority as you have placed yourself under the Lord's authority" (translation mine).

To violate Leadership 101 is to frustrate a husband. He may get angry and dictatorial or he can rebel by becoming Mr. Passive and deserting his God-given responsibility, allowing his wife to be head. During many years of counseling, I have seen both kinds of husbands and neither approach leads to a happy marriage. I am not saying all this is easy, especially for the wife who is capable, verbal, and aggressive. But allowing the husband to be head pays off in the long run, as one wife discovered. She and her husband are both professors at a major American university. Recently, they had one of their few major stalemates. The decision involved purchasing a vacation home. She wanted it, but he did not, for financial reasons. Rather than yielding to her husband's authority she insisted that they do things her way. Her letter continues:

"Until the vacation home stalemate, we had been conscious to not live a lifestyle that was dependent on my income. [But] I wanted a vacation home and pushed the point, even though my husband didn't support the purchase. Turning this decision back to my husband was one of the first things I did after reading your book. Apart from the fact that I violated my husband's authority, I also realized that the 'issue wasn't the issue' and that purchasing something we couldn't afford on my husband's income was inconsistent with a commitment to honor his desire to provide for me and felt very disrespectful to him."

With no regrets, this wife told her husband she would support whatever he decided to do with the vacation condo. After telling her how critically important it was to him that she had stepped back and allowed him to be the leader, he decided to sell the condo sometime in the future. What surprised her the most, however, was how right it felt to respect her husband's authority. She had feared being stripped of her dignity; instead all she lost was her initial sense of contentiousness.

Session 11, Question 4

What I say here is for good-willed wives and good-willed husbands who are willing to practice Love and Respect as they discuss a problem that affects the entire family. The wife should keep in mind that her husband may be more open to feedback and suggestions than she first thought. And the husband should remember that spiritual leadership is his responsibility.[i] As a husband, realize that spiritual leadership is not rocket science; it is more of an art that you can master if you are willing to do three things:

a. Show your wife that Christ is an important part of your life: pray and read Scripture on your own and with her; talk together about what Scripture means in your lives; pray together for guidance in parenting and in being a Love and Respect couple who want to honor the Lord.

b. Be there, part of whatever is going on—family devotions, praying before bed, going to church, and other spiritual endeavors. If you are not as verbal as your wife, delegate certain duties (like the Bible story) to her. Leaders delegate all the time; it is part of being a leader. Your job is be sure everyone is listening as they see that you are interested and "into" what is happening.

c. As you make decisions, from small ones to big ones, make it clear to your wife and children that you are depending on Christ for wisdom. Make Proverbs 3:5–6 a family motto. Once or twice a week, as your wife may share a concern about one of the children, or some other problem, stop right there and lead in a short prayer about the situation. Take the issue that may be burdening your wife and carry it up to God. You don't have to solve her problem; give it to the One who can solve it. This will mean more than the world to your wife.

In short, to be a spiritual leader the husband needs to show up and be interested. And, just as important, his wife needs to step back a bit if necessary and let him lead. He may be halting, unsure, a bit clumsy at times, but he can do it if given a chance. If a wife undercuts, criticizes, shows disapproval because all is not being done as well as she thinks it should be done, the husband will sense this in an instant and back off. A leader needs followers. A husband's wife should be his most supportive and enthused follower.

Session 13, Question 3

That you may be suffering right now, I have no doubt. But have you considered that God is allowing this suffering in order to reward you? The writer of Hebrews instructs us to fix "our eyes on Jesus, the author and perfecter of faith, who for the joy set before Him endured the cross, despising the shame, and has sat down at the right hand of the throne of God" (Hebrews 12:2). When I began teaching people in deeply troubled marriages that their present suffering would be rewarded in heaven, I thought they would turn me off. Instead, I found many of them saying things like, "I never thought about God using my spouse in my life," or "This gives me a desire to endure since what I do matters to God." Following are some typical letters:

"One question I was asking God was, 'How can someone you love so much be so hurtful and just turn their back on you?' I was feeling really let down and pushed away. . . . [But God's] answer to me was: 'I've been there, I know how you feel and I died for you.' Oh my, what a revelation! This was not an issue of whether my [spouse] was treating me correctly, but whether I was looking at this whole relationship the way God does. [My suffering] is a form of worship, obedience and praise to God. . . . That is a tall order to meet, but what a joy to know I am doing it all for the glory of God."

"I have been married for 37 years . . . What an eye opener for me that I should be loving and respectful, not for my [spouse], but for God."

"Even if I see no change in my marriage, I know I am doing what pleases God and this alone gives me peace and takes the edge off the hurt and pain. The emotions are less and less significant and there is hope. When I fail, I just thank God for His mercy and patience."

ⁱ The husband's responsibility for spiritual leadership is strongly implied in Ephesians 5:23–27. Note especially v. 23: "For the husband is the head of the wife, as Christ also is the head of the church." The parallel is clear: because Jesus Christ is the responsible spiritual leader of the church, so a husband is to be the responsible spiritual leader in relationship to his wife.

www.loveandrespect.com

facebook.com/loveandrespectministries

twitter.com/emersonEE